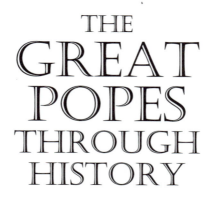

THE
GREAT
POPES
THROUGH
HISTORY

THE
GREAT POPES
THROUGH HISTORY

An Encyclopedia
VOLUME I

EDITED BY FRANK J. COPPA

GREENWOOD PRESS
Westport, Connecticut • London

Library of Congress Cataloging-in-Publication Data

The great popes through history : an encyclopedia / edited by Frank J. Coppa.
    p. cm.
    Includes bibliographical references and index.
    ISBN 0–313–29533–6 (set : alk paper)—ISBN 0–313–32417–4 (v. I : alk. paper)—
    ISBN 0–313–32418–2 (v. II : alk. paper)
    1. Popes—Biography—Encyclopedias.   2. Papacy—History—Encyclopedias.
I. Coppa, Frank J.
BX955.3.G74   2002
282'.092'2—dc21   2002023254
    [B]

British Library Cataloguing in Publication Data is available.

Library of Congress Catalog Card Number: 2002023254
ISBN: 0–313–29533–6 (set)
     0–313–32417–4 (vol. I)
     0–313–32418–2 (vol. II)

First published in 2002

Greenwood Press, 88 Post Road West, Westport, CT 06881
An imprint of Greenwood Publishing Group, Inc.
www.greenwood.com

Printed in the United States of America

∞™

The paper used in this book complies with the
Permanent Paper Standard issued by the National
Information Standards Organization (Z39.48–1984).

10 9 8 7 6 5 4 3 2 1

CONTENTS

— V —

CONTENTS

CONTENTS

CONTENTS

INTRODUCTION: NOTABLE POPES THROUGH THE CENTURIES

The papacy is among the oldest and most controversial institutions. The interest continues as questions are posed about the projected beatification of Pius XII (1939–58) and the papal response to the Holocaust, as well as the premature death of John Paul I after thirty-three days in office in 1978. Various mechanisms have emerged to satisfy this curiosity, including the opening of the John Paul II Cultural Center in Washington, D.C., in the spring of 2001, which has been designed to bring papal teachings to American public attention. However, interest in the papacy is far from a recent phenomenon. Publications on the institution and its holders have long been a staple of scholarship. Through the centuries the papacy has generated inquiry and study, as have the more than 260 men who have held the office of bishop of Rome and visible head of the Catholic church. Not surprisingly, the literature on the papacy and the popes is vast. There are a series of multivolume works on the chair of Peter and the papacy, and most popes have been examined in numerous books, articles, dictionaries, and encyclopedias, Catholic and otherwise.

A number of volumes examine the institution as a whole. Among the most recent of these overviews is P.G. Maxwell-Stuart's *Chronicle of the Popes: The Reign-by-Reign Record of the Papacy from St. Peter to the Present* (London: Thames and Hudson, 1997). The volume I edited, *Encyclopedia of the Vatican and Papacy* (Westport, CT: Greenwood, 1999), focuses on papal developments from the Renaissance to the present, but includes all the popes, antipopes, and councils, as well as Rome's reaction to ideological and religious movements, past and present. Matthew Bunson's *The*

Pope Encyclopedia (New York: Crown Trade, 1995) likewise covers the popes, antipopes, and papal institutions and includes a useful article on papal selection. Richard P. McBrien's *Lives of the Popes: The Pontiffs from St. Peter to John Paul II* (San Francisco: Harper, 1997) offers chronologically arranged biographies of the popes while providing information on how popes are elected and removed from office. Somewhat broader in scope but extremely useful and important is Richard P. McBrien's edited one-volume *The HarperCollins Encyclopedia of Catholicism* (San Francisco: Harper, 1995), which treats numerous aspects of the papacy and the church with clarity and balance. Eamon Duffy, *Saints and Sinners: A History of the Popes* (New Haven, CT: Yale University Press, 1997), designed as a companion volume to the History Channel's six-part history of the papacy, remains among the most comprehensive single-volume studies of the papacy, at once accurate and readable.

The flood of publications continues. There are critical volumes such as John Cornwell's *Hitler's Pope: The Secret History of Pius XII* (New York: Viking, 1999) and Garry Wills, *Papal Sin: Structures of Deceit* (New York: Doubleday, 2000). The papacy's position toward the Jews is explored in James Carroll's *Constantine's Sword: The Church and the Jews* (Boston: Houghton Mifflin, 2001) and in more balanced studies including *Christianity in Jewish Terms*, edited by Tivka Frymer-Kensky and others (Boulder, CO: Westview, 2000), and Jeremy Cohen's *Living Letters of the Law: Ideas of the Jew in Medieval Christianity* (Berkeley: University of California Press, 1999). Somewhat broader in scope are William J. La Due's *The Chair of Peter: A History of the Papacy* (Mary Knoll, NY: Orbis Books, 1999) and Allan Hall's *A History of the Papacy* (San Diego: Advantage, 1998). J.N.D. Kelly's somewhat older, but still immensely important, *The Oxford Dictionary of Popes* (Oxford: Oxford University Press, 1986) contains chronological coverage of popes and antipopes as well as a wealth of information on the papacy, as does J.V. Bartlett's *The Popes: A Papal History* (Scottsdale, AZ: Sim Ridge, 1990).

In light of this extensive and expanding literature on the papacy and the individual popes, one might ask, why another study? We believe that the present volume fills a need that has hitherto been ignored—that is, a focus on the most important popes through the centuries. At present, there is no biocritical study of these notable popes in English. Unlike most of the other studies, which present minientries on all the popes from Peter to John Paul II; the present volume focuses on those deemed the most important and interesting in five historical periods, providing longer critical entries that include appended bibliographies. Our volume examines those popes who have influenced the development of the church and the course of history in five broad periods: (1) the early papacy, from Peter through Pelagius II (590 A.D.); (2) the medieval papacy, from Gregory I through Boniface VIII (1303); (3) the Renaissance and Reformation papacy, from

Benedict XI through Pius IV (1565); (4) the early modern papacy, from Pius V through Clement XIV (1774); and finally (5) the modern papacy, from Pius VI through John Paul II.

Specialists were selected as part editors for each of these periods: Gerard H. Ettlinger, professor of patristics and church history at St. John's University, New York, for the early papacy; Glenn Olsen, professor of history at the University of Utah, for the medieval papacy; Margery A. Ganz, professor of history at Spelman College, for the Renaissance papacy; William V. Hudon, professor of history at Bloomsburg University, for the early modern papacy; and Frank J. Coppa, professor of history at St. John's University, New York, for the modern papacy. The latter also served as general editor of the volume.

The volume is a cooperative and interdisciplinary effort par excellence, involving the collaboration of the general editor, the five part editors, and the more than forty contributors of the individual entries. The authors hail from the United States and abroad, and the work has drawn scholars from various institutes, colleges, and universities, as well as the Secret Vatican Archives in Vatican City and the Villa I Tatti in Florence. In the pages that follow, some ten different fields of interest are represented, including history, political science, theology, religious studies, patristics, philosophy, classics, medieval studies, and Byzantine studies, among others. The notable popes included in each of the five periods were selected by the part editors in consultation with the general editor. In narrowing the papal list to forty-six, difficult choices had to be made by the part editors and general editor based on our assessment of the importance of the various popes and the availability and willingness of scholars able to undertake the task of research and writing. Not everyone will agree with our every decision and final selection, but we trust that the reader will concur with most of our choices. In many cases, popes not accorded separate treatment are considered within the context of the introduction for each part. We have sought some uniformity of format and length in the forty-six entries that follow, but not at the expense of stifling the individual contributor's creativity, style, and judgment.

The part editors were responsible for inviting the various specialists to write on each of the popes included therein, received and edited the first drafts produced, and subsequently transmitted them to the general editor for review. In one case, the part editor had to translate the article from another language into English. Each editor and many of the contributors had at least one opportunity to assess the revisions and additions made by the general editor. In addition, the five part editors each composed an introduction for his/her section that included a historical overview and analysis of the period and the literature on it, placing the articles on the individual popes that follow in perspective. Ultimate responsibility for the work and its contents rests with the general editor.

CHRONOLOGY

A number of the dates for the early popes remain disputed, even by scholars and specialists. Those provided below are drawn from the annual Vatican directory and J.N.D. Kelly, *The Oxford Dictionary of Popes*.

Names in **bold** type are entries in the encyclopedia.

St. Peter (d. c. 64 A.D.)

St. Linus (c. 66–c. 78)

St. Anacletus (Cletus) (c. 79–91)

St. Clement I (c. 91–c. 101)

St. Evaristus (c. 100–c. 109)

St. Alexander I (c. 109–c. 116)

St. Sixtus I (116–25) (also called Xystus I)

St. Telesphorus (125–136)

St. Hyginus (c. 138–c. 42)

St. Pius I (142–55)

St. Anicetus (155–66)

St. Soter (166–74)

St. Eleutherius (174–89)

St. Victor I (189–98)

St. Zephyrinus (199–217)

St. Callistus I (217–22) (also called Calixtus I)

St. Urban I (222–30)

St. Pontian (230–35)

St. Anterus (235–36)

St. Fabian (236–50)

St. Cornelius (251–53)

St. Lucius I (253–54)

St. Stephen I (254–57)

St. Sixtus II (257–58)

St. Dionysius (260–68)

St. Felix I (269–74)

St. Eutychian (275–83)

St. Caius (283–96) (also called Gaius)

St. Marcellinus (296–304)

St. Marcellus I (306–8)

St. Eusebius (309 or 310)

St. Miltiades (311–14)

St. Sylvester I (314–35)

St. Marcus (336)

St. Julius I (337–52)

Liberius (352–66)

St. Damasus I (366–84)

St. Siricius (384–99)

St. Anastasius I (399–401)

St. Innocent I (401–17)

St. Zosimus (417–18)

St. Boniface I (418–22)

St. Celestine I (422–32)

St. Sixtus III (432–40)

St. Leo I (the Great) (440–61)

St. Hilarius (461–68)

St. Simplicius (468–83)

St. Felix III (II) (483–92)

St. Gelasius I (492–96)

Anastasius II (496–98)

St. Symmachus (498–514)

St. Hormisdas (514–23)

St. John I (523–26)

St. Felix IV (III) (526–30)

Boniface II (530–32)

John II (533–35)

St. Agapetus I (535–36) (also called Agapitus I)

St. Silverius (536–37)

Vigilius (537–55)

Pelagius I (556–61)

John III (561–74)

Benedict I (575–79)

Pelagius II (579–90)

St. Gregory I (the Great) (590–604)

Sabinian (604–6)

Boniface III (607)

St. Boniface IV (608–15)

St. Deusdedit (Adeodatus I) (615–18)

Boniface V (619–25)

Honorius I (625–38)

Severinus (640)

John IV (640–42)

Theodore I (642–49)

St. Martin I (649–53)

St. Eugenius I (654–57) (also called St. Eugene I)

St. Vitalian (657–72)

Adeodatus (II) (672–76)

Donus (676–78)

St. Agatho (678–81)

St. Leo II (682–83)

St. Benedict II (684–85)

John V (685–86)

Conon (686–87)

St. Sergius I (687–701)

John VI (701–5)

John VII (705–7)

Sisinnius (708)

Constantine (708–15)

St. Gregory II (715–31)

St. Gregory III (731–41)

St. Zachary (741–52) (also called St. Zacharias)

Stephen II (752)

Stephen III (752–57)

St. Paul I (757–67)

Stephen IV (768–72)

Hadrian I (772–95) (also called Adrian I)

St. Leo III (795–816)

Stephen V (816–17)

St. Paschal I (817–24)

Eugenius II (824–27) (also called Eugene II)

Valentine (827)

Gregory IV (827–44)

Sergius II (844–47)

St. Leo IV (847–55)

Benedict III (855–58)

St. Nicholas I (858–67)

Hadrian II (867–72)

John VIII (872–82)

Marinus I (882–84)

St. Hadrian III (884–85)

Stephen VI (885–91)

Formosus (891–96)

Boniface VI (896)

Stephen VII (896–97)

Romanus (897)

Theodore II (897)

John IX (898–900)

Benedict IV (900–903)

Leo V (903)

Sergius III (904–11)

Anastasius III (911–13)

Lando (913–14)

John X (914–28)

Leo VI (928)

Stephen VIII (928–31)

John XI (931–35)

Leo VII (936–39)

Stephen IX (939–42)

Marinus II (942–46)

Agapetus II (946–55)

John XII (955–63)

Leo VIII (963–65)

Benedict V (964)

John XIII (965–72)

Benedict VI (973–74)

Benedict VII (974–83)

John XIV (983–84)

John XV (985–96)

Gregory V (996–99)

Sylvester II (999–1003)

John XVII (1003)

John XVIII (1003–9)

Sergius IV (1009–12)

Benedict VIII (1012–24)

John XIX (1024–32)

Benedict IX (1032–45)

Sylvester III (1045)

Benedict IX (1045)

Gregory VI (1045–46)

Clement II (1046–47)

Benedict IX (1047–48)

Damasus II (1048)

St. Leo IX (1049–54)

Victor II (1055–57)

Stephen IX (X) (1057–58)

Nicholas II (1058–61)

Alexander II (1061–73)

St. Gregory VII (1073–85)

Blessed Victor III (1086–87)

Blessed Urban II (1088–99)

Paschal II (1099–1118)

Gelasius II (1118–19)

Callistus II (1119–24)

Honorius II (1124–30)

Innocent II (1130–43)

Celestine II (1143–44)

Lucius II (1144–45)

Blessed Eugenius III (1145–53)

Anastasius IV (1153–54)

Hadrian IV (1154–59)

Alexander III (1159–81)

Lucius III (1181–85)

Urban III (1185–87)

Gregory VIII (1187)

Clement III (1187–91)

Celestine III (1191–98)

Innocent III (1198–1216)

Honorius III (1216–27)

Gregory IX (1227–41)

Celestine IV (1241)

Innocent IV (1243–54)

Alexander IV (1254–61)

Urban IV (1261–64)

Clement IV (1265–68)

Blessed Gregory X (1271–76)

Blessed Innocent V (1276)

Hadrian V (1276)

John XXI (1276–77)

Nicholas III (1277–80)

Martin IV (1281–85)

Honorius IV (1285–87)

Nicholas IV (1288–92)

St. Celestine V (1294)

Boniface VIII (1294–1303)

Blessed Benedict XI (1303–4)

Clement V (1305–14)

John XXII (1316–34)

Benedict XII (1334–42)

Clement VI (1342–52)

Innocent VI (1352–62)

Blessed Urban V (1362–70)

Gregory XI (1370–78)

Urban VI (1378–89)

Boniface IX (1389–1404)

Innocent VII (1404–6)

Gregory XII (1406–15)

Martin V (1417–31)

Eugenius IV (1431–47)

Nicholas V (1447–55)

Callistus III (1455–58)

Pius II (1458–64)

Paul II (1464–71)

Sixtus IV (1471–84)

Innocent VIII (1484–92)

Alexander VI (1492–1503)

Pius III (1503)

Julius II (1503–13)

Leo X (1513–21)

Hadrian VI (1522–23)

Clement VII (1523–34)

Paul III (1534–49)

Julius III (1550–55)

Marcellus II (1555)

Paul IV (1555–59)

Pius IV (1559–65)

St. Pius V (1566–72)

Gregory XIII (1572–85)

Sixtus V (1585–90)

Urban VII (1590)

Gregory XIV (1590–91)

Innocent IX (1591)

Clement VIII (1592–1605)

Leo XI (1605)

Paul V (1605–21)

Gregory XV (1621–23)

Urban VIII (1623–44)

Innocent X (1644–55)

Alexander VII (1655–67)

Clement IX (1667–69)

Clement X (1670–76)

Blessed Innocent XI (1676–89)

Alexander VIII (1689–91)

Innocent XII (1691–1700)

Clement XI (1700–1721)

Innocent XIII (1721–24)

Benedict XIII (1724–30)

Clement XII (1730–40)

Benedict XIV (1740–58)

Clement XIII (1758–69)

Clement XIV (1769–74)

Pius VI (1775–99)

Pius VII (1800–1823)

Leo XII (1823–29)

CHRONOLOGY

Pius VIII (1829–30)

Gregory XVI (1831–46)

Blessed Pius IX (1846–78)

Leo XIII (1878–1903)

St. Pius X (1903–14)

Benedict XV (1914–22)

Pius XI (1922–39)

Pius XII (1939–58)

Blessed John XXIII (1958–63)

Paul VI (1963–78)

John Paul I (1978)

John Paul II (1978–   )

PART I

THE EARLY PAPACY

INTRODUCTION

GERARD H. ETTLINGER

It is not difficult to identify the most significant leaders of the Roman church during the first six centuries of Christian history. It can, however, be deceptive to group them with their successors in the next fifteen centuries, since the Roman episcopacy in the early church was quite different in form and function from its later manifestations. To link a second-century bishop of Rome with a medieval or modern pope is, therefore, a complex task that could lead to gross misconceptions. History shows that the Roman bishop's position in the church evolved from one of important, but limited competence to the institution that is the modern papacy. The acknowledgment of such development does not deny Christ's role in establishing the papacy, nor does it imply that the papacy is merely a human invention or the result of cultural or political circumstances. In fact, historical evidence shows that from earliest times the importance of the Roman bishop was based, first of all, on the scriptural record that Christ gave a special mandate to Peter, and then on the tradition that both Peter and Paul, the two great apostles, had been martyred there. This introduction will, therefore, place the most notable Roman bishops of the first six centuries in their historical context.

One must begin with a comment on the title of pope, which is the English translation of a word that in both Greek and Latin signifies "father." From about the third century it was used to designate various church dignitaries, although in Eastern Christianity the title appears to have been restricted to the bishop of Alexandria, who still retains it today; from the sixth century in the Western church it was applied primarily to the bishop of Rome, a practice that became fixed in the eleventh century. Before the third century, therefore, to refer this title to the bishop of Rome in the sense that it is used today is anachronistic. But in light of the development already noted, the earliest leaders of the Roman church are, of course, to be discussed, in their own context, as part of the papal succession.

Although Peter cannot literally be called bishop of Rome or pope, he is included here as the defining figure that links the papacy to Christ, because the power attributed to the bishop of Rome was believed to flow from Christ through him. Christ's words to Peter in the New Testament are interpreted as making him the leader of the apostles and the head of the church, and this power is transmitted to the bishop of Rome. For a discussion of scriptural references and the citation of the first Vatican council, see the entry on Peter by Jean-Pierre Ruiz in this volume.

One of the earliest testimonies to the importance of the Roman See in Christian life comes from Irenaeus, bishop of Lyons in the last quarter of the second century. In attempting to refute Gnostic heretics who claimed to have a secret tradition that did not derive from Christ or the apostles, Irenaeus says that the truth of the church's teaching can be discovered by looking at the succession of bishops in all the churches, because, according to him, they are the ones to whom the apostles entrusted all that was needed for salvation. He goes on to say that in order to avoid the tedium of documenting all the churches, he will refute his opponents by pointing to the

> tradition of the very great and very ancient church known to all, founded and established by the very glorious apostles, Peter and Paul—that tradition which it has from the apostles, as well as the faith which has been preached to the people and comes down to us through the succession of bishops. . . . For every church, that is, the faithful everywhere, must agree with this church because of its preeminent authority, since the apostolic tradition has been preserved continuously by those [faithful] everywhere. (Iraneus, *Adversus haeraesus* 3, 3, 2)

Although the Roman church is not mentioned by name, it is clearly the church of which Irenaeus is speaking, and it is equally obvious that he considers it to have been established by both Peter and Paul. The meaning of the final sentence is highly controversial, and it may be impossible to determine it exactly, since the text exists only in a Latin translation. But whatever Rome's "preeminent authority" or, in another translation, "authoritative preeminence" means, it certainly attributes special power and influence to the church of Rome, although it does not necessarily imply the kind of juridical authority claimed by later popes.

Irenaeus goes on to say that "the blessed apostles . . . committed into the hands of Linus the office of the episcopate" (Iraneus, *Adversus haeraesus* 3,

3, 30). The manner of enumeration shows that Irenaeus did not consider Peter the first bishop of Rome; he says that after Linus there came Anacletus and Clement, the latter being "third in line after the apostles." He then names the successors of Linus up to Eleutherius, who, at the time of Irenaeus, "[inherited] the episcopacy twelfth in line after the apostles." Irenaeus portrays a Roman church that stands out among all the churches of the world, primarily, it would appear, because its bishops are successors of the great apostles Peter and Paul.

Clement I authored the earliest extant document written by a bishop of Rome. In this regard see the entry on Clement by Margaret Schatkin. The personality of the episcopal author was not considered an important factor at the time of composition, since his name was not mentioned in the document, which simply says that it was sent "from the church of God that dwells in Rome." The author urges the church of Corinth to foster unity and peace, but since he does not insist upon the church's compliance, the extent of his authority appears to be limited. Clement's text "must primarily be seen as a letter and not as a juridical document. As such it does not speak with authority. . . . [It] lacks anything that represents authority, law, and order. What can be said is that the letter strives towards such structures" (Fullenbach, p. 10).

Opposition to authority is perhaps the clearest sign that the authority in question is not insignificant. If this is true, then even though the accusations made by Hippolytus against Callistus I in the first quarter of the third century are of dubious value, as shown by Michael Slusser in his entry, they seem to show that little more than a century after the shadowy Clement I, the bishop of Rome had become an important person, deeply involved in the church's life and responsible for the purity of doctrine and the preservation of sound ecclesiastical discipline. In any event, the episcopal office was clearly desirable, since Hippolytus apparently allowed himself to be elected antipope. But the fact that the bishop can be opposed and attacked with relative impunity shows that his authority at this time was neither absolute nor definitive.

Less than fifty years after Callistus I the scope of the Roman bishop's activity is seen to extend far beyond the city itself through its relationship with the more highly structured form of episcopacy that prevailed in the church of North Africa. Cyprian, the bishop of Carthage from around 248 to 258, was the leader among a group of local bishops who often met in council to discuss questions of doctrine and discipline. His extant letters reflect, with certain limitations, relatively close links of collegiality and responsibility between the North African bishops and the bishop of Rome.

A major persecution under the emperor Decius (250–51) gave rise to a dispute over the penitential discipline to be imposed on those who had denied their faith during the persecution. Cyprian, who had gone into hiding during the persecution, favored a moderate approach, as did Cornelius, who became bishop of Rome (251–53) after his predecessor died in the persecution. Cornelius was opposed by the rigorist Novatian, but was supported by Cyprian, who, by speaking in his letters about the election of Cornelius and his relations with other bishops, provides information about the Roman episcopacy of the time.

Cyprian says that his view of Cornelius is based "on the judgment of God, who made him a bishop, and on the testimony of his fellow bishops, who without exception the whole world over, have given him their approbation in unanimous accord" (55.8.1, G.W. Clarke, *The Letters of St. Cyprian of Cathage*, New York: Newman Press, 1984–1989). He describes the election of Cornelius at length: "Moreover, Cornelius was made bishop by the choice of God and his Christ, by the favorable witness of almost all of the clergy, by the votes of the laity then present, and by the assembly of some sixteen bishops, men of maturity and integrity" (55.8.4). Cyprian clearly has great respect for Cornelius and supports him in his conflict with Novatian. Cyprian's attitude changed, however, during the term of Stephen I (254–57), the second bishop of Rome after Cornelius, in a controversy concerning the baptism conferred by schismatics and heretics; in this case Cyprian adopted a rigorist position and demanded the rebaptism of any convert who had received such a baptism. Stephen, however, espoused a moderate approach, which he described as Roman tradition, and rejected rebaptism. Using very negative language in describing both Stephen and his practice, Cyprian wrote a number of letters to and about Stephen in which he stated that Stephen was simply wrong.

It is possible to unravel the theology underlying Cyprian's protean attitude toward Rome through his treatise *On the Unity of the Catholic Church*, written at the time of the controversy concerning Cornelius. In chapter 4 Cyprian discusses church unity in terms of Peter, bishops, and their interrelationships. This chapter exists in two versions: one says that Peter was first among the apostles and therefore had a central role in the unity of the bishops and the church, while the other calls Peter a first among equals and shifts the focus of unity in the church to the apostles and the bishops themselves. They describe two contradictory structures of unity and authority in the church; one seems to favor papal primacy, while the other stresses the importance of the individual bishops acting in harmony with the bishop of Rome and one another.

Maurice Bévenot explains the two versions of chapter 4 in the context of Cyprian's conflict with Stephen (De Lapsis and De Ecclesiae Catholicae Unitate in Oxford Early Christian Texts, Oxford: Clarendon, 1971). He maintains that this is not a case of interpolation, for Cyprian was responsible for both versions. According to Bévenot, the text favoring the primacy of Peter and the bishop of Rome was the original, written on behalf of Cornelius and therefore prior to the conflict with Stephen; the other text, which gives all the bishops an equal share in power with one another, would have been written after the controversy over rebaptism to justify Cyprian's actions and to prevent his own words from being used against him. Cyprian's theology of the episcopate was, therefore, driven by his episcopal praxis. He obviously felt that Peter and Rome were very important, but the relationship between Carthage and Rome was, for him, not one of dependence and absolute authority. Despite these views and his rejection of Stephen, he died in 258, a revered martyr, during a persecution under the emperor Valerian.

The legalization of Christianity by Constantine I provided the opportunity for increased activity by church authority, but the power of Rome did not take immediate advantage of this potentiality. Even as Constantine was acting, the church faced what it saw as a major crisis in the teachings of Arius, a priest from Alexandria. His opponents felt that his apparent denial of the divinity of the word of God attacked the very core belief of Christianity; but episcopal opinion concerning Arius was sharply divided, and the fierce conflict that arose as a result threatened the peace both of the church and of the empire whose ruler supported it. Constantine therefore convened a meeting of church leaders in the city of Nicaea in 325.

This gathering, known as the first general council of the Christian church, debated the case of Arius and, with the help of the emperor, concluded and decreed that he and his teaching should be condemned. The bishop of Rome, Sylvester I, was represented at the council by two priests, but he and they appear to have had little direct influence on the council or its aftermath. The Arian controversy broke out with renewed force after the council, but the main battles were fought largely in the Eastern church. The most important proponents of orthodoxy were Greek-speaking bishops such as Athanasius of Alexandria and the Cappadocians, Basil of Caesarea, Gregory of Nazianzus, and Gregory of Nyssa.

The influence of the bishop of Rome grew stronger during the reign of Theodosius I (379–95), after Christianity became the state religion of the Roman Empire and Arianism was at least officially defeated. Damasus I (366–84) made certain papal claims that initiated a process that would lead to Leo I (440–61) and Gelasius I (492–96). Since imperial authority favored the Christian church, Damasus was able to exercise the authority that he saw lodged in his office because of Christ's words to Peter, whose successor he was. He, therefore, referred to the Roman See as apostolic and strongly emphasized its primacy.

Unlike Cyprian, Damasus based his praxis on his theology and exercised his authority in matters of doctrine and discipline in both Eastern and Western churches. His efforts were not always successful, but the many Roman synods that he directed, and the Council of Constantinople (381), to which he sent delegates, were instrumental in the rejection of a variety of heresies and heretics and in strengthening the structure of authority within the church. Yet it was during his reign that the Council of Constantinople declared that "because it is new Rome, the bishop of Constantinople is to enjoy the privileges of honor after the bishop of Rome." This ruling caused displeasure in Rome (because it based ecclesiastical significance on a political factor rather than on the martyrdom of the apostles) and in Alexandria, which had formerly been second after Rome.

Damasus was bishop of Rome at a time when the great trinitarian controversy that began with Arius was coming to a close with the condemnation of those who impugned the divinity of the Holy Spirit. At the same time, the condemnation of Apollinarius was the beginning of a new controversy concerning Jesus Christ, the Savior. Through synods in Rome Damasus had a hand in these actions, and from his time on the bishop of Rome would play a role in the major doctrinal controversies that ensued. While this is true in principle, it must be said that Damasus did not have as strong an influence as Leo I, under whom papal authority overcame even the limitations imposed upon Damasus.

Exactly fifty years after the Council of Constantinople, during the episcopacy of Celestine I (422–32), a council at Ephesus (431) condemned Nestorius, bishop of Constantinople, and approved the Christology of Cyril of Alexandria (412–44). Celestine had faced problems earlier in his pontificate with the church of North Africa, where he was forced to yield, and in Illyria in the East, where he met with greater success. The Nestorian controversy was a difficult matter for the bishop of Rome and exposed the fragility of papal claims to universal jurisdiction.

Others had complained to Celestine about Nestorius before Cyril provided a full exposé of the errors to be found in Nestorius's teaching. Celestine and a Roman synod condemned Nestorius and entrusted the execution of the sentence to Cyril. The actions of the emperor in convening a council, the actions of Cyril in holding a council before the Roman delegates arrived, and the actions of the supporters of Nestorius doing that council all serve to show the lack of concern that the parties involved had for papal authority. In the end, however, the Roman delegates did approve the findings of Cyril's council, and papal authority had its day. But it was nonetheless still possible to achieve one's own ends by circumventing both the pope and the papacy.

Cyril and the supporters of Nestorius, who had been deposed and exiled, made peace in 433 when Cyril accepted the so-called *Formula of Union*, a compromise that had been proposed by John, bishop of Antioch (429–41). Followers of both of the principals in this agreement objected because they felt that their beliefs had been betrayed. The years that followed were stormy ones. In 447 Theodoret, bishop of Cyrus, composed a dialogue called *Eranistes* in which he attacked an unnamed heresy; the teachings described there could have been attributed to a rising school of thought later described as Monophysitism, or to Cyril of Alexandria, if one chose to interpret Cyril in this way. A year later Cyril's successor, Dioscorus (444–51), offered his support to Eutyches (378–454), an archimandrite of a monastery in Constantinople and a leading advocate of so-called Monophysite doctrine. When Flavian, bishop of Constantinople (446–49), deposed Eutyches in 448, he appealed his deposition, unsuccessfully, to the bishop of Rome, Leo I.

The emperor Theodosius II called a council at Ephesus in 449 to settle these disputes. Dioscorus presided at the council. It rehabilitated Eutyches, condemned Theodoret and other opponents of Eutyches, mistreated Flavian, who died soon after, and insulted delegates from Rome, who had come to deliver Leo's *Tome*, a document addressed in 449 to Flavian, in which Leo condemned the teaching of Eutyches and presented his own teaching about Christ. The actions of this council were later annulled, and it came to be known as the Latrocinium, or Robber Council. A year later Theodosius II died, and the new emperor, Marcian, called for a new council of the whole church, which met at Chalcedon in 451.

The Council of Chalcedon rejected the Latrocinium, rehabilitated those whom it had condemned, deposed Dioscorus, and condemned Eutyches and Monophysitism. It published an expression of its faith in language taken from Cyril of Alexandria, John of Antioch, and the *Tome* of Leo I. Council records state that the assembled bishops declared that Leo spoke with the voice of Peter, thus acknowledging the link between Peter and the bishop of Rome. Although Leo did not attend the council in person, he emerged as a forceful leader who could now press further the claim of papal primacy, and whose papacy would be a focal point for the development of the future power of the Roman bishop. See the entry on Leo I in this volume by Philip A. McShane.

A considerable number of churches rejected the Council of Chalcedon, generally out of loyalty to Cyril of Alexandria, who they felt had been misrepresented and betrayed. The struggle over Monophysitism, therefore, survived the council's condemnation, and more than two centuries and two general councils, both held at Constantinople, would pass before it was effectively ended. The theological conflict became embroiled, as before, with political differences, and the issue was further complicated by the continuance of the so-called barbarian invasions, some of which succeeded in taking control of large segments of the empire.

The legacy of Leo passed at the end of the fifth century to Gelasius I (492–96), who was a strong defender of the teachings of Chalcedon and of the primacy of Rome against Constantinople. During his pontificate a new title was accorded to the pope when a Roman synod in 495 referred to Gelasius as the vicar of Christ. A major achievement that influenced later political thought on monarchy and church-state relations was his articulation, in a letter to the emperor Anastasius, of a two-power structure in the world. The pope incarnated the spiritual power, which was concerned with spiritual goods, while the emperor embodied the temporal power, which dealt correspondingly with temporal matters. While each received power from God, was subject to Christ, and was independent of the other, the pope, for Gelasius, possessed spiritual supremacy, since the emperor was a member of the church, through which he received the offer of eternal salvation. This theory represented another step in the development and consolidation of papal authority.

This discussion of the context of the early papacy will close with a few comments on Pelagius I (556–61). See the entry on Pelagius I in this volume by Robert B. Eno. As a deacon, Pelagius was intimately linked with his predecessor Vigilius (537–55) in his defense of the theology of Chalcedon against the emperor Justinian and the Second Council of Constantinople (553), which took a strongly anti-Chalcedonian position. Since Vigilius maintained his position to the end of his life, the most striking aspect of the accession of Pelagius to the papacy is the fact that he was chosen by the emperor himself. The choice was apparently based on a change of heart on the part of Pelagius, who therefore began his papacy with a severely tarnished reputation.

Pelagius spent most of his papacy resolving specific problems in a variety of geographical areas, trying to repair the damage caused by his supposed vacillation. Papal authority as such had not been diminished, but the influence that the emperor in the East exerted over the pope in the West was a sign of the problematic church-state relationship that had developed. The issues disputed by both the defenders and opponents of the Council of Chalcedon were extremely complex, and in light of compromises struck in the late twentieth century, one is hard put today to assess guilt in the early period. But after almost two centuries of a steady defense of tradition by papal authority, from Damasus to Vigilius, the wavering of Pelagius stands as a warning sign for future generations of popes. The legacy of Leo I, called "the Great," probably the most outstanding pope of the early period, would pass to Gregory I, the only other pope called "the Great," the last pope chosen in the sixth century and the first major figure in the next stage of the papacy.

PETER (D. C. 64 A.D.)

Jean-Pierre Ruiz

Chapter 3 of *Lumen gentium*, the Second Vatican Council's dogmatic constitution on the church, identifies the Roman pontiff as vicar of Christ and successor of Peter (*Lumen gentium* 22). In so doing, the council relies on traditions that date to the second century A.D. (Ignatius, *Romans* 4, 3; Irenaeus, *Adversus haereses* 3, 1, 2f; 3, 3, 3; Tertullian, *De praescriptione haereticorum* 36; *Scorpiace* 15), which place Peter (and Paul) in a position of foundational preeminence in Rome. According to the New Testament, the road that eventually led Peter to the capital city of the empire began in first-century Galilee, where he was among the very first to take up the call to follow Jesus. The fact that the documents of the New Testament mention no follower of Jesus more often than Peter (he is mentioned by name more than two hundred times) makes these texts indispensable sources for any investigation of the historical Peter who underlies these traditions.

Of course, the retrieval of such data must proceed with due attention to the nature of the New Testament texts themselves, since these documents yield biographical information only indirectly. Likewise, investigators must be careful to recognize the likelihood that later understandings have been read back into the New Testament portrait of Peter. In the Gospels Peter functions mainly in a supporting role in narratives that focus the attention of readers on Jesus. The extent to which the gospel portraits of Peter prior to the resurrection are influenced by the experience of Peter subsequent to the resurrection and the image of Peter in the post-Easter church is often hard to establish. Where Peter appears in the letters of Paul, Paul mentions him in the service of the rhetorical ends of that correspondence in comparisons that underscore Paul's integrity and legitimate apostolic authority. In the Acts of the Apostles the speeches attributed both to Peter (2:14–36; 3:12–26; 4:8–12; 5:29–32; 10:34–43; 11:2–18; 15:7–11) and Paul exhibit common patterns of Christian preaching that were familiar to Luke and probably do not reflect their own words. There is much controversy among New Testament scholars over the historical value and accuracy of the material in Acts. Finally, in the two New Testament epistles attributed to Peter the apostle appears as a larger-than-life figure whose abiding authority remained crucial even after his death.

Turning first to the canonical New Testament documents attributed to Peter himself, most scholars now regard 1 Peter as a pseudonymous epistle, written in Peter's name and invoking the apostle's authority. Probably written between 73 and 92 A.D., it presents a portrait of Peter as an apostolic pastor addressing himself to Christians in Asia Minor. In Peter's voice, the author urges: "exhort the presbyters among you, as a fellow presbyter and witness to the sufferings of Christ and one who has a share in the glory to be revealed. Tend the flock of God in your midst" (1 Peter 5:1–2a). Second Peter is also pseudonymous, written perhaps as late as the early second century A.D. and presenting itself as the work of "Simeon Peter, a servant and apostle of Jesus Christ" (2 Peter 1:1). This document, depicting Peter as an apostle whose death is imminent (2 Peter 1:14), presents his eyewitness experience of Jesus as the foundation of true doctrine, presented to counteract the threat of false teaching. In addition to these two canonical epistles, several apocryphal writings also bear Peter's name. Among these are the Acts of Peter; the Acts of Peter and the Twelve Apostles, found among the Nag Hammadi Coptic Gnostic codices; three Apocalypses of Peter, one extant only in Arabic, another available in Ethiopic translation and in fragmentary form in Greek, and a third found among the Nag Hammadi codices; and the Gospel of Peter. The Pseudo-Clementines (c. 220-300 A.D.) include the so-called Letter of Peter to James and the *Kerygmata Petrou*.

The New Testament itself provides only the scantiest bits of personal information about Peter prior to his becoming a follower of Jesus. His father's name was Jonah (Matthew 16:17; John 1:42, 21:15–17), and his own given name was Simon. His brother Andrew was also a follower of Jesus (Matthew 4:18, 10:2; Luke 6:14; John 1:40, 44; 6:8), and both they and Philip came from Bethsaida in Galilee (John 1:44, 12:21). Like James and John, Simon and Andrew were fishermen by trade (Matthew 4:18–22; Mark 1:16–20; Luke 5:1–11; John 21:1–7). It is very likely that Peter lived in Capernaum, a town located on the northwestern shore of the Sea of Galilee, since the synoptic Gospels speak of Jesus entering the house to heal Peter's mother-in-law (Matthew 8:14–15; Mark 1:29–31; Luke 4:38–39). Mention of his mother-in-law makes it clear that Peter was married, though we do not know his wife's name, and on the basis of 1 Corinthians 9:5 we know that she accompanied him on his missionary travels.

Concluding their detailed analysis of the biblical data, the Roman Catholic and Protestant scholars, whose background work for ecumenical discussions of the role of the papacy in the church appeared as *Peter in the New Testament* (Brown, Donfried, and Reumann), arrived at the following minimal conclusions about the career of the historical Simon Peter beginning with his call to follow Jesus:

1. Simon during the ministry of Jesus:
   a) Simon was one of the first called of those who became disciples of Jesus and who continued to follow Jesus after the resurrection;
   b) Simon held a prominent place among this group of followers of Jesus prior to and after the resurrection;
   c) Simon probably made a confession of faith in Jesus during Jesus' earthly ministry, a confession probably made in terms drawn from contemporary Judaism;
   d) Simon failed, at least in part, to fully understand Jesus.

2. Peter in the early church:
   a) Simon came to be known as Cephas (Peter), probably because Jesus himself had given him this name;
   b) Simon Peter was granted an appearance of the risen Jesus, probably among the first of these appearances;
   c) Peter was the most important of the Twelve in Jerusalem;
   d) Peter engaged in missionary activity among Jews and possibly among Gentiles;
   e) Peter's theological stance probably represented an intermediate position between James and Paul.

Statue of Peter in the papal robes displayed in St. Peter's in Rome. (Courtesy of the Vatican Library)

With these conclusions as a starting point, the following will focus on four specific features of Peter's career: first, Jesus' response to Peter's confession (Matthew 16:17–19); second, Peter's denial of Jesus and his post-resurrection rehabilitation; third, the controversy between Peter and Paul at Antioch; fourth, the evidence of Peter's presence in Rome.

Among the New Testament texts in which Peter appears, none has figured more prominently in shaping subsequent Roman Catholic understanding of the Petrine office than Matthew 16:17–19, the unique Matthean version of Jesus' response to Peter's confession in the preceding verse, "You are the Messiah, the Son of the living God" (Matthew 16:16). The confession itself is found, in slightly different terms, in each of the synoptic Gospels (Mark 8:29, "You are the Christ"; Luke 9:20, "You are the Christ of God"). Luke follows Mark closely in reporting Jesus' command that the disciples are to tell no one of this; Matthew diverges from the other synoptics by preceding this order with Jesus' declaration:

> Blessed are you, Simon, son of Jonah! For flesh and blood has not revealed this to you, but my Father in heaven. And I tell you, you are Peter, and on this rock I will build my church, and the gates of Hades will not prevail against it. I will give you the keys to the kingdom of heaven, and whatever you bind on earth will be bound in heaven, and whatever you loose on earth will be loosed in heaven.

This text, which reflects pre-Matthean tradition, includes three distinct elements: first, a macarism announcing that Simon's identification of Jesus as "the Messiah, the Son of the living God" is the result of divine revelation; second, the bestowal of the name "Peter" and an explanation of its significance; third, the conferral of the "keys to the kingdom of heaven," the power to bind and loose. The first element is one of several instances in Matthew's Gospel where Jesus reminds the disciples that they are privileged recipients of divine revelation. In Matthew 13:11 Jesus tells them, "To you it has been given to know the secrets of the kingdom of heaven," a knowledge not entrusted to the general public, a gift reinforced by the macarism found in 13:16: "Blessed are your eyes, for they see, and your ears, for they hear." Even though the reception of privileged divine revelation is granted to the disciples as a group, Matthew 16:17 is the only instance in the Gospels where a named individual is singled out as the recipient of a blessing from Jesus. Matthew thus underlines the particular prominence of Peter among the disciples, a prominence that goes well beyond Peter's role as spokesperson on behalf of the other disciples.

The second element, the renaming of Simon as Peter, is attested elsewhere in the synoptic Gospels (cf. Matthew 4:18; 10:2; Mark 3:16; Luke 6:14). It is also described in John 1:42, " 'You are Simon son of John. You are to be called Cephas,' (which is translated Peter)." Only in Matthew does the renaming of Simon follow immediately upon his christological confession, whereas in John 1:42 the conferral of the name takes place the very moment Simon is first brought into Jesus' presence by Andrew. Mark 3:16 makes mention of Simon's new nickname in the course of listing the names of the Twelve chosen by Jesus. The different contexts in which the

Gospels relate Jesus' nicknaming of Simon as Peter make the historical occasion of that renaming uncertain. As for the name itself, the name "Rock" is not attested as a normal personal name in contemporary Greek, Aramaic, or Hebrew, so that its conferral on Peter has the quality of a nickname, perhaps somehow indicative of his character. A number of commentators suggest that the renaming of Peter recalls instances in the Old Testament in which the Israelite patriarchs Abram and Jacob receive new names—Abraham (Genesis 17:1–8) and Israel (Genesis 32:22–32), respectively—from God that signify their divinely appointed roles. The conferral of the name Peter on Simon, whatever the historical occasion, symbolizes the divinely appointed role he would play in the church.

The third element, the conferral on Peter of the keys to the kingdom of heaven, is a motif based on Isaiah 22:22, in which the prophet announces to Shebna, king Hezekiah's steward, that he will be removed from this position and replaced by Eliakim, of whom Isaiah prophesies, "I will place on his shoulder the key of the house of David; he shall open, and no one shall shut; he shall shut, and no one shall open." The use of this motif here indicates that Jesus constitutes Peter as a majordomo, with a steward's responsibility for the kingdom of heaven. While the giving of keys undoubtedly represents the bestowal of authority (see, for example, Revelation 1:18; 2 Enoch 40:9–11; b. Sanhedrin 113a), there is substantial scholarly controversy over the significance of "binding" and "loosing." Hypotheses range from the suggestion, based on the use of "binding" and "loosing" in the intertestamental literature with reference to exorcisms, that Peter is receiving power over demons to the suggestion that Peter is being granted authority to forgive sins (cf. John 20:23) and to an interpretation of binding and loosing in terms of teaching authority, the standard Roman Catholic understanding, which is in accord with the rabbinical usage of "binding" and "loosing."

All four Gospels narrate Jesus' prediction of Peter's threefold denial (Matthew 26:30–35; Mark 14:26–31; Luke 22:31–34; John 13:36–38), pronounced after the Last Supper after Peter's protestation of singular loyalty to Jesus (Matthew 26:33; Mark 14:29; Luke 22:33; John 13:37), and the denial itself (Matthew 26:69–75; Mark 14:66–72; Luke 22:54–62; John 18:15–18, 25–27). Luke softens the blow of the prediction of Peter's denials by prefacing it with Jesus' announcement of the role the repentant Peter will play: "Simon, Simon, behold Satan has demanded to sift all of you like wheat, but I have prayed that your own faith may not fail; and once you have turned back, you must strengthen your brothers" (Luke 22:31–32). The postresurrection fulfillment of this positive prediction and charge entrusted to Peter begins in Acts 1:15–26 when Peter is said to take the lead in appointing a successor to Judas, thereby reconstituting the Twelve.

The rehabilitation of Peter is handled differently in John 21, where it appears between an appearance of the risen Jesus to the disciples as they are fishing on the Sea of Galilee (John 21:1–14) and an exchange between Peter and Jesus about the Beloved Disciple (John 21:20–23). In John 21: 15–19 we find Jesus asking Peter three times whether he loves him, and Peter's increasingly insistent threefold positive response. To each of Peter's three affirmations Jesus responds by entrusting Peter with pastoral responsibility (21:15, "feed my lambs;" 21:16, "tend my sheep;" 21:17, "feed my sheep").

Together with Matthew 16:17–19, John 21:15–17 was cited by *Pastor aeternus*, the First Vatican Council's Dogmatic Constitution on the Church of Christ (1870), in its solemn definition of the pope's primacy of jurisdiction as successor of Peter:

> We, therefore, teach and declare, according to the testimony of the Gospel, that the primacy of jurisdiction over the whole church of God was immediately and directly promised to and conferred upon the blessed apostle Peter by Christ the Lord. . . . After his resurrection, Jesus conferred upon Simon Peter alone the jurisdiction of Supreme Shepherd and ruler over his whole flock with the words: "Feed my lambs . . . feed my sheep" (John 21:15–17). (Denzinger and Schönmetzer 3053)

Because the Johannine Jesus declares that being a good shepherd involves the willingness to lay down one's life for the sake of the sheep (John 10:11), it is not surprising that the risen Jesus' conferral of pastoral responsibility on Peter is followed by stark words about what would await Peter: "Amen, amen, I say to you, when you were younger, you used to dress yourself and go where you wanted; but when you grow old, you will stretch out your hands and someone else will dress you and lead you where you do not want to go" (John 21:18). The narrator then explains, "He said this signifying by what death he [Peter] would glorify God" (John 21:19a).

In Paul's letter to the Galatians, after describing his visit to Jerusalem, at the end of which "James, Cephas and John, who were acknowledged pillars . . . gave to Barnabas and me the right hand of fellowship, agreeing that we should go to the Gentiles and they to the circumcised" (Galatians 2:9), Paul describes a confrontation between himself and Peter (to whom he consistently refers as "Cephas") during Peter's stay in Antioch:

> But when Cephas came to Antioch, I opposed him to his face, because he stood self-condemned; for until certain people came from James, he used to eat with the Gentiles. But after they came, he drew back and kept himself separate for fear of the circumcision faction. And the other Jews joined him in this hypocrisy, so that even Barnabas was led astray by their hypocrisy. But when I saw that they were not acting consistently with the truth of the gospel, I said to Cephas before them all, "If you, though a Jew, live like a Gentile and not like a Jew, how can you compel the Gentiles to live like Jews?" (Galatians 2:11–14)

Paul provides no explanation for Peter's presence in Antioch, for the description of his encounter with Peter there serves not to inform his Galatian audience about Peter, but to enhance his own apostolic stature by comparison with a figure who was well known and well respected among them. It was Paul who accused Peter of hypocrisy when Peter withdrew from table fellowship with Gentile Christians upon the arrival of "certain people from James," that is, Jewish Christian representatives of the Jerusalem church. Whatever the description in Galatians of the controversy at Antioch may tell us about Paul, it indirectly supplies us with valuable information about Peter: first, that, together with James and John, Peter was among those "reputed to be pillars" of the Jerusalem church; second, that Peter's prominence among the apostles was recognized far beyond Jerusalem; third, that Peter himself traveled at least as far as Antioch.

With the credibility of his recent preaching in the Galatian Christian community imperiled by the arrival of "some who are confusing you and want to pervert the gospel of Christ" (Galatians 1:7), Paul defends the divine origin of the gospel he preached among the Galatians, employing an autobiographical narrative of his divine commission to proclaim the gospel among the Gentiles (Galatians 1:11–20). Paul emphasizes that he did not "go up to Jerusalem to those who were already apostles before me," and that only three years later did he go to Jerusalem, where he visited Cephas and stayed with him for fifteen days (Galatians 1:18). After fourteen years he returned to Jerusalem, together with Barnabas and Titus, to present to the leaders of the Christian community there "the gospel that I proclaim among the Gentiles, in order to make sure that I was not running, or had not run, in vain" (Galatians 2:2).

Stepping back to review the presentation of the relationship between Paul and Peter presented in Galatians, we find a three-stage progression. At first, Paul came to Jerusalem as Peter's guest (1:18); then Paul and those with him engaged as equals in discussion with the leadership of the Jerusalem community (2:1–10); finally, Paul judged Peter and found him guilty of hypocrisy (2:11–14). While Paul himself recognized Peter's stature as one of those "who were acknowledged pillars" (Galatians 2:9) and affirmed Peter's privilege as a witness to the resurrection of Jesus (1 Corinthians 15:5), he did not hesitate either to defend the authenticity of his own apostolic calling or to take Peter to task for the sake of the gospel.

While John 21 testifies to Peter's martyrdom as an event that had already taken place by the time the Fourth Gospel was completed in its final form (c. 90 A.D.), it does not specify the location of Peter's death. Early Christian tradition affirms that Peter's martyrdom occurred in Rome, but precisely how Peter eventually made it to Rome is entirely uncertain. The statement of the second-century Roman presbyter Gaius notwithstanding, neither Peter nor Paul were founders of the Roman church. There is evidence indicating the presence of Christians in Rome as early as the 40s, since Paul's letter to the Romans speaks of his long-standing but as yet unrealized desire to visit the already-established Christian community there (Romans 15:22–23). Despite his familiarity with Peter, Paul makes no mention of him in Romans, which concludes with an extensive list of Roman Christians whom Paul greets by name (Romans 16:1–23). This makes it highly unlikely that Peter had arrived in Rome prior to A.D. 55–58, the range of years during which most scholars fix the composition of Romans. The only New Testament evidence of Peter's presence in Rome is provided by 1 Peter 5:13, "The chosen one in Babylon sends you greetings." "Babylon" was a symbolic designation of Rome frequently found in Jewish and early Christian literature (for example, Revelation 14:8, 17:5, 18:2), metaphorically connecting the fall of Jerusalem to Babylon in 586 B.C. with the destruction of Jerusalem by the Romans in A.D. 70.

1 Clement 5 provides the earliest evidence of Peter's death in Rome, noting of Peter and Paul that "through jealousy and envy the greatest and most righteous pillars of the church were persecuted and contended unto death." According to Eusebius (c. 260–340 A.D.), both Peter and Paul suffered martyrdom in Rome during the reign of Nero, around 62 A.D. (*Ecclesiastical History* 2, 25, 1). Eusebius records the legend that Peter was executed by crucifixion, head downwards (*Ecclesiastical History* 3, 1), and quotes the second-century Roman presbyter Gaius's identification of Peter's funeral monument on the Vatican hill: "I can point out the monuments of the victorious apostles; if you go to the Vatican or to the Ostian Way, you will find the monuments of those who founded this church" (*Ecclesiastical History* 2, 25, 7). Archaeological excavations undertaken beneath St. Peter's Basilica have discovered that by the beginning of the third century a monument had been erected over the site where Peter was believed to have been buried, and graffiti etched onto the walls of the site indicate that this monument was a popular pilgrimage site. The suggestion that bones discovered there can be identified as those of Peter, despite the 1968 announcement to that effect by Pope Paul VI, remains highly speculative.

SELECTED BIBLIOGRAPHY

Brown, Raymond E., Karl P. Donfried, and John Reumann, eds. *Peter in the New Testament*. New York: Paulist Press; Minneapolis: Augsburg, 1973.

Cullmann, Oscar. *Peter: Disciple—Apostle—Martyr*, 2nd ed. Trans. Floyd V. Filson. London: SCM, 1962.

Dietrich, Wolfgang. *Das Petrusbild der Lukanischen Schriften*. Stuttgart: W. Kohlhammer, 1972.

Droge, Arthur J. "The Status of Peter in the Fourth Gospel." *Journal of Biblical Literature* 109 (1990): 307–11.

Farmer, William R., and Roch Kereszty. *Peter and Paul in the Church of Rome: The*

Ecumenical Potential of a Forgotten Perspective. Theological Inquiries. New York: Paulist Press, 1990.

Guarducci, Margherita. *The Tomb of St. Peter.* Trans. Joseph McLellan. New York: Hawthorn, 1960.

Karrer, Martin. "Petrus im paulinischen Gemeindekreis." *Zeitschrift für die neutestamentliche Wissenschaft* 80 (1989): 210–31.

Karrer, Otto. *Peter and the Church: An Examination of Cullmann's Thesis.* Trans. Ronald Walls. Quaestiones Disputatae. 8. New York: Herder & Herder, 1963.

Kirschbaum, Engelbert. *The Tombs of St. Peter and St. Paul.* Trans. John Murray. New York: St. Martin's Press, 1959.

Lohse, Eduard. "St. Peter's Apostleship in the Judgment of St. Paul, the Apostle to the Gentiles: An Exegetical Contribution to an Ecumenical Debate." *Gregorianum* 72 (1991): 419–35.

O'Connor, Daniel William. *Peter in Rome: The Literary, Liturgical, and Archeological Evidence.* New York: Columbia University Press, 1969.

Perkins, Pheme. *Peter: Apostle for the Whole Church.* Studies on Personalities of the New Testament. Columbia: University of South Carolina Press, 1994.

Pesch, Rudolf. *Simon-Petrus: Geschichte und geschichtliche Bedeutung des ersten Jüngers Jesu Christi.* Päpste und Papsttum 15. Stuttgart: Anton Hiersemann, 1980.

Smith, T.V. *Petrine Controversies in Early Christianity: Attitudes towards Peter in Christian Writings of the First Two Centuries.* WUNT, 2 Reihe, 15. Tübingen: J.C.B. Mohr (Paul Siebeck), 1985.

CLEMENT I
(C. 91–C. 101)

MARGARET A. SCHATKIN

In Christian antiquity Clement of Rome enjoyed great esteem, though he is known only as the author of one small writing, the Epistle to the Corinthians. So religiously useful did the letter prove that it passed into an early New Testament manuscript, the famous Codex Alexandrinus, where it follows immediately (with the so-called 2 Clement) the Apocalypse of John. This suggests that at an early period in some parts of the Christian world the epistle was regarded as canonical, as part of the New Testament.

The actual name of the writer of the Epistle to the Corinthians (hereafter cited as 1 Clem.) is not mentioned in the letter itself. According to the salutation, it is a letter from the church of Rome written to the church of Corinth: "The church of God which sojourns in Rome to the church of God which sojourns in Corinth." But all the ancient authors agree with one another on the authorship of Clement. Already Bishop Dionysius of Corinth (about 170) calls Clement of Rome the author of this epistle (Eusebius, *H.E.* 4.23), and it would be difficult to find anyone in a position to be better informed than he was. To his testimony we may add those of Irenaeus (*Adv. haer.* 3.3.3), of Hegesippus (Eusebius, *H.E.* 4.22), and of Clement of Alexandria, by whom the epistle appears to be treated as Scripture. D. Völter tried to disprove the attribution to Clement, but the reasons he adduces are not convincing (*Die Visionen des Hermas, die Sybille, und Clemens von Rom*, Berlin: Schwetschke und Sohn, 1900, 31). There is no reason for rejecting the tradition that has always ascribed the letter to Clement.

The information we have regarding the origin and life of Clement is limited. Irenaeus tells us that he (Clement) had seen and had contact with the apostles, and furthermore that he was the third successor of St. Peter in the episcopal dignity at Rome: Petrus, Linus, Anacletus, Clement (*Adv. haer.* 3.3.3). Origen (*Comm. in Joh.* 6.54.36) identified him with the Clement of the Epistle of Paul to the Philippians 4:3: "Clement and the rest of my fellow workers, whose names are in the book of life." Eusebius (*H.E.* 3.15), Epiphanius (*Adv. haer.* 27.6), and Jerome (*De vir. ill.* 15) all agree with him. Since Origen was a critical scholar, this identification seems to be more than a mere conjecture.

A Clement is also mentioned in the Shepherd of Hermas, in which it is stated that it was his (Clement's) duty to write to other churches: "Clement is to send his copy (or rescripts of it) to the cities abroad, for this function is his" (*Vis.* 2.4.3). This allusion in an early Roman document" points to a Clement in Rome exercising the same functions as the writer of our epistle.

Altogether improbable are the accounts of the so-called Pseudo-Clementinae (Recognitiones, Homiliae), which represent Clement, the future bishop of Rome, as a descendant of the imperial house. The Recognitions of Clement are considered a fictionalized account, using the theme of "recognition" often found in ancient novels. It is a common plot in ancient Greek comedy: the girl, loved by the son of a family of good standing, is a slave, but at the end she is found to be the daughter of a highly esteemed family, fallen into the hands of slave traders in her youth. The comedy finishes with the recognition of their parents and the wedding. Thus also Clement is represented as traveling to Palestine and meeting St. Peter there. Later on he rediscovers his parents and brothers. From this recognition the novel has its name. But the tale is only the frame for theological argumentations of Jewish-Christian character. These frame narrations represent a very old literary form in classical literature: for example, books 9 to 12 of the *Odyssey* are such a narrative. In one night Odysseus tells the Phaeacians his wanderings during ten years beginning with his departure from Troy, during the farewell banquet given to him by the king of the Phaeacians. The Pseudo-Clementinae (Recognitiones and Homiliae) belong to the third century and cannot be used as a reliable source for the life of Clement.

Some nineteenth-century scholars attempted to identify our Clement with the Roman consul Titus Flavius Clemens. This Flavius Clemens was accused of impiety by his cousin, the emperor Domitian, because of his Jewish proclivities (Dio Cassius, *Hist. Rom.* 67.14). In 95 Flavius Clemens was put to death, and his wife, Domitilla, was banished to the island of Pandateria. There is no absolute proof that Flavius Clemens was really a Christian, but there is a great probability, since one of the oldest catacombs in Rome belonged to Domitilla (via Ardeatina) and certainly was connected with this family. But it is probably not the case that Titus Flavius Clemens was the author of our letter, because contemporary writers, Christian or pagan, certainly would have laid stress upon the fact that a cousin of the Roman emperor was bishop of Rome. However, the Christianity that had taken root in the household of Domitian's cousin is memorialized in the person of the Alexandrian church father Titus Flavius Clemens (c. 150–215). Indeed, the name Clemens is frequent in later Latin, perhaps made popular by Stoicism. Pope Clement, who wrote in Greek, bears the Greek form of the Latin name. The name was common among slaves and freedmen, including those of Jewish descent.

Tillemont drew the conclusion, upheld by many scholars, that the author, Pope Clement, was a Jew by birth from 1 Clem. 4.8, where Jacob is called "our father," and from 1 Clem. 31.2, where Abraham is likewise called "our father" (*Mémoires pour servir à l'histoire ecclésiastique*, Vol. 2, 149, *St. Clément Art. I*). In conclusion, we can state that there is no reason for rejecting the very old and good tradition that Clement, one of the first successors of St. Peter, really is the author of 1 Clement.

According to Irenaeus, Clement was the third successor of Peter as bishop of Rome: Linus (cf. 2 Tim. 4: 21) and Anacletus preceded him. Eusebius (*H.E.* 3.15, 34) states that in the twelfth year of the reign of Emperor Domitian (92), Clement became bishop of Rome and died in the third year of Trajan's reign (101). Others date his pontificate between 88 (?) and 97 (?). There can be little

Mosaic of procession of martyrs detail of Saint Clement carrying crown, in Saint Apollinare Nuovo Ravenna, sixth century. (The Art Archive/San Apollinare Nuovo Ravenna/Dagli Orti)

doubt, however, that from the time of Peter (died 64 or 67) through the pontificates of Linus (67–79?) and Anacletus (79–88?), Clement was a powerful presence in Rome. No bishop of Rome until Leo I, the Great, made as deep an impression upon the Christian community, as is witnessed by the literature, genuine and fictitious, surrounding his name.

Most critics, including Lightfoot (1890) and Harnack (1929), have assumed that the letter was written by Clement at the time when he was actually pope, that is, the last decade of the first century. Internal evidence, however, suggests that the epistle was indited earlier, perhaps around 69–70, when Clement was still functioning as "secretary of state" (cf. Hermas, *Vis.* 2.4.3). Some of the evidence for the date of the epistle is as follows:

1. The temple at Jerusalem is not yet destroyed, for Clement speaks of the temple cultus as being carried on (1 Clem. 41). This points to a date before 70.

2. Clement does not quote from the written Gospels and evidently relied upon other traditions for the sayings of Jesus.

3. Clement refers to the persecution of Nero (64) as "very recent" and "within our generation," in which Peter and Paul were martyred along with a "great multitude of the elect" (1 Clem. 5–6).

4. The allusion at the beginning of the epistle to "a series of sudden misfortunes and accidents that have come upon us" may refer to the civil war that took place in the city of Rome in 69, the "year of four emperors." According to Tacitus, "the streets were choked with carnage, the squares and temples reeked with blood, for men were massacred everywhere as chance threw them in the way" (*Hist.* 4.1). If Clement were writing when the civil war was raging in Rome, in 69, it would explain his abhorrence of strife and faction and his emphasis on the value of peace and concord.

The occasion for writing 1 Clement was a schism that emerged in the church of Corinth. One or two ringleaders had stirred up the faithful against the presbyters, of whom several of irreproachable life had been driven from office. The church of Rome learned of these troubles through public rumor and/or informants, and Clement, then presbyter-secretary of Rome, intervened in an authoritative form: "We consider therefore that it is not just to remove from their ministry those who were appointed by them [the apostles], or later on by other eminent men, with the consent of the whole church, and have ministered to the flock of Christ without blame" (1 Clem. 44.3). The letter is a proof that the Roman church at that very early time was conscious of its primacy.

The epistle is divided into two main parts. The first part (1–36) contains general exhortations to the practice of charity, penance, obedience, humility, faith, and hospitality, calculated to ensure a spirit of concord among the faithful. The second part (37–61) deals with the troubles at Corinth and, referring to the organization of an army and of the human body, as well as of the hierarchy of the Old Testament, demands that the Corinthians subordinate themselves and yield ready obedience to the ecclesiastical superiors appointed by the apostles or their successors. In the conclusion (62–65) the author expresses the hope that the bearers of the letter will soon return with the information that peace and concord reign again in the church of Corinth.

Clement intended to write a real letter, a letter in the strict sense of the word. This conclusion can be drawn from the occasion that induced the author to write the letter: the schism that had broken out in the church of Corinth. He seems to have been a convert from Judaism who, knowing the Old Testament well, was also trained in Greek literature. This particular Jewish-Hellenistic education can be observed in Clement and enabled him to follow, as regards style, Greek models, not as a master, it is true, but as a skilled imitator. He wished to write a real letter with an important subject matter, but, unlike St. Paul, was compelled to give general exhortations, since he was informed about the Corinthian situation only in general, or else chose, for diplomatic reasons, to suppress the details. As a result, he turned the real letter he intended to write into a pure treatise on Christian community and church governance. His epistle may thus be compared to some works of the contemporary Roman Stoic philosopher Seneca.

The manuscripts that give the text of the epistle are as follows: the Codex Alexandrinus, a Greek uncial of the fifth century in the British Museum, contains the whole text with the exception of one page (chaps. 57.6–64.1). There exists a photographic edition of the whole codex published by the trustees of the British Museum. The Codex Constantinopolitanus is a Greek minuscule written by the notarius Leo in 1056 and discovered by Philotheus Bryennius, metropolitan of Nicomedia, in 1873. A photographic edition of the text is given in Lightfoot's edition of Clement (*The Apostolic Fathers* 1.1, London: MacMillan and Co., 1892, 425–74). The codex is usually called Codex Hierosolymitanus because it is now kept in the Patriarchal Library of Jerusalem.

The Syriac version, extant in only one manuscript written in 1169 and now in the library of Cambridge University (MS. add. 1700), a version perhaps of the eighth century, was published by R.L. Bensly and R.H. Kennet (*The Epistles of St. Clement to the Corinthians in Syriac*, Cambridge: Cambridge University Press, 1899). Under the name Second Epistle of Clement to the Corinthians there survives a sermon that is found in the two Greek manuscripts already mentioned and in the Syriac version, but not in the Latin and Coptic version. Eusebius doubts its authenticity (*H.E.* 3.38.4).

The Latin version of 1 Clement is of a very early date (late second or early third century) and seems to have been used by Lactantius. The manuscript of the eleventh century in the seminary of Namur was published by Dom Germanus Morin (*Anecdota Maredsolana*, vol. 2, Maredsous, 1894) as *Sancti Clementis Romani ad Corinthios Epistulae versio latina antiquissima*. The Coptic version exists in two manuscripts: the older and better preserved, in the Königliche Bibliothek at Berlin in MS. Orient., fol. 3065 (of the fourth century), was published by C. Schmidt in the serbes Texte und Untersuchungen 32, 1, as *Der erste Clemensbrief in altkoptischer Übersetzung*

(Leipzig, 1908). The later (seventh-century) and more fragmentary manuscript is in Strassburg and was published in Strassburg in 1910 as *Bruchstücke des ersten Clemensbriefes* by F. Rösch.

SELECTED BIBLIOGRAPHY

Bumpus, Harold Bertram. *The Christological Awareness of Clement of Rome and Its Sources.* Cambridge Mass.: University Press of Cambridge, 1972.

Denzinger, Heinrich, and Adolf Schönmetzer, eds. *Enchiridion symbolorum: definitionum et declarationum de rebus fidei et morum.* Barcelona: Herder, 1976.

Fuellenbach, John. *Ecclesiastical Office and the Primacy of Rome: An Evaluation of Recent Theological Discussion of First Clement.* Catholic University of America Studies in Christian Antiquity, no. 20. Washington, D.C.: Catholic University of America Press, 1980.

Glimm, Francis X, trans. *The Letter of St. Clement of Rome to the Corinthians. The So-Called Second Letter of St. Clement, Being an Ancient Homily by an Anonymous Author.* The Fathers of the Church, vol. 1: *The Apostolic Fathers.* Washington, D.C.: Catholic University of America Press, 1947.

Grant, Robert M., and Holt H. Graham. *The Apostolic Fathers: A New Translation and Commentary.* Vol. 2: *First and Second Clement.* New York: Thomas Nelson and Sons, 1965.

Guidobaldi, Federico. *San Clemente: Gli edifici romani, la basilica paleocristiana, e le fasi altomedievali.* 2 vols. Rome: Collegio San Clemente, 1992.

Harnack, Adolf von. *Einführung in die alte Kirchengeschichte: Das Schreiben der römischen Kirche an die Korinthische aus der Zeit Domitians (I. Clemensbrief).* Leipzig: J.C. Hinrichs, 1929.

Hooijbergh, Wilhelm A.E. "A Different View of Clemens Romanus." *Heythrop Journal* 16 (1975): 266–88.

Jaubert, Annie. *Clément de Rome: Épître aux Corinthiens.* Sources Chrétiennes 167. Paris: Cerf, 1971.

Lake, Kirsopp. *The Apostolic Fathers.* Greek text with an English translation. Vol. 1. Loeb Classical Library no. 24. 1912. Reprint, Cambridge, Mass.: Harvard University Press, 1985, 1–163.

Lightfoot, Joseph Barber. *The Apostolic Fathers. First Part: S. Clement of Rome: A Revised Text with Introductions, Notes, Dissertations, and Translations.* Vol. 1: Nachdruck der 2. Auflage, London, 1890. Vol. 2: Nachdruck der Ausgabe London, 1890. Hildesheim: Georg Olms Verlag, 1973.

Sanders, L. *L'Hellénisme de S. Clément de Rome et le paulinisme.* Studia Hellenistica 2. Louvain: Universitas Catholica Louvaniensis, 1943.

Tillemont, M. Lenain de. *Memoires pour servir l'Histoire Ecclesiastique de six premiers siecles.* Venice: Pitteri, 1732.

CALLISTUS I (217–22)

Michael Slusser

St. Callistus I is the best known of all the bishops of Rome following Peter in the first two centuries of Christianity. He owes this unusual visibility to the fact that he incurred the bitter enmity of a contemporary, Hippolytus, who wrote a *Refutation of All Heresies* that culminates with an attack on Callistus. Apart from the information that Hippolytus gives in book 9 of that treatise, we have only a brief mention in Eusebius's *Ecclesiastical History* by which to date his episcopate. He followed Zephyrinus as bishop shortly after Marcus Antoninus Elagabalus became emperor, and survived five years. A late tradition represented in the *Martyrologium Romanum* describes a violent death, but we are ignorant of the circumstances. Callistus's rival Hippolytus, in book 9 of the *Refutation of All Heresies*, gives us more details about Callistus than we have about any other early bishop of Rome. These details are probably by and large founded on fact, since even a libel is enhanced by verisimilitude, but his charge that Callistus embodied in his own person the essentials of all previous heresies is so obviously the fruit of his enmity with his rival that it must be viewed with skepticism. Let us first cover Callistus's life as Hippolytus describes it and then turn our attention to his alleged errors.

According to Hippolytus, Callistus was a slave in the household of a Christian named Carpophoros, who himself is described as being of the imperial household. Carpophoros was engaged in banking, and his good reputation attracted many deposits from widows and fellow Christians. He entrusted a portion of this banking business to Callistus, who lost everything and went bankrupt. He attempted to flee the day of reckoning with his master by hiding on a ship about to leave from Portus, but Carpophoros was informed and pursued him there. Callistus, either in desperation or, according to Hippolytus, in an attempt at suicide, threw himself overboard, but was retrieved and brought back to Rome to work at the grinding mill as punishment. After a while, when he told some of the Christians that he could get their money back, they asked Carpophoros to release him, and he did so, in the hope of recovering some of the reputation he had lost. But Callistus failed to turn up the missing money, and when he saw that he had no chance to flee, he broke in on a synagogue service and started a riot. Arrested and sent to the prefect of the city, Fuscianus, he was sentenced to the mines in Sardinia.

Shortly thereafter, Marcia, a Christian who was a concubine of the emperor Commodus, sought to use her influence to rescue some of the Christian martyrs held in Sardinia, using a list given her by Bishop Victor. Callistus is said by Hippolytus not to have been on that list, but to have prevailed upon Marcia's messenger to bring him back anyway, much to the dismay of Victor. Rather than tarnish the reputation of the others by returning Callistus to custody, Victor sent him out of Rome to Anzio, with a monthly living allowance from the community as a confessor and therefore a cleric. After Victor's death his successor Zephyrinus brought him back to Rome to help lead the clergy and take charge of the cemetery. This would have been an important position, as the Christian communities could gain legal status as burial societies even though their religion was not protected by law. When Zephyrinus died, Callistus rose to the leadership of the church in Rome, according to Eusebius of Caesarea; Hippolytus does not accord him such an unambiguous position. Whether the Christians in Rome were by this time organized in some sort of unitary body, or whether their congregations were still rather loosely associated, is unclear from his account. At this point in the *Refutation*, Hippolytus leaves off his account of Callistus's life: either Callistus was still alive at the time Hippolytus was writing, or his death in a genuine martyrdom (if the legend in the so-called *Calendar of 354* is based on fact) was an embarrassment to his bitter enemy.

After giving these biographical details, Hippolytus transfers his attention to what he considers the heresies of Callistus. These were primarily in the area of the doctrine of the Trinity, but also in regard to penitential practice, the recognition of clergy, and marriage across the class divisions of Roman society. Since each charge has its peculiar interest, we shall examine them separately here. The heaviest charge is the doctrinal one. Hippolytus has prepared the way for it by the way he structures the list of heresies that leads up to Callistus. Callistus is alleged to have advocated a form of the heresy of a certain Noetus, who identified Jesus with God the Father to the point where it was the Father himself who died on the cross, was buried, and rose again. Hippolytus saw himself as reacting against this denial of distinction within the Godhead; he apparently upheld some form of Logos Christology. In any case, he accused Callistus of, first, when he was a deacon, misleading Pope Zephyrinus into making ambiguous statements on the subject, such as, "I know one God, Jesus Christ, and apart from him no one else who was born and suffered," and "It was not the Father who died, but the Son." When Hippolytus tried to refute these statements, Callistus had called him a "ditheist" (believer in two Gods), an accusation that earned him Hippolytus's lasting hatred.

Apparently Callistus did not make any unequivocal statement that would link him directly with Noetus. No matter; Hippolytus charged him all the more vigorously with deviousness and blamed him for pushing another contemporary, Sabellius, into a heresy that Callistus shared but was not honest enough to espouse. When Callistus expelled Sabellius from the Roman church, Hippolytus thought that he was motivated not by uprightness but by a devious spirit, along with fear of Hippolytus's own reproofs. Callistus, Hippolytus claimed,

An idealized portrait of Pope Callistus I by Fra Diamante. (Courtesy of the Vatican Library)

> said that the Logos himself is Son, and himself Father, called Son and Father in name, but the indivisible Spirit being one. The Father is not one thing, the Son another, but they are one and the same. And everything is full of the divine Spirit, both things above and those below. And the Spirit which was enfleshed in the virgin was not other than the Father but one and the same thing. And this is what he said: "Do you not believe that I am in the Father and the Father in me?" For what is visible, which is a human being, is the Son, but the Spirit which is contained in the Son is the Father. "For," he says, "I shall not say 'two Gods, Father and Son,' but one; for the self-originate Father, when he took flesh, made it divine by uniting it to himself and made one thing, so that Father and Son are called one God. And this being a single person cannot be two, and thus the Father suffered along with the Son." (Hippolytus, *Refutatio omnium haeresium*, ed. Marcovich, 353–54)

Hippolytus denounced such language as intentionally deceptive, "for he is unwilling to say that the Father suffered and is one person—the devious fool hopes to avoid blasphemy against the Father" (Hippolytos, *Refutatio omnium haeresium*, ed. Marcovich, 354). Despite Callistus's efforts, Hippolytus claimed that he combined the heresy of Sabellius with that of Theodotus. If in fact Callistus did not deserve either accusation, Hippolytus may have found it more effective to charge him with both. In the comparatively fluid state of trinitarian terminology in the early third century, Callistus's words may have fallen within acceptable limits; his real offense may have been to accuse Hippolytus himself of heresy.

The next charge against Callistus was that he made penance, and therefore readmittance to Communion, available to Christians whom more rigorous pastors (including Hippolytus himself, significantly) had expelled from their churches. Hippolytus thought this policy a blatant ploy to win popular support. Closely related to it was a willingness to turn a blind eye to the sins of bishops, priests, and deacons who were "twice or thrice married"; furthermore, Hippolytus claimed that Callistus had allowed someone in the clergy to marry. On these two latter charges, we should remember that among some early Fathers, most notably Tertullian, even for a lay person remarriage after the death of a spouse was considered a mark of excessive slavery to sexual impulse. There need not have been many clergy who fell into these categories; one or two would be enough for Hippolytus if they preferred Callistus to him. Common to Callistus's decisions in these matters seems to have been a sense that Christianity was not a sect of the pure but a church that included all its members, pending the judgment of God. Hippolytus claimed that Callistus liked to cite Romans 14:4, Matthew 13:29–30, and the juxtaposition of clean and unclean beasts in Noah's ark as biblical warrants for his policy of inclusion of sinners.

The special treatment that Callistus accorded to women of high station who took slaves as concubines in lieu of husbands has long interested scholars. One view, advocated by Jean Gaudemet, notes that Roman law limited marriage between people of different social classes: free citizens could not marry slaves, and women of senatorial class could not even marry freedmen. It did, however, recognize stable relations of a less formal sort across class boundaries, and inscriptions record the faithful love of the partners in such unions: they were hardly clandestine. In Gaudemet's judgment Callistus was simply extending the logic that governed admission of slaves and concubines to baptism to the similar situations involving marriage: "When civil law forbade marriage, the church accepted a concubinal relationship" (Gaudemet, 343). Henneke Gülzow ascribes the situation to the fact that during the brief reign of Elagabalus the old, strict marriage regulations were in abeyance; if women of high degree who could find no Christian husbands in their own class married slaves in the church, this was simply recognized by Callistus, even though civil legislation had not caught up. Though the hostile portrait that Hippolytus gives us of Callistus must be read with more than ordinary suspicion and the resulting details are tantalizingly fragmentary, we can still get a fascinating glimpse into the difficult tasks that faced an early pope.

SELECTED BIBLIOGRAPHY

Adam, Karl. *Der sogenannte Bußedikt des Papstes Kallistus*. Munich: J.J. Lentner, 1917.

Alès, Adhémar d'. *L'Edit de Calliste: Étude sur les origines de la pénitence chrétienne*. Paris: Beauchesne, 1914.

———. "Zephyrin, Calliste, ou Agrippinus?" *Recherches de science religieuse* 10 (1920):254–56.

Baruffa, Antonio. *Le catacombe di San Callisto: Storia, archeologia fede*. Turin: Elle Di Ci, 1988.

Beyschlag, Karlmann. "Kallist and Hippolyt." *Theologische Zeitschrift* 20 (1964): 103–24.

Brent, Allen. *Hippolytus and the Roman Church in the Third Century: Communities in Tension before the Emergence of a Monarch-Bishop*. Leiden: E.J. Brill, 1995.

Capelle, Bernard. "A propos d'Hippolyte de Rome." *Recherches de théologie ancienne et médiévale* 19 (1952): 193–202.

———. "Hippolyte de Rome." *Recherches de théologie ancienne et médiévale* 17 (1950): 145–74.

Dal Covolo, Enrico. *I Severi e il cristianesimo: Ricerche sull'ambiente storico-istituzionale delle origini cristiane tra il secondo e il terzo secolo*. Rome: Libreria Ateneo Salesiano, 1989.

Döllinger, Johann Joseph Ignaz von. *Hippolytus und Kallistus; oder, Die römische Kirche in der ersten Hälfte des dritten Jahrhunderts*. Regensburg: Josef Manz, 1853. Reprint, Aalen: Scientia, 1977. Translated by Alfred Plummer as *Hippolytus and Callistus; or, The Church of Rome in the First Half of the Third Century*. Edinburgh: T. & T. Clark, 1876.

Donini, Ambrogio. *Ippolito di Roma! Polemiche teologiche e controversie disciplinari nella chiesa di Roma agli inizi del III secolo*. Rome: Libreria di cultura, 1925.

Esser, Gerhard. *Der Adressat der Schrift Tertullians "De pudicitia" und der Verfasser des römischen Bußediktes*. Bonn: Hanstein, 1914.

Frend, W.H.C. "Open Questions Concerning Christians and the Roman Empire in the Age of the Severi." *Journal of Theological Studies*, n.s., 25 (1974):333–51.

Gaudemet, Jean. "La décision de Callixte en matière de mariage." In *Studi in onore di Ugo Enrico Paoli*. Ed. Luisa Banti. Firenze: Lemonnier, 1955, 334–44. Reprinted in Jean Gaudemet, *Sociétés et mariage*. Strasbourg: Cerdic-Publications, 1980, 104–15.

Gieseler, J.C.L. "Über Hippolytus, die ersten Monarchianer, und die römische Kirche in der ersten Hälfte des dritten Jahrhunderts." *Theologische Studien und Kritiken* 26 (1853): 759–87.

Gülzow, Henneke. "Kallist von Rom: Ein Beitrag zur Soziólogie der römische Gemeinde." *Zeitschrift für die neutestamentliche Wissenschaft* 58 (1967): 102–21.

Hall, Stuart George. "Calixtus I." *Theologische Realenzyklopädie* 7 (1981):559–63.

Hippolytus. *Refutatio omnium haeresium*. Ed. Miroslav Marcovich. Patristische Texte und Studien, 25. Berlin: Walter de Gruyter, 1986.

Koschorke, Klaus. *Hippolyt's Ketzerbekämpfung und Polemik gegen die Gnostiker: Eine tendenzkritische Untersuchung seiner "Refutatio omnium haeresium."* Wiesbaden: Otto Harrassowitz, 1975.

Mansfeld, Jaap. *Heresiography in Context: Hippolytus' "Elenchos" as a Source for Greek Philosophy.* Leiden: E.J. Brill, 1992.

Poschmann, Bernhard. *Paenitentia secunda: Die kirchliche Büße im ältesten Christentum bis Cyprian und Origenes.* Bonn: P. Hanstein, 1940.

Prestige, G.L. "Callistus; or, Faith in a Divine Saviour." In *Fathers and Heretics.* London: S.P.C.K., 1954, 23–42.

Preysing, K. von. "Existenz und Inhalt des Bußediktes." *Zeitschrift für katholische Theologie* 43 (1919): 358–62.

Rolffs, Ernst. *Das Indulgenz-Edikt des römischen Bischofs Kallist kritisch untersucht und reconstruiert.* Texte und Untersuchungen 11, 3. Leipzig: J.C. Hinrichs, 1893.

Rossi, Giovanni Battista de. "Esame archeologico e critico della storia di s. Callisto narrata nel libro nono dei Filosofumeni." *Bollettino di archeologia cristiana* 4, no. 4 (1866): 1–99.

Simonetti, Manlio. "Sabellio e il Sabellianismo." *Studi storico religiosi* 4 (1980): 7–28. Reprinted in Manlio Simonetti, *Studi sulla cristologia del II e III secolo.* Rome: Institutum Patristicum Augustinianum, 1993, 217–38.

Slusser, Michael. "The Scope of Patripassianism." *Studia Patristica* 17, no. 1. Oxford: Pergamon Press, 1982, 169–75.

DAMASUS I (366–84)

LOUIS J. SWIFT

Damasus, who reigned from 366 to 384, was both successor to Pope Liberius and heir to the passionate religious conflicts that had marked his predecessor's years as bishop of Rome. Born in 304/5, Damasus was the scion of a prominent Christian family in the capital city, where his father was a Roman ecclesiastic of fairly substantial means. Both his sister Irene and his mother Laurentia were devout members of the community. Irene lived a life of consecrated virginity prior to her early death, and Laurentia, who lived to a very old age, was a consecrated widow for many years following the death of Damasus's father.

As a young man, the future pope grew up in the city and became a deacon in the Roman church under Liberius. Although he seems to have abandoned the pontiff for a time and to have supported the antipope, Felix, upon Liberius's death (366) he was elected the pope's successor by the vast majority of the Christian community and was installed in S. Lorenzo in Lucina. A week earlier a small group of dissidents, who had apparently remained committed to Pope Liberius during that pope's enforced exile, had anticipated Damasus's election by choosing the deacon Ursinus and having him installed as pope in the Julian Basilica (S. Maria in Trastevere). Violent struggles over competing claims of legitimacy and over control of the churches in Rome ensued. Attacks made on Ursinus's supporters by Damasus's friends eventually caused more than a hundred deaths and provoked the intervention of the civil authorities, including that of the emperor himself.

In his desire to maintain public order, Valentinian I initially attempted to settle matters by driving Ursinus and his supporters from Rome. A year later, however, they were readmitted, only to be exiled once more within three months of their return. The churches held by Ursinians were restored to Damasus, but Ursinus and his followers continued directly or indirectly to challenge the new pope for more than a decade. Included in their attacks were the notorious criminal charges (perhaps for public violence or adultery) brought against the pope by the converted Jew Isaac during the 370s. Damasus was exonerated, but ongoing conflicts with Ursinus's supporters, as well as with Arians, Donatists, and Luciferians, made his years as bishop of Rome a time of continued turmoil.

To a degree not seen before, Damasus used the authority of the Roman See to promote doctrinal and juridical uniformity within the church in both the Western and Eastern parts of the empire. In the West he used a series of synods at Rome to oppose Arian bishops in Illyricum and Milan, he invoked the aid of civil authorities in efforts to expel the Donatists and other heretical churches from Rome, and he attacked the schismatic supporters of Lucifer of Cagliari. Damasus involved himself in civic issues by supporting Ambrose of Milan and the Christian senators at Rome in opposing pagan attempts to restore the Altar of Victory to the Roman Senate House. He also enlisted the cooperation of civil authorities in establishing the church's independence with regard to its own internal affairs and its personnel. Through a synod at Rome in 378, he persuaded the emperor to place bishops accused of wrongdoing in religious matters under the practical jurisdiction of episcopal courts.

Damasus's relationship to the East was both more distant (physically and ideologically) and less successful. There is a particular irony in this fact because of the strenuous and oft-expressed desires of St. Basil, bishop of Caesarea, to establish closer union with the papacy in his conflict with the Arians. Misunderstandings about terminology in the homoousian controversy, Damasus's suspicions about the orthodoxy of Meletius (whom Basil supported in the schism of Antioch), and an apparent difference of opinion between himself and Basil about the terms of communion between Eastern and Western churches all contributed to frustration at both ends of the Mediterranean.

Basil's assessment of the relationship between Damasus and the Eastern church is summed up in his remark about the pope's being a "proud man" who had little knowledge of the needs of his Eastern colleagues. At the same time, it is apparent that Damasus experienced extreme difficulty in getting an accurate picture of orthodox and heretical groups in the Eastern part of the empire, a fact that is reflected in the pope's initial acceptance and subsequent rejection of Vitalis, who promoted Apollinarian views on the Trinity. In the long dispute over the bishopric of Antioch, Damasus endorsed Paulinus's claim as the only legitimate one and clarified his own stance vis-à-vis the church in the East through a series of anathemata that enunciated a trinitarian doctrine in quite traditional formulae.

Damasus exercised his influence and authority in church affairs in other parts of the empire as well. In 380 he enjoined a synod of Spanish bishops meeting at Saragossa to avoid condemning Priscillian's supporters who had not received a hearing. He urged Macedonian bishops to be cautious about ordaining unworthy candidates to the episcopacy and about allowing bishops to move from one see to another. He refused to recognize Flavianus as bishop of Constantinople and rejected communion with his consecrators. If Damasus is the actual author of the work entitled *Ad Gallos episcopos*, the pope offered extensive pastoral advice to other bishops concerning the selection and training of the clergy. In all of these activities the pope continued to assert the primacy of the Roman See, and in 380 he gained civil endorsement of this idea when the emperor Theodosius declared that Damasus and Peter of Alexandria (whose episcopacy the pope had supported) were to be considered the touchstones of orthodoxy for all Christians. Damasus appears to have been the very first to cite the pericope of Mt. 16:18 as evidence for the primacy of Rome.

Pope Damasus I wearing his mitre surrounded by a halo. (Hulton/Archive by Getty Images)

Administrative and pastoral activities occupied much of Damasus's eighteen years as bishop. Not the least of these was his interest in seeing to the proper management of papal archives and in promoting both the study of Scripture and devotion to the Roman martyrs. In the latter area he is particularly noteworthy for composing epigrams for the Roman catacombs and other burial places. Many of these were inscribed, or at least designed, by the talented and well-known contemporary artist Furius Dionysius Filocalus, who was a friend of the pope. The inscriptions, of which about fifty-nine have been judged genuine by modern scholars, exhibit the influence of classical authors like Vergil and Epicurus, and they provide important *testimonia* about early Christian witnesses to the faith.

The value of these epigrams as literature is much disputed. Scholars have traditionally criticized the poetry for being obscure, derivative, repetitive, and lacking in inspiration, and these comments seem apt for more than a few of the extant pieces. Nonetheless, several recent critics have followed the lead of Jerome, who spoke of Damasus's "sophisticated talent" (*elegans ingenium*), and have seen his epigrams on the martyrs as a very important stage in the development of Christian poetry. The bishop, they argue, is an author engaged in "continual catechesis" whose elegies in hexameter verse extol the life and death of Christian heroes and invite passersby to reflection and prayer. Thus the epigrams form a kind of liturgical text by using-images and descriptions of suffering and triumph to unite the church in devotion, as the pope had sought through other means to unite it in the expression of faith.

Appearing, as they did, at actual or supposed burial sites of martyrs or of Christian friends and relatives of the pope, the inscriptions drew attention to the holy places in Rome and were part of Damasus's overall purpose of providing a Christian identity to the Eternal City. Perhaps one of the best examples of the simplicity, the scriptural basis, and the classical echoes that characterize Damasus's poetry is the epitaph that he composed for himself (Ferrua 12):

> Qui gradiens pelagi fluctus conpressit amaros,
> vivere qui prestat morientia semina terrae,
> solvere qui potuit letalia vincula mortis
> post tenebras, fratrem post tertia lumina solis
> ad superos iterum Martae donare sorori,
> post cineres Damasum faciet quia surgere credo.

> I believe that He whose step brought calm to the
> turbulent sea, who made the earth's dying seeds come to
> life, who could burst the destructive bonds of death,
> who after three days and nights could restore to Martha
> her brother, once again among the living, will bring
> about Damasus's rise from the ashes.

An excellent example of Damasus's devotion to Roman martyrs as models of Christian virtue and as encouragement for visitors to the shrine is the epitaph that he composed for the converted soldiers Nereus and Achilleus (Ferrua 8).

Nereus et Achilleus Martyres

> Militiae nomen dederant saevumq. gerebant
> officium, pariter spectantes iussa tyranni,
> praeceptis pulsante metu servire parati
> mira fides rerum: subito posuere furore,

conversi fugiunt, ducis inpia castra relinquunt,
proiciunt clipeos, faleras telaq. cruenta,
confessi gaudent Christi portare triumfos.
credite per Damasum possit quid gloria Christi.

Nereus and Achilleus Martyrs

They had pledged the army and were exercising
that cruel office. Matching one another in
observing the orders of the tyrant, they were
ready to heed his commands with fearful blows.
O wondrous faith in events. Suddenly they
cast off their madness; as converts they take
flight; they leave the frightful camp of their
commander; they throw down their shields, their medals,
and their cruel weapons. Professing their faith
they rejoice to carry the trophies of
Christ. Through Damasus believe what
Christ's glory can bring about!

No doubt the most famous inscription erected by Damasus and the one that has provoked the most commentary among scholars is that which marked a shrine of SS. Peter and Paul on the Via Appia (Ferrua 20).

Hic habitasse prius sanctos cognoscere debes
nomina quisque Petri pariter Paulique requiris.
Discipulos Oriens misit, quod sponte fatemur;
sanguinis ob meritum Christumque per astra secuti
aetherios petiere sinus regnaque piorum:
Roma suos potius meruit defendere cives.
Haec Damasus vestras referat nova sidera laudes.

You who inquire about the names of Peter and Paul should know that the saints occupied this place in an earlier time. The East sent these disciples; we freely admit that fact. By their blood and by following Christ through the starry heights they gained a heavenly refuge in the kingdom of the saints. But it was Rome that deserved to claim them as citizens. O new stars, permit Damasus to offer these verses in your praise.

Another part of Damasus's plan for "Christianizing" the city was the churches that he founded. These included the Basilica of the Apostles, San Lorenzo in Damaso, and the Basilica of Saints Mark and Marcellianus. He chose a place near the latter of these as the burial place for his sister, his mother, and himself.

Some of Damasus's works have been preserved. The most significant of the extant pieces is surely the *Tomus Damasi confessio fidei* (377 A.D.), which is the pope's profession of faith that he sent to Paulinus of Antioch. This document has been seen as a precursor to Nicene orthodoxy, and in subsequent years its close association with the Nicene Creed is indicative of the influence that it exercised in the West. Tradition has it that Damasus was also the author of the *Decretum Gelesianum*, but scholars now commonly believe that he was, at most, responsible for the first three chapters (the last two being products of the sixth century).

One of Damasus's most fruitful and personally satisfying relationships was that with St. Jerome. The latter assisted the pope with official correspondence and with responses to inquiries from various synods throughout the empire. On more than one occasion Damasus also called upon Jerome's expertise as an interpreter of Scripture. Whether the pope was wrestling with the meaning of a Hebrew word, the explanation of a parable, or a series of difficult texts, he was obviously impressed with Jerome's brilliance and did not hesitate to avail himself of this ready resource for theological argument or devotional practice. A bit of Damasus's own literary preferences is reflected in his statement that he expected Jerome's replies to be succinct and to the point because the pope often found himself bored by what he considered the turgid style of Lactantius.

The relationship between Jerome and Damasus was a genuine friendship, and Jerome acknowledged the pope's affection by dedicating more than one of his exegetical works to him. Perhaps the most important result of their mutual respect was Jerome's revised translation of the Gospels, which grew out of Damasus's original request that Jerome revise the Latin translations of the Bible. In all probability Jerome's revision of the Latin text of the Psalter was also prompted by the Roman pontiff.

At Damasus's death on 11 December 384, the church of Rome was quite different from what it had been when his pontificate began. The authority of the Roman See was more centralized and the structure of the Roman church better organized. More important, perhaps, a sense of tradition, especially that which is associated with the apostles and martyrs, had become deeply entrenched in the thinking and the practices of the Christian community in the Eternal City. That development had an influence on Christianity in both East and West that can scarcely be measured.

SELECTED BIBLIOGRAPHY

Amand de Mendieta, E. "Basile de Césarée et Damase de Rome: Les causes de l'échec de leurs négociations." In *Biblical and Patristic Studies in Memory of Robert Pierce Casey*, ed. J.N. Birdsall and R.W. Thomson. Freiburg im Br., 1963, 122–66.

Chadwick, H. "Pope Damasus and the Peculiar Claim of Rome to St. Peter and St. Paul." In *Neotestamentica et patristica*. L. Leiden: 1962, 313–18.

———. "St. Peter and St. Paul in Rome: The Problem of the *Memoria Apostolorum ad Catacumbas.*" *Journal of Theological Studies*, n.s., 8 (1957):31–52.

Di Berardino, Angelo. *Patrology.* Trans. P. Solari. Westminster, Md., 1986, 4:273–78.

Ferrua, A. *Epigrammata Damasiana.* Rome, 1942.

Fontaine, J. "Damase poète Théodosien: L'imaginaire poétique des epigrammata." In *Secularia Damasiana: Atti del Convegno internazionale per il XVI centenario della morte di Papa Damaso I.* Rome, 1986, 115–45.

———. "Un sobriquet perfide de Damase: *Matronarum auriscalpius.*" In *Hommages à Henri le Bonniec: Res Sacrae*, ed. D. Porte et J.-P. Néraudau. Collection Latomus 201. Paris, 1988, 177–92.

Lawler, T.C. "Jerome's First Letter to Damasus." In *Kyriakon: Festschrift Johannes Quasten*, ed. P. Granfield and J.A. Jungmann. Münster: 1970, 2:548–52.

Lippold, A. "Ursinus and Damasus." *Historia* 14 (1965):105–28.

Norton, M.A. "Prosopography of Pope Damasus." In *Leaders of Iberian Christianity, 50–650 A.D.*, ed. J.M.-F. Marique. Boston, 1962, 13–80.

Pietri, C. "Damase et Théodose, communion orthodoxe et géographie politique." In *Epektasis: Mélanges patristiques offerts au Cardinal Jean Daniélou*, ed. J. Fontaine and C. Kannengiesser. Paris, 1972, 627–34.

———. "Damase évêque de Rome." *Saecularia Damasiana: Atti del Convegno internazionale per il XVI centenario della morte di Papa Damaso I.* Rome, 1986, 31–58.

———. *Roma Christiana: Recherches sur l'église de Rome (311–440).* Rome: 1976, 1, chaps. 6–10.

Saghy, M. "Prayer at the Tomb of the Martyrs? The Damasan Epigrams." In *La preghiera nel tardo antico: Dalle origini ad Agostino.* Studia Ephemeridis Augustinianum 66. Rome: 1999, 519–37.

Shepherd, M.H. "The Liturgical Reform of Damasus I." In *Kyriakon: 2: Festschrift Johannes Quasten*, ed. P. Granfield and J.A. Jungman. Münster, 1970, 847–63.

Taylor, J. "St. Basil the Great and Pope St. Damasus I." *Downside Review* 91 (1973): 186–203, 262–74.

Turner, C.H. "Latin Lists of the Canonical Books: The Roman Council under Damasus, A.D. 382." *Journal of Theological Studies* 1 (1899–1900): 554–60.

CELESTINE I (422–32)

JOSEPH F. KELLY

The *Liber Pontificalis* relates that Celestine was by birth a Campanian, the son of a man named Priscus; the date of his birth is unknown, but was probably around 375 to 380. He apparently migrated to Rome and joined the clergy there, becoming a deacon under Innocent I (401–17). He likely gained some prestige in Rome, since he corresponded with Augustine. The African mentions a letter that Celestine wrote to him in his reply, Epistle 192, written in 418. Significantly, Augustine's letter makes no reference to any doctrinal or disciplinary problem but rather discusses, in a mild philosophic fashion, the nature of love. It is a personal letter from which Augustine apparently did not expect direct assistance with any pending matter, not a small point since the exchange occurred during the pontificate of Zosimus (417–18) when Roman-African relations were descending to a new low over the pope's tactless behavior in the Pelagian controversy.

Boniface I (418–22) succeeded Zosimus and became embroiled in a dispute with Eulalius, who for a year disputed the papal election and even held the advantage until he foolishly disobeyed the Western Roman emperor Honorius (395–423), who then recognized Boniface. Celestine supported Boniface and gained enough influence in the city to win election for himself in 422. The *Liber Pontificalis* says that the see remained vacant for only nine days after Boniface's death. Having just survived a schism, the Romans clearly wanted to elect a new and recognized pope before any more trouble, possibly from former supporters of Eulalius, could break out.

Celestine's pontificate proved a turning point in the Western struggle against heresies, a struggle in which the pope used his primatial power and authority. Indeed, the questions of heresy and primacy dominated his busy, troubled, and productive reign. In the struggle against the Pelagians, the African episcopacy had expected papal support. They loathed the temporizing Zosimus and went over his head to the emperor to get him to force the pope to condemn the Pelagians. Boniface had pacified the Africans, particularly Augustine, by his anti-Pelagian stance. Celestine took the same tack, but even more vigorously. The Pelagians had established a beachhead in Rome; furthermore, in the 420s Julian of Eclanum, an Italian bishop, had emerged as the Pelagian leader. In the fourth century the African Donatists had actually established a rival community with its own bishops in Rome, and followers of the third-century antipope Novatian still survived. Celestine determined to extinguish any taint of heresy from the city.

With the support of the civil authority, he confiscated the churches of the Novatianists, thus forcing them to worship in private houses. As for the Pelagians, he supported the imperial policy of expelling Pelagian leaders from the West. He strongly opposed Julian of Eclanum and vigorously opposed the policy of Nestorius, patriarch of Constantinople (428–31), who in 429 gave a hearing to the Pelagian leader Caelestius, whom the Romans had already condemned. Nestorius also gave brief sanctuary to Julian of Eclanum. As will be seen later, the struggle against Pelagianism even led to the founding of an episcopate in Ireland.

The Africans were naturally pleased by the pope's effort against their theological nemesis, but they could not accept the theoretical basis for his action. Celestine did not consider himself a local bishop fighting against an intrusive heresy; rather, he considered himself the successor of St. Peter, who spoke through him. His anti-Pelagian activity formed but one part of his paternal care for the church, a care that extended to Africa, Gaul, Britain, and the East.

Scholars cannot always reach the minds of their subjects, and thus there is no way to tell how Celestine viewed this Roman prerogative. To some bishops, he seemed to invoke Peter in order to spread his own authority, but Celestine claimed that he had a duty to care for the other churches, a duty that he took seriously and found onerous. Given the odds against him in trying to further papal authority, it is difficult to believe that he undertook to assert it purely for aggrandizement. But the Africans had good reason to be concerned.

Around 416 Augustine had made a terrible pastoral mistake. He had recently won a great victory over the Donatists, getting them outlawed by the emperor, and he turned next to the problem of winning back the hearts of Donatist believers. In his diocesan town of Fussala he chose a lector named Antoninus to be bishop. Antoninus had not achieved the canonical age for consecration, but he had lived in Augustine's monastery at Hippo.

Furthermore, he spoke Punic, as did many Donatists. But this promising young bishop turned out to be a thief, and a brutal one at that.

Responding to complaints, Augustine called a council at Hippo and deposed Antoninus, although he allowed him to keep his title of bishop if he made restitution for his thefts. Antoninus claimed that if he were to be bishop, he had to have a see, and he appealed over the heads of the Africans to Rome. Boniface infuriated Augustine by agreeing to hear the complaint and sent an investigative commission to Africa. Because Boniface died soon after, the papal commission deferred to an African council, which denied Antoninus's appeal. Nonetheless, Antoninus appealed to Rome again, this time to Celestine. Augustine moved quickly; his Epistle 209 to Celestine provided the case against Antoninus. Perhaps their earlier friendship bore fruit because the matter disappeared after this, thus heading off an almost certain confrontation.

S.CÆLESTINVS filius, creatus die 3, Sedit an.8.mens.5. April.an.432.Vac. I. Roman? Prisci Nouemb. an.423. dies 3.Obijt die 6. Sed.dies 20.

Pope Celestine I. (Hulton/Archive by Getty Images)

But a second and more serious case arose that again focused on the question of primacy. In 417 a rogue priest named Apiarius had been deposed and excommunicated by his bishop Urbanus for outrageous behavior bordering on the criminal. Following Antoninus's lead, he appealed to Rome, knowing full well that African ecclesiastical legislation forbade appeals outside the province. Zosimus, who had been burned by the African bishops in the Pelagian affair, agreed to hear the case and sent legates to inform the Africans that the papacy could indeed hear appeals from their province and that Rome would excommunicate Urbanus if he did not reinstate Apiarius.

In 419 the Roman legates, representing the new pope Boniface I (418–22), attended an African council and insisted on the appellate role of the papacy, which they based upon canons of the ecumenical Council of Nicaea. The Africans knew that the canons were false, but the Romans did not. Surprisingly, the Africans decided to keep the peace by giving Apiarius a second chance.

After a few years Apiarius resorted to his old behavior, was again deposed and excommunicated, and again appealed to Rome, this time to Celestine. The pope supported his case and restored him to his priesthood. To make sure that the Africans obeyed him, Celestine sent a personal legate, the arrogant Faustinus, who treated the African bishops in a condescending way. Around 426 at a council in Carthage, Apiarius broke down and confessed to his misdeeds. The triumphant Africans wrote to Celestine to remind him of their right to deal with their own clergy; they also pointed out that their right derived from the canons of Nicaea, a direct rebuke to papal claims. With no subtlety, they told Celestine never to send Faustinus to Africa again. The chastened Celestine made no further attempt to assert papal primacy in Africa.

He did, however, fare better in Gaul, which had long been under Roman influence. Zosimus had raised Bishop Patroclus of Arles (412–16) to a metropolitan status, to the resentment of other Gallic bishops. Celestine feared that a metropolitan of Arles might assert rights detrimental to Rome. He also feared the influence of the monks of Lérins on the Gallic episcopacy. The very conservative monks resented what they perceived to be the predestinationist innovations of Augustine, and they advocated a moderate position that suggested that the human would cooperate with divine grace. This position, commonly and wrongly labeled Semi-Pelagianism, raised questions about the orthodoxy of the Gallic church. A Gallic layman, Prosper of Aquitaine, stoked the Augustinian fires and even went to Rome to get Celestine to condemn the Semi-Pelagians. The pope backed away from such a radical step, but he did use the opportunity to warn the Gallic bishops to keep their house in order, to look to Rome for guidance on such matters, and to obey papal authority.

Celestine also strove to maintain Roman dominance in Illyricum, long a bone of contention between Rome and Constantinople and which as recently as 421 had been assigned to the patriarch of the Eastern capital by the Eastern emperor Theodosius II (408–50). Boniface I successfully lobbied the Western emperor Honorius to get Theodosius to halt the transfer of territory, but matters remained tense. Celestine convinced the Illyrian bishops to accept Bishop Rufus of Thessalonica as his vicar, and problems in the Balkans were comparatively minor, at least compared to those that his predecessors had faced and to another Eastern problem he was about to face.

When Nestorius became patriarch of Constantinople in 428, he tried to root out heresy, including the veneration of the Virgin Mary as Theotokos, Mother of God. The patriarch said that no human could be the parent of God and Mary should thus be called Christotokos, Mother of Christ. This raised the suspicions of Cyril of Alexandria (412–44), who believed that Nestorius was excessively separating the human and the divine in Christ. In Alexandrian theology, the human and divine were so linked that Mary, as mother of the person Jesus Christ, could legitimately be honored as the Mother of God.

But Cyril had more in mind. In the third century Alexandria had ruled the Greek world theologically and had managed to extend its influence throughout the East. When Constantine I (307–37) established his new capital on the Bosphorus, the Alexandrians watched their influence wane before the patriarchs of Constantinople, who combined the prestige of the imperial see with access to the emperor. But the Arian controversy offered hope. The Alexandrians stood fast behind the Council of Nicaea, as did the Romans, while Constantinopolitan bishops wavered or became Arians. When Athanasius of Alexandria (328–73) had to flee his see, Pope Julius I (337–52) welcomed him to Rome, thus forming a Roman-Alexandrian alliance.

The Constantinopolitan bishops attempted to have their position in the church legitimated by the Council of Constantinople (381), which decreed that the Eastern capital's status stood only behind Rome. But Pope Damasus I (366–84) realized that if the secular status of a see determined its ecclesiastical status, Rome might one day fall behind Constantinople. The Romans always watched their new rivals, and Cyril would exploit this.

Alexandrian opposition to Constantinople had been successful before. In 403 the patriarch Theophilus of Alexandria engineered the deposition of John Chrysostom from the imperial see at a synod in which his nephew Cyril participated. In 428 Cyril revived the Roman-Alexandrian alliance in order to emulate his uncle Theophilus and bring down a hated Constantinopolitan rival. Nestorius proved an easy target. His willingness to allow Pelagians such as Caelestius and Julian of Eclanum to reside in his city had infuriated Celestine. Cyril, who always wrote in Latin to Celestine (who could not read Greek), made a case against Nestorius to the pope; furthermore, papal representatives in Constantinople sent unfavorable reports of the bishop's teachings.

Cyril was a wolf when it came to ecclesiastical politics, Nestorius a comparative lamb. He wrote to Celestine in Greek, wanting to know why he should not receive Pelagian exiles. He simply did not recognize that Celestine considered a Roman condemnation binding upon all other bishops. Nestorius also did not realize how serious the theological issue had become or the extent to which Cyril had exploited it. In 430 Cyril forced Nestorius to clarify his views. Cyril next wrote to Celestine, detailing Nestorius's errors. The Roman-Alexandrian alliance, the sanctuary for the Pelagians, Roman fear of Constantinople's primatial designs, and Cyril's shameless propagandizing all worked toward Nestorius's downfall. In August 430 a Roman synod condemned him and ordered him to recant his errors or be excommunicated. Celestine entrusted Cyril with carrying out the sentence of the synod.

But the Alexandrian's victory was not complete. The Eastern emperor

Theodosius II had appointed Nestorius, and no one believed that Cyril acted solely from theological concerns. The emperor decided that only an ecumenical council could settle matters, and he called one for Ephesus in June 431. This put Celestine in an awkward position. Rome had condemned Nestorius, so, in the pope's view, the matter had been settled and there was no need for a council. But Roman primatial claims had little influence in the East and virtually none with the emperor. Celestine had no choice but to send legates to the council, although he instructed them to work with Cyril, avoiding the daily business of the council unless it impinged upon Rome's authority. Furthermore, they should try to make sure that the council came to the same conclusion the Roman synod had and should reject its decision if it did not.

Cyril demonstrated that he did not really accept Roman primacy but had used it only to strengthen his hand against Nestorius. When travel difficulties prevented the Roman legates from getting to the council on schedule, Cyril simply opened it without them and presided over the condemnation of Nestorius on 22 June 431. Also arriving late were bishops from Syria who supported Nestorius. When they arrived on 26 June and asked when the council would open, they learned that it had already been held and Nestorius had been condemned. They promptly held their own council and rehabilitated him. In early July the papal legates, two bishops and a priest, arrived to find to their astonishment that not one but two councils had been held without Roman representation. Cyril diplomatically agreed to hold another session on 10 July, at which a letter of Celestine was read to the assembled bishops, who approved it. On the next day the legates gave their approval to the proceedings of Cyril's council of 22 June. Nestorius was condemned, and Mary was honored as Theotokos.

In fact, matters were not yet finished. Both Greek parties engaged in postconciliar political maneuvering; Cyril emerged as the victor. Celestine, who died the year after the council, had nothing to do with any of this. He was satisfied that Ephesus had followed the way set out by the Roman synod.

Celestine's concern for heresy lies behind a little-known episode of his pontificate but one of great importance for the British Isles. Pelagius was a Briton, and apparently his teaching had made some headway in his home province. The Gallic writer Prosper of Aquitaine records in his chronicle that in 429, at the urging of a deacon named Palladius, Celestine sent the Gallic bishop Germanus of Auxerre to combat Pelagianism in Britain. Clearly the pope felt that the British episcopate was not up to the task and possibly had Pelagian sympathies. Since Britain and Gaul both belonged to the Roman diocese of Gaul, Germanus might have been familiar with the situation. The written accounts show Germanus routing the enemy, but, significantly, he had to make a second visit to Britain in 447, when Celestine had been dead for some time.

The pope's concern for British orthodoxy lay behind another very important move he made in the West. Prosper says that in 431 Celestine sent a bishop named Palladius to be the first bishop of the Irish Christians. These Irish Christians are unknown; information about Christianity in Ireland comes only after the mission of Patricius (St. Patrick), probably beginning around 435. Medieval accounts tell of pre-Patrician saints, all on the southeast coast. These largely legendary accounts probably reflect the historical situation that Christianity made its way to Ireland from Britain. Furthermore, the Irish community must have had some size or organization, since the popes did not use bishops as missionaries.

Possibly the sheer number of the Irish Christians required the presence of a bishop, but most scholars assume that this Palladius is identical to the deacon who had recommended the mission of Germanus only two years before. The reason is the British connection. If, as seems inevitable, the Irish had gotten their Christianity from Britain, probably Celestine worried that the British might also have exported Pelagianism. Thus Palladius, who had worked to eliminate Pelagianism from the Roman province, would be the ideal bishop for the barbarian community—a man the pope knew and could trust as well as one who would not underestimate the Pelagian threat.

Regrettably, only two sentences in Prosper's chronicle contain all the known historical information about Palladius, which means that scholars know nothing of his work in Ireland. Later accounts of Patrick play down Palladius's role, having him die as a martyr or even leave Ireland for Britain, but since these accounts wish to glorify Patrick, they contain no reliable information about Palladius. Prosper neatly sums up Celestine's work in the western isles claiming he made the barbarian island Christian while keeping the Roman island Catholic.

From the fourth to the nineteenth century the popes had some responsibility for the physical condition of Rome. Celestine saw to the rebuilding of the Basilica of Santa Maria in Trastevere, which had suffered damage during the Gothic pillage of 410. He also saw to the building of the Basilica of Santa Sabina on the Aventine Hill, which many art historians consider the finest example of the classical architectural tradition in the late Roman period. Two rows of columns with Corinthian capitals support high-pitched arches that are surmounted by marble and tall windows. Scholars are uncertain to what extent Celestine was involved in the particulars, but he can take responsibility for the founding of the church.

The *Liber Pontificalis* records that in addition to giving some gifts to the Roman church, Celestine also introduced psalmody into the liturgy, apparently between the reading of the epistle and the gospel, thus bringing to Rome a practice known in several other Western churches. Celestine's writings consist of letters that have not yet been translated into English. These include his missives to the Gallic and Illyrian bishops and to many of the participants in the Nestorian controversy. They offer his view of papal primacy in his own words, including his assurance to the people of Constantinople that the blessed apostle Peter (in the person of Celestine) would not desert them (*Ep.* 25.9). Traditionally, the collection of his letters has included a series of decretals known as the *Capitula Caelestini*; these are not authentic, and most scholars believe that Prosper of Aquitaine prepared them.

The Roman church venerates Celestine as a saint; his feast is 6 April, the date of his death. The *Liber Pontificalis* sites his grave in the cemetery of Priscilla. Celestine was not a remarkable man with ingenious solutions to seemingly inextricable dilemmas but rather an intelligent, solid, faithful administrator who had ideals and who worked carefully to achieve them. His achievements had their limits: Germanus had to return to Britain, the Illyrian question continued long after the pope's death, and the aftermath of Ephesus proved so confused and even traumatic that two more councils, the so-called Ephesus II in 449 (the Latrocinium or "Robber Council," as Leo I called it) and then the ecumenical Council of Chalcedon in 451 has to deal with it. Africa proved to be a sad experience for Celestine, as it had for many Roman bishops.

But Celestine's insistence on the papal position on Nestorius guaranteed that future christological discussion would include Rome, and Leo's *Tome* played a significant role at Chalcedon. If Celestine did not clear up matters in Illyricum, he kept them from deteriorating and continued the Roman presence. Pelagianism had roots too deep in Britain for one mission to eliminate, but Celestine made the Roman presence felt. His intervention in Gaul did prove both successful and lasting, and to him goes the credit of bringing Ireland into the Latin church. He extirpated heresy in Rome, beautified the city, and reformed the Roman liturgy. All of this occurred in one decade. How many other pontificates of such length have had such significance?

SELECTED BIBLIOGRAPHY

Davis, Leo Donald. *The First Seven Ecumenical Councils (325–787): Their History and Theology*. Wilmington Del.: Michael Glazier, 1987.

Dekkers, Eligius, ed. *Clavis Patrum Latinorum*. 2nd ed. Bruges: In Abbatia S. Petri, 1961, 1650–54.

De Paor, Liam. *Saint Patrick's World*. Notre Dame, Ind.: University of Notre Dame Press, 1993.

Di Berardino, Angelo, ed. *Encyclopedia of the Early Church*. New York: Oxford University Press, 1992, 1:154.

———. *Patrology*. Vol. 4. Westminster, Md.: Christian Classics, 1986, 587–88.

Duchesne, Louis, ed. *Le Liber Pontificalis*. Paris: E. Thorin, 1886–92, 1:cxxi, 230–31. English translation in *The Book of the Popes*, ed. Louise R. Loomis. New York: Columbia University Press, 1916, 92–93.

Ferguson, Everett, ed. *Encyclopedia of Early Christianity*. 2nd ed. New York: Garland Pub., 1997, 228.

Jeffrey, Peter. "The Introduction of Psalmody into the Roman Mass by Pope Celestine I." *Archiv für Liturgiewissenschaft* 26 (1984): 147–65.

Kelly, J.N.D. *The Oxford Dictionary of Popes*. New York: Oxford University Press, 1986, 41–42.

Merdinger, Jane. *Rome and the African Church in the Time of Augustine*. New Haven: Yale University Press, 1997.

Milburn, Robert. *Early Christian Art and Architecture*. Berkeley: University of California Press, 1988.

Pietri, Charles. *Roma Christiana: Recherches sur l'Église de Rome, son organisation, sa politique, son idéologie de Miltiade à Sixte III (311–440)*. 2 vols. Rome: École française de Rome, 1976.

Rendina, Claudio. *I Papi: Storia e segreti*. 5th ed. Rome: Newton Compton editori, 1990, 105–7.

Spiegl, Jakob. "Die Päpste in der Reichskirche des 4. und frühen 5. Jahrhunderts von Silvester I. bis Sixtus III." In *Das Papsttum*, ed. M. Greschat. Stuttgart: W. Kohlhammer, 1988, 43–55.

Vogt, Hermann Josef. "Papst Cölestin und Nestorius." In *Konzil und Papst*, ed. Georg Schwaiger. Munich: Ferdinand Schöningh, 1975, 235–54.

LEO I (440–61)

PHILIP A. MCSHANE

A mural attributable in part to Raphael depicts the scene in which Pope Leo I (440–61) dissuades Attila the Hun from attacking the city of Rome (452)—though it is likely that the plague and a lack of provisions had as much to do with Attila's departure as did Leo's entreaties. This, of course, was far from being the only crisis that faced the Western empire in the fifth century: vast territories were lost to the barbarians, the economy was in ruins, and political assassination was rife. As a boy or young man, Leo would have witnessed Alaric's sack of Rome (410). Later, as pope and sole authority in Rome (the emperors had long since sought refuge in the more secure city of Ravenna), he had to negotiate with the Vandal Geiseric, who occupied and pillaged the city in 455. These diplomatic missions, however, are by no means the sole reason why Leo is the first of only two popes (the other being Gregory I) to be surnamed "the Great." In addition to his political and social activity, his theological contributions (notably in Christology and the nature and exercise of the Petrine function) became landmarks as a clear exposition of Christian tradition.

Little is known of Leo's background either from his own writings or from those of his contemporaries. Of Tuscan descent, Leo was born toward the end of the fourth century, possibly in Velathri (the modern Volterra) or perhaps in Rome itself, his parents having migrated there to escape the barbarian incursions. Raised and educated in Rome, Leo entered the Roman clergy at an early age and quickly rose to a position of importance. Augustine of Hippo mentions an acolyte named Leo (the future pontiff?) bearing messages from Pope Zosimus (417–18). Some years later Cyril of Alexandria, embroiled in christological dispute and desirous of Western support, enlisted the aid of Pope Celestine I's deacon, Leo, who in his turn commissioned John Cassian to prepare a treatise *De incarnatione*. According to Prosper of Aquitaine, Leo's intervention was decisive in persuading Pope Sixtus III (432–40) not to reinstate the Pelagian-bishop Julian of Eclanum. Finally, just before his election as pope in 440, Leo was called upon to arbitrate between the Roman general, Aetius, and the praetorian prefect, Albinus, whose quarrel could well have spelled disaster for the Western empire. All this while, Leo, as deacon, archdeacon, and subsequently as pope, had to preoccupy himself with the material relief of the city and of the many refugees who flocked to it for protection.

In typical Roman fashion, where the person is subsumed by the office, Leo's writings tell us practically nothing of this. His sermons, covering the liturgical year, contain but a few allusions to contemporary events. In the main, they are concise, authoritative statements of doctrine, to which the letters often enough pronounce the corresponding disciplinary measures. Despite the obvious differences between the sermons and letters as to style, content, and date of composition, there is a basic unity between them. The more doctrinal letters, in particular, contain numerous passages from the sermons, quoted literally or reworked. Leo's consciousness of the essential unity of all Christians is such that he felt obliged in his preaching to expound to the faithful at Rome, truths that were questioned only at the opposite end of the empire. The first major extant collection of works by a bishop of Rome, the 97 sermons and some 143 letters are concerned with furnishing brief, straightforward expositions of traditional church doctrine and discipline; as such, they are remarkable for their freshness and clarity, so much so that they have provided a veritable quarry for precise, well-rounded statements.

Leo would be described today as an existentialist thinker and not as a systematic one. In no sense did he construct a doctrinal system. Everything he says results from his reaction to events and from a gradual and progressive appreciation of his responsibilities. Certainly he was obliged to elaborate rationally the position he took, but he did so always in the light of actual circumstances and faced with a concrete situation. With Leo, *theoria* is always the repercussion of *praxis* and not the reverse. Consequently, his thought cannot be reduced to a system. While it preserves a real continuity, it is subject to continual development owing to the events of his time, many of which had a profound effect on Leo.

Leo was particularly exercised by the questions of orthodoxy and unity, both of which were constantly threatened during the turbulent years of his pontificate. He was the first to bring together traditional understandings of the papacy and, by expanding on the recent and exclusively Roman exegesis of Mt. 16:18, to elaborate a coherent theology of its nature and function. Thus, pressured by the manifest needs of the church of his day, Leo drew on Scripture and tradition to stress the distinctive Petrine ministry (this notably in the sermons on the anniversary of his episcopal consecration). By divine inspiration the first to confess Christ, Leo asserts, Peter received the primacy and was explicitly commissioned to bear responsibility and concern for the whole church. This primary responsibility was unique, for while the other apostles were heads of the church and all believers participate in Christ's priesthood, this general participation implies and requires a symbolic representation. The Petrine ministry provides just such a representation. For what all the apostles received from Christ, they received through Peter. Peter's faith, therefore, effactually symbolizes—is a "sacrament" of—the unity of the church's faith. Further, Peter's mission was, to Leo's mind, clearly associated with the city of Rome. For not only had Peter been deputed by Christ to come to the capital, but, continues Leo, by his martyrdom there, Peter had become the special patron of the city—a patronage that was recognized by the universal church. In this way Leo steered a middle course between Eusebius's virtual identification of church and empire and Augustine's rejection of the earthly city. Leo envisaged, rather, the transformation of pagan Rome to a renewed Christian Rome (29 June, the feast of SS. Peter and Paul, had formerly been dedicated to Romulus and Remus). By the blood of its martyrs, Rome had, as it were, been baptized; because of this apostolic foundation, and not because of its imperial prestige, it held pride of place as Peter's See.

Pope Leo I. (Courtesy of the Vatican Library)

"The solidity of Peter's faith," Leo writes, "is enduring; and just as what Peter believed abides in Christ, so there abides what Christ instituted in Peter" (*Serm.* 3, 2). Leo insists on the continuity and permanence of Peter's special ministry, his symbolizing of the faith and unity of the church, and his active concern for the whole church from the presidency of his own particular see. Peter, then, remains actively present, and his enduring mission finds its visible expression in each of his successors. Rather than a linear succession, there is a direct sacramental identity between Peter's function and that of each bishop of Rome. Consequently, the ministry of the bishop of Rome is to be a symbol of faith in unity, a sacramental representation of the church's being one in Christ.

Leo borrowed the occasional term from imperial Roman law on succession to express this. In Roman law the deceased lived on in the heir, though this was qualified by the concept of *haeres indignus* according to which the heir, though "unworthy" as to personal qualities, could validly succeed to the office. Thus the pope inherited Peter's function but not Peter's subjective merit. The inevitable juridical element in Leo's thought nonetheless remained subordinate to the sacramental. In subsequent interpretations of Leo, however, the juridical aspect has been more and more emphasized, to the extent that some have accused him of self-aggrandizement. That this is unfounded and indeed anachronistic can best be illustrated from his actual exercise of that ministry.

The word "priesthood" for Leo connotes the priesthood of all. He invariably describes his own function in terms of ministry and service. This was no pious rhetoric. At no time did Leo claim universal jurisdiction. Such an idea would have been unthinkable to a Roman: in the empire there was never a universal law applicable everywhere and to all. One of the salient traits of the Roman character was precisely respect for the local situation, and Leo was very much a Roman in this regard. Thus we need to distinguish different levels in Leo's relationship to the churches: as metropolitan of suburbican Italy, as patriarch of the Latin West, and as minister of the communion of the universal church.

As metropolitan, Leo exercised immediate jurisdiction over central and southern Italy, though he did so with far more moderation than obtained, for example, at Alexandria. Leo never lost sight of the principle that general rules need to be adapted to individual persons and circumstances. Certainly he expected and demanded from his suffragans conformity to the canons and to established discipline and summoned them each year to a synod at Rome, usually held on the anniversary of his consecration. He warned them to be watchful for heresy and himself initiated an investigation of the Manichaeans who, refugees from Africa, had infiltrated Rome. As part of this campaign, he persuaded Emperor Valentinian III to enforce penal legislation against heretics—this being typical of Leo's conviction that the two authorities of the one Christian republic should work closely together.

In the wider Latin patriarchate, Rome, in addition to its apostolic prestige, had acquired a reputation (at least outside Africa) as an impartial arbiter and consequently acted as a final court of appeal. In this, too, the principle of subsidiarity prevailed. Leo stressed the need for, and the importance of, local councils and respected their decisions. On at least one occasion he rebuked an appellant who had bypassed the intermediate authority, pointing out that only when this latter could not deal competently with a matter should it be referred to Rome.

At this period, however, many of the Western churches were in disarray. Successive invasions had disrupted church life in Gaul, of which only the southeastern provinces remained in contact with Rome. Dominated by Arian Vandals and Sueves, disorder in the Spanish churches had facilitated a resurgence of the Priscillianist heresy and had effectively prevented the convocation of a council. In Africa a once-flourishing church with its own distinctive tradition had been reduced to the two Mauritanias and a part of Numidia. While Leo's concern for peace and unity arose ultimately from his theology of Christ living in the church and making of it one body, it was these actual circumstances that provoked his immediate response.

In 447 Turibius of Asturica, the metropolitan of Galicia, sought Leo's advice in countering heresy. Leo's reply (*Ep.* 15) included a commentary on Turibius's report, an account of his own dealings with the Manichaeans at Rome, and a recommendation that a council of the five Spanish provinces be held, or at least a provincial council in Galicia. Neither council proving practicable, Turibius could only forward Leo's letter to his fellow bishops.

Similarly, the church in Africa, formerly very jealous of its autonomy, accepted Leo's decisions on various electoral irregularities and other infractions of discipline. Once again, Leo, who maintained that all bishops share the same dignity and pastoral responsibility regardless of the importance of their sees (*Ep.* 14), recognized that the regional authority is often better informed and so better able to deal with a local situation. He therefore urged the Africans (*Ep.* 12) to meet in council should similar cases arise in the future.

As to Gaul, in 444 the dispute involving Vienne and Arles, due largely to the growing importance and pretensions of the latter, had been decided by Leo with perhaps unusual severity toward Hilary, the saintly though overly zealous bishop of Arles. Backed once again by Valentinian III, Leo (*Ep.* 10) deprived Hilary of all authority outside the limits of his see and reaffirmed the metropolitical privileges of Vienne. The issue remained unresolved until, in 450, the metropolitan of Vienne and the new bishop of Arles, Ravennius, both appealed to Rome. Leo's solution was a practical one: Vienne would have jurisdiction over the regions occupied by the barbarians, Arles over those under Roman control. This compromise seemed acceptable to both sides.

In Illyricum (the Balkans), part of the Italian prefecture, Leo confirmed the papal vicariate that had been established by his predecessors principally to ward off encroachments by Constantinople. Nonetheless, he felt obliged to rebuke Anastasius of Thessalonica, his haughty and tactless agent, ordering him to respect the rights of the local metropolitans (*Ep.* 14). As a papal delegate, Leo pointedly observed, Anastasius did not enjoy the *plenitudo postestatis*, or complete power.

Leo's attempts to be the symbol and agent of church communion found more scope but less success in the East. The major Eastern sees had a long history of strife both in doctrine and discipline. Alexandria and Constantinople were continually at loggerheads over ecclesiastical preeminence, and both frequently infringed on the privileges of Antioch. It was precisely in the interest of peace and order that the Roman bishops, Leo in particular, had appealed to the Council of Nicaea, which had ratified the then-established order of churches, each with its demarcated sphere of influence.

A worse disorder was to prevail in doctrinal matters. In 448 Leo received an appeal from the archimandrite Eutyches against the deposition issued by his bishop, Flavian of Constantinople. Eutyches was suspected of Monophysitism, teaching that there was only one (divine) nature in Christ. Leo confirmed Eutyches' condemnation and asserted the permanent distinction of Christ's two natures in one person. Dioscorus of Alexandria, however, openly supported Eutyches, Domnus of Antioch proved timid and vacillating, Juvenal of Jerusalem, ambitious for his see, blatantly changed with the wind, and Flavian of Constantinople seemed overwhelmed by the court of Theodosius II. This comparative isolation and the apparent unreliability of his fellow bishops only served to heighten Leo's consciousness of his special role, as Peter's heir, to defend orthodoxy.

Faced with a dispute that, experience taught, could well split the church, Leo dispatched an important letter (*Ep. 28*) to Flavian (449). This letter, the *Tome*, really a short treatise, affirms the necessity of Christ's full humanity and full divinity if our redemption is to be possible, and has become a classical statement of traditional Western Christology.

Leo's insistence that his *Tome* represented the final word was really an all-out attempt to preserve harmony and unity. His reluctance to allow the matter to be opened to further debate seemed justified when Theodosius II summoned the Second Council of Ephesus (449). This council, branded by Leo as a "robber council," "in which Dioscorus displayed his malice and Juvenal his ignorance" (*Ep. 85*), resulted in the vindication of Eutyches, the deposition of Domnus, and the assassination of Flavian.

Leo pleaded with Theodosius to restore the status quo ante until a more representative council could meet, preferably in Italy, for, to his mind, the Eastern bishops had scarcely shown themselves capable of withstanding heresy, let alone of combatting it. His reluctance was no doubt strengthened by the fact that Flavian's successor, Anatolius, a former apocrisiary of Dioscorus, was consecrated by Dioscorus himself and so was presumably of his party.

The death of Theodosius and the accession of Marcian and Pulcheria provided Leo with an ally in the East but did not lessen his wariness of a new council. Marcian's determination to proceed, however, forced Leo to resign himself to the idea. But when the Council of Chalcedon (451) reversed the decisions of Ephesus and "canonized" the *Tome* ("Peter has spoken through Leo"), Leo was both gratified and relieved. This was short lived, however. The council went on, in the absence of the Roman delegates, to pass a number of canons, the 28th of which accorded to Constantinople, the new Rome, a status second only to that of the old Rome on the grounds that both were imperial cities. This was so unacceptable to Leo that he delayed endorsing the council for almost two years, maintaining all the while that canon 28 was invalid.

Leo was not seeking to impose his own theological expression. In a second *Tome*, addressed to the monks of Palestine (*Ep.* 124), he refers the Easterners to their own Fathers and traditions. He insisted repeatedly, however, that all the churches should subscribe to the formula "two natures in one person" and to no other. Here again, circumstances played their part. Anatolius was, in Leo's view, still suspect. Proterius, Dioscorus's successor, failed to win over the Egyptian churches and was brutally assassinated, and his see was usurped by Timothy Aelurus. Juvenal, once more among the Dyophysites, was expelled from Jerusalem by rebellious monks who had the backing of Eudocia, the widow of Theodosius. Despite Leo's efforts, the East was yet again in turmoil.

Not only did Leo live totally for the church, but his whole personality seems devoted, almost abandoned, to the cause he served. His personal feelings are rarely expressed in the terse, austere antitheses of his epistolary style. His sermons, though, breathe a tone of simplicity and practical piety, with an underlying serenity despite the constant activity of public life. In the narrower circle of suburbican Italy, he was a pastor, vigilant and exacting for the observance of discipline, admitting no remissness in himself or in others. In the wider sphere, he displayed the qualities and authority of an ecumenical leader. Convinced that Rome was the divinely established center of unity for the church universal, he had that truly "imperial" ability of overseeing, without pettiness, even the most distant of churches.

SELECTED BIBLIOGRAPHY

Arens, H. *Die christologische Sprache Leos des Grossen*. Freiburg B., 1982.

Ballerini, P., and H. Ballerini. *Sancti Leonis Magni romani pontificis opera*. Venice, 1753–57. Reproduced in J.P. Migne, *P.L.* 54. Paris: 1881.

Bartnik, C. "L'interprétation théologique de la crise de l'empire romain par Léon le Grand." *Revue d'histoire ecclésiastique* 63 (1968): 745–84.

Chavasse, A. *Sancti Leonis Magni romani pontificis tractatus septem et nonaginta*. Corpus Christianorum, Series Latina 138 and 138A. Turnhout, 1973.

Conroy, J.P. "The Idea of Reform in Leo the Great." Ph.D. Diss., Fordham University, 1981.

Dekkers, E. "Autour de l'oeuvre liturgique de saint Léon le Grand." *Sacris Erudiri* 10 (1958):363–98.

Deneffe, A. "Tradition und Dogma bei Leo dem Grossen." *Scholastik* 9 (1934): 543–54.

De Soos, M.B. *Le mystère liturgique d'après saint Léon le Grand*. Liturgiewissenschaftliche Quellen und Forschungen, Heft 34. Münster, 1958.

Dolle, R. *Léon le Grand: Sermons*. Sources Chrétiennes 22, 49, 74, 200. Paris, 1964–1976.

Dvornik, F. *Byzantium and the Roman Primacy*. New York: Fordham University Press, 1966.

———. *The Idea of Apostolicity in Byzantium*. Dumbarton Oaks Studies 4. Cambridge, Mass., 1958.

Ernst, C. "The Primacy of Peter: Theology and Ideology." *New Blackfriars* 50 (April/May 1969): 347–55, 399–404.

Feltoe, C.L. *The Letters and Sermons of Leo the Great, Bishop of Rome*. In *A Select Library of Nicene and Post-Nicene Fathers of the Christian Church*. 2nd ser., vol. 12. New York, 1895. Reprint, Grand Rapids, Mich.: Eerdmans, 1976.

Freeland, J.P., and A.J. Conway. *St. Leo the Great: Sermons*. The Fathers of the Christian Church Inc., vol. 93. Washington, D.C., 1996.

Grillmeier, A., and H. Bacht, eds. *Das Konzil von Chalkedon*. Würzburg: Echter Verlag, 1951.

Hervé de l'Incarnation. "La grâce chez saint Léon le Grand." *Recherches de théologie ancienne et médiévale* 22 (1955): 17–55, 193–212.

Horn, S.O. *Petrou Kathedra*. Paderborn: Bonifatius, 1982.

Hudon, G. *La perfection chrétienne d'après les sermons de saint Léon*. Paris, 1959.

Hunt, E. *St. Leo the Great: Letters*. The Fathers of the Christian Church Inc., vol. 34. New York: 1957.

Jalland, T.G. *The Life and Times of St. Leo the Great*. London: SPCK, 1941.

McShane, P. *La Romanitas et le pape Léon le Grand*. Paris and Montreal: Desclée/Bellarmin, 1979.

Nicolas, M.J. "La doctrine christologique de saint Léon le Grand." *Revue Thomiste* 51 (1951): 609–62.

Paschoud, F. *Roma Aeterna*. Rome, 1967.

Pietri, C. *Roma Christiana*. Rome: École française de Rome, 1976.

Quasten, J. *Patrology*. Vol. 4B. Westminster, Md.: Christian Classic, 1986, 589ff.

Schwartz, E. *Leonis Papae I epistolarum collectiones*. In *Acta Conciliorum Oecumenicorum*, vol. 2, p. 4. Berlin, 1932.

Silva-Tarouca, C. *Sancti Leonis Magni Epistolae*. Textus et Documenta, Series Theologica, fasc. 9, 15, 20, 23. Roma: Pontificia Universitas Gregoriana, 1932–35.

Stockmeier, P. *Leo I des Grossen Beurteilung der kaiserlichen Religionspolitik*. Munich, 1959.

Ullmann, W. *The Growth of Papal Government in the Middle Ages*. 2nd ed. London, 1962.

———. "Leo I and the Theme of Papal Primacy." *Journal of Theological Studies*, nos., 11, no. 1 (1960): 25–51.

PELAGIUS I (556–61)

ROBERT B. ENO

Pelagius I is rarely placed in the ranks of the great popes of history, yet he deserves to be better known for the dilemmas he faced. The context of his brief papacy (16 April 556–3 March 561) was the Three Chapters controversy. His predecessor, Vigilius (537–55), was caught between the conflicting interests of an emperor in Constantinople, Justinian (527–65), and the traditions of the Western church. After being imprisoned and mistreated in Constantinople, Vigilius died on his way back to Rome. Pelagius was left to deal with the fallout as best he could.

The roots of the Three Chapters controversy go back at least to the Council of Chalcedon (451), which saw the triumph of the Christology outlined in Leo I's *Tome*: that Christ has a human nature and a divine nature united in one divine hypostasis or person. Many Easterners, especially in Egypt, saw this as a fatal betrayal of the Christology of Cyril of Alexandria (d. 444), whose views had prevailed at Ephesus in 431. After Chalcedon there was not only theological dissent but also violence in the streets of Alexandria. Dissatisfaction with the Chalcedonian settlement later spread to Palestine and Syria. The dissenters would become known as Monophysites.

From this time on, Eastern emperors were faced with a threatening reality: the increasing alienation of important sectors of their empire because of religious controversies. Successive rulers tried various forms of compromise, but to no avail. The Monophysites found the compromise statements insufficient, while Chalcedonians, especially Westerners, saw in such attempts at compromise a veiled attack on and a betrayal of the council and Leo. The accession of Justin I as emperor in 518 brought an end to the Acacian schism that had arisen precisely because of such compromise attempts and had split East from West for some thirty-seven years. His nephew and successor, Justinian I, was persuaded by Theodore Askidas, an accused Origenist, to try another tack. This maneuver would become known as the affair of the Three Chapters (543), an attempt to appease the Monophysites by condemning three men long dead and some or all of their writings.

Theodore of Mopsuestia (d. 428) was an exegete of the school of Antioch and teacher of Nestorius; Theodoret of Cyrus (d. c. 466) was both an important theologian and historian of that school. Ibas (d. c. 457) was bishop of Edessa and had attacked Cyril in a letter to a Persian bishop. Theodoret and Ibas were both regarded as clear enemies of Cyril but were unjustly labeled Nestorians. Apart from the reluctance to condemn those long dead, there was the fact that Chalcedon had examined the cases of Theodoret and Ibas and had approved them both. Earlier, Pope Leo had received an appeal from Theodoret from his condemnation at the "robber council" of 449, and Leo had approved his orthodoxy. So, in Western eyes, the belated attempt to condemn the three men and some of their writings was an ill-disguised attack on the authority of both council and pope.

With the deposition of Pope Silverius (536–37) by Byzantine forces in Italy, Vigilius became pope, allegedly because he had assured the empress Theodora, a Monophysite sympathizer, that he would be "more flexible" in matters dear to her heart. In pursuit of his plan, Justinian brought Vigilius to Constantinople (25 January 547), where pressure could be applied to make him conform. We cannot go into detail here about the various desperate measures taken by Vigilius to follow the emperor's wishes while at the same time avoiding giving offense to the West. In the spring of 553 the emperor called the fifth ecumenical council, II Constantinople, to do his will on the Three Chapters. The pope did not attend. When Vigilius in his *Constitutum* attempted to walk a tightrope, condemning offending documents but refusing to condemn individuals, Justinian rejected it as too little too late. After six more months of imperial pressure Vigilius abandoned his opposition and accepted the conciliar condemnation of the Three Chapters. After an absence of nine years he was allowed to return to the West. When he died en route in Sicily, his successor was left to face the wrath of an unhappy and indignant Latin church.

According to the *Liber Pontificalis*, Pelagius was the son of John, a *vicarianus*, a Roman civil servant. He first appears in history already a deacon, accompanying Pope Agapitus to Constantinople in the winter of 535–36. The papal mission was a failure, but it did succeed in reviving Chalcedonian fortunes against the pro-Monophysite machinations of the empress Theodora. Before dying there, Agapitus made Pelagius the apocrisiarius, his official representative in Constantinople. In this capacity, he attended the anti-Monophysite synod of June 536, whose acts he, together with another deacon, signed as the representatives of the Roman church. While Byzantines and Goths struggled for control of Italy, the subdeacon Silverius was elected pope. But those in power in Constantinople had other ideas. They chose another Roman deacon, Vigilius. Upon his return to Rome in early 537, Vigilius was installed as pope by the Byzantine army, and his short-lived predecessor was rushed into exile.

During his time in Constantinople Pelagius exercised a degree of influence at court. He helped to choose a Chalcedonian, the monk Paul, as bishop of Alexandria. When Paul turned out badly, Pelagius was sent to depose him in favor of Zoilus. On his way back, monks in Jerusalem complained to him about the Origenist problem. In 543, thanks to the efforts of Pelagius, among others, the emperor prepared a treatise against the Origenists that he sent to the patriarchs for their approval. A former Palestinian monk and suspected Origenist, Theodore Askidas, who had sufficiently impressed the emperor to be made bishop of Caesarea in Cappadocia, was forced to accept this condemnation. He blamed Pelagius for this and, according to some sources, suggested the condemnation of the three "Nestorians" to Justinian as a sort of riposte.

The emperor's condemnation of 543 or 544 was sent to the bishops. Opposition quickly arose. Even the Eastern patriarchs were dubious. The African bishops saw it as a Monophysite ploy.

Saint Pelagius I. (Hulton/Archive by Getty Images)

When Vigilius temporized, Justinian had him brought to Constantinople. In the meantime, Pelagius returned to Rome. He found that the seesaw Byzantine-Gothic struggle was turning the country in general and the city in particular into a wasteland of famine and disease. Pelagius spent most of his time and much of his personal resources trying to relieve the misery of the Roman people. In December 546, when the city was betrayed to the Goth Totila, Pelagius's pleading saved the lives of some Romans but did not spare the city from being sacked. Totila sent him to Justinian seeking some accommodation, but the emperor would have none of it. The war went on, and Rome was retaken by Byzantine forces under Belisarius in the spring of 547.

Now Pelagius began his involvement in the growing controversy surrounding the Three Chapters. In April 548 Vigilius issued his *Judicatum*, following the emperor's wishes. Western bishops quickly reacted negatively. Pelagius, back in Rome, wrote to a leading theologian, the Carthaginian deacon Ferrandus, for his opinion. His reply was critical of the emperor's efforts. A synod in Illyricum defended the Three Chapters, while an African synod excommunicated the pope. In view of this firestorm of protest, Vigilius withdrew his *Judicatum*, and sought a new meeting of Western bishops. After further investigation Justinian issued a new edict of condemnation in July 551. Vigilius rejected the new edict and excommunicated bishops like Menas of Constantinople and Theodore Askidas who accepted it.

It was at this point that Pelagius returned to the Eastern capital, where he supported Vigilius in his current, more intransigent stand. In December 551 Vigilius, accompanied by Pelagius, sought refuge across the water from Constantinople in Chalcedon, in the Basilica of St. Euphemia where the council had been held a century before. The site of Leo's triumph became the place of Vigilius's abasement. In February 552 Vigilius returned to the city, where Menas, Theodore, and other bishops offered their submission. All now placed their hopes for an amicable settlement in a council to be held in the coming year. But Justinian had not altered his goals in the slightest. Pelagius acted as an intermediary between Vigilius and the council. He supported the pope in his refusal to attend and was a signatory to Vigilius's *Constitutum* of May 553, forbidding any attempt to detract from the authority of Chalcedon. This put Vigilius and Pelagius in direct conflict with the decisions of the council, which was doing the emperor's bidding. When Vigilius finally succumbed to imperial pressure at the end of 553, he lost the support of Pelagius. Refusing to follow Vigilius in accepting the council, Pelagius was exiled and imprisoned. It was during this period that he wrote his treatise in defense of the Three Chapters, a work heavily dependent on the earlier book of the African bishop Facundus of Hermiane.

That might have seemed to be the end of Pelagius, but, surprisingly, when Vigilius died, Pelagius was Justinian's choice to be his successor. Whatever his motives for making such an unexpected selection, the obvious condition was the reversal of Pelagius's former views, the condemnation of the Three Chapters, and the acceptance of the council recently held in Constantinople. Pelagius chose conformity to the wishes of the emperor. Given his previous benefactions to the Roman people, one might have expected a warm reception for him in the city, but such was not the case. Some Romans blamed him for the troubles and even the death of

Vigilius. Others saw him as tarred with the same anti-Chalcedonian brush as Vigilius. Facundus in a renewed attack referred to the "Roman prevaricators."

Pelagius the deacon was finally ordained bishop of Rome on 16 April 556 by the bishops of Perugia and Ferentinum. A priest of Ostia is always mentioned as participating, but since even in the sixth century priests did not ordain bishops, it may be presumed that he was simply present, filling in for the absence of his bishop, who as ordinary of one of the suburbicarian sees normally ordained the bishop of Rome. Was there a general shortage of bishops due to the desolation caused by the endless warfare in the area or a general reluctance on the part of bishops to participate in the ordination of one viewed as a turncoat? Given his public relations problem, Pelagius's first act as pope was to confer with Justinian's military commander in Italy, Narses. His second was to proceed immediately to St. Peter's Basilica, where, holding aloft a cross and the book of the Gospels, he swore that he had had nothing to do with the death of Vigilius and that he had done nothing against the first four ecumenical councils. In other words, the policy would be (1) to deny any wrongdoing and (2) to be prepared to use force to counter any dissenters.

The writings that have survived from Pelagius's papacy are his letters. If it were not for the problems raised by the Three Chapters controversy and his part in it, his pontificate of barely five years probably would have been uneventful and would have been remembered principally for his efforts to reestablish ecclesiastical discipline. But, in the event, the suspicion that something very wrong had taken place in the East during Vigilius's long sojourn there and that the Catholic faith of Leo had been endangered, if not betrayed, overshadowed Pelagius's exertions in other fields. His correspondence indicates that his general declarations did not suffice to allay suspicions about him in the West.

Pelagius's first attempt at damage control was made with Childebert, king of the Franks, whose power now extended south to embrace Provence. In a letter of December 556 (*Ep.* 3) he told the king that neither he nor his bishops should pay any attention to the "fables of men who delight in scandals." To reassure the king, Pelagius condemned anyone who departed from the faith of Pope Leo or the Council of Chalcedon by even a syllable. It was true that letters allegedly from Pelagius in Constantinople were in circulation, claiming that the Catholic faith had been corrupted. Pelagius denied the authenticity of any such letters, but one has to wonder if his earlier writings, letters or otherwise, in defense of the Three Chapters might be at the root of such rumors. He admitted that while Theodora (d. 548) was still alive, he had been concerned for orthodoxy, but he was sure that Childebert's father (i.e., Justinian) would never allow the faith to be violated. To render Childebert more receptive to his soothing message, he sent some Roman relics to the monks of Lerins. Within two months he had also made Bishop Sapaudus of Arles his vicar in Gaul, awarding him the *pallium* (*Ep.* 5).

But the king was not satisfied. He wanted further reassurance that Pelagius really stood by the faith outlined in the *Tome* of Leo. Pelagius sent him a lengthy (c. seventy-eight lines) confession of faith in his own words (*Ep.* 7), one that went into great detail on trinitarian and christological doctrine, ending: "This is my faith and hope which I have by the gift of God's mercy. The blessed Peter the Apostle commands us to be 'always ready to give an explanation to anyone who asks you for a reason' " (1 Pet. 3:15). These last words almost became for Pelagius a new standard Petrine text. Pelagius would use it frequently in the years to come. He concluded by again warning the king to be on guard against people who spread false rumors and sowed dissension.

Pelagius's problems were not confined to Gaul. In April 557 he wrote to the bishops of northern Tuscany (*Ep.* 10) to assure them of his orthodoxy. He marveled that they, forgetful of apostolic authority, expected him, Pelagius, to approve their separation from the universal church. They should be the ones to overcome popular ignorance and misconceptions. Instead, they were following the slanders being spread against the Apostolic See. He confirmed his own assertions with otherwise unknown "citations" from Augustine. The sign of their alienation from him was their omission of his name from the liturgy. He then reiterated his loyalty to and defense of the first four councils, whose words, he insisted, he had neither added to nor detracted from. He had not changed a word. He had kept inviolate Leo's *Tome*, adopted by Chalcedon, allowing no one to weaken it or to call it in doubt. He closed by inviting all who were still hesitant or dubious to come to him in person to satisfy their curiosity. He cited 1 Pet. 3:15 again.

Such continued to be the general skepticism in the West that Pelagius felt compelled to send an unusual declaration of faith in 557 or 558 addressed simply to the "whole people of God." His detractors were people who were zealous but "not according to knowledge" (Rom. 10:2). Those who were currently tearing themselves away from the body of mother church through an evil animosity were acting out of ignorance. He would therefore try now to silence such rumors by assuring them that he had done nothing against the faith of the Fathers or the firmness of the four councils. He then wrote his act of faith. Unlike his earlier statement for the Frankish king, this declaration of faith centered on his fidelity to the councils and to the teachings of his predecessors. He would defend them with his whole soul and strength until the end. He singled out for special mention the one "who lived up to his name," Leo the lion, whom he sought to follow and imitate. He mentioned by name Celestine, Sixtus, Leo, and his successors through Agapitus. He condemned those whom they condemned and honored as orthodox those whom they received, notably Theodoret and Ibas. Once more he cited 1 Pet. 3:15. How many doubters were reassured by this exercise is unknown. But if some were not, it may well have been because the names of Vigilius and the Council of Constantinople of 553 were conspicuous by their absence from his statement (*Ep.* 11).

Perhaps out of frustration, Pelagius at the end of 558 or the beginning of 559 struck out in a different and, for a pope, surprising direction. In his letter 19 to Sapaudus of Arles, he admitted that he had changed. Let those who wish to blame him for that do so, he began. He had corrected himself and in so doing was in good company. In support of his new candor, he cited Cyprian, who, in his letter 73, warned against those who cling to their own ideas, and Augustine, who at the end of his life wrote a book of "Reconsiderations." "These are the ones that I, albeit not of comparable strength, compelled by a greater fear, have striven to imitate." He followed with a sentence from the prologue to Augustine's book: "Let those who are going to read this book not imitate me when I err but rather when I progress toward the better" (*Prol.* 3). He urged Sapaudus not to follow the erring path of a few bishops or even of a few provinces, but the way of "thousands" of Eastern bishops or the six hundred or so who had spoken in the council. In particular, the path chosen by the apostolic sees should be followed. We note in passing the new emphasis on apostolic sees in the plural.

For most of the remainder of his papacy, Pelagius was concerned with the northern Italian sees such as Milan and Aquileia that had withdrawn from communion with him. His policy was to promise leniency to those who returned on their own but to keep urging Byzantine officials to coerce those who were slow. In his letter to the patrician John (*Ep.* 24 of February 559) he condemned the ordination of Paulinus as bishop of Aquileia by the bishop of Milan. Moreover, Paulinus had now assumed the title of patriarch. Such schismatic ordinations were not consecrations but execrations, he quipped. Such actions by those separated from the church and the apostolic sees were a profanation, not a making holy ("dissecrat, non consecrat").

Two laymen had written to Pelagius, seeking counsel about their relations with the schismatics (*Ep.* 35). Pelagius expressed astonishment at their ignorance. Of course, they must stay away from a schismatic Eucharist. Continuing to indulge his penchant for wordplay, he asserted that these were sacrileges, not sacrifices. "Either you believe that they are the church, and since there cannot be two churches, you will judge, God forbid, that we are the schismatics, or, if it is clear that the true church is to be found with the apostolic sees, know both that they are cut off from unity and that there can be no question of communion since true communion can only be found in unity."

Increasingly, Pelagius took a harder line against the dissidents. To the patrician Valerian he said that the schismatics were arrogant and presumptuous in excommunicating the patrician John (*Ep.* 52). Byzantine officials hesitated to use force against the schismatics, partially because their authority was very limited in northern Italy but also because they did not wish to be called persecutors. Pelagius denied that such coercion was a persecution. Persecution was to make someone do something bad. On the contrary, he who punished a bad action or stopped someone from doing evil was not a persecutor but was showing love. On the other hand, anyone who thought that evil should not be punished had something wrong with him. Therefore, John should arrest the offending bishops and send them to the emperor in Constantinople (*Ep.* 53).

Apparently Valerian was not convinced by this reasoning and sought to have Paulinus of Aquileia readmit John to Communion. Pelagius then reverted to an earlier tactic, saying that if Paulinus was not satisfied, he should choose three or four learned men to come to Rome to discuss the matter with him. Yet no local or regional council had a right to stand against an ecumenical council (*Ep.* 59).

Continuing his policy of urging coercion, he wondered why the general Narses hesitated to use force against the dissidents (*Ep.* 60). He sinned by negligence in declining to do so. Until his death in 561, Pelagius persisted in his efforts to have the northern Italian schism suppressed by force, but to little avail. These difficulties continued to plague his successors, including Gregory I (590–604). Aquileia was not reunited until the end of the seventh century.

Pelagius's efforts to reestablish ecclesiastical discipline were largely overshadowed by the problems that arose from the Three Chapters controversy. Today we see Justinian's condemnation of the Three Chapters in the hope of reconciling the Monophysites as one more exercise in futility. A more subtle and historically sensitive exegesis would both hesitate to condemn the three authors, on the one hand, and be less narrow in the interpretation of Chalcedon, on the other. John Meyendorff has said that the stubbornness of certain regions of the Western church that insisted on making the defense of the Three Chapters a test of loyalty to Leo and Chalcedon arose from a distinct Chalcedonian fundamentalism. He also noted that the Monophysite phenomenon in the East had arisen from a certain Cyrillian fundamentalism as well. Indeed, some have labeled the disputes that arose after Chalcedon a "schism about language."

The troubles of Vigilius showed that the papacy was entering a period in which the Eastern emperors would exercise a growing power in Italian ecclesiastical circles. Pelagius was caught in the middle, trying to claim complete loyalty to an interpretation of the past and, at the same time, reinterpreting one aspect of that past to accommodate the demands of a strong emperor. Whether out of ambition or of necessity, he eventually decided that his earlier hesitations as a deacon had been a mistake, and he began to extol the virtues of admitting one's mistakes and of change. But the authority of the papacy lay in the defense of tradition, not in switching sides.

SELECTED BIBLIOGRAPHY

Devreesse, R., ed. *Pelagii diaconi ecclesiae romanae in defensione trium capitulorum.* Studi e Testi 57. Rome: Biblioteca Apostolica Vaticana, 1932.

Duchesne, Louis, ed. *Le Liber Pontificalis.* Paris: 1886–92, 1:cxxi, 230–31. English translation in *The Book of Pontiffs*, trans. R. Davis. Translated Texts for Historians. Liverpool: Liverpool University Press, 1989, 59.

Eno, Robert. *The Rise of the Papacy.* Wilmington, Del.: M. Glazier, 1990.

Facundus, bishop of Hermiane. *Opera.* CCL 90A.

Gassó, P., and C. Batlle, eds. *Pelagii I Papae Epistulae quae supersunt (556–561).* Abbey of Montserrat, 1956.

Jedin, H., ed. *History of the Church.* Vol. 2. New York: Seabury, 1980.

Levillain, P., ed. *Dictionnaire historique de la papauté.* Paris: Fayard, 1994, "Vigile" (by C. Sotinel), 1724–27; "Pélage Ier" (by C. Fraisse-Coué), 1293–96.

Liberatus, Deacon of Carthage. *Breviarium causae Nestorianorum et Eutychianorum*, PL 68.

Meyendorff, John. *Imperial Unity and Christian Divisions: The Church, 450–680 A.D.* Crestwood, N.Y.: St. Vladimir's Seminary Press, 1989.

Mommsen, T., ed. *Victor, Bishop of Tunna: Chronicle.* MGH, Auct. Ant. 11.

Sotinel, C. "Autorité pontificale et pouvoir impérial sous le règle de Justinien: L'exemple du pape Vigile." *Mélanges de l'École française de Rome: Antiquité* 104, no. 1 (1992): 439–63.

BIBLIOGRAPHIC NOTE

There is very little original source material available for the earliest popes, and there is considerable controversy among New Testament scholars over the historical value and accuracy of the material in the Acts of the Apostles. An introduction to and English translation of the Nag Hammadi Gnostic Apocalypse of Peter is available in James Brashler and Roger A. Bullard, "Apocalypses of Peter," in *The Nag Hammadi Library* (ed. James M. Robinson, rev. ed., San Francisco: Harper and Row, 1988, 372–78). Two major collections offer some testimony. One is P. Jaffe's *Regesta pontificum Romanorum ab condita ecclesia ad annum post Christum natum MCXCVII*, 2nd ed. by G. Wattenbach (Leipzig, 1885–88); reprint, Graz: 1956), and the second is L. Duchesne, ed., *Le Liber pontificalis* (Paris: 1886–92). For a modern overview and perspective, see the volumes by Robert B. Eno and J.N.D. Kelly in the appended bibliography. Useful references to specific personages and popes are noted in the bibliographies appended to the entries on the various popes in this part.

On Peter, see also Pheme Perkins, *Peter: Apostle for the Whole Church*, Studies on Personalities of the New Testament (Columbia: University of South Carolina Press, 1994), and the volume edited by Raymond E. Brown, Karl P. Donfried, and John Reumann. *Peter in the New Testament* (New York: Paulist Press, 1973). The first of these offers useful suggestions on using the Gospels to ask historical questions about Peter. It also provides a good socioeconomic class position of the Galilean fisherman. On the archaeological excavations at Capernaum, where some claim to have discovered the house of Peter, see Jerome Murphy-O'Connor, *The Holy Land: An Archaeological Guide from Earliest Times to 1700* (New York, 1986).

On Clement I there are important primary sources, including Joseph Barber Lightfoot, *The Apostolic Fathers. First Part: S. Clement of Rome: A Revised Text with Introductions, Notes, Dissertations, and Translations*, 2 vols., (London, 1890, 1973), which remain invaluable. Also useful is Kinsopp Lake, *The Apostolic Fathers* (reprint, Cambridge, Mass.: Harvard University Press, 1985). Francis X. Glimm has provided a translation, *The Letters of St. Clement of Rome to the Corinthians. The So-Called Second Letter of St. Clement, Being an Ancient Homily by an Anonymous Author* (Washington, D.C.: Catholic University of America Press, 1947). Finally, Robert M. Grant and Holt H. Graham have edited *The Apostolic Fathers: A New Translation and Commentary*, vol. 1, *First and Second Clement* (New York: Thomas Nelson and Sons, 1965), which provides insightful, critical notes. Among the secondary literature, John Fuellenbach's *Ecclesiastical Office and the Primacy of Rome: An Evaluation of Recent Theological Discussion of First Clement* (Washington, D.C.: Catholic University of America Press, 1980), provides a vast survey of the literature on Pope Clement. Meanwhile, a good introduction to the religious thought of Clement is provided in H.B. Bumpus, *The Christological Awareness of Clement of Rome and Its Sources* (Winchester, Mass.: University Press of Cambridge, 1972.) On Callistus, much of the work is in German, but Ignaz von Döllinger's work has been translated as *Hippolytus and Callistus or the Church of Rome in the First Half of the Third Century* (Edinburgh: T and T Clark, 1876).

Starting with Damasus and his successors, there is generally more information to be found in Jaffé and Duchesne on the early popes. In the bibliography on Damasus a number of articles are particularly useful, including those by H. Chadwick, "Pope Damasus and the Peculiar Claim of Rome to St. Peter and St. Paul," in *Neotestamentica et patristica* 6 (Leiden, 1962), 313–18, and Armand de Mendieta, "Basile de Césarée et Damase de Rome: Les causes de l'échec de leurs négociations," in *Biblical and Patristic Studies in Memory of R.P. Casey*, ed. J.N. Birdsall and R.W. Thomson (Freiburg im Br.: 1963). The writings of Hermann Josef Vogt and Jakob Spiegl are useful for Celestine I. Charles Pietri's *Roma Christiana: Recherches sur l'Église de Rome* (Rome: École Française de Rome, 1976) offers a magisterial history of the Roman church before the pontificate of Leo the Great and provides much material on Celestine's dealing with the Gallic and Illyrian bishops. Robert Milburn's *Early Christian Art and Architecture* (Berkeley: University of California Press, 1988), provides a general account of the Roman basilicas, including those with which Celestine was involved.

Leo I is by far the most extensively documented of the popes of the early period. In this regard see R. Dolle, *Léon le Grand: Sermons, Sources Chrétiennes* 22, 49, 74, 200 (Paris, 1963–73), and C.L. Feltoe, *The Letters and Sermons of Leo the Great, Bishop of Rome*, in *A Select Library of Nicene and Post-Nicene Fathers of the Christian Church*, 2nd ser., vol. 12 (New York: William B. Eerdmans 1895; reprint, Grand Rapids, Mich.: Eerdmans, 1976). There are concise accounts of Leo's pontificate in the church histories and histories of the papacy by E. Caspar, H. Jedin, and J.N.D. Kelly. Though now questioned in some of its details, the most comprehensive account is still T.G. Jalland, *The Life and Times of St. Leo the Great* (London: SPCK, 1941). The writings of Pelagius are to be found in the relatively recent edition of R. Devreesse, *Pelagii diaconi ecclesiae romanae in defensione trium capitulorum* (Rome: Biblioteca Apostolica Vaticana, 1932).

Additional and useful general sources include the following:

Dvornik, F. *Byzantium and the Roman Primacy*. Paris: Les Editions du Cerf, 1964.

Eno, Robert B. *The Rise of the Papacy*. Collegeville, Minn.: Michael Glazier Books/ The Liturgical Press, 1990.

Farmer, William R., and Roch Kereszty. *Peter and Paul in the Church of Rome*. New York: Paulist Press, 1990.

Grabowski, S.J. "Saint Augustine and the Primacy of the Roman Bishops." *Traditio* 4 (1946): 89–114.

Granfield, Patrick *The Limits of the Papacy: Authority and Autonomy in the Church*. New York: Crossroad/Continuum, 1987.

Kelly, J.N.D. *The Oxford Dictionary of Popes*. New York: Oxford University Press, 1986.

McCue, J.F. "The Roman Primacy in the Second Century and the Problem of the Development of Dogma." *Theological Studies* 25 (1964): 161–96.

Twomey, V. *Apostolikos Thronos: The Primacy of Rome as Reflected in the Church History of Eusebius and the Historico-Apologetic Writings of Saint Athanasius the Great*. Münster: Aschendorff Verlag, 1982.

PART II

THE MEDIEVAL PAPACY

INTRODUCTION

Glenn W. Olsen

A widespread convention views Gregory I, the Great (590–604), as the first of the medieval popes. Prominent among Gregory's many accomplishments was his initiative in sending a monk from the urban Roman Monastery of St. Andrew on the Coelian Hill, which Gregory had established in his family home and in which he had lived before becoming pope, with the mission to convert the Anglo-Saxons. This monk, St. Augustine of Canterbury, named after the location in Kent in which King Ethelbert established Augustine and his fellow missionaries upon their arrival in England, brought with him Gregory's monastic theology, which the pope adapted to English conditions. Specifically, since this was a missionary enterprise, Gregory allowed Augustine to mix modes of life, monastic and clerical, generally kept apart in Rome. Monks, clerics, and boys training to become priests all were to live around Augustine in a family imitating the life of the first Christians. Such adaptation was characteristic of Gregory and foreshadowed much early medieval papal policy.

Though missionary enterprises sponsored by others in the church had been common, the papacy itself had not previously generally initiated missions to preach to pagan peoples. The normal form of evangelization up to Gregory's day had been through the secular arm, the Roman state. Like his predecessors ever since Christianity had become the official Roman religion in the late fourth century, Gregory came to the papal office taking for granted the state's interest in evangelization and enforcing orthodoxy within the imperial boundaries, and on this basis he called various matters to its attention, a pocket of pagans here, a heresy there. Beyond this, we cannot really speak of a "missionary policy" in the early Middle Ages. At the time he initiated the English mission, the geography of the old empire was still alive, and Gregory in part saw the mission to the English as an expression of traditional imperial concern that all within the boundaries of the empire be Christian. Though, like Augustine (354–430), Gregory had never seen Christianity as simply coextensive with the empire, but had thought of it as having a universal mission, in his mind the Anglo-Saxons were exceptional in that they were an entire pagan people living within the long-established boundaries of the Christian Roman Empire. As such, like earlier pagan peoples who had entered the empire, they should become Christian.

Gregory seems to have hoped that the English kings would play a role in the conversion of England similar to that the Roman emperors played in enforcing orthodoxy in the empire generally. He was quickly disabused of this notion or came to a clearer understanding of the tenacity of paganism in England, and in the event the conversion of England took more than his lifetime. Still, it was from his pontificate that the papacy took seriously Christ's command to preach the gospel to every nation. When the patriarch of Alexandria addressed Gregory, rather than the patriarch of Constantinople, as "ecumenical patriarch," Gregory rejected the title because his view was that to claim it would be to undercut the status of his fellow bishops. He saw no one, the patriarch in the East or himself in the West, as a prince placed above the other bishops, ruling the church through them. The bishop of Rome held primacy within the church, but was not a monarch. He was, to use the phrase Gregory coined, "servant of the servants of God." Following St. Paul (1 Cor. 9:19; 2 Cor. 1:24, 4:5) and St. Augustine, the apostolic ideal was service, not domination. Gregory expressed this ministerial ideal of pastoral care in his *Pastoral Rule*. Though Rome was no longer the political center of Europe, which had been shifting northward out of the Mediterranean basin, initiatives such as Gregory's mission to England prevented the city of Rome from becoming completely isolated from developments in the north. Indeed, while the profound decay of governments, institutional structures, and communications across Europe, especially in the seventh and eighth centuries, left Rome in considerable isolation, it also presented an opportunity.

The papacy from the fourth century into the sixth had in many respects fallen under tutelage of the empire and had become part of an integrated sacral society, the Christian Roman Empire. Then increasingly from Gregory's day the institutions of the ancient world, at least in the West, disappeared, the papacy itself partially excepted. Though the popes generally into the eighth century continued to accept the traditional imperial orientation toward Constantinople, gradually the papacy passed over from being in tutelage to becoming tutor, to becoming teacher of the Germanic peoples who had replaced the Romans as the governors of the Western regions that had composed the empire. In the eighth century anti-Greek sentiment in the West increased, in part a result of dispute over whether the church in Illyricum should be controlled from Constantinople or from Rome. Much of the subsequent history of Central and Eastern Europe, of the lands converted by either German or Greek missionaries, was centered on clashes between the competing claims of the Latin and Greek churches. While Gregory I had taken Constantinople's claims to sovereignty for granted, the embracing of iconoclasm, the rejection of the use of icons in worship, by eighth-century Eastern emperors led the West to reconsider its attitudes. Early on, Pope Gregory II (715–31), reiterating the teaching of Pope Gelasius I (492–96), declared in a letter of 727 to Emperor Leo III: "The pontiffs who preside over the church do not meddle in affairs of state, and likewise the emperors ought not to meddle in ecclesiastical affairs, but to administer the things committed to them" (Tierney, p. 19).

In France the Carolingian dynasty, founded in 751, gained identity by distinguishing itself and the West from the East. Despite the fact that such popes as Hadrian I (772–95) continued to approve the conclusions arrived at by councils held in the East such as II Nicaea, Carolingian theological works criticized the East for having distorted the patristic heritage and thus suggested that it was the West that was in most direct continuity with the Christian past. Hadrian had not personally attended II Nicaea, but he had through two legates approved its decision to return to an iconophile position, that is, to permit the use of icons or images in worship. Late in his pontificate he had to admonish and correct Charlemagne's advisors for their attacks on the teachings of II Nicaea. This they accepted, and learned Carolingians continued to define the West by obedience to Rome. They continued also to associate the Pauline vision (Eph. 5:27) of the church without blemish with the church of Rome. The court theologian Theodulf insisted that Rome be consulted in every matter of faith and placed Rome's authority above that of all the other apostolic sees.

The culmination of anti-Greek sentiment, the emancipation of the West from Byzantine leadership, came when, in 800, Charlemagne received the imperial crown himself from Pope Leo III (795–816). War against the Lombards in defense of the papacy, the price the Carolingians had paid earlier in the century for the recognition of their line as royal by Pope Zachary (741–52), now received its reward, the foundation of the Papal States in the 750s. From that time until the nineteenth century, the pope was the temporal ruler of a band of land running across Italy from Rome to Ravenna. Learned men increasingly claimed that the empire had been transferred to the Franks. Byzantium was rejected, but the idea of empire lived on. This, however, was an attenuated empire, for the pope had essentially become the head of the Latin church, and in some measure of Latin Christendom, at the cost of being cut off from the rest of the Christian church.

Henry Mayr-Harting has shown how "Rome centered" St. Boniface, the apostle to the Germans in the early eighth century, was (*Coming of Christianity to Anglo-Saxon England*, 3rd ed., University Park: Pennsylvania University Press, 1991). Especially since the seventh century, Rome had become a pilgrimage site, and much thought in the north of Europe thereafter looked toward the city of the apostles. Such an orientation, common also in England among the "Roman party" of which Bede (d. 735) was a member, expressed itself in the flood of relics from Roman basilicas and catacombs that flowed north in the eighth and ninth centuries, connecting the chief holy site of the Latin world with individual churches and monasteries in the north. A focus on Rome continued to dominate ninth-century reformers north of the Alps. For instance, during his tenure as abbot of Fulda beginning in 822, Hrabanus Maurus avidly collected relics from Rome, where a thriving relic trade flourished. A younger contemporary, Rudolf, who recorded the itinerary of relics passing from Rome to Germany, was particularly concerned in his *Miracula* about Fulda's relationship with Rome. The Roman relics Fulda possessed confirmed the relation of its foundation to St. Boniface and Pope Zachary and its continuing relation to Rome.

Reverence for Rome was also evident in the large place in the life of the church played by papal decretal letters. Modeled on imperial responses, the papal decretals had begun in the late fourth century, had developed in the fifth, and were gathered together in early medieval canonical collections, books containing the law of the church. More than five hundred decretals were cited in the *Hispana*, a canonical collection composed in seventh-century Spain. In comparison to Eastern canonical collections, which contained patriarchal and episcopal letters by many writers, the canonical letters of the Western collections were solely papal, and it was only papal letters that were thought of as having universal import. This development gave the West a jurisdictional centralization that the East lacked. The most important of the Roman collections, of the sixth century, was the *Dyonisiana*. This gathered the universal canon law as it was then understood, and was the main Western collection in the early Middle Ages, competing with the *Hispana*. It was later augmented by the *Hadriana*, given by Pope Hadrian I to Charlemagne in 774. The early-sixth-century *Decretum Gelasianum*, which at various times was attributed to various authors, including Gelasius, gave a list of "orthodox Fathers" who have not strayed from the communion of the Holy Roman church. This was subsequently used to the end of our period to determine who were the orthodox writers.

Reverence for Rome lay behind the steps taken in the ninth century in the direction of papal monarchy, that is, in the direction of a view of the church in which the bishops were seen as placed in a hierarchy under the papal primacy. This was the view especially of Popes Nicholas I (858–67) and John VIII (872–82). If over the previous century the influence of Byzantium over Rome had declined, this did not mean that Rome was now free to do what it pleased. In many ways the former domination-from-a-distance of the Byzantines had been replaced by various more local forms of domination, and the papacy had been freed from Byzantium only to fall under the control of a variety of Western powers ranging from the nobility of the city of Rome itself to Charlemagne, who in traditional Germanic fashion fancied himself a theocratic monarch, responsible, among other things, for the government of the church itself, whether in Frankland or at Rome.

Against such theocratic domination Nicholas I and John VIII in some measure protested and offered the alternative of a pyramidal church hierarchy under the pope as a way for the church to live its own life. In the long run, it might be argued, conditions favored the development of such a hierarchical view of the relation of the authority of the pope to that of the bishops, for the pope had become not just the chief priest in the church, but almost the last bearer of ancient imperial ideas and practices. In the short run, however, the papacy now passed through one of its most difficult periods. During the tenth century, when Europe was attacked from the east by the Magyars, from the south by the Moslems, and from the north by the Vikings, the bishop of Rome largely became captive to struggles internal to the city of Rome. At times the papacy was little more than a prize to be awarded to some family member by the victorious side in the unceasing struggles between the principal Roman families. We might speak of a secularization of the papacy, if by that we mean that some popes conceived of their office in the way that laymen commonly conceive of theirs, as something to be used to enrich one's family and supporters. Simony, the payment of money to receive an ecclesiastical office, and lay investiture, the investiture of an ecclesiastical official by a layman, were common throughout the church and influenced the papacy. No more than bishops were popes free from the pressures and control sought over them by kings and nobles. Theocratic monarchy and the proprietary church, that is, a Germanic tendency to view ecclesiastical institutions as property, especially of the laity, ruled.

There has been much controversy over the interpretation of the tenth and eleventh centuries. According to traditional German theocratic and proprietary notions, the king, though not a cleric, was a sacral figure placed at the head of society to direct and integrate everything in it, including the church. Catholic historians have often adopted the viewpoint of the later eleventh-century reformers and viewed this as a system in which the laity oppressed the church. They have often seen a so-called Gregorian reform, named after Gregory VII (1073–85), as injecting into society a healthy dualism by which the church was made more independent of secular rulers than it previously had been, and thus was enabled more clearly to specify the nature of Christian society. Lutheran historians such as Gerd Tellenbach, defending the sacral order of tenth- and eleventh-century Germany, have argued that the role of the German kings and emperors in church affairs, ruling "by the grace of God," was largely positive, and that their record was later unfairly blackened by the reformers of the time of Gregory VII, who in their condemnation of simony and clerical marriage were, the argument goes, largely opportunistic (Tellenbach, *Church, State and Christian Society at the Time of the Investiture Contest*, trans. R.F. Bennett, Oxford: Basil Blackwell, 1959).

Tellenbach thinks that the idea that there was an "imperial church system" was largely a later construct and insists that there was no deep conflict before the mid-eleventh century between king and pope. He vigorously defends Gregory VII's opponent, Henry IV (1056–1106) of Germany, and views Gregory as a failure. Though such a view successfully shows that Henry, too, was religiously motivated, it leaves unexplained (1) why in the tenth century itself voices were raised against the oppression of the church by powerful laymen, and (2) why the drive from about 1050 for what reformers called *libertas ecclesiae*, freedom of the church, resonated in as many hearts as it did. As Tellenbach himself showed in *Church, State and Christian Society at the Time of the Investiture Contest*, the church's drive for freedom did much to unify Europe, not at the political level but at the level of forming a greater consciousness of common membership in Christendom, a shared Christian culture. Indicative of tenth-century protest are the words of the Council of Troslé of 909, describing the conditions of the monasteries: "They no longer have legitimate superiors, owing to the abuse of submitting to secular domination. We see in the monasteries lay abbots with their wives and their children, their soldiers and their dogs" (*Sacorum Conciliorum*, ed. Giovanni Mansi, trans. Christopher Dawson in Dawson, *Religion and the Rise of Western Culture*, Garden City, N.Y.: Doubleday, 1958, 121). Such resentment was only to increase with time.

However we assess the tenth-century church, its general contours remained into the eleventh century, though here and there movements seeking some kind of reform, usually of a moral nature, always existed. At this time the city of Rome had a population of about 10,000. Families such as the Crescentii and the Tusculans continued to dominate the city. In 1032 the latter again succeeded in gaining the papacy for a member of their family, who became Benedict IX (1032–44). In 1045 his archenemies, the Crescentii, selected their own pope, Sylvester III, who almost immediately was forced out of the city. Benedict returned to office, only to resign in return for a payment of money and to be replaced by Gregory VI (1045–46). At this point Henry III of Germany (1039–56), operating from a deep sense of responsibility for Christendom, decided to intervene in the scandalous situation in Rome. A synod held at Sutri deposed both Gregory and Sylvester, and Henry sent Gregory into exile in Germany. Gregory was accompanied in this exile by a Roman monk, Hildebrand, the future Gregory VII.

The new pope, Clement II (1046–47), gave Henry the imperial crown and the title *patricius* to signify that Clement recognized Henry as his defender. Since at this time the first vote in papal elections was cast by the patricius, Clement was thus trying to limit the influence on papal elections of the Roman nobility. The pontificates of the following four popes, all German, were brief, and there is evidence that Clement himself was poisoned. One of these German popes, Leo IX (1049–54), was particularly successful in communicating the nature of the reforms he desired. Spending only six months of his pontificate in Rome, Leo constantly traveled and held synods to explain the reforms he thought the church needed. Already at a Lateran council of 1049 he proposed, unsuccessfully, that all ordinations given by simonists were invalid. To end clerical marriage, he similarly proposed that the wives and children of priests become church serfs. While Henry III of Germany accepted these decisions, Henry I (1031–60), vigorously opposed them in France. Similarly, in England a little later William the Conqueror (1066–87) jealously watched communications between England and Rome to make sure that no royal prerogatives were lost to the reviving papacy. He may himself have won England under a papal banner, a sign, like the papal banner and blessing given the Normans to conquer Sicily about the same time or like the First Crusade another generation later, of the increased willingness of the papacy to pursue the reordering of the world through warfare, but to William this itself meant that the pope bore watching. To return to Leo IX, the Normans had entered southern Italy earlier in the century and were in Leo's day expanding northward: A holy war proclaimed against them by Leo ended in disaster at Civitate in 1053, with the papal volunteers cut to pieces and Leo held as a captive for eight months. Negotiations with Constantinople to resolve a range of disputes between the Greek and Latin churches over dogma and liturgy only worsened relations and resulted in Humbert of Silva Candida excommunicating the patriarch of Constantinople in 1054.

The Lotharingians Leo IX brought with him to Rome were, like indigenous Roman and Italian reformers, outspoken in their attempts to purify the church. Increasingly such reformers understood the needed reforms to be not simply of a moral nature but to involve exclusion of all lay influence in, for instance, the election and deposition of bishops. One step in this direction was the establishment of the college of cardinals in 1059 under Pope Nicholas II (1058–61). Thenceforth the popes were to be elected by the members of this college. However, only from about the time of Alexander II (1061–73) did the reformers center their hopes on the papacy itself. Henceforth Roman centralism was to be the prime agent of reform.

It expressed itself in all manner of ways, for instance, in the insistence that all Latin Christendom worship in Latin according to a papally approved rite.

From this time the popes rapidly introduced ecclesiastical government more centralized than anything that previously had existed. They shortly became the sponsors of such Europe–wide projects as the Crusades. Papal monarchy had appeared, with attendant shifts in ecclesiology, that is, in how the church was understood. Just as increasingly the popes insisted that they must be independent from lay control, they simultaneously insisted on a pyramidal structure of authority within the church, with themselves as the "universal ordinary." As individual bishops stood to their dioceses, the pope was to be seen as standing to the church itself, including the bishops. Such views effectively clericalized the church in the sense that a hierarchical clergy was more clearly than ever before distinguished from the laity. The "church" itself was ever more closely identified with the clergy. The subordination of the bishops to the pope found in such views was to remain, though it received various adjustments over time. Thus a relatively more proepiscopal attitude appeared in the 1120s. In this the popes came to see the danger in the exemption of monasteries from local episcopal control, which had been a feature of Cluniac life since the tenth century.

Wherever one's sympathies lie in regard to the positions taken by Gregory VII and Henry IV, there were many ironies in the situation of the papacy in Gregory's time. Gregory clearly advanced the articulation of Christianity as a universal faith, but against the background of a very diverse European world. Sometimes, as in Germany, his claims were resisted in principle, but sometimes, as in Norway or Poland, his claims were received politely but because of cultural differences or distance were not possible to implement. Tellenbach's statement that "the vision Gregory and Humbert had of the right order in the world was magnificent, naive, and unrealistic" is in an obvious sense and for the short run true, but Gregory had changed forever how the papacy viewed itself and was viewed by others (*The Church in Western Europe from the Tenth to the Early Twelfth Century*, trans. Timothy Reuter, New York: Cambridge University Press, 1993, 264). In this sense the very idealism of Gregory's views powerfully changed the world. Until the twentieth century the papacy was to be a powerful force prodding local churches to a larger view of the world than that of a single cultural tradition.

The "investiture contest," the quarrel over the freedom and nature of episcopal elections, raged long after the death of Gregory VII. Gregory's claim that he could judge and depose kings, expressed in such acts as his deposition of Henry IV and the election of Rudolf of Rheinfelden in 1077 in the presence of papal legates to replace Henry, struck at the claims of theocratic monarchy and blood right. His successors and defenders, if they were sometimes more flexible than Gregory, maintained his stance. Thus Fulcher of Chartres could declare in the early twelfth century that it is "the Roman church which holds the superior power of correcting the whole of Christendom," (Robert Bartlett, *The Making of Europe: Conquest, Colonization, and Cultural Change, 950–1350*, Princeton: Princeton University Press, 1993, 243). The successor of Urban II (1088–99), who in 1095 at Clermont called the First Crusade, was Paschal II (1099–1118). In 1102 Paschal renewed the excommunication originally made by Gregory VII of Henry IV of Germany. A more or less final resolution of the quarrel was achieved by Callistus II (1119–24) in the Concordat of Worms of 1122. In this the papacy won the essential point that ecclesiastical offices are spiritual and not mere appendices of material possessions or temporal offices. Though conflicts between church and state never were to disappear, and lay rulers continued to exercise considerable influence over episcopal elections, subsequent conflicts typically formed around issues other than direct lay election of bishops or lay ownership of ecclesiastical property.

In the early twelfth century Rome was comparable in neither size nor level of trade to the chief cities of northern Italy. Though the German emperor remained Rome's nominal lord, the old pattern of struggle between the papacy and aristocratic factions in the city continued. This struggle centered on the attempt to dominate the highest local official, the prefect of Rome, who was the deputy of the emperor, but over whom the pope had the right of confirmation. The struggle also expressed itself in periodic threats to the papacy of schism. In 1124, at the death of Callistus II, a turbulent election followed. Again in 1130, on the death of Honorius II (1124–30), the college of cardinals divided, with the majority favoring the antipope Anacletus II (1130–38), and a minority Innocent II (1130–43). This division reflected both family feuding and division within the papal court. One party, that of Innocent, favored new religious orders such as the Cistercians and Premonstratensians and won the support of the most prominent churchman of the day, the Cistercian Bernard of Clairvaux, as well as of Norbert of Magdeburg. The other party, that of Anacletus, favored Cluny and disapproved the growing tendency of the papacy to support bishops against monasteries. Old tensions also remained between the city and the nobility of the surrounding Campagna. These later came to a boil in 1143 when Pope Innocent II refused assent to the desire of the Romans to destroy Tivoli. The Romans rebelled and in recollection of their ancient past proclaimed a senate.

This rebellion was the work of the Roman middle class, which now aimed at freeing the city from papal control. Rome remained turbulent through the time of Celestine II (1143–44) and Lucius II (1144–45). In 1145 a monk, a student of Bernard of Clairvaux, was elected Eugenius III (1145–53), and the situation changed. Eugenius refused recognition to the newly formed Roman commune or independent city government, though this meant that he had to live outside the city. He subsequently fled to France. A radical reformer, Arnold of Brescia, while holding no office, prodded the city to an ever more antipapal stance. In 1148 Eugenius excommunicated him, but the situation remained difficult, and Eugenius died in exile unreconciled with the Roman populace. With Hadrian IV (1154–59) and especially Alexander III (1159–81), though the papal position in Rome remained precarious, a new breed of man, commonly educated in law or theology in the schools of Bologna and Paris and concerned with the details of law and administration, ascended to the papacy.

In the twelfth century discussion in canon law of the respective authority of the writings of the church fathers, of church councils, and of papal letters increasingly grew. About 1140 the great canonist Gratian took up this discussion in Distinction 20 of his *Decretum* (translated by Jean Werck-meister) and said that the authority of papal letters was equal to that of conciliar canons. He saw the Fathers as arguably superior in knowledge and grace to the other authorities, and thus as superior commentators on the Bible, but said that they lacked *potestas* in cases, that is, judiciary power for making legal decisions. Thus "ecclesiastical causes are . . . settled . . . by the decrees of the Roman pontiffs and by the holy canons of the councils" (Irena Backus, ed., *The Reception of the Church Fathers in the West from the Carolingians to the Maurists*, New York: Brill, 1977, I, 75). Here Gratian established a hierarchy of authority with general councils and papal decretals on the same plane, followed by the Fathers. Increasingly after him the authority of the Fathers declined, and new ecclesiastical law was seen as simply what was contained in papal decretals, as in the *Decretals* of Gregory IX (1227–41), and in conciliar decisions. In this development the papal *potestas* (authority) in the form of new papal decretals tended to return canon law to a base in legislative texts rather than in patristic authority. Papal power asserted itself over patristic authority. Already in the thirteenth century writers such as Roger Bacon regretted this change, and to the present there has been in certain circles a desire to return to what has been perceived as an older tradition in which canon law was sacramental, a participation in mystery, rather than legislative. Other circles, while acknowledging the important shift that took place after Gratian, have seen views such as Bacon's as romantic and ahistorical, as based on an ancient church that never was.

Though it is a commonplace that the pontificate of Innocent III (1198–1216) initiates the high point of papal influence in the Middle Ages, which runs through the pontificate of Innocent IV (1243–54) to the pontificate of Boniface VIII (1294–1303), a culmination of the papal monarchy toward which the papacy had been inclining since the time of Gregory VII, in fact, under Innocent III the pope's position in Rome and the Papal States was not much improved over what it had been earlier. Elsewhere, just as in the time of the investiture struggle, strong kings continued to control the appointment of bishops. Thus in 1217, as one aspect of its deep-rooted anti-Irish racial policies, the English Crown directed its justiciar in Ireland "that henceforth you allow no Irishman to be elected [bishop] in our land of Ireland or preferred in any cathedral" (Bartlett, 225). Nevertheless, in spite of such continuing attempts to bend the church to political purposes, to "integrate society" on royal terms, in certain obvious ways all Europe was increasingly oriented toward the papal curia.

By the early thirteenth century the papacy issued hundreds of letters each year, and papal legates were found pursuing the pope's affairs all across Christendom. By 1200 about eight hundred bishoprics fell under obedience to Rome and followed the Latin liturgy. This number continued to increase in the thirteenth century as various forms of force and crusade continued Latin Christianity's penetration into areas such as Livonia and Prussia. The final lines between the Greek and Latin churches were drawn along the Baltic in the fourteenth century, but as early as 1222 Pope Honorius III (1216–27) tried to force the Russians to observe the Latin rite. The expansion of Latin Christianity that had proceeded especially along the eastern and northern frontiers of Europe all through the early Middle Ages received an unexpected, if precarious, increase through the conquest of Constantinople in the Fourth Crusade. From 1204 to 1261 and beyond, a new string of Latin dioceses was found in Greece, the Aegean, and the eastern Mediterranean. Everywhere, even as far away as Mongolia, new religious orders such as the Franciscans and Dominicans, both approved by Innocent III, helped advance papal policy.

An interesting study by Michael Borgolte of papal burials over the centuries has revealed how secure papal ideology had become by the thirteenth century. We may conclude with its findings. From about 500 to about 900 the popes had been buried at old St. Peter's, the predecessor of the present St. Peter's. In the tenth and eleventh centuries the popes were buried in various places, some in Rome, but some even in Germany. Ten of sixteen popes were buried at the Lateran in the twelfth century. Innocent III saw burial at St. Peter's as customary, but he and the majority of thirteenth-century popes were buried elsewhere, often someplace in the Papal States. Although the theory was that papal burials were "Petrine," in continuity with St. Peter, over the centuries they had become less literally Petrine, that is, less at St. Peter's. In fact, popes could be buried anywhere. Partly this was a necessity caused by the continuing strife at Rome, but partly the principle "Ubi est papa, ibi est Roma" (Rome is where the pope is) had established itself.

GREGORY I, "THE GREAT" (590–604)

CAROLE E. STRAW

Gregory I, "the Great" (b. 540; papacy: 590–604), as an administrator and political leader, marks the beginning of the medieval papacy. As a theologian and exegete, he is considered the fourth doctor of the church and the founder of a truly medieval spirituality. Gregory's background was privileged. While Gregory's extended family was no longer considered a member of the *gens* Ancia or Decia, it was influential and had given the church Felix III (483–92), Gregory's great-great-grandfather, and Agapitus (535–36), a distant cousin. Gregory's father was a minor church official, and his aunts had adopted monastic vows. Gregory's education, praised extravagantly by Gregory of Tours as "second to none" (*Hist. Franc.* 10.1), included rhetorical and probably legal training.

Gregory began public service as urban prefect (cf. *Ep.* 4.2) and was converted to monastic life in 573. The years he spent in monastic life at St. Andrew's on the family estate he deemed the happiest of his life (574–79). But soon Gregory was thrust back into the world as deacon and apocrisiarius for Pelagius II: until 585/86 Gregory served as papal representative to the Byzantine court. Gregory chose to live apart in a monastic community of friends, which included Leander of Seville. To this community, Gregory originally preached his exposition of Job, *Magna Moralia*. Despite the friendships Gregory made at court, he never learned Greek fluently, and he seemed always to suspect the Greeks of cleverness and over-sophistication. On his return to Rome, Gregory resumed his office of deacon and returned to his life at St. Andrew's.

Gregory never became abbot, nor is St. Andrew's believed to have been a Benedictine monastery, despite the admiration of Benedict evident in Gregory's *Life* of the saint. Gregory was elected pope in 590, when Pelagius II had succumbed to the plague and the city was in turmoil. Gregory wrote unsuccessfully to the emperor Maurice protesting his election. While awaiting the emperor's reply, Gregory organized a penitential procession to avert the wrath of God manifested in the plague. According to legend, Gregory saw the archangel Michael atop Hadrian's tomb, returning the sword of the Lord's vengeance to its scabbard. Today a statue of Michael on the Castel Sant'Angelo commemorates this vision.

Gregory's times justify the apocalypticism found in his works. Justinian's reconquest, formalized in the Pragmatic Sanction of 554, had left Italy ravaged by wars, famine, and the plague. As the Byzantine presence weakened, independent military leaders came to dominate society, and the church fell prey to the influence of such strongmen in a variety of ways ranging from simony to the usurpation of privileges and to the ill education of clergy who simply saw the church as another means of advancing their career in society. Across the sea, tension with the Byzantine government existed over several ecclesiastical and political issues, the chief of which was how to deal with the Lombards' invasion of Italy. Despite these adversities that demanded his active attention, Gregory continued to write and cultivate the spiritual life. In 591 Gregory published the *Regula pastoralis*, dedicating it to John of Ravenna. This blueprint for the good ruler became enormously influential and is known particularly in a translation authorized by King Alfred into Anglo-Saxon. Gregory also undertook the preaching of homilies on Ezechiel in 591–92. In 593 Gregory preached *Homilies on the Gospel*, and four books of *Dialogues* were published in 594. A partly edited copy of the *Magna Moralia* was dedicated and sent to Leander of Seville in 595. All of these works assume an audience primarily composed of clergy and monks. From 595–598 he continued to preach to the monastic community around him. Some of these works (on Proverbs, the Prophets, and the Heptateuch) are lost. Gregory's commentaries on the Song of Songs and the first book of Kings do survive through redactions by Claude of Ravenna and are both considered authentically Gregorian.

Gregory's activities as pope are witnessed by a register of more than 860 surviving letters. Since those of the second indiction seem fairly complete—240 for book 2 (September 598–August 599)—other books are obviously fragmentary. The original corpus must have been very lengthy. The *Liber Pontificalis*, the lives of Gregory by an anonymous monk of Whitby, by Paul the Deacon, and by John the Deacon, and references to Gregory by Gregory of Tours and by Bede comprise most of our early knowledge of him. The contributions of Gregory as pope fall into diverse categories. When the Lombards invaded Italy, Gregory became de facto ruler of Rome and defender of southern Italian interests in general. Byzantine interests focused on defending the imperial capital of Ravenna: the exarch ignored the plight of Rome, which was surrounded by Lombard dukes at Spoleto and Benevento. Gregory secured the grain supply for Rome (*Ep.* 1.70), sent troops against the Lombards (*Epp.* 2.4, 2.27, 2.28), secured defense of Naples (*Epp.* 2.20, 2.47), paid ransoms when necessary to buy off soldiers, and was eventually forced to become paymaster, defraying the daily expenses of defending Rome (*Ep.* 5.39). He even sought to make a separate peace with the Lombards, although this infuriated the Byzantine emperor Maurice (*Epp.* 5.34, 5.36). A short peace was formalized in 599, but lasted only two years. In 601 the Byzantine government renewed the war against the Lombards.

Thus wars with the Lombards and tensions with the Byzantine government overshadowed Gregory's papacy. While Gregory had no intention of supplanting the Byzantine government, his response at least asserted the importance of Rome on a political map whose center was shifting north and eastward. What enhanced the papacy's position most were internal reforms in the Roman church and the position Rome took against potential rival sees. Gregory continued the practice of living in common with his *familia* of monks and clerics in the Lateran palace and assembled a circle of trusted friends to help him rule. Indeed, the "monasticization" of his administration and the displacement of the clerical party were such that they led to a reaction against Gregory after his death. With this core of supporters, Gregory hoped to establish a church purified of various abuses of

Tenth-century book illumination depicts Pope Gregory I and his scribe. (Courtesy of the Vatican Library)

worldliness, such as simony, the seizure of land, and usurpation of privileges (*Epp.* 1.9, 1.18, 1.23; see esp. *CCL Append.* 1). More esoteric problems of ecclesiastical reform were addressed in the one synod held under Gregory's rule, in 595 at St. Peter's. For instance, deacons were forbidden from singing in the Mass, popes could no longer be buried wearing dalmatics, lay attendants were excluded from service of the pope in the Lateran palace, slaves were allowed to become monks, and so on. Scholars reject the notion that he redacted the *Sacramentary* that passes under his name, and they also reject any role in establishing Gregorian chant, although he did apparently establish a school for cantors.

Perhaps Gregory achieved most in his administration of the papal patrimony, consisting of between 1,360 and 1,800 square miles in Italy, Sicily, Sardinia, and Corsica. Gregory developed a highly organized staff to manage these estates and utilized a hereditary grant of land that anticipates medieval practices of land use (*Ep.* 1.42). Several letters testify to an attempt to mitigate the plight of peasants (*Epp.* 1.42, 9.46, 13.35) or eradicate residual paganism (*Ep.* 4.46). His attitudes toward Jews reflect the prejudice of his age, consisting of a mixture of severity and "persuasion" that Jews be converted (*Epp.* 2.6, 3.37, 4.31). Other letters reveal Gregory's attempt to mitigate the abuses of secular strongmen and show the limits of his power. Theodore, duke of Sardinia, was a case in point. A decade of letters reveals Gregory's futile protests; even appeals to the emperor could not check Theodore's malfeasance (*Epp.* 1.47, 1.59, 5.38, 14.2). While abuses were often difficult to eradicate, under Gregory, tenants prospered and revenues were sufficient to fund various projects, from the ransoms paid to Lombards to the welfare extended to the Roman population—records were even kept of welfare payments.

The Catholic church in the late sixth century did not have a cogent hierarchical order with Rome at its head, and there is no evidence that Gregory held such a vision. Other cities had their bishops and their own senses of autonomy, such as Milan and Ravenna, not to mention churches of the East. The extent of Gregory's authority was limited. When Gregory was called upon to forward an imperial law to bishops "within his writ," he contacted only bishops in Italy, Sicily, Sardinia, Greece, and the Balkans, omitting Africa, much of the East, and the lands to the north. While Gregory made no claims of Roman primacy, as is later understood by the term, he did believe that bishops were subject to the Holy See when they had committed a fault (the ability "to bind and to loose" given Peter), but otherwise he asserted the equality of all churches (*Ep.* 8.29). Yet respect for Gregory's authority on moral issues was open to question. Appeals to secular authorities generally led to frustration, because the Byzantine authorities were ready to make many compromises to preserve peace and stability. In the early years of his pontificate Gregory was more active in trying to assert his position. This was followed by a period of adjustment to the limits of his effective power. Gregory did exercise discretion in his behavior and did learn by experience. He was generally more successful closer to home. His effective authority weakened with distance.

One dispute that divided West and East and caused innumerable problems in the West was over the imperial policy supporting the condemnation of the "Three Chapters" (certain writings by Theodore of Mopsuestia, Theodoret of Cyrus, and Ibas of Edessa) at the Fifth Ecumenical Council in Constantinople. Westerners believed that Justinian was trying to placate certain Monophysite groups, and they resented the papacy's change of position to fall in line with imperial policy. Gregory was faced with rebellion by churches in Istria and sent troops to discipline the patriarch of Aquileia and summon him to Rome. The Istrians appealed to the emperor and threatened to ally with neighboring bishops in Gaul if they were not left alone. The emperor wanted to avoid the political consequences of such an alliance and ordered Gregory to desist. Gregory complied, although his conscience as pastor must have been wounded. While he did try to persuade schismatics to return to Roman views, the last years of his pontificate still show some letters to him calling for imperial suppression of schismatics (see, for example, *Ep*. 13.34).

Schism also threatened in Africa, where so-called Donatists resisted conformity to the Roman church. Gregory complained of simony, and it seemed that some Catholic bishops had even been bribed to tolerate Donatists (*Epp*. 2.39, 1.82). Gregory's attempt to reform the primatial system that favored age over merit was resisted by Catholic bishops, and a synod in Numidia in 593 ended not in reform, but in the violation of many canons (*Epp*. 4.1; cf. 3.47, 3.48). Imperial authorities sided against at least one Catholic bishop, Paul, who persecuted Donatists. While Gregory did succeed in getting a council at Carthage to condemn Donatists in 594, the imperial edict issued to suppress Donatists went unenforced. Authorities ignored Gregory's requests to institute a persecution of Donatists. By 596 references to Donatists disappear from his letters; Gregory seems to have let the matter drop.

In Dalmatia and other churches of Illyricum Gregory scarcely fared better. He tangled with the Byzantine government over the appointment of Bishop Maximus, whom Gregory excommunicated, to the see of Salona. In something of a compromise, the emperor ordered Gregory to accept Maximus, but did send Maximus to Rome. Gregory insisted on his authority to discipline the bishop, saying that he would "rather die than see the church degenerate" (*Ep*. 5.6). Maximus agreed to do public penance in Ravenna, an act that must have enhanced the authority of Rome. In other churches of Illyricum Gregory tried to extend his authority, but found the emperor more influential. A dispute between Bishop Adrian of Thebes and John of Prima Justiniana was mediated by the emperor; when Gregory tried to assert jurisdiction, no one came to the hearing he called. Later, when it was time to replace the bishop of Prima Justiniana, Gregory used discretion, saying that he would conform to the emperor, should he act in accordance with the canons. If not, still he "would submit to it, as far as [he] could do so without sin" (*Ep*. 11.29; cf. *Ep*. 13.6). These are the words of a careful politician.

Gregory's relations with Constantinople and the Eastern churches were marred by the adoption of the title of ecumenical patriarch by John of Constantinople. Gregory's reaction was dramatic: the incident seems to have struck at the core of how he perceived the nature of authority. True authority should be grounded in humility and service to others, not a desire to have power over others or enjoy the honors of high status. Gregory saw himself as *servus servorum dei* (servant of the servants of God) very sincerely. John had allowed himself to be called ecumenical patriarch as early as 588, and this had been protested by Pelagius II. While this title had been used by patriarchs at the Synod of Constantinople in 518, John was the first to use the term for himself. Gregory protested, only to be commanded by Emperor Maurice to desist. But Gregory continued to object, sending letters to John himself and various members of the Byzantine court, and sought support from the patriarchs of Alexandria and Antioch. Schism was averted by John's death and the emperor's shrewd appointment of a more amiable man, Cyriacus, as patriarch. Still, Cyriacus would not give up the title. Gregory's strongest action came in 599 when a synod was called in Constantinople, inviting bishops under Gregory's jurisdiction. Gregory wrote, reminding them that the synod was invalid without the authority and consent of the Holy See, and he threatened to excommunicate his bishops if they countenanced the offensive title (*Ep.* 9.156). Gregory appears to have been ignored. Hope came in the form of the new emperor Phocas, who issued a decree that the "Apostolic See of Peter, that is, the Roman church, should be the head of all churches." This did not stop the patriarch's use of the title, and ironically, Gregory's successors decided that the best strategy was co-option and began to style themselves as ecumenical bishops and popes.

On balance, Gregory had little success outside Rome and the patrimony he so carefully administered and endeavored to reform. He was constantly frustrated by an emperor whose interests lay elsewhere. Furthermore, the desire of individual cities and regions for autonomy often put them at odds with Gregory. He was frequently forced to compromise. In fact, Gregory's aims and claims were quite modest, namely, that other sees were accountable to the moral authority of the See of Peter. Gregory was firm in asserting this, and such claims would have consequences for the future.

Gregory's greatest contribution to posterity was his writing. The French historian Jean Leclerq said of Gregory's influence in the Middle Ages, "Everyone . . . had read him and lived by him" (Leclerq, *The Love of Learning and the Desire for God*, 34). Gregory's concern with the moral meaning of Scripture, his concerns with suffering and evil, his attitudes defining the proper exercise of power, and his view of the centrality of the church and its sacraments all foreshadow later medieval views, as does his vision of an invisible world of demons and angels surrounding men and women in everyday life, ready to wreak havoc or extend aid as executors of God's will. Gregory is also important as a translator of tradition. Through Gregory, the works of Augustine especially are made more accessible. But Gregory also read deeply the more ascetic and Neoplatonic Ambrose, and he was steeped in the works of Cassian and the Sayings of the Desert Fathers. Traces of Gregory Nazianzen, Gregory of Nyssa, and Origen are also evident. (Gregory may have grown familiar with these writings during his stay in Constantinople.) The Stoicism absorbed by Christian writers such as Ambrose was very influential, but it appears that Gregory knew Seneca's works directly. Despite his debt to others, Gregory's writings have a distinctive structure and impact that make his spiritual message very much his own.

Gregory addressed theodicy most directly in his exegesis of Job, *Magna Moralia*. All evils, including suffering and temptation, were defined as "adversities" sent by God to try the Christian. The puzzle was that each individual could never presume to understand the ultimate purpose of the trial: whether God sent it to discipline him for previous sins or to try him that his virtue might increase. Nor could one's final end be prejudged. Adversity might be sent to chasten and thus restore a soul to God, or it might be the trial that would break the weak and thus foreshadow one's damnation. Adversity, then, is fundamentally ambiguous; it can even be a good thing, a "prosperity," if it saves the soul and increases reward. Thus a complementarity exists between virtue and temptation, activity and contemplation, and even virtue and sin.

Gregory prescribed that the soul should always balance and moderate these dynamic oppositions through discretion. The soul should remain in hope as well as salutary fear, using all adversities in ways to achieve spiritual equilibrium and health. In this program Gregory is very Stoic. In sum, Gregory spelled out and systematized much of what was mysterious and indeterminate in Augustine and other earlier Fathers. Through his various writings, be they a manual for rectors (*Pastoral Care*), questions and answers on various spiritual questions and on the lives of saints (*The Dialogues*), homilies preached publicly (*Homilies on the Gospel*), or more elevated works of exegesis (on Job, the first book of Kings, and the Song of Songs), Gregory gave diverse Christians an understandable "guidebook" of precepts for behavior in various circumstances, be it for the regulation of a ruler in the temptations of power and the most effective way to mold subjects, the frustrations of a monk who must alternate the safety of contemplation with dangerous worldly activity, or the dismay of average Christians, who saw their fragile achievements easily undermined by unwilling sins. Gregory held that all life was to be a sacrifice to God; as long as one's intentions were pure, and one's actions were performed in a spirit of penitential offering, the Christian could hope that God would have mercy toward his own creation. In his clear and systematic answers to fundamental spiritual problems, Gregory laid the foundation for medieval spirituality. His attitudes toward spiritual martyrdom and the centrality of the sacraments led to a renewed interest in Gregory during the Counter-Reformation.

The church and its provision of the sacrament of the Mass came to structure the Christian's life in a way perhaps more central to Gregory than to Augustine and earlier Fathers; here again Gregory anticipates the Middle Ages. The church was Christ's body in which all members played their various, complementary assigned roles. The church was a unity, a *compago*, whose very interconnection with others offered one the opportunity for self-sacrifice and allowed one to participate in the virtues of others. The intercession of saints helped the weak, while the Mass daily repeated the sacrifice of Christ for the benefit of his members. Christians need never feel alone or overwhelmed by trials. Prayer, the sacrifice of the Mass, and the *caritas* connecting the members of the body of Christ existed to fortify them in the particularly urgent challenges they faced as the world neared its end.

SELECTED BIBLIOGRAPHY

Baus, Karl, Hans George Beck, Eugen Ewig, and Hermann Joseph Vogt. *The Imperial Church from Constantine to the Early Middle Ages*. Trans. Anselm Biggs. Vol. 2 of *Handbook of Church History*. New York: Seabury Press, 1980, 602–756.

Caspar, Erich. *Geschichte des Papsttums von den Anfängen bis zur Höhe der Weltherrschaft*. Vol. 2. Tübingen: J.B.C. Mohr 1933 II, 306–514.

Cavadini, John, ed. *Gregory the Great: A Symposium*. Notre Dame Studies in Theology. Notre Dame, Ind.: University of Notre Dame Press, 1995.

Dagens, Claude. *Saint Grégoire le Grand: Culture et expérience chrétiennes*. Paris: Études Augustiniennes, 1977.

Dudden, F. Homes. *Gregory the Great: His Place in History and Thought*. 2 vols. Reprint, New York: Russell & Russell, 1967.

Fontaine, Jacques, Robert Gillet, and Stan Pellistrandi, eds. *Grégoire le Grand*. Colloques internationaux du Centre National de la Recherche Scientifique. Paris: Editions du Centre National de la recherche scientifique, 1986.

Gillet, Robert. "Grégoire le Grand." In *Dictionnaire de spiritualité ascétique et mystique, doctrine et historie*, vol. 6, ed. Marcel Viller. Paris: G. Beauchesne & ses fils, 1967, 872–910.

Godding, Robert. *Bibliografia di Gregorio Magno: Opere di Gregorio Magno*. Complement./1. Rome: Città nuova editrice, 1990.

Grassi, Vittorino, ed. *Gregorio Magno e il suo tempo*. 2 vols. XIX Incontro di studiosi dell'antichità cristiana in colloborazione con l'École Française de Rome. Rome: Institutum Patristicum "Augustinianum," 1991.

Gregory I. *Dialogues*. Ed. Adalbert de Vogüé. Sources chrétiennes 251. Paris: Les éditions du Cerf, 1978.

———. *Sanctus Gregorius Magnus in Canticum Canticorum, in Librum Primum Regnum*. Ed. Patrick Verbraken. Corpus Christianorum, Series Latina 144. Turnholt: Brepols, 1963.

———. *Homiliae in Hiezechihelem prophetam*. Ed. Marcus Adriaen. Corpus Christianorum, Series Latina 142. Turnholt: Brepols, 1971.

———. *The Homilies of St. Gregory the Great: On the Book of the Prophet Ezekiel*. Trans. Theodosia Gray. Etna, Calif.: 1990.

———. *Forty Gospel Homilies*. Trans. David Hurst. Cistercian Studies 123. Kalamazoo, Mich.: Cistercian Publications, 1990.

———. *Moralia in Iob*. Ed. Marcus Adriaen. Corpus Christianorum, Series Latina 3 vols. 143, 143A, 143B. Turnholt: Brepols, 1979–85.

———. *Morals on the Book of Job*. The Library of Fathers of the Holy Catholic Church 18, 21, 23, 31. Oxford: John Henry Parker, 1844–50.

———. *Opera Omnia*. In *Patrologia Latina* 75–79, ed. J-P. Migne. Reprint, Turnholt: Brepols, n.d.

———. *Pastoral Care*. Trans. Henry Davis. Ancient Christian Writers 11. Westminster, Md.: Newman Press, 1950.

———. *Register of the Epistles of Saint Gregory the Great*. In Nicene and Post-Nicene Fathers 12–13. Trans. James Barmby. Reprint, Grand Rapids, Mich.: Wm. B. Eerdmans Publishing Company, 1989.

———. *Registrum Epistularum*. Ed. Dag Norberg. Corpus Christianorum, Series Latina 140–140A. Turnholt: Brepols, 1982– .

———. *Règle pastorale*. Ed. Bruno Judic and Floribert Rommel. Trans. Charles Morel. Sources chrétiennes 381–82. Paris: Les éditions du Cerf, 1992.

Leclerq, Jean. *The Love of Learning and the Desire for God*. Trans. Catharine Mishrahi. 3rd ed. New York: Fordham University Press, 1985.

Leclercq, Jean, François Vandenbroucke, and Louis Bouver. *The Spirituality of the Middle Ages*. A History of Christian Spirituality 2. Trans. the Benedictines of Holme Eden Abbey. London: Burns & Oates, 1968, 3–30.

Lieblang, Franz. *Grundfragen der mystischen Theologie nach Gregors des Grossen Moralia und Ezechielhomilien*. Freiburg im Breisgau: Herder, 1934.

Markus, Robert. *Gregory the Great and His World*. Cambridge: Cambridge University Press, 1997.

Richards, Jeffrey. *Consul of God: The Life and Times of Gregory the Great*. London: Routledge & Kegan Paul, 1980.

Straw, Carole. *Gregory the Great*. Berkeley: University of California Press, 1988.

Vogüé, Adalbert de. "L'Auteur du commentaire des Rois attribué à saint Grégoire: Un moine de Cava?" *Revue Bénédictine* 106 (1996): 319–31.

Weber, Leonhard. *Hauptfragen der Moraltheologie Gregors des Grossen*. Freiburg in der Schweiz: Paulusdruckerei, 1947.

GREGORY VII
(1073–85)

UTA-RENATE BLUMENTHAL

Born around 1025 in southern Tuscany, Hildebrand, as Gregory VII was called before his elevation to the papacy, grew up and was educated among the canons of the Church of the Lateran in Rome. A later account, alleging that he also spent some time in the Benedictine Monastery of S. Maria on the Aventine Hill, is of questionable authenticity. Since it is now certain that Hildebrand never became a monk at Cluny, the famous Burgundian abbey, the issue of his presumed monastic profession remains open. The first firm date for Hildebrand is January 1047, when he accompanied Pope Gregory VI—deposed because of simony at the Synod of Sutri (20 December 1046)—as chaplain into exile at Cologne, Germany. At this city's famous cathedral school he continued his studies before returning to Rome in early 1049 in the company of the future pope Leo IX (1049–54). Leo ordained Hildebrand subdeacon, distinguishing him with the title cardinal, and named him rector of the Abbey of S. Paolo fuori le mura.

Hildebrand served the papacy as legate in France (1054, Tours; 1056, Chalon-sur-Saône), at the imperial court in Germany (1054/55, 1057/58), and briefly in Milan (1057). He was also a member of the papal chancery. Emperor Henry III (d. 5 October 1056) held Hildebrand in high esteem. At some point Hildebrand participated in an election of Henry's heir, the infant Henry IV, and swore never to accept the papacy without the royal consent. In a letter of December 1073 (Register 1.19) he apologized for his inability to keep this oath in the face of the divine providence that had brought about his election as the successor of St. Peter. Under Stephan IX (1057–58), Nicholas II (1059–61), and Alexander II (1061–73), Hildebrand became a leading figure at the papal court. As early as 1058/59, Peter Damian described him as an "unmovable column of the apostolic see" (Letter 63, trans. Owen Blum in *The Fathers of The Church, Medieval Continuation*, Washington, D.C.: The Catholic University of America Press, 1992). He actively furthered the alliance with the southern Italian Normans (this was a reversal of former papal policy) and supported the reforming efforts of the Milanese faction known as the Pataria, as well as the monks of Vallombrosa, in their struggle against the bishop of Florence, who was accused of simony.

Fragmentary minutes of a session of the Lateran Synod of 1059 include an address Hildebrand delivered before the assembly in the presence of the pope. Acting as archdeacon of the Apostolic See, he demanded the removal of a provision in the Aachen Rule of 816 that had allowed canons to possess private property. He perceived this as a perversion of the declarations of the church fathers. Contemporary manuscripts of the rule, primarily from Rome, evidence Hildebrand's success at the council, for they omit the objectionable passages. Pope Nicholas II had elevated him to archdeacon at the latest in 1059. This office entailed financial, liturgical, judicial, and military duties. Hildebrand was responsible for the Papal States and acted as papal vicar during a papal absence from Rome. However, it is difficult to differentiate the office (it ceased to exist in the early twelfth century) from the personality of Hildebrand, or his activities as archdeacon from his policy as pope. It is more likely than not that Hildebrand's responsibilities at this time reflected his personal influence in Rome rather than duties attached to the office per se.

Gregory's pontificate is relatively well documented. His official register is still preserved in the Archivio Segreto at the Vatican. It contains numerous letters as well as minutes and decrees from his councils and the formulae of oaths that the pontiff required from lay vassals and ecclesiastics and thus provides a reliable, albeit limited, basis for the interpretation of his reign, limited because only a small percentage of his correspondence has been registered (selection criteria are unknown), and especially because it was customary to supplement the most important points of a letter by oral messages. The famous *Dictatus papae*, however, is part of the register (Reg. 2.55a, dated March 1075). It consists of twenty-seven brief and pointed declarations that extol the papal primacy and even include the radical claim that the pope had the right to depose emperors. Scholars agree that Gregory was the author of the sentences. Sources and purpose are still in dispute, however. On 22 April 1073, during the funeral of Pope Alexander II in Rome, a tumultuous crowd raised Hildebrand to the papacy as Gregory VII (after Gregory I?). Cardinals, clerics, and laity subsequently formally elected and enthroned him at S. Pietro in Vincoli.

Gregory interpreted his election as a specific call by God to continue the struggle for the right ordering of human and ecclesiastical affairs. In particular, he saw it as his inescapable duty to restore the church to its ancient, original splendor as conceived and understood by ecclesiastical reformers. He linked the fight against simony and unchastity of the clergy with a pronounced insistence on the papal primacy. Primacy did include the subordination of secular power—if it were Christian—to papal authority, but it primarily affected ecclesiology, the definition and internal ordering of the church. From Gregory's point of view, all Christians, including kings and emperors, owed the pope unquestioned obedience, for only the pope would always remain a true Christian and cognizant of the will of God, thanks to his special link to St. Peter, whose successor he had become. According to Gregory, it was St. Peter himself who directed and led the church in a very realistic manner by means of the person of the pope.

Obedience to God thus became obedience to the papacy, an assumption that was bound to have far-reaching implications. It is fashionable today as well as justified to emphasize the religious components of the thought of Gregory VII; however, it should not be forgotten that the pope had an astute grasp of political realities and was always willing to take them into account, provided they would further his own reforming efforts.

Papal territorial claims intensified markedly. Gregory tried to assert the overlordship of St. Peter, that is, the papacy, with regard to several regions of Europe. The alliance with the Norman leaders Richard of Aversa (1073) and Robert Guiscard (1059) is the most successful example of the use of secular feudal arrangements by the papacy. Vassalic obligations included, besides fealty, military as well as financial aid and investiture on the part of the pope. Aragon was commended to St. Peter in 1068. French knights were promised conquered Spanish lands as papal benefices. In 1076 Duke Demetrius-Zwonimir of Croatia-Dalmatia had to swear a vassalic oath in the hands of two papal legates, who crowned him king.

Engraving of Pope Gregory VII from the twelfth century. (Courtesy of the Vatican Library)

Less clearly defined are the relationships envisioned by the pope with Denmark, Hungary, the Kingdom of Kiev, Brittany, Poland, and Bohemia. William I of England, whose invasion of 1066 Hildebrand had supported, refused the vassalic oath requested by Gregory, although he resumed the Anglo-Saxon payment of Peter's pence. With the exception of southern Italy, the Pyrenean region, and the islands of Sicily, Corsica, and Sardinia, Gregory's attempts to expand the role of the papacy as a secular overlord were not very successful. Behind these efforts lay Gregory's concern for financial and military support for papal reform policies, as expressed also in episcopal oaths that promised obedience as well as military aid to the papacy in case of need.

Attempts by the pope to claim England as a fief for St. Peter were unsuccessful. He left it at that, given William the Conqueror's support of the church in general. Rulers in northern Spain accommodated papal requests and/or sought papal support. However, in France as well as in Germany serious discords were the results of Gregory's efforts to ensure canonical elections of bishops. As early as December 1073 Gregory called King Philip I (1060–1108) the worst of all princely tyrants oppressing the church because the king refused to invest a canonically elected bishop with the bishopric. Gregory threatened excommunication and interdict. A year later Gregory announced in a letter that he would do everything in his power to depose Philip from the throne. This extraordinary and hitherto unheard-of threat fell on deaf ears in France, and Philip continued in office. His quarrels with Gregory were smoothed over, especially after 1075 when Gregory named standing legates for France. This meant that Gregory could remain in the background and occasionally blame the legates for apparent excesses in severity regarding French bishops who had been excommunicated by the legates. In late 1082 or early 1083 Gregory, relying on forged texts in the canonical collection known as the *Pseudoisidorian Decretals*, named Hugh of Die archbishop of Lyons and primate of Gaul. This constituted a serious infringement and reordering of French ecclesiastical affairs, but Gregory's general attitude toward the French church was conciliatory.

Gregory was conciliatory also toward Henry IV (1056–1106), at least in the beginning of his pontificate. He saw in the young king a ruler in the image of Emperor Henry III (1039–1056), writing to him in late 1074 that he would entrust the king with the protection of Rome and the Roman church, while he himself would lead a Christian army on a crusade to the East. The chief obstacle to the elimination of simony and nicolaitism (clerical marriage) in the German church appeared to be the German episcopate. When bishops refused to appear at his synods to account for their actions, Gregory counted on Henry's support. In this struggle with the episcopate he also requested the active aid of the laity, just as in France and Italy. These untraditional summons to the laity contradicted canon law, as did Gregory's willingness to allow accusations of superiors by inferiors. Henry, however, failed to live up to papal expectations, in particular regarding episcopal nominations to Italian bishoprics in 1075 (Milan, Ferno, and Spoleto). At the Diet of Worms (24 January 1076) Gregory's severe reproaches (excommunication threatened?) resulted in a royal demand for Gregory's renunciation of the papacy and a withdrawal of obedience by a majority of German bishops. Northern Italian bishops joined in. Gregory received their letters during the Lenten synod of 1076 (14–20 February) and replied immediately. At the conclusion of the council, in a solemn prayer addressed to St. Peter, the pope declared Henry deposed and excommunicated. At the same time, the pope absolved all royal subjects of Henry from their oaths of loyalty.

The effect was tremendous, causing the almost complete isolation of the king, who was deserted by many followers. Gregory now also permanently prohibited investiture of bishops and abbots by secular rulers (November 1078), depriving Henry IV in particular of all means to select and retain the loyalty of bishops and abbots on whom much of his government depended. Gregory's actions were a logical reflection of his absolute conviction that the papal primacy, granted by Christ to St. Peter and through the Apostle to the Roman church, was not only valid within the church but even more so in the secular sphere (*regnum*). This meant the subordination of the secular to the spiritual, replacing the Carolingian vision, in which ruler and priest stood side by side as leaders of the one church whose head was Christ. When Henry IV submitted to Gregory (28 January 1077) at Canossa, he rescued his throne but implicitly recognized the papal claims. The encounter at the castle of Canossa had interrupted Gregory's journey to Augsburg, Germany. The pope was to be met by German princes who had planned to elect a new ruler in the presence of the pope. Although Gregory had returned to Rome after reluctantly absolving Henry at Canossa, the German princes proceeded with their plans without the pope. They elected Rudolf of Rheinfelden (anti)king on 15 March 1077 in the presence of papal legates. Gregory hesitated until the Lenten synod of 1080 to accept Rudolf, but then deposed and anathematized Henry for a second time.

The second excommunication had little effect on the civil war in Germany compared to the first. A synod held under the aegis of Henry IV at Brixen formally deposed Gregory on 25 June 1080 and nominated Archbishop Guibert of Ravenna as pope. Guibert called himself Clement III after his and Henry's armies had finally entered Rome in March 1084 and he was formally elected to the papacy. By then Gregory had been rejected by major segments of the Roman clergy, including thirteen cardinals, because of his uncompromising attitude, and the Romans had opened the city gates to the king. Clement crowned Henry IV emperor (31 March 1084). Gregory had fled into Castel Sant'Angelo. His Norman vassal, Robert Guiscard, came to his rescue in May. Guiscard's troops plundered the city, however, and Gregory was obliged to leave Rome together with them. On 25 May 1085 he died at Salerno, under Norman protection, leaving the church in turmoil. He was canonized by Pope Paul V in 1606, and Benedict XIII extended the celebration of his feast day (25 May) from

Salerno to the entire church in 1728. The nine hundredth anniversary of his death was celebrated at Salerno in the presence of Pope John Paul II in 1985.

Without any doubt, Gregory was one of the greatest of all popes, whether he is considered a religious genius, a revolutionary, or both. His reign represents a significant turning point in the evolution of the papal primacy, especially though by no means exclusively with regard to the expansion of papal claims over secular rulers, who were now considered laymen. With elemental force and unhesitatingly, Gregory translated his personal religious and mystical experience into direct action in the world at large. His intuitive vision of the role of the papacy in the world was formally elaborated in schools and universities of the twelfth and thirteenth centuries. His immediate legacy for his successors up to Pope Callistus II (1119–24), however, was the prohibition of investiture. Its purpose was to exclude the influence of lay rulers from the church and its territorial possessions. It could not be enforced, however, and the investiture struggle ended with a compromise between church and secular government at Worms in 1122.

SELECTED BIBLIOGRAPHY

Autenrieth, Johanne. "Der bisher unbekannte Schluss des Briefes Gregors VII. an Mathilde von Tuscien (Reg.I.47)." *Deutsches Archiv fur Erforschung des Mittelaters* 13 (1957): 534–38.

Benson, Robert L. *The Bishop-Elect: A Study in Medieval Ecclesiastical Office*. Princeton: Princeton University Press, 1968.

Beumann, Helmut. "Tribur, Rom, and Canossa." In *Investiturstreit und Reichsverfassung*. Konstanzer Arbeitskreis für mittelalterliche Geschichte 17. Sigmaringen: Thorbecke, 1973, 33–60.

Blaul, Otto. "Studien zum Register Gregors VII." *Archiv für Urkundenforschung* 4 (1912): 113–228.

Blumenthal, Uta-Renate. *The Investiture Controversy: Church and Monarchy from the Ninth to the Twelfth Century*. Philadelphia: University of Pennsylvania Press, 1988.

Borino, Giovanni Battista. "Il decreto di Gregorio VII contro le investiture fu 'promulgato' nel 1075." *Studi Gregoriani* 6 (1959): 329–48.

———. "Un' ipotesi sul Dictatus papae di Gregorio VII." *Archivio della deputazione romana di storia patria* 67 (1944): 237–52.

Brooke, Christopher. "Hildebrand." In *Medieval Church and Society: Collected Essays*. New York: New York University Press, 1972, 57–68.

Caspar, Erich, ed. *Das Register Gregors VII*. Monumenta Germaniae Historica, Epistolae selectae, vol. 2, parts 1 and 2. Berlin: Weidmann, 1920, 1923.

———. "Studien zum Register Gregors VII." *Neues Archiv* 38 (1913): 144–226.

Cowdrey, H.E.J. *The Cluniacs and the Gregorian Reform*. Oxford: Clarendon Press, 1970.

———. ed. and trans. *The epistolae vagantes of Pope Gregory VII*. Oxford Medieval Texts. Oxford: Clarendon Press, 1972.

———. "The Papacy, the Patarenes, and the Church of Milan." *Transactions of the Royal Historical Society*, 5th ser., 18 (1968): 25–48.

———. "Pope Gregory VII and the Anglo-Norman Kingdom." *Studi Gregoriani* 9 (1972): 79–114.

———. *Pope Gregory VII, 1073–1085*. Oxford: Clarendon Press, 1998.

Emerton, Ephraim, trans. *The Correspondence of Pope Gregory VII: Selected Letters from the Registrum*. Columbia University Records of Civilization, Sources and Studies 14. New York: Columbia University Press, 1932.

Fornasari, Giuseppe. "Del nuovo su Gregorio VII? Riflessioni su un problema storiografico 'non esaurito.' " *Studi medievali*, 3rd ser., 24 (1983): 315–53.

Fuhrmann, Horst. " 'Quod catholicus non habeatur, qui non concordat Romana ecclesiae': Randnotizen zum Dictatus Papae." In *Festschrift für Helmut Beumann*, ed. K.-U. Jäschke and R. Wenskus. Sigmaringen: Thorbecke, 1977, 263–87.

Gilchrist, John T. "Gregory VII and the Primacy of the Roman Church." *Tijdschrift voor Rechtsgeschiedenis* 36 (1968):123–35.

Goez, Werner. "Zur Erhebung und ersten Absetzung Papst Gregors VII." *Römische Quartalschrift* 63 (1968):117–44.

Hilpert, Hans-Eberhard. "Zu den Rubriken im Register Gregors VII." *Deutsches Archiv für Erforschung des Mittelaters* 40 (1984):606–11.

Hoffmann, Hartmut. "Zum Register und zu den Briefen Papst Gregors VII." *Deutsches Archiv für Erforschung des Mittelaters* 32 (1976): 86–130.

Kämpf, Hellmut, ed. *Canossa als Wende*. Wege der Forschung 12. Darmstadt: Wissenschaftliche Buchgesellschaft, 1969.

Kempf, Friedrich. "Ein zweiter Dictatus papae?" *Archivum historiae pontificiae* 13 (1975):119–39.

———. Review of Rudolf Schieffer's *Die Enstehung des papast lichen Investiturverbots fur den deutschen Konig*. *Archivum historiae pontificiae* 20 (1982): 409–14.

Kuttner, Stephan. "Liber canonicus." *Studi Gregoriani* 2 (1947):387–401.

Ladner, Gerhart Buridan. "Gregory the Great and Gregory VII: A Comparison of Their Concepts of Renewal," with "A Note on the Computer Methods Used," by David W. Packard. *Viator* 4 (1973):1–31.

———. "Two Gregorian Letters: On the Sources and Nature of Gregory VII's Reform Ideology." *Studi Gregoriani* 5 (1956):221–42.

Laudage, Johannes. *Priesterbild und Reformpapsttum im II, Jahrhundert*. Beihefte zum Archiv für Kulturgeschichte 22. Cologne and Vienna: Böhlau Verlag, 1984.

Leyser, Karl. "The Crisis of Medieval Germany." *Proceedings of the British Academy* 69 (1983): 409–43.

Meulenberg, Leo. *Der Primat der römischen Kirche im Denken und Handeln Gregors VII*. The Hague: Pontificia Universitas Gregoriana, 1965.

———. "Une question toujours ouverte: Grégoire VII et l'infaillibilité du pape." In *Aus Kirche und Reich: Studien zu Theologie, Politik und Recht im Mittelater: Festschrift für Friedrich Kempf*, ed. Hubert Mordek. Sigmaringen: Thorbecke, 1983, 159–71.

Miccoli, Giovanni. "Gregorio VII, papa, santo." *Bibliotheca Sanctorum* 7 (1966): cols. 294–379.

Monumenta Germaniae Historica: Libelli de lite imperatorum et pontificum saeculis XI et XII conscripti. 3 vols. Hanover: Hahnsche Buchhandlung, 1891–93.

Mordek, Hubert. "Proprie auctoritates apostolice sedis: Ein zweiter Dictatus Papae Gregors VII.?" *Deutsches Archiv für Erforschung des Mittelaters* 28 (1972): 105–32.

Murray, Alexander. "Pope Gregory VII and His Letters." *Traditio* 22 (1966): 149–202.

Robinson, Ian Stuart. *Authority and Resistance in the Investiture Contest: The Polemical Literature of the Late Eleventh Century.* Manchester: Manchester University Press, 1978.

———. "Gregory VII and the Soldiers of Christ." *History* 58 (1973): 184–91.

———. "*Periculosus homo*: Pope Gregory VII and Episcopal Authority." *Viator* 9 (1978): 103–31.

———. "Pope Gregory VII, the Princess, and the *Pactum*, 1077–1080." *English Historical Review* 94 (1979): 721–56.

Santifaller, Leo. *Quellen und Forschungen zum Urkunden- und Kanzleiwesen Papst Gregors VII.* Vol. 1, *Quellen.* Studi e testi 190. Vatican City: Biblioteca Apostolica Vaticana, 1957.

Schieffer, Rudolf. *Die Entstehung des päpstlichen Investiturverbots für den deutschen König.* Monumenta Germaniae Historica, Schriften 28. Stuttgart: Anton Hiersemann, 1981.

Schieffer, Theodor. "Gregor VII." *Lexikon für Theologie und Kirche.* 2nd, rev. ed., vol. 4 (1960):1183–85.

Schneider, Christian. *Prophetisches Sacerdotium und heilsgeschichtliches Regnum im Dialog, 1073–1077.* Munich: Wilhelm Fink Verlag, 1972.

Struve, Tilmann. "Gregor VII., Papst." *Lexikon des Mittelalters*, vol. 4 (1989): 1669–71.

Studi Gregoriani per la storia di Gregorio VII e della riforma Gregoriana. Rome: Libreria Ateneo Salesiano, 1947– .

Tellenbach, Gerd. *The Church in Western Europe from the Tenth to the Early Twelfth Century.* Trans. Timothy Reuter. Cambridge: Cambridge University Press, 1993.

———. *Church, State, and Christian Society at the Time of the Investiture Contest.* Trans. R.F. Bennet. Oxford: Blackwell, 1970.

Vitae Gregorii VII. Ed. I.M. Watterich. In *Pontificum romanorum vitae*, vol. 1. Leipzig: Guilhelm Engelmann, 1862, 293–546.

Vogel, Jörgen. *Gregor VII und Heinrich IV. nach Canossa.* Schriftenreihe des Instituts für Frühmittelalterforschung der Universität Münster 9. Berlin and New York: Walter de Gruyter, 1983.

Werminghoff, Albert. "Die Beschlüsse des Aachener Concils im Jahre 816." *Neues Archiv* 27 (1901): 669–75.

Wojtowytsch, J.-Myron. "Proprie auctoritates apostolice sedis: Bemerkungen zu einer bisher unbeachteten Uberlieferung." *Deutsches Archiv für Erforschung des Mittelaters* 40 (1984): 612–21.

Zimmermann, Harald. *Der Canossagang von 1077: Wirkungen und Wirklichkeit.* Akademie der Wissenschaften und der Literatur in Mainz, Abhandlungen der Geistes-und Sozialwissenschaftlichen Klasse, Jahrd. 1975, Nr. 5. Mainz: Akademie der Wissenschaften und der Literatur, 1975.

URBAN II (1088–99)

ROBERT SOMERVILLE

Pope Urban II (1088–99) was born under the name Odo around the year 1035 in the diocese of Soissons in northern France, probably at Châtillon-sur-Marne. He was educated in the cathedral school at Rheims, where one of his masters was St. Bruno of Cologne, who later established the Carthusian order, and with whom Odo/Urban maintained a cordial relationship even after becoming pope. From Reims, where he also served the church as archdeacon, Odo entered the great monastery of Cluny in Burgundy, eventually becoming prior and building a strong relationship with Abbot Hugh on which he would later draw, especially during the early, tempestuous years of his reign as Roman pontiff. In 1079/80, however, he left the monastery, having been named by Pope Gregory VII to the important position of cardinal-bishop of Ostia. In this capacity he was employed by Gregory as a trusted legate during the tense and often-chaotic final years of his pontificate.

Gregory VII died in May 1085, at a time of great difficulty for the reforming cause that often bears his name (the Gregorian reform). Gregory's distinctive efforts to advance reform of church life and structure, in the process highlighting the claims of the Roman church to a unique position of leadership in church and society, collided with other interests, and perhaps nowhere was this collision more vivid than in the territory of the German ruler Henry IV. The struggle between Gregory and Henry often is described as a classic medieval "church-state" conflict.

The reality cannot be spelled out in such simple terms, but by the time of Gregory's death, it would have been difficult to see the outcome of the clash other than as a victory for Henry. Gregory's last years were increasingly a time of crisis at Rome, and the pope died away from the city, in Salerno, to which he escaped after being rescued by the southern Italian Normans in the face of a siege by Henry and his forces. Henry supported the creation of a papal competitor, the so-called antipope Clement III (Archbishop Guibert of Ravenna), and through Henry's assistance Guibert/Clement had access to Rome. Gregorian support throughout the Latin church is difficult to measure at this juncture, yet without question papal leadership of the eleventh-century reforming movement had been sidetracked (e.g., no legislation is known to survive from any council of Gregory VII after the year 1080).

Near the end of Gregory's reign, in 1084, he sent Cardinal Odo to Germany on an important legatine mission. Odo thus was in a position to assess for himself the political and ecclesiastical conditions there and to make contact with the few Gregorian supporters in the empire. He was, in fact, still in the north when Gregory died, and he probably did not return to Italy until the spring of 1086. There is some evidence to indicate that Pope Gregory wished for Odo to be his successor, but the direct successor of Gregory VII was Abbot Desiderius of Monte Cassino. His election as Pope Victor III occurred nearly a year after Gregory's death, thus indicating the confused and perilous situation of the Gregorians, huddled in Norman territory south of Rome. But Desiderius reigned for only a brief period, dying in September 1087.

Victor III may also have designated Cardinal Odo as his successor, and at Terracina, in March 1088, he finally was elected bishop of Rome. Odo now took the name Urban, which, among other things, probably signified his claim on Rome and his intention to be the city's bishop, with all that entailed. But regrouping the shattered reforming papacy would not be an easy task after the debacle of the last years of Gregory VII, which not only saw creation of an antipope and Gregory's flight from Rome, but also the desertion of a number of Gregorian cardinals to the obedience of Clement III. Traditionally the reign of Urban II has been seen principally in light of the First Crusade, but this is a distortion and, indeed, ought to be reversed. The launching of that great expedition to the East in November 1095, at the Council of Clermont, should be viewed within the context of several factors, for example, overcoming the vicissitudes of Urban's early years as pope, his relations with the Greek would that were fostered in southern Italy in those early days of his reign, and, in general, a significant revival of the Gregorian fortunes. Without these factors between the years 1088 and 1094 as background, mustering support in France for the crusade in 1095–96 would have been unthinkable.

Urban's reign can be split into two parts, divided by his return to Rome from southern Italy late in the year 1093. The first five years were spent south of Rome, in a land where political and ecclesiastical structures were confused. The Norman princes of the region struggled against each other, against non-Normans, and against whatever influence the Byzantine emperors could exert from Constantinople. The church also was split between Greek and Latin prelates and usages. During these years Urban worked to consolidate Latin claims, both religious and political, and to enhance his own authority and undermine the claims of his rival Clement III. In the process he established contacts with the emperor and patriarch of Constantinople. He also tried to destabilize Henry IV's power in any manner possible and to pave the way for his own return to Rome. Yet the particulars of church reform were not neglected, and during his sojourn in the south, Urban convened papal councils at Melfi (1089), Benevento (1091),

Pope Urban II giving papal bull to Abbot Oderisi, from twelfth-century manuscript *Regesto de St. Angelo in Formis*. (The Art Archive/Montecassino Abbey Archives/ Dagli Orti)

south and Troia (1093). These synods treated a number of substantive issues of church discipline and reform such as clerical mores, canonical election to church offices, the relation of clergy and laity, and secular influence in ecclesiastical matters, including a decree from Melfi condemning lay investiture of bishoprics and abbeys. Disciplinary canons from all three assemblies circulated throughout the church, and the legislation from Melfi in particular seems to have had a surprisingly large diffusion and influence in canon law.

With his return north, the second phase of Urban's reign began. By this time he clearly had gained the upper hand in his maneuvers against Clement and Henry, and although he never would be totally free from trouble that they or their supporters might cause for him, between 1094 and his death in 1099 Urban was able to focus on relationships with those who were outside of Italy and the empire, church reform throughout Latin Christendom, including attention to the monastic life and the life of regular canons, and, of course, the crusade. Pivotal for his initiatives were another group of synods over which Urban presided between 1095 and 1099, including several assemblies larger than those that he had convened in southern Italy. Between March 1095 and April 1099 Urban held seven councils: at Piacenza and Clermont (1095), at Tours and Nîmes (1096), at the Lateran (1097), at Bari (1098), and at St. Peter's (April 1099). Piacenza and Clermont issued many decrees dealing with church discipline and practice, some of which became classical statements in the evolving tradition of Latin canon law, for example, Piacenza's canons on the ordination of schismatics and Clermont's ruling about episcopal-abbatial claims on various church revenues. Decrees from both synods on these issues are to be found in the great collection of canon law assembled toward the middle of the twelfth century by Gratian, which became the textbook for canonical studies in the medieval universities. Bari, one of the largest of the councils that Urban held, but from which no legislation is known to survive, dealt particularly with relations between Latins and Greeks and even witnessed a discourse by St. Anselm of Canterbury—in exile from England—that defended the Latin theology of the double procession of the Holy Spirit, that is, the belief that the Holy Spirit proceeds from the Father "and from the Son" (filioque).

No pope since Leo IX in the middle of the eleventh century had traveled so widely and been so visible throughout the Latin church, yet it is not insignificant to note that when Urban II died, he was in Rome, and despite the fact that Clement was still alive, Urban would have been regarded as bishop by most of the city's inhabitants. The uncertain prospects faced by the Gregorians in 1085 had been replaced by fresh initiatives for reform under papal leadership, by increasingly firm papal ties to the churches in lands beyond Italy, and by a political landscape on which the fortunes of Henry IV and the antipope had to be seen as dicey. Not every problem was solved, by any means—for example, the nagging question of lay investiture of bishops and abbots, which had come to stand at the heart of the reform movement, remained to be settled—but it is with some justification that writers of the twelfth century could see Urban II instead of Gregory VII as the great eleventh-century reforming pope. Historians in recent years have questioned how useful the venerable notion "Gregorian reform" is as a label for the conglomerate of movements under way in Latin Christendom between 1050 and the early twelfth century, emphasizing that if the term is employed, it should be used with care and precisely defined. While there can be no question that Gregory's agenda was far-reaching, and that the papacy never could be seen in the same light after his reign, his rulings and pronouncements are found less frequently in twelfth-century canon law than might be expected. Rulings from Urban II are far more prominent therein, thus providing a useful gauge of his legacy in restructuring and refocusing the papal side of the movement for reform in the Latin church.

The First Crusade must be seen, as already noted, in this wider context. Urban had been interested in Latin relations with Byzantium since the early days of his reign as an exile in southern Italy. Perhaps an emissary from Emperor Alexius I appeared before the Council of Piacenza in 1095 to seek armed assistance in the fight in Asia Minor against the Turks. Exactly how Urban's thoughts about formal plans for the crusade developed has been the subject of much debate and speculation by modern scholars. As a Cluniac, the pope would have been aware of various campaigns against the Muslims in Spain, in which Cluny played a prominent role, and as an advisor to pope Gregory VII, Cardinal Odo probably came to know Gregory's thoughts about the East (although by the time that Odo came into papal service, the press of Western affairs must have been paramount). At Clermont in late 1095 Urban publicly announced plans for an armed expedition to rescue the churches of the East, including Jerusalem, "from the power of the Saracens." He set the goods of those who participated under the Peace of God and also proclaimed for them a penitential indulgence. He probably repeated and perhaps even amplified these regulations in subsequent councils and in public appearances after Clermont when he urged men to take part in this venture. Clermont appears, furthermore, to have legislated in greater detail about the crusade than the surviving decrees show, but the Eastern expedition certainly was not the only, or even the most important, matter on the synodal agenda.

Urban II died at the end of July 1099, shortly after the Latin armies had captured Jerusalem, undoubtedly unaware that this had occurred. His legacy is multifaceted. Urban is, of course, "the pope of the First Crusade," but he also is more. His work to neutralize his rival Clement III and to end the papal schism, to counter the influence of Henry IV in the German and northern Italian church, and to advance the process of ecclesiastical reform all marked Urban's pontificate as a turning point in the history of the "Gregorian reform." Even though he did not end the papal schism, and both Henry and Clement survived him, as much as any pope of that age, the Cluniac Urban II helped prepare the way for the papal monarchy of the High Middle Ages. The line between Gregory VII and Innocent III might seem, from some vantage points, to be straight, but its passage through the reign of Urban II is a significant moment and must not be overlooked.

SELECTED BIBLIOGRAPHY

Becker, Alfons. *Papst Urban II*. 2 vols. to date. Monumenta Germaniae historica, Schriften 19.1–2. Stuttgart: A. Hiersemann, 1964, 1988.

Constable, Giles, and Robert Somerville. "The Papal Bulls for the Chapter of St. Antonin in Rouergue in the Eleventh and Twelfth Centuries." *Speculum* 67 (1992):828–64.

Fuhrmann, Horst. "Una papa tra religiosità personale e politica ecclesiastica: Urbano II (1088–1099) e il rapimento di un monaco benedettino." *Studi medievali*, 3rd ser., 17 (1986):1–21.

———. "Das Papsttum zwischen Frommigkeit und Politik: Urban II. (1088–1099) und die Frage der Selbstheiligung." In *Deus qui mutat tempora: Menschen und Institutionen im Wandel des Mittelalters: Festschrift für Alfons Becker*, ed. Ernst-Dieter Hehl, Hubertus Seibert, and Franz Staab. Sigmaringen: J. Thorbecke, 1987, 157–72.

———. *Papst Urban II. und der Stand der Regularkanoniker*. Bayerische Akademie der Wissenschaften, Phil.-hist. Klasse, Sitzungsberichte 1984, 2. Munich: C.H. Beck, 1976.

———. "Pseudoisidor, Otto von Ostia (Urban II.), und der Zeitatenkampf von Gerstungen (1085)." *Zeitschrift der Savigny-Stiftung für Rechtsgeschichte*. Kan. Abt., 68 (1982): 52–69.

Gossman, F.J. *Pope Urban II and Canon Law*. Catholic University of America, Canon Law Studies, 403. Washington, D.C.: Catholic University of America Press, 1960.

Hiestand, Rudolf. *Initienverzeichnis und chronologisches Verzeichnis zu den Archivberichten und Vorarbeiten der Regesta pontificum romanorum*. Monumenta Germaniae Historica, Hilfsmittel 7. Munich, 1983.

Jaffé, P., and G. Wattenbach, eds. *Regesta pontificum romanorum ab condita ecclesia ad annum post Christum natum MCXCVIII*. 2nd ed. Leipzig: 1885–88, vol. 1, under "Urbanus II."

Riley-Smith, Jonathan. *The First Crusade and the Idea of Crusading*, Philadelphia: University of Pennsylvania Press, 1986.

Somerville, Robert. *The Councils of Urban II*. Vol. 1, *Decreta Claromontensia*. Annuarium historiae conciliorum, Supplementum, 1. Amsterdam: Hakkert, 1972.

———. *Papacy, Councils, and Canon Law in the 11th–12th Centuries*. Variorum Reprints 312. Aldershot: Variorum, 1990.

Somerville, Robert, in collaboration with Stephan Kuttner. *Pope Urban II, the Collectio Britannica, and the Council of Melfi (1089)*. Oxford: Clarendon Press, 1996.

ALEXANDER III (1159–81)

KENNETH PENNINGTON

Alexander III was a Tuscan, born in Siena, named Rolandus, the son of Rainucci. Sienese tradition has assigned him to the Bandinelli family. If this attribution is correct, his family had been active in the political life of Siena since the eleventh century. But his affiliation with the Bandinelli may be a later tradition; there is no contemporary evidence for the conception. More important, Alexander's biography has recently undergone radical changes under the scalpel of modern scholarship. Historians had long thought that he had studied canon law and touted him as the first great jurist-pope of the High Middle Ages by attributing a *Stroma iuris* on Gratian's *Decretum* to his pen. John T. Noonan and Rudolf Weigand have definitively proven that the Rolandus who wrote the legal treatise was not the Rolandus who later became pope. Recently scholars have determined that the same Rolandus who wrote the *Stroma* also composed a theological treatise, the *Sententie Rodlandi Bononiensis magistri*. Rolandus son of Rainucci cannot be credited as the author of any legal or theological work. He was, nonetheless, most probably a learned theologian who taught for a while at Bologna (before around 1142). The canonist Huguccio (C.2 q.6 c. 3 1: "et Alexandro tertio Bononie residente in cathedra magistrali in divina pagina ante appellatum eius.") and the abbot of Mont Saint Michel, Robert de Torigny, noted that Rolandus taught theology in Bologna. Since Rolandus has left no known works, we cannot judge the depth and breadth of his education in his formative years. Since he taught at Bologna, we might assume that he was a student there.

His biographer, Boso, said nothing about his education but asserted that he achieved great fame in the church of Pisa. Pisan documents record a "Rolandus" (among others) who was a canon in the cathedral chapter between 1142 and 1147. He attracted the attention of Pope Eugenius III, who most likely met Rolandus when he stayed in Pisa during the month of October in 1148. Eugenius summoned him to Rome in the same year and quickly raised him to the cardinalate, first as cardinal-deacon of SS. Cosmas and Damian (1150) and a short time later as cardinal-priest of St. Mark (1151). His rapid rise through the ranks of the papal curia culminated with Eugenius appointing him chancellor of the Roman church in 1153, an office that he held through the pontificates of Anastasius IV (1153–54) and Hadrian IV (1154–59). Boso's description of Rolandus's character and learning rings true and helps explain his success in Rome: "He is a man of letters, fluent with polished eloquence, a prudent, kind, patient, merciful, gentle, sober, chaste man" (trans. Boso, 43). Arnulf of Lisieux, who became his staunch supporter and who very likely knew Rolandus during his stay in Italy studying law, described him as possessing "the perfection of knowledge and of all virtues" (letter 28 in Barlow, 39).

During the years 1148 to 1159 Rolandus played a role in the diplomatic negotiations between the papacy and secular monarchies. In 1153 he took part in a legation of seven cardinals who negotiated the terms of an imperial-papal treaty at Constance. Shortly afterwards, in May 1153, he was rewarded with the chancellorship, an officer of the curia responsible for the diplomatic correspondence of the papacy. In 1156 Rolandus concluded a treaty at Benevento with King William I of Sicily. The treaty established an alliance with the Normans and granted the king of Sicily a number of ecclesiastical rights. In Apulia and Calabria the king recognized the right to appeal to Rome and the pope's right to authorize an episcopal deposition or translation; on the island of Sicily, on the contrary, these rights were exercised only with the consent of the king. William took the feudal oath to the pope and promised an annual tribute in coin or gold and silver. Rolandus revealed himself to be pragmatic, cautious, and prudent when dealing with secular princes. In contrast, Thomas Becket held the rights granted to the Norman kings to be a tyrannous usurpation.

The most dramatic diplomatic mission in which Cardinal Rolandus participated was a legation to the imperial diet of Besançon in October 1157. Frederick Barbarossa called the diet to hear papal complaints about his treatment of the archbishop and primate of Scandinavia, Eskil of Lund. The emperor had captured Eskil, a vociferous foe of imperial pretensions, on his return from Rome and had resisted papal requests to free him. Pope Hadrian sent Rolandus and Bernard, cardinal-priest of St. Clement, with a letter for Frederick. Some historians have described Rolandus as the leader of the "anti-imperial, pro-Sicilian" faction of the curia at this time. It is unlikely, however, that Hadrian would have sent a legate known to be inimical to the emperor to Besançon. Rahewin, Frederick's court historian, described the two legates as being "distinguished for their wealth, their maturity of view, and their influence, and surpassing in authority almost all others in the Roman church." The imperial chancellor, Rainald of Dassel, read Hadrian's letter to the assembly in German. At a crucial passage, Rainald translated Hadrian's words as "but if the emperor had received still greater fiefs [beneficial] from us [the pope] . . . we would have rejoiced." The assembly erupted. One of the cardinals responded by saying, "If our lord pope does not confer the empire on the emperor, who does?"

Fresco in Palazzo Pubblico, Siena, depicts Pope Alexander III receiving an ambassador. (Courtesy of the Vatican Library)

This comment has often been attributed to Rolandus, but he rarely demonstrated an inclination to confront issues or persons so directly. Frederick immediately issued a letter that asserted that his power derived from God, not the pope. Hadrian wrote a second letter in which he disputed Rainald's translation of "beneficium." "Beneficium," he stated, "means gifts or benefits, not fiefs." Even if Rolandus was not responsible for the challenging statements at Besançon, his presence at that tumultuous meeting probably permanently damaged his relationship with the emperor. Significantly, Rolandus was not sent back to Frederick by Hadrian with another letter explaining that the pope did not mean "fiefs" when he wrote "beneficia," but "favors."

When Hadrian IV died on 1 September 1159, a split between the pro-imperial cardinals and those cardinals who had supported Hadrian's policy to use the Norman kingdom of Sicily as a counterweight to imperial ambitions resulted in a contested election. Rolandus was elected by the majority of cardinals. A lesser number of cardinals elected Octavian, cardinal-priest of St. Cecilia. Octavian was consecrated as Pope Victor IV at the imperial abbey of Farfa. When Arnulf of Lisieux compared the two candidates, he noted caustically that if one would have taken away Octavian's noble lineage, he would not have dared aspire to the papal throne. Rolandus was consecrated as Pope Alexander III at Ninfa. Frederick Barbarossa sent an encyclical to all European bishops asking them to assemble at Pavia. He announced with sorrow that although the pope and emperor were the two heads and two beginnings by which the whole world was ruled, two popes had been elected and consecrated after the death of Hadrian. Papal decretals and ecclesiastical statutes dictated that when schism erupted within the church, the emperor should choose between them, according to the opinion and counsel of the orthodox. Frederick invited Alexander and his cardinals, but Alexander refused since, as he wrote to the emperor, only the pope may convene a council. The council commenced in February 1160. Pavia became a council of German and Italian prelates, in which Alexander was excommunicated and Victor acclaimed as the rightful pope.

A diplomatic campaign ensued in which Alexander and Victor wooed the other European monarchs. In October 1160 King Henry II of England and King Louis VII of France, together with bishops from England, France, and Spain, met at Beauvais. The assembly gave its allegiance to Alexander. Frederick continued to support Victor. Because of imperial strength in Italy and the long duration of the schism, Alexander was forced to reside outside of Rome for a large part of his pontificate. The schism persisted for eighteen years, but it would be the last until the Great Schism of 1378. Frederick's successors, especially Frederick II, used other means to oppose papal authority.

Frederick's opposition was not the only reason that Alexander could not reside in Rome for most of his pontificate. Like most of the Italian communes, the people of Rome began to rebel against ecclesiastical rule in the twelfth century. Popes Eugenius III and Hadrian IV dealt with a Roman populace that, under the leadership of Arnold of Brescia, challenged the legitimacy of papal governance in the city. Although Hadrian had, with the help of Frederick Barbarossa, temporarily quelled Roman ambitions for self-rule and had arranged for the arrest and execution of Arnold in 1155, the city had new opportunities under the schism. Alexander resided in Rome during the second year of his pontificate, but after losing most of the Papal States to imperial forces, he sought refuge in the Kingdom of Sicily, among the Normans whom he had supported as cardinal-legate. In 1162 he and his entourage sailed to France in four galleys provided by William I of Sicily. Delayed by a shipwreck shortly after departing from Terracina, he finally arrived in France and established his curia in Sens from 1163 to 1165. He returned to Rome in 1165 but could not prevent Victor's successor, Paschal III, from being consecrated at Rome in July 1167 in the presence of the emperor. Alexander retreated to Norman Benevento. During the next ten years he moved among the papal strongholds of southern Italy: Anagni, Palestrina, Ferentino, Tusculum, and Veroli. He finally returned to Rome in 1178, but even after having concluded a peace with Frederick, he was forced out of the city shortly after the Third Lateran Council had been held in March 1179 and spent his last two years moving among cities that remained loyal to him in the Papal States: Civita Castellana in the north and Tusculum in the south. When his body was brought back to Rome for burial in August 1181, Sigebert of Gembloux reported that the people of Rome threw rocks and mud at his funeral cortege. Not until the pontificate of Clement III (1187–91) did the pope reside regularly again in Rome.

Alexander's inability to control Rome and the Papal States was due to his conflict with Frederick. Although he attempted to support the cities of Lombardy, he had neither the power nor the resources to render effective assistance. Frederick and his popes ruled central and northern Italy. From 1164 the Lombard League resisted imperial ambitions with greater and greater success. Finally, in May 1176 Frederick's army was decisively defeated at the Battle of Legnano, and the emperor was forced to conclude a peace with the league and the pope. Alexander and Frederick met in Venice in July 1177. They concluded a treaty on 1 August 1177 in which the emperor recognized Alexander as pope and Frederick's excommunication was raised. Schismatic bishops and cardinals were pardoned. Even the antipope Callistus III was eventually appointed by Alexander to the governorship of Benevento in 1178. Obduracy was not part of Alexander's makeup.

This aspect of Alexander's character may shed some light on his relationship with Thomas Becket. Historians have generally disapproved if not condemned Alexander's refusal to support Becket in his conflict with Henry II, king of England and lord of Angevin lands in France. However, as some historians have correctly shown, Becket's position on the contested legal issues of the dispute was not clearly supported by contemporary canon law. Furthermore, Alexander's experience dictated that secular rulers were to be persuaded, not confronted. His experiences as a legate had perhaps taught him the virtues of compromise. Alexander advised Becket in 1165 while Becket was in exile that he should "not act hastily or rashly . . . regain the favor and goodwill of the illustrious English king . . . the

Lord will grant better times." Probably the pope never had second thoughts about the advice that he had given to the archbishop. Further, the Becket controversy, a centerpiece of English historiography of the twelfth century, may not have seemed as important from the perspective of Rome. Although he lived through the events, Boso, Alexander's biographer, did not even mention Becket's dispute with Henry until Becket's death. Then the crucial issue was whether Henry had been responsible for the archbishop's murder. Alexander satisfied himself quickly that Henry was not guilty. Immediately afterwards he endorsed Henry's conquest of Ireland and congratulated the king for conquering that barbarous nation. He also ordered the kings and princes of Ireland to honor their oaths to the conqueror. By the end of his reign, in spite of a pontificate wracked with turmoil, Alexander had a series of diplomatic successes with European monarchs. He maintained his claims to overlordship in the Kingdom of Sicily. In 1169 he reached a concordat with Bela, the king of Hungary, that protected the rights of the pope in the translations and depositions of bishops. The provisions were very similar to those worked out by Alexander when, as cardinal, he negotiated the Treaty of Benevento. In 1179 he confirmed Alfonso I as king of Portugal in return for tribute.

Alexander may have been a moderate, but he was also a reformer. His program can be most clearly seen in the canons of the two most important councils that he presided over during his pontificate, the Council of Tours in 1163 and the Third Lateran Council of 1179. The pope called a council at Tours shortly after he arrived in France and summoned clergy and prelates from England, France, Italy, and Spain. The conciliar canons dealt with the unlawful division of ecclesiastical benefices, clerical usury, lay possession of tithes, prosecution of heretics in southern France, simony, and a ban on monks studying medicine and law after they had taken religious vows. The only mention of the schism was a condemnation of all measures and actions established by Pope Victor and his supporters. Although the Council of Tours took place in France at a time when the church was in schism, Alexander made it clear that it should be considered a general council of the church, and it was. All of its canons were incorporated into the canonical collections of the twelfth and early thirteenth centuries.

The Third Lateran Council marked the end of Alexander's pontificate, his triumph over his adversaries, and the culmination of twelfth-century papal conciliar activity. At the opening of the Third Lateran Council an anonymous preacher addressed Alexander and the assembled prelates: "The great pontiff, namely the highest patriarch, presiding over [the Blessed Roman church], who recently rose from the ocean of raging waves of persecution like a serene sun . . . illuminates not only the present church but the entire world with his worthy brilliance of shining splendor." The sermon was preached in the Church of St. John in the Lateran to more than three hundred bishops, a greater number of abbots, twenty-one cardinals, and laymen from all over Christendom. There was even a small group of Waldensians from Lyons. The twenty-seven conciliar canons dealt with a wide range of topics. Canons regulated the elections of bishops and stipulated the age necessary to be a bishop. The curia was definitively established as being the last court of appeal in ecclesiastical law. *Licet de evitanda* determined the rules that should govern future papal elections. Alexander did not want another schism like that after his election. Henceforth, a valid papal election required that two-thirds of the cardinals must have voted for the successful candidate. This rule has governed papal elections to the present day. Heresy had become an even greater concern within the church than it had been at the Council of Tours. In *Sicut ait beatus Leo* Alexander named the heretics who presented a danger to the church, Albigensians, Cathars, and Paterines, and expanded the categories of persons who could be punished for heresy to include those who defended or harbored them. As at Tours, benefices were a concern. Canon 5 forbade dividing benefices in half. A cleric must be given an adequate stipend to live on. Canons 3 and 8 ordained that if a benefice were vacant for more than six months, the right to bestow it was transferred to the next highest authority. These canons were an attempt to prevent bishops and chapters from profiting from the income of unoccupied benefices. Other canons dealt with simony, celibacy of the clergy, and commercial relationships with Muslims and Jews. The canons of the Third Lateran Council were immediately included in collections of canon law and incorporated into theological *summae* (treatises) of Peter the Chanter, Alan of Lille, Peter of Poitiers, and Thomas of Chobham.

The decretal letters of Alexander represent the most lasting legacy of his pontificate. In spite of a pontificate that was peripatetic, chaotic, and confused, his chancellery produced thousands of letters sent to those who remained loyal to him. Not surprisingly, his registers of letters have been lost. We do know, however, that his letters were registered in four volumes at the curia. Of the letters that have survived, the overwhelming majority have been preserved from canonical collections or from the archives of recipients. Although more than 700 of his decretal letters survive in canonical collections, these represent only a small part of his correspondence. It is remarkable, however, that 470 of these 700 decretals found a permanent place in the law of the church, the *Corpus iuris canonici*. That is more than those of any other medieval pope except for Innocent III (1198–1216).

Alexander's total correspondence must have been formidable, but we shall never know how many letters were issued during his pontificate. Some idea of the problem that his chancellery must have faced can be had from one example. Bishop Arnulf of Lisieux collected 141 of his letters written between 1144 and 1181. Eight of them were addressed to three of

Alexander's predecessors, 41 to Alexander. All the letters requested answers. Although Arnulf was trained in law and had an interest in the judicial system, the amount of correspondence cannot be attributed to his individual interests.

Alexander's decretal legislation made significant contributions to all areas of law, but especially to three: appeals, procedure, and marriage. During Alexander's pontificate the Roman curia became the accepted court of last resort and was flooded with cases. The number of cases appealed to Rome reached such proportions that Alexander issued decretals that tried to define and limit the circumstances under which appeals could be made from episcopal courts to the curia. The importance of Alexander's pontificate in shaping the whole system of appeals can be seen from the contents of title 28 in the *Decretals* of Gregory IX: almost half of the seventy-three decretals that Raymond of Peñafort placed under *de appellationibus* were Alexander III's. These decretals stressed that the pope exercised jurisdictional primacy within the church, that an appeal to the pope could, in most cases, bring local proceedings to a halt, and that even the decisions of judges-delegate whose letters granted them final authority, "non obstantibus appellationibus" (not withstanding appeals), could be appealed for a number of different reasons.

The procedural system taken from Roman law and adapted by the jurists of the twelfth century, called the *ordo iudiciarius*, was accepted as the only proper mode of proof in Alexander's decretals. His letter repeatedly stated that clerics and ecclesiastical institutions could only be judged by using the *ordo iudiciarius*. No other systems of proof were legitimate in canon law.

The law of marriage underwent fundamental changes during the twelfth century, and Alexander's decretals were primarily responsible for moving the canon law of marriage in new directions. The freely given mutual consent of the man and woman became the cornerstone of a valid marriage, replacing parental consent as a key element of marriage law. The right of a person to consent to marriage became a benchmark of law in the twelfth century. The importance of intercourse was diminished, although a consummated marriage continued to have a stronger legal basis than an unconsummated one. From Alexander's pontificate on, Rome became the court of last resort and increasingly evolved as the arbiter of disputes among Christian princes. The pope also became the supreme judge of martial cases in Christendom. At the beginning of the twelfth century local episcopal synods were still rendering decisions in marriage disputes within the noble families of Europe. By the end of the century Pope Innocent III insisted that all issues of law involving marriages fell under the jurisdiction of the pope, whether the litigants were of noble families or not. This change would have a profound effect on the future relations between the papacy and European rulers.

Alexander's pontificate marked the apogee of papal power and authority in the twelfth century. In extraordinarily difficult circumstances he laid the foundations for a centralized church, a pan-European canon law, and an efficient papal bureaucracy. His successors may have pointed the papacy in directions that he might not have approved, but they owed much to his perseverance and ability.

SELECTED BIBLIOGRAPHY

Alexander III. *Epistolae*. In *Epistolae pontificum Romanorum ineditae*, ed. S. Löwenfeld. Leipzig: Palme, 1885, 149–209.

———. *Epistolae*. In *Patrologia latina*. ed. J.-P. Migne, vol. 200. Reprint, Turnholt: Brepols, n.d., cols. 69–1320.

———. *Epistolae*. In *Recueil des historiens des Gaules et de la France*. vol. 15. Paris: Palme, 1878, 744–977.

Baldwin, Marshall. *Alexander III and the Twelfth Century*. The Popes through History, vol. 3. Glen Rock, N.J.: Newman Press, 1968.

Barlow, Frank, ed. *The Letters of Arnulf of Lisieux*. 3rd series, vol. 6. London: The Offices of the Royal Historical Society, 1939.

Boso. *Boso's Life of Alexander III*. Trans. G.M. Ellis. Totowa, N.J.: Rowman & Littlefield, 1973.

Brundage, James A. "Marriage and Sexuality in the Decretals of Pope Alexander III." In *Miscellanea Rolando Bandinelli, Papa Alessandro III*, ed. Filippo Liotta. Siena: Accademia senese degli intronati, 1986, 57–83.

Duggan, Charles. "Decretals of Alexander III to England." In *Miscellanea Rolando Bandinelli, Papa Alessandro III*, ed. Filippo Liotta. Siena: Accademia senese degli intronati, 1986, 85–151.

Fliche, Augustin, and Victor Martin. *Histoire de l'Eglise depuis les origines jusqu'à nos jours*. Vol. 9, *Du premier Concile du Latran à l'avènement d'Innocent III*, pt. 2. Paris: Bloud & Gay, 1953, 50–188.

Foreville, Raymonde. "Alexandre III et la canonisation des saints." In *Miscellanea Rolando Bandinelli, Papa Alessandro III*, ed. Filippo Liotta. Siena: Accademia senese degli intronati, 1986, 217–36.

———. *Latran I, II, III, et Latran IV*. Histoire des conciles oecuméniques 6. Paris: Éditions de l'Orante, 1965.

Garcia y García, Antonio. "Alejandro III y los reinos ibéricos." In *Miscellanea Rolando Bandinelli, Papa Alessandro III*, ed. Filippo Liotta. Siena: Accademia senese degli intronati, 1986, 237–57.

Jedin, Hubert, ed. *Handbuch der Kirchengeschichte*. Vol. 3, *Die mittelalterliche Kirche*, part 2, *Vom kirchliche Hochmittelalter bis zum Vorabend der Reformation*. Freiburg: Herder, 1968, 67–143.

Noonan, John T. "Who Was Rolandus?" In *Law, Church, and Society: Essays in Honor of Stephan Kuttner*, ed. Kenneth Pennington and Robert Somerville. Philadelphia: University of Pennsylvania Press, 1977, 21–48.

Pacaut, Marcel. "Alexandre III." *Dictionnaire historique de la papauté*, ed. Philippe Levillain. Paris: Fayard 1994, 64–67.

———. *Alexandre III: Étude sur la conception du pouvoir pontifical dans sa pensée et dans son oeuvre*. L'Église et l'État au Moyen Age 11. Paris: J. Vrin, 1956.

Paravicini-Bagliani, Agostino. "Évolutions ecclésiologiques: Le pontificat d'Alexandre III." In *Histoire du Christianisme des origines à nos jours*, vol. 5, *Apogée de la papauté et expansion de la Chrétienté (1054–1254)*, ed. André Vauchez Paris: Desclee, 1993, 223–29.

Somerville, Robert. *Pope Alexander III and the Council of Tours*. Publications of the Center for Medieval and Renaissance Studies 1163. Berkeley and Los Angeles: University of California Press, 1977.

Ullmann, Walter. "Alexander III and the Conquest of Ireland: A Note on the Background." In *Miscellanea Rolando Bandinelli, Papa Alessandro III*, ed. Filippo Liotta. Siena: Accademia senese degli intronati, 1986, 369–87.

Weigand, Rudolf. "Glossen des Magister Rolandus zum Dekret Gratians." In *Miscellanea Rolando Bandinelli, Papa Alessandro III*, ed. Filippo Liotta. Siena: Accademia senese degli intronati, 1986, 391–423.

———. "Magister Rolandus und Papst Alexander III." *Archiv für katholisches Kirchenrecht* 149 (1980):3–44.

INNOCENT III (1198–1216)

James M. Powell

The author of the *Gesta Innocentii III*, a member of the papal court close to the pope, undertook to explain Innocent's attitude toward secular politics in order to justify his deep involvement in reforming the Patrimony of St. Peter. He tells us that Innocent found "this concern in some ways abhorrent" (Lotario dei Segni, *Opera Omnia*, vol. 214, xxix–xxx). Some historians have treated this statement as a disingenuous effort to absolve the pope of blame for paying more attention to secular than spiritual matters. For this reason, they have not taken it seriously. But in following this course, they have missed the important role his efforts to deal with the tensions involved in the conflict between the spiritual and the material worlds played in his pontificate. It is, indeed, almost a touchstone of his reign that he tried so hard to balance spiritual and temporal concerns. If his thought tended to be unduly complex, it was because he could seldom make a direct statement without resort to images such as those of Melchisedech or his reliance on such descriptive terms as "vicar of Christ."

The result has created more than a little difficulty for those attempting to explain his positions to modern audiences. This is not to suggest that Innocent approached the relations between the secular and the spiritual ambivalently. He certainly had strong ideas about what he was attempting to accomplish. He was, however, very much a product of his age, and that age was itself pulled in various directions by the complex forces and personalities that have come to dominate our own historical understanding of the period. If Innocent III occupied the same world as a Francis of Assisi, a Philip Augustus, a King John of England, a Jacques de Vitry, or a Peter

Waldo, he was no less a product of that world than they were. In fact, his dramatic emergence as pope in 1198 signaled not merely the coming of a new century but a new generation.

What influenced the cardinals, on the very day (8 January 1198) of the death of Pope Celestine III, a man who himself had been very much aware of the pulsating currents of his age, to select the youngest of their number, Lothar, from the family of the counts of Segni, to succeed him? In conventional terms, the author of the *Gesta* began his explanation with family relationships. Innocent was the son of Transmundus, "from the family of the counts of Segni," and of Clarina, "the daughter of a noble Roman line," the Scotti (Lotario dei Segni, *Opera Omnia*, vol. 214, xvii). This genealogy was important to understand not merely Innocent's local roots, but the motives behind his Roman policies, which could not be divorced from family ties and interests. Indeed, these family ties were essential to his success in the city. The *Gesta* especially stresses his building program, mentioning not merely the Torre dei Conti, a symbol of growing family power, but his numerous projects both in Rome and the Patrimony of St. Peter. But it was also important that he was educated not merely in Rome, where he drank deeply of the local religious culture and formed his views of the papacy, but also in Paris and Bologna. What was important to the author of the *Gesta* was that he "surpassed his contemporaries both in philosophy and theology, as his opuscula, which he drafted and dictated at various times, demonstrate." The author goes on to say that he authored, as a cardinal, books *On the Misery of the Human Condition*, *On the Mysteries of the Mass*, and *On the Fourfold Types of Marriages*. He speaks also of his sermons, letters, registers, and decretals, "which clearly show how expert he was in both human and divine law." Until recently, scholarship has played down the importance of his treatises and has questioned this judgment on his work in philosophy and theology, while focusing on the importance of his legal learning. But the cardinal-electors knew him chiefly for those early writings and the views expressed in them. In fact, these were important popularizations that struck at the heart of some of the most controversial issues of the age. They put Innocent in the forefront of those who were attempting to respond to fundamental concerns over the relation between the material and the spiritual worlds, the essential nature of the human condition, and the central position of the sacraments in twelfth-century theology, especially the Eucharist, as well as the symbolism of marriage as a binding together of the spiritual and material worlds. It is not surprising that Lothar rose so rapidly. Nor is it entirely surprising that he was chosen to succeed Celestine III, despite that pope's preference for the experienced and deeply spiritual John of St. Paul, cardinal-priest of St. Prisca. The cardinals seem to have preferred youthful insight to age and experience.

From the beginning of his pontificate it was apparent that Innocent stood firmly within the tradition of the reform papacy, which had become the mainstream position at Rome during the course of the twelfth century. If, however, the main lines of meaning of papal reform had become clear, there remained much that still provoked differences even among those committed to it. Among these factors, the relationship with the empire was particularly prominent, bearing as it did on the relations between the popes, the Lombard communes, and the Kingdom of Sicily. Less visible,

Medallion of Pope Innocent III that hangs over the door of the gallery of the House chamber at the U.S. Capitol. (Courtesy of the Library of Congress)

but probably more important in the long run, were those issues that touched the internal constitution of the church, especially the relationship between pope and bishops. This remained one of the largely unresolved issues from late antiquity. The reformers had also been in the forefront of a program of centralization aimed at strengthening the juridical role of the papacy. But there were also bases for conflict among the bishops, monasteries, cathedral chapters, and a growing number of local powers that were competing among themselves for greater independence in their own affairs. Add to these issues differences over the nature of Christian practice among an increasingly more involved laity, and it becomes apparent that Innocent confronted a world in which commitment to reform on the part of the papacy could hardly be defined; it had to be shaped within a continuing process. It is from this perspective that we may try to understand his policies and his formulation of his office and its objectives.

In general, it may be useful to divide Innocent's pontificate into two parts, though it is not possible to specify a precise date that separates one from the other. During the first period, which lasted more than a decade, Innocent largely responded to the problems that were brought before him. It is to this period that his decretals on the relations between the church and temporal authorities, as well as his vivid rhetorical formulations of papal power, belong. During the second period he tried to control the agenda and shape policy much more directly. Throughout his pontificate, however, he was extremely active, and from the beginning he demonstrated a willingness to innovate, even to the point of reversing previous courses of action.

The centerpiece of his commitment to reform was his effort to restore and develop the Patrimony of St. Peter, which he initiated within a short time of his accession. As the *Gesta* makes clear, he toured central Italy and appointed legates to further the task of establishing existing rights and making good on papal claims, using force where necessary. The basis for his actions lay in a disparate collection of rights and privileges stretching back to the Carolingians or even earlier. What appears somewhat new in his approach is the degree of systematization of government that he applied, making it valid to speak of him as the founder of the papal state. Defense of these rights formed the core of his policy toward the competing interests in thirteenth-century Italy.

Historians have often pointed out how fortunate Innocent was that the emperor Henry VI died in 1197, that England and France were locked in conflict, and that the heir to the Kingdom of Sicily was a child. Of course, this view assumes that Innocent had a clear view of the advantages he would gain thereby. But the example provided by the imperial vacancy suggests a more cautious appraisal. The death of Henry's widow, Constance of Sicily, and the moves on the part of Henry's brother, Philip of Swabia, to secure the imperial throne for his nephew and then for himself, culminated in a conflict among the princes that led to the double election of Philip and Otto of Brunswick. Innocent's slow response and lack of decisiveness in dealing with this crisis suggest that, whatever his attitude toward the candidates, he was unwilling to make an immediate commitment to either. He seems to have developed his policy as circumstances unfolded. His most complete rationale for his policy became clear only in

1202 (*Venerabilem*), more than three years after the disputed election of June 1198 and well after his chancery had begun the *Regestum super negotio Romani imperii*. (May 1199) to preserve the critical record of the conflict. Even after the decision in favor of the Welf candidate, Otto IV, in 1202, he does not seem to have entirely closed the door to Philip and his supporters. In 1206 he spoke of Philip as *princeps* rather than as duke, revealing a shift toward him that was only terminated by Philip's assassination by Otto von Wittelsbach in a private quarrel that had broad political consequences. The coronation of Otto IV and his subsequent conflict with the pope over lands in the Patrimony of St. Peter and the Kingdom of Sicily merely reinforce the view that Innocent's failure to commit irretrievably to either candidate probably stemmed from a realistic appraisal of imperial goals in Italy, regardless of party or candidate. Otto's subsequent invasion of the Kingdom of Sicily in defiance of Innocent and the pope's decision to support his ward, Frederick Roger of Sicily, for the imperial succession suggest how fluid the situation was. Innocent clearly wanted to preserve the Patrimony of St. Peter and the independence of the Kingdom of Sicily, but was willing to risk the latter in defense of the former.

A number of key elements emerged in the development of Innocent III's relations with secular rulers. Very often these were most innovative where Innocent tried to establish his right to intervene in particular situations. Thus his argument that the pope could judge the suitability of imperial candidates, contained in the decretal *Venerabilem* came in response to arguments put forward by supporters of Philip of Swabia. *Per venerabilem*, in which he defended his right to judge in secular matters where there was no superior secular power involved, should perhaps be read in relation to his later decretal *Novit*, in which he argued that he could intervene in the dispute between King John of England and Philip Augustus of France, not on feudal grounds, but because sin was involved (*ratione peccati*). Both suggest a certain probing of potentialities. He defended his powers in vivid language, evoking such images as that of the priest-king, Melchisedech, and that of the church as the sun compared to the secular power as the moon. Yet as his reign progressed, both the nature of his interventions and his defense of them underwent important changes. His conflict with King John over the election of an archbishop of Canterbury in 1207 and his imposition of the interdict and his subsequent excommunication of the king because of the royal refusal to accept Stephen Langton as archbishop of Canterbury remained throughout a dispute over jurisdictional rights. Even John's acceptance of vassal status to the Holy See as part of the settlement should be read chiefly in ecclesiastical terms, though it certainly had a political dimension. This device had been widely used by the papacy since the eleventh century to bolster papal jurisdiction over the episcopacies of lands where the ecclesiastical situation was in a state of flux. What seems most clear is that this period was one in which Innocent was trying very hard to find better ways of coping with the problems of his age. It was a period that called for flexibility and one in which success came only seldom and with difficulty.

This description certainly characterized his planning for the Fourth Crusade at the very beginning of his pontificate. Although some scholars have argued that Innocent was strongly committed to papal leadership of the crusade and cite various statements of his to demonstrate this conclusion, the pope actually played little part in the actual planning of the Fourth Crusade and only intervened after it was clear that the crusade faced real problems. In the absence of clear statements, we cannot know to what degree Innocent blamed himself for its failure. In fact, however, most of his initiatives aimed at keeping the Fourth Crusade on track were ineffective. It was not until 1213 that a fully developed crusade policy began to emerge from the rubble of the Fourth Crusade.

Perhaps the greatest challenge faced by the medieval church was the fundamental transformation of its spirituality and the new role of the laity that was already very evident in the generation before Innocent's pontificate. Efforts by the Third Lateran Council and by Pope Lucius III in 1184 to deal with these changes were little more than gut reactions. Innocent's own approaches during the first years of his pontificate have provoked some to see his policy as combining both the carrot and the stick. The decretal *Vergentis* (1200) subjected heretics to the penalties of secular law, decreeing the confiscation of their goods. On the other hand, Innocent showed considerable understanding of the complexities of the changes taking place at this time in his dealings with the Humiliati at the very beginning of his pontificate, as well as his openness to the ideas of Dominic de Guzman, the founder of the Order of Preachers, concerning the approach to be taken in dealing with the Cathar heretics, and in his dealings with the Waldensian factions of Durandus of Huesca and Bernard Prim. Although Innocent is known for summoning a crusade against the Cathars in southern France after the murder of his legate, Peter of Castelnau, in 1208, most recent historical discussion of his efforts to come to grips with the new religious movements of the period has focused more on his relationship with Francis of Assisi. That still-enigmatic figure certainly holds the key to an understanding of many aspects of this period.

The appearance of Francis of Assisi at the Roman curia in 1209/10 remains controversial in large part because it is closely tied to various views of Francis himself advanced in modern scholarship. What is evident is that Francis was already a respected figure, supported by his bishop and by Cardinal John of St. Paul. Moreover, he quickly found other strong supporters at the curia, including Innocent's own relative, Cardinal Hugolino, later Pope Gregory IX. Given the tangled state of early Franciscan sources, chiefly because of efforts to solve "problems" in the early history of the

Franciscan order, modern scholarship has become a process of selection aimed at bolstering particular interpretations. Yet Innocent's role does seem much clearer than it is often presented as being. He approved a *propositum* presented verbally by Francis of Assisi. He ordered that Francis and his followers be tonsured. Thus he established their clerical status. This point is interesting in light of disputes that seem to have broken out relatively soon in the order over the distinctions between priests and "lay" friars. Innocent did not apply the model he had adopted in granting recognition to the Humiliati, distinguishing the various types of membership. He apparently accepted Francis's own view of his "little brothers" and gave him verbal approval to carry out his work of preaching and recruitment. The evidence that Francis had in mind a new kind of monastic order seems clear from his subsequent actions.

The second phase of Innocent's pontificate was already under way after 1210. However, it may be said to have begun to take a public aspect with the issuance of his letter *Vineam Domini* in 1213, in which he enunciated the program that would dominate the remainder of his pontificate: the reform of the church and the promotion of the crusade. The scope of the program he envisaged was very large. He did not merely summon a council to meet in 1215 and launch the preaching of the Fifth Crusade, but put in motion an investigation of the state of the church by "prudent men." He not merely appointed legates for various Western churches, but charged Cardinal Pelagius of Albano with establishing peace between the Latin Empire of Constantinople and Theodore Lascaris, who, from his seat in Nicaea, was emerging as the effective ruler of the remnant of the Byzantine Empire still in Greek hands. Pelagius was also to promote the unity of the Latin and Greek churches and to secure Eastern participation in the forthcoming council. At least in conception, Innocent's view of reform embraced the whole church. His approach to the crusade at this time seems also to have solicited the views of others. Anxious as he was to move the crusade forward and detailed as was the program he developed for it and published in *Quia maior*, he left the important issue of crusade taxation to be dealt with at the council. He had learned from his previous experience that the bishops and abbots affected would support only what they approved. The Fourth Lateran Council would mark a major step in the implementation of this vast vision.

No other medieval council achieved the participation from both East and West, the numbers of bishops and abbots, and the presence of so many lawyers and theologians, that this council did. Only very gradually have we come to recognize that this grand council, the pinnacle of Innocent III's achievement, was indeed a mirror of the church of its time. Innocent deserves recognition for the scope of its agenda and the reform program laid down in many of its decrees, for its role as a forum in trying to bring international conflicts to an end, and for the enormous impact that it would have on the thirteenth-century church. He also suffered some defeats, endured various setbacks, and made compromises in the process. His successes on the political front were uneven. There was victory in his effort to install Frederick II as emperor-elect, but that had already been assured by Otto's defeat at Bouvines in 1214. The English baronial party, which had rebelled against the tyranny of King John and had exacted Magna Carta as the price of peace, found no support from the pope, but that was clear before the council. On the other hand, the effort of the pope to rein in Simon de Montfort and his crusaders and to support Raymond VI of Toulouse and his son ended in a compromise that frustrated the papal desire to secure the participation of Raymond in the crusade. Many of the most important canons suggest that they had undergone some revision, notably, that on the reform of preaching, whose remaining restrictions were soon to be further eroded by papal privileges, and that which prohibited the foundation of religious orders not based on existing rules, which probably reflected demands from some in the curia as well as many bishops. One decision that has caused much difficulty for historians is that regulating the dress of Jews and Muslims. It is most likely that this decree, often taken to express Innocent's views, reflected mounting pressure from the French bishops, who had been much influenced by the controversy over the Talmud. Apparently, Innocent himself modified this decree in a letter to the French hierarchy soon after the council limiting the kinds of distinctive garb to be worn by the Jews—Muslims are not mentioned—to those that would not endanger their way of life. On the other hand, those reforms touching the sacraments, such as the requirement regarding confession, may well bear Innocent's personal stamp. This is certainly true of much of the legislation that aimed at strengthening the structures of the church.

From early in his pontificate Innocent had been concerned with the performance of the papal chancery. It was under him that the progress of specialization began to make real progress. He continued the policies of centralization that had marked the development of the reform papacy during the twelfth century. The council extended these efforts and, for the first time, provided something that approached a coherent program in dealing with all of the issues of the age. The achievement of Innocent III was in his perseverance to reach this critical moment. It was, unfortunately, a beginning that he would not be able to carry forward. His plans for reform and for the crusade were left to his successors when he died on 16 July 1216 in Perugia. Able though many of these successors were, it is arguable whether any ever achieved his breadth of vision in dealing with the issues facing the medieval church.

SELECTED BIBLIOGRAPHY

Andrews, Francis. *The Early Humiliati*. Cambridge: Cambridge University Press, 1999.

Cheney, Christopher. *Pope Innocent III and England*. Stuttgart: Hiersemann, 1976.

Foreville, Raymonde. *Le pape Innocent III et la France*. Stuttgart: Hiersemann, 1992.

Hageneder, Othmar, Anton Haidacher, Werner Maleczek, Alfred A. Strand, and Karl Rudolf, eds. *Die Register Innocenz III*. 7 vols. Graz: H. Böhlaus, 1964– .

Imkamp, Wilhelm. *Das Kirchenbild Innocenz' III (1198–1216)*. Stuttgart: Hiersemann, 1983.

Kempf, Friedrich. *Papsttum und Kaisertum bei Innocenz III*. Rome: Pontificia università gregoriana, 1954.

Lambert, Malcolm. *The Cathars*. Oxford: Blackwell, 1998.

Lauf, Manfred. *Politik und Recht bei Innocenz III*. Cologne: Böhlau, 1980.

Lotario dei Segni (Innocent III). *De miseria condicionis humane*. Ed. and trans. Robert E. Lewis. Athens: University of Georgia Press, 1978.

———. *Opera Omnia*. In *Patrologia Latina*, ed., J.-P. Migne, vols. 214–17. Paris: Migne, 1844–64.

———. *Selected Letters of Pope Innocent III Concerning England (1198–1216)* ed. Christopher Cheney and W.H. Semple. Edinburgh: Nelson, 1953.

Luchaire, Achille. *Innocent III*. 6 vols. Paris: Hachette, 1905–8.

Moore, John C., ed. *Pope Innocent III and His World*. Aldershot, Hants: Ashgate, 1999.

Morris, Colin. *The Papal Monarchy: The Western Church from 1050 to 1250*. New York: Oxford University Press, 1990.

Pennington, Kenneth. *Pope and Bishops: The Papal Monarchy in the Twelfth and Thirteenth Centuries*. Philadelphia: University of Pennsylvania Press, 1984.

Powell, James M. *Anatomy of a Crusade, 1213–1221*. Philadelphia: University of Pennsylvania Press, 1986.

———, ed. *Innocent III: Vicar of Christ or Lord of the World?* 2nd ed. Washington, D.C.: Catholic University of America Press, 1994.

Sayers, Jane. *Innocent III: Leader of Europe, 1198–1216*. London: Longman, 1994.

Tillmann, Helene. *Pope Innocent III*. Trans. Walter Sax. Amsterdam: North-Holland Publishing Company, 1980.

Waley, Daniel. *The Papal State in the Thirteenth Century*. New York: St. Martin's Press, 1961.

GREGORY IX (1227–41)

ROBERT C. FIGUEIRA

Ugo or Ugolino dei Conti, son of a Count Mathias and a descendant of the counts of Segni, was born around 1170 at Anagni in Campania. Some historians have been misled by Matthew Paris's description ("fuit . . . fere centenarius") into placing the date decades earlier, but Matthew probably wanted to stress the pope's great age at death. He was a relative (nephew or grandnephew or cousin) of Innocent III and—though this is disputed by some—the uncle of Rainaldo of Segni, the later Alexander IV (1254–61). We still possess three contemporary pictorial representations of him: an ink miniature portrait in a manuscript of his papal register, a mosaic fragment from old St. Peter's, and a wall painting of him as cardinal in the lower Church of Sacro Specco in Subiaco.

Ugo was perhaps educated as a boy in the cathedral school of Anagni; it is possible that he eventually belonged to the clergy of that church, for on at least two occasions he referred to himself as a "son" (*filius*) of the church of Anagni. He studied at university in Paris (probably theology); perhaps he also studied law at Bologna (a contemporary account calls him *iuris peritus*). Named papal subdeacon and chaplain in 1198 by his papal relative, he remained a close advisor and confidant throughout Innocent's pontificate. He was soon (sometime between September and December 1198) made cardinal-deacon of St. Eustace. Innocent's sometime confessor, the Cistercian Rainer of Ponza, acted for a time as teacher and spiritual advisor. Hugo himself served often during these years as an auditor of cases at the curia.

In May 1206 Innocent named him cardinal-bishop of Ostia and Velletri, and thereby the most senior of the college (equivalent to dean, a title not then in use); as such, he would serve as consecrator of a new pope (assisted by cardinal-bishops of Albano and Porto), anointer of a new emperor, and in consistory or council the cardinal next in precedence to the pope. As bishop of Ostia and Velletri, he strengthened the former's fortifications and founded a monastery in the latter diocese. In December 1206 he tried to patch up a quarrel between Velletri and neighboring communities; around 1222–23 he was successful in arranging peace between Velletri, Cori, Sermoneta, Ninfa, Sezze, and Acqua Putrida.

During these years Cardinal Hugo continued to act as auditor of many cases at the curia. From perhaps 1207 onwards he—along with two other cardinals—received annual stipends from King John of England; perhaps there was a connection between said payments and John's diplomacy in favor of his nephew and imperial claimant Otto of Brunswick. Broken off at a later time, these payments were resumed by the king's order in July 1214. Thomas of Evesham sought on behalf of his monastery the cardinal's counsel and protection at the curia. At the Fourth Lateran Council Hugo was asked to arbitrate a settlement of a conflict between the monastery of Cîteaux and its four immediate daughter houses.

After the death of his papal uncle on 16 July 1216, Hugo and Guido of Praeneste were the two electoral commissioners entrusted by the other cardinals to perform an *electio per compromissum*; on 18 July, with unanimous approval of their colleagues, they chose Cencio Savelli to become the next pope, Honorius III (1216–27).

Hugo's legatine missions for the former pope dealt largely with German affairs or with Germans, while legations undertaken for the latter pope largely concerned the affairs of Italian cities and towns. In 1199 Hugo was one of three legates (the others being Cardinals Octavian of Ostia and Guido of St. Mary in Trastevere) sent to treat with Markward of Anweiler, the German commander whose military and political activities in central and southern Italy following his master Henry VI's death caused Pope Innocent considerable concern. Hugo was clearly the junior member of the legation.

Markward had prompted this particular legation by his apparent willingness to treat regarding his excommunication and offer to resign the regency of the Kingdom of Sicily (or Regno). The *Gesta Innocentii III* reported that when Markward nonetheless lured the legates to a banquet meeting where his troops could threaten the cardinals with arrest, Hugo dramatically produced Pope Innocent's legatine mandate naming the conditions of Markward's reconciliation, read it aloud, and declared that the mandate was inviolable. Despite the ensuing uproar, Markward backed down, requested and received a stay of the mandate after acknowledging its receipt, and declared his intention to conclude negotiations personally with the pope.

In September–October 1202 Hugo traveled as Innocent's legate over the northern border of the Regno to make peace between the archbishop-elect of Capua and a neighboring castellan regarding alleged rights and properties of the church of Capua. During 1207–9 Hugo was dispatched on three separate missions to Germany in order to deal with the throne dispute between Philip of Swabia and Otto of Brunswick, as well as various local ecclesiastical disputes.

His companion for the first legation—which would effect Pope Inno-

Medallion of Pope Gregory IX that hangs over the door of the gallery of the House chamber at the U.S. Capitol. (Courtesy of the Library of Congress)

cent's diplomatic turn in favor of Philip—was Leo Brancaleone, cardinal-priest of Santa Croce. In July 1207 they first met with Philip, whom in the next month they released from excommunication at a large meeting of princes in Worms. Hugo and Leo further negotiated a truce between the contenders that was to hold until late June 1208; they also wrung from Philip an agreement to permit the return of Archbishop Siegfried to his see of Mainz. Both legates were present at the November 1207 Reichstag at Augsburg. During early 1208 they accompanied envoys from both parties back to Rome.

After a final peace was concluded between Philip and the pope in May 1208, the two cardinals were again appointed legates on a mission to Germany to cement Innocent's diplomatic shift in policy. Their travel northward got no further than Lombardy, where their progress was halted by Leo's illness and by the news of Philip's murder. In the changed situation, Innocent decided nonetheless to send the two legates to Otto to remind him of his promises made in 1198 and 1201 in preparation for an imperial coronation. Hugo and Leo treated with Otto in March 1209 and prompted the latter's 22 March diploma repeating promises to allow free ecclesiastical elections of prelates, to respect the property rights of the same, to acknowledge the papal recuperation of territories in central Italy, and to protect the Regno as a fief of the Roman church. Incidentally, Otto's failure to keep these promises soon after his imperial coronation would cause the break in amicable relations between him and Innocent and the renewal of war between Welf and Hohenstaufen. Before they returned south in advance of Otto's coronation expedition to Rome, the legates also attended a festive royal court at Würzburg. By mid-September 1209 at the latest, Hugo and Leo were both back at the curia.

In 1217 Hugo was dispatched by Honorius III to northern Italy to promote peace and further the cause of the crusade in accordance with recent legislation of the Fourth Lateran Council. Pisa and Genoa were locked in rivalry over competing Sardinian claims. Hugo's diplomacy in this matter was capped in December by a solution finalized before Pope Honorius and the curia. The legate's actions in the internal affairs of Lucca and Volterra had a similar goal in the promotion of civic concord. In the case of the latter city Hugo utilized the bishop of Pistoia as a legatine subdelegate. Finally, there is reason to suppose that Hugo perhaps also journeyed as legate to Hungary to promote the crusade and King Andrew's participation therein. In any event, the legate returned to Rome before the end of the year.

During the late spring of 1218 Honorius once more sent Hugo to northern Italy, this time again for furtherance of communal peace in assistance of the contemporary crusading campaign in Egypt. In Tuscany the legate encouraged an end to internal strife in Siena and Florence; he arbitrated a dispute between Pistoia and Bologna as well. Hugo's major challenge, however, lay in Lombardy, where warfare had broken out between contentious groups of cities led, respectively, by Milan and Cremona. Here the legate cooperated smoothly with Frederick II's vicar, Bishop James of Turin. In December Hugo presided over an arbitrated peace between Milan and Cremona at Lodi that led to a general pacification. During early 1219 the legate moved on to Venetia, where he negotiated with Doge

Pietro Zeno for a lower price for transporting a crusader contingent on Venetian ships.

By May the legate was back in Rome, but Honorius immediately sent him northward again to supervise (successfully) recuperation of some Mathildine territories (properties descendant from Countess Mathilda of Tuscany) for the papacy and to attempt (unsuccessfully) to dissuade the Ferrarese from creating a new town on territories claimed by the church. By August Hugo was back at the curia.

Hugo's final series of legatine missions for Honorius III occurred in 1221. Here again the aims included furtherance of communal peace and promotion of the crusade by preaching and recruitment of troops. In addition, the legate was to cement support for the newly crowned emperor Frederick II, campaign against heresy, and assist the collection of papal revenues. The emperor even empowered the legate to act in the capacity of an imperial vicar to release persons and places from the imperial ban. Hugo began his journey in March, recruiting crusaders, collecting money, and pacifying civil discord as he traveled to Siena, Florence, Piacenza, Pistoia, Lucca, Milan, Venice, Treviso, Padua, Mantua, and Reggio.

During July and August the legate arbitrated a particularly persistent territorial dispute among the patriarch of Aquileia, the bishop of Belluno-Feltre, and the commune of Treviso. Where the legate could not solve a specific conflict, he often committed it to local ecclesiastics for solution. In several towns Hugo either canceled or prevented communal legislation that diminished ecclesiastical liberties or fostered alienation of ecclesiastical lands. During his 1219 visit Hugo had been unable to bring the Ferrarese to heel regarding what the papacy considered their encroachments in the Massa Fiscaglia. Now, in the late summer of 1221, he placed the town under the interdict and excommunicated its podestà, or chief official, to force submission some months later.

During the summer and autumn the recruitment of crusaders and the collection of crusading funds continued; in addition, Hugo ordered the communes of Padua, Modena, and Parma to restore ecclesiastical property and enact statutes to prevent such confiscation in the future. The legate also was active against heresy within the territories of his legation. In Piacenza, Bergamo, and Mantua he published the sanctions of the Fourth Lateran Council against heretics and ordered their codification in communal statues. Furthermore, Hugo commanded that the heretics' meeting places be destroyed and the heretics themselves banished.

Three further disputes occupied his time. The feud between the commune of Milan and that city's archbishop regarding the latter's punishment of Monza had led to the prelate's exile. Hugo's blandishments and threats of interdict were of no avail; it would be left to Pope Honorius to resolve this quarrel in 1225. The legate also intervened in the conflict regarding disputed territory between the archbishop of Ravenna and Imola, on the one hand, and the cities of Faenza and Bologna, on the other. While Hugo's successful arbitration brought peace and arranged mutual reparations, he wisely refrained from passing definitive sentence regarding the disputed territory, no doubt in cognizance of an imperial judgment in the matter. The legate's arbitration of Piacenza's internal strife met with less success. His compromise judgment between aristocratic and popular factions only momentarily reestablished political unity and softened the harsh prior actions of the imperial vicar against the popular party; soon the situation deteriorated once again.

Interestingly enough, Hugo's actions as legate in Italy also showed his considerable sensitivity to the concerns of Frederick II; as shown earlier, he often worked to further the young ruler's interests in northern Italy, and on several occasions he effectively cooperated with imperial officials. Upon the death of Honorius III the cardinals present at the curia met on the following day in the Septizonium (19 March 1227) and delegated to a commission of three of their number (among them Hugo) the decision regarding who would be the next pope (i.e., they authorized an *electio per compromissum*). The papacy was offered first to Konrad of Urach, cardinal-bishop of Porto, who refused. Then Hugo himself was unanimously elected, immediately enthroned, consecrated on 21 March, and crowned on 11 April 1227.

The new pope influenced higher education in two ways, namely, through his policies regarding two universities and through his actions concerning the teaching of Aristotle's philosophy. In 1231 Gregory reopened the University of Paris after a two-year-long closure prompted by a secession of masters and scholars in the aftermath of violence between them and Parisian police. The pope's activities in the immediately preceding period had included appointing an investigating commission, reprimanding the bishop of Paris (William of Auvergne) for his unsatisfactory handling of the situation, and politicking on behalf of the university with young Louis IX and his mother Blanche of Castile, the regent. As university functions resumed, Gregory promulgated on 13 April 1231 the bull *Parens scientiarum*, the "great charter," which gave to the university of masters considerable powers of self-government by their own statutes. On another front two years later, the pope founded a university of Toulouse with the same liberties as those at Paris; this was the second instance (after Frederick II's 1224 foundation at Naples) wherein a medieval ruler created by fiat an institution of higher learning.

Ever since the 1210 provincial council of Sens, many of Aristotle's metaphysical and natural philosophical works had been forbidden in the arts curriculum at Paris due to their alleged conflict with theological tenets. Gregory repeated the prohibition in *Parens scientiarum*, but in effect modified the ban by softening penalties and by appointing on 23 April 1231 a commission of three Parisian theologians (William of Auxerre, Stephen of Provence, and Simon d'Authie) to prepare a sanitized collection of these texts for further study. Although we know nothing about the commission's further activities, if any, in subsequent decades the entire then-extant corpus of Aristotelian and pseudo-Aristotelian texts was the object of comprehensive study and comment.

Since 1217 (after their first meeting in Florence) Cardinal Hugo had been the steady friend and patron of Francis of Assisi (whom he was to canonize on 16 July 1228 less than two years after the latter's death). After the death of Francis's prior patron, Cardinal John of St. Paul, Hugo was named by Honorius III in late 1220 at Francis's request to be the first protector of the Franciscan order. Immediately Hugo set to his charge, directing various prelates by letter not to impede the activities of the friars and interceding with the pope to send similar letters. An indispensable advisor to the saint during the years of explosive growth of the Friars Minor, Hugo attended various general chapter meetings of the order at the Portiuncula in 1219 and 1221. In 1220, in Francis's absence, he copresided with the founder's two vicars over a general chapter, and in 1222 he presided in Francis's presence at the so-called Chapter of the Mats.

A participant in the drafting of the *Regula non bullata* of 1221, the cardinal was very influential in shaping the *Rule* of 1223 and rules for the "Poor Clares" or Second Order (1218–19, strongly based on Benedictine practices) and Tertiaries (1221, no longer extant). As a quasi-founder of the Second Order, Hugo established convents of Poor Clares in northern and central Italy. A possible meeting with Francis in 1222, at Subiaco, is perhaps the reason why the cardinal's portrait can be found in the Chapel of San Gregorio in the lower Church of Sacro Specco. He also fostered the growth of Franciscan Tertiaries. In short, as an active protector, Hugo played a major role in determining the path whereby the Franciscan orders would grow and develop in the years following the founder's death. His legalistic frame of mind also provided comfort for the founder's concern for the order's future.

As pope, Gregory also personally laid the foundation stone to the saint's sepulchral basilica, wrote hymns in honor of Francis, and even commissioned the first biography of the saint, written by Thomas of Celano. The pope supported an enlarged competence of the Franciscans in preaching and in hearing confessions. He forced the convocation of and presided at the general chapter of the order at Pentecost 1239, where Minister-General Elias of Cortona was deposed.

After Francis's death the order called upon Gregory for guidance in dealing with the former's *Testament* as well as in explicating doubtful passages of the 1223 *Rule*. Gregory's bull *Quo elongati* (28 September 1230) clarified many of these doubts, among other matters declaring Francis's *Testament* to be juridically nonbinding vis-à-vis the *Rule* of 1223 and further authorizing the collection of money, books, and utensils for the use (*usus*) of the friars (i.e., a use without ownership) through the mediation of third parties (whose ownership was presumed still to exist). The pope relied here not only upon principles of canon law regarding the limits of authority, but also upon his personal familiarity with Francis's intention as well as his role as cardinal-protector of the order at the time that the 1223 *Rule* was written and received papal approbation.

In short, although Gregory's bull indicated on a number of points both a stricter and looser interpretation of current Franciscan practice, it in effect represented a turning point in the history of the First Order away from some of the impractical elements of Francis's ideals. Interestingly enough, Gregory also endeavored—in distinction from his policy for the friars—to provide endowments for houses of Clarisses that they might support themselves in a life of strict claustration.

The pope canonized Anthony of Padua (d. 1231) on 30 May 1232 and Landgravine Elizabeth of Thuringia (d. 17 November 1231) on 27 May 1235 (the first German Franciscan Tertiary); he had been a close spiritual advisor to the latter during her lifetime, and among other things he had commanded Konrad of Marburg in early 1228 to resume his position as Elizabeth's confessor during her widowhood and to provide her counsel in worldly matters as well. In the early fourteenth century Phillip of Perugia related that he had heard two stories concerning Gregory from a friar in the pope's entourage: the pope is reported not only to have washed the feet of the poor while dressed in a Franciscan habit and assisted by other friars, but also to have worn said habit in the company of Franciscans while visiting holy places within Rome.

Before his elevation to the papacy Hugo had also cultivated friendship with the other great mendicant founder, Dominic of Osma, whom he first met perhaps in 1215 at the Fourth Lateran Council. Other meetings of the two are noted for 1217, 1219/20, and 1221. In 1221 Hugo celebrated Dominic's funeral mass in Bologna and as pope canonized him on 13 July 1234. Hugo was a strong supporter of the Preachers during their formative years, even though this order did not then possess an official protector. As pope, he issued to the Dominicans the privilege of preaching and hearing confessions in any diocese in September 1227.

As cardinal, he was a frequent donor of religious houses and hospitals; in 1208 he established a hospital at Anagni and gave it to the Crucifer order. He was supportive of followers of Joachim of Fiore, founding houses for the latter at Velletri, at Anagni, and near Ninfa. As both cardinal and pope, he assisted the reform and spread of Cistercians, Carmelites, Cluniacs, Camaldolese, Premonstratensians, and the Teutonic Knights (especially the latter's "mission" to the Baltic, where he preached a crusade against the pagan Lithuanians).

As legate in northern Italy, Hugo introduced Frederick II's antiheresy statute of March 1224 (*Cum ad conservandum*) into the ordinances of several cities. As pope, he oversaw efforts, begun in 1229, to organize episcopal inquisitorial activities against heretics in southern France. Count Raymond VII of Toulouse was impelled by treaty (12 April 1229) to provide assistance in the suppression of Cathars and Waldensians in his lands. In January 1231 Gregory had the imperial antiheresy statute copied into papal registers. In the next month he promulgated a constitution (*Excommunicamus et anathematisamus*) that became an important milestone for inquisitorial activities, stipulating the death penalty at the hands of the civil power for obstinate heretics and life imprisonment for unrepentant heretics.

Eventually Gregory did much to centralize inquisitorial activities across diocesan boundaries and appoint clergy other than bishops—most often Dominicans—as inquisitors. In France the pope empowered (20 April 1233) the Dominican provincial prior of Provence to select inquisitors who would act as direct papal agents. Soon thereafter a similar arrangement was made effective for northern France. Between 1232 and 1235 inquisitorial activities throughout Italy were also put on a firmer footing as Dominican inquisitors were established throughout the peninsula. From October 1235 to May 1236 Gregory himself sojourned at Viterbo and personally issued judgments against professed heretics before popular assemblies. In Germany Konrad of Marburg was authorized in 1231 to investigate and suppress heresy, activities that would lead to his murder two years later. In Aragon, with the support of King James I, the pope also organized inquisitorial activities under the supervision of bishops and Dominicans.

Dozens of private collections of decretals were compiled in the years following the appearance and general use of Gratian's *Decretum* in the mid-twelfth century. By Gregory's pontificate many factors called for the promulgation of a comprehensive and officially recognized work as a solution to legal insecurity caused by the explosive growth in the circulation of decretals by the popes, by the varied contents of the private collections, by questions of authenticity and validity of individual decretals, by the often-differing opinions found in individual decretals on a single subject, and by the absence of a handy compendium drawn from the multitude of more recent source texts.

In 1230 the pope commissioned his chaplain and penitentiary Raymond of Peñafort to compile and edit a decretal collection to fill these needs; on 5 September 1234 in the bull *Rex pacificus* Gregory officially sanctioned the resulting compendium and sent it to the universities of Bologna, Padua, and Paris. The use of other decretal collections in school or in court was expressly prohibited.

The texts collected by Raymond included decretals circulating since the compilation of Gratian's *Decretum*, including two hundred of Gregory's own, some issued specially for the compilation. The pope's decretals found their way especially into the civil, criminal, and procedural portions of the collection. Raymond's collection became ultimately known as the *Decretales* or *Liber extra* or *Gregoriana*, an important portion of the *Corpus iuris canonici* in force until the early twentieth century. An additional seven decretals by Gregory were included in the next official papally authorized collection, the *Liber sextus*, promulgated in 1298 by Pope Boniface VIII.

During his pontificate Gregory upheld the Latin Empire of Constantinople through his own financial support, diversion of money confiscated from Jewish usurers by the French Crown, taxes on clergy, preaching of crusade against resistant Byzantines, commutation of crusading oaths in return for service in defense of the Latin Empire, and penance imposed by inquisitors on penitent heretics. As Innocent III and Honorius III had previously held, this pope also saw the fortuitous conquest of Constantinople and the erection of the Latin Empire as divine punishment for Greek disobedience, as an opportunity to reconcile the Greek church to papal headship, and as an important factor in assuring the ultimate success of the Franks in Outremer. Innovatory, however, was Gregory's insistence that those Greeks or Bulgarians who as schismatics resisted the authority of the Latin church also promoted heresy and thereby incurred the penalties set forth by the Fourth Lateran Council, canon 3 (*Excommunicamus*).

In 1232 Patriarch Germanus II of Constantinople (Nicaea), at the behest of his emperor, John III Vatatzes, made contact with Gregory and the cardinals. In a reply (26 July 1232) the pope affirmed his claims for ecclesiastical primacy. In another letter (18 May 1233) Gregory laid the entire blame for schism on the Greeks and dispatched four friars (a pair each of Franciscans and Dominicans) as nuncios to the East with the aim of reconciling the two churches. Meetings took place between the Greeks and the nuncios at Nicaea and near Smyrna in January 1234, but agreement foundered on Greek refusal to accept the Latins' views on the procession of the Holy Spirit from the Son and the licitness of unleavened bread in the eucharistic consecration.

After 1235 the pope spent considerable time and effort in complex negotiations to coordinate two military expeditions to aid the Latin Empire, one by Bela IV of Hungary, the other composed of Western European troops under the command of the Latin emperor Baldwin II himself. A major object of the pope's diplomatic efforts was to ensure the cooperation and support of John II Asen, the congenitally untrustworthy king of the Bulgarians. The two expeditions took place in a fitful manner in 1239–40 and made no appreciable change in the military situation.

The new pope's relations with his Roman flock were at first amicable; Gregory's procession through the city was the scene of a splendid welcome. On 31 May 1227 the pope left Rome for Anagni and a summer vacation. The only scandal that occurred in his absence was the activity of a fraudulent representative who presumed to absolve crusading oaths for money. While the pope was absent, he pronounced his first excommunication of Frederick II (September). He returned to the city on 10 October. During November one of the emperor's representatives even managed to publicly read aloud on the Capitol the emperor's defense of his position.

But when, on Maundy Thursday of the next year, Gregory renewed his ban of the emperor, imperialist partisans disrupted the ceremony. On another front, when in April 1228 the communal government embarked upon military operations against Rome's archfoe Viterbo, the pope prudently left the city for Rieti and subsequently Perugia. His absence lasted almost two years.

The terrible floods of February 1230 were seen by many Romans as divine judgment for their estrangement from the pope. Gregory returned in March, upon receiving an invitation from communal officials, and immediately took energetic steps to assist the city's inhabitants with provisions and rebuilding efforts. Later that same year the pope also undertook a large operation against heretics in the city, involving identification, arrest, trial, and condemnation. Under papal influence communal officials promulgated an antiheresy edict early in 1231.

Nonetheless, the Romans' desire for renewed aggression against Viterbo led to repeated offensive operations during April and May 1231. The pope, who did not share this antagonism, left the city again in late spring for Rieti and Anagni. Military operations continued into the next year, with Gregory eventually arranging a truce. In March 1233 a Roman deputation invited the pope back. Gregory returned, continued his diplomatic activity, negotiated a peace treaty between Romans and Viterbans in April, saw to its ratification in June, and, after a summer sojourn outside Rome, finally returned to the city in November.

During 1234 considerable disagreement arose between the pope and Romans regarding three points. The Romans asserted that the pope could not excommunicate any of them or lay an interdict upon the city. Furthermore, they maintained that an annual communal tax—paid by the Roman church on occasion in the past—should be recognized as customary. Finally, the Roman municipal government persisted in its expansionist policy by attempting to create a *contado* (country district) including nearby Tuscan and Campanian towns.

In late May, when the pope and curia departed the city for Rieti, plundering occurred at the Lateran and in the houses of several cardinals. The senator Luca Savelli, who had emerged as the leading spokesman of the just-named policies, was thereupon excommunicated along with his associates. Frederick II lent Gregory his assistance, himself leading troops to protect the pope and cardinals. After the emperor's departure some German troops were left behind; Gregory meanwhile began to organize an economic blockade of the city.

When the Roman forces advanced on Viterbo in October 1234, they were decisively defeated in battle. Soon the Romans and the pope entered into negotiations that bore fruit by the late spring of 1235. The former had to compensate their opponents for damages, free hostages, return occupied territory and properties, drop their attempts to build a *contado*, and recognize ecclesiastical and clerical immunity from secular jurisdiction and taxation. The treaty was ratified in May.

Gregory and the curia, nonetheless, continued to reside outside Rome. At the end of 1236 a revolt in the city led by Pietro Frangipani against the pope and the then-propapal senator was crushed by municipal forces and propapal partisans. During 1237 political infighting between various Roman factions probably led to power sharing between two senators who represented propapal and proimperial interests. The pope returned to the city in October, and shortly thereafter the emperor won his great victory over the Lombards at Cortenuova (27 November). Frederick informed the Romans that his triumph was also theirs and subsequently (in January 1238) ordered that his battle trophy, the captured Milanese *carroccio* (war chariot) be brought to Rome and placed on the Capitol.

During 1238 persistent political jockeying for advantage by the city factions continued. After the pope left for his summer vacation, a loyal senator managed to forestall an attempted revolt. Gregory returned in October, when his ongoing conflict with the emperor subsequently led to the latter's second excommunication in March 1239, the pope received, surprisingly enough, no overt opposition from the Romans. It had become clear even to the latter that Frederick's policy of strict centralization of power had led to the subjugation of other Italian cities; if it were successful, then Rome's municipal autonomy would certainly also suffer. Even the emperor's letter of 20 April 1239 to the Romans, wherein he all but called for a revolt against Gregory, prompted no response.

When imperial forces threatened the city and its resident pontiff in February 1240, Gregory rallied the hesitant population by staging a great procession led by the sacrosanct relics of Peter and Paul, thereby rousing such enthusiastic preparations for defense that they smothered any local proimperial sentiment and dissuaded Frederick from any direct assault. The Romans persisted in their loyalty to Gregory until the pope's death in August 1241. A final comment regarding Gregory's rule over the papal patrimony, the so-called lands of St. Peter, is that the pope promulgated a constitution (*Habet utilitas stimulos*), probably in January 1234, whereby henceforth only cardinals were to be entrusted with rectorships in the patrimony, and one-third of net patrimonial revenues were to be paid, respectively, to the papal camera, to the college of cardinals, and to the treasury of the Roman church.

Before his election as pope, Hugo's relations with Frederick II, Roman emperor and king of Sicily, had been friendly. As cardinal of Ostia, he had been present at Frederick's imperial coronation on 22 November 1220 and on that occasion had given the crusading cross to this ruler, thereby confirming Frederick's spontaneous act of 1215 at his royal coronation. But the emperor's nonfulfillment of his crusading vow greatly exasperated Honorius III as promised deadlines for departure came and went. In 1227 Gregory's announcement to Frederick of his own election to the papacy stressed the latter's need to speed up crusade preparations.

The emperor's inexcusable years-long delay to fulfill his sworn commitment would prove to be the first point of discord between the two men. But the background to papal-imperial conflict lay also in various other circumstances, namely, in the disputed status of the March of Ancona and the Duchy of Spoleto (lands of St. Peter or imperial territory?), in Frederick's political ambitions in Lombardy and Tuscany, in papal fears of a strengthening of the bonds between the Sicilian kingdom and the empire, and in Frederick's actions to control the Sicilian church.

When, in early September 1229, Frederick claimed illness and ordered his crusading fleet and army concentrated at Brindisi to turn back to Otranto, Gregory's patience was at an end. Mindful of the emperor's procrastination during his predecessor's pontificate, he excommunicated Frederick on 29 September 1227 and renewed the excommunication on 18 November 1227 and 23 March 1228, interdicting automatically any place where the emperor chose to reside. To the initial charges of nonfulfillment of his crusading oath the pope added the additional charge that Frederick oppressed the church in the Regno.

The emperor replied to his penalty on 6 December 1227 in a manifesto (*In admiratione vertitur*) defending himself and declaring his intention to sail east the following spring. A revolt of the proimperial Frangipani-led faction in Rome against the pope during the 1228 Easter season forced Gregory to withdraw for a time to Perugia. At this time Frederick also charged the pope with hindrance of the crusade and support of rebellious Lombard cities.

Frederick sailed off from Brindisi for Outremer on 28 June 1228. Allegedly without his master's authorization, the Sicilian regent, Rainald of Urslingen (duke of Spoleto), invaded certain territories in the lands of St. Peter first recuperated decades before by Innocent III. Rainald thereby reestablished a land corridor between Frederick's territories in northern and southern Italy. For his part, Gregory released from fealty first Frederick's imperial subjects resident in the Regno and subsequently all of his royal and imperial subjects. At the same time the pope preached a crusade against the emperor, raised an army (the "soldiers of the Keys," so named after their insignia) to eject invading imperial forces from papal territories, and ordered an invasion of the southern kingdom commanded by cardinal-legates Pandulf and Pelagius. John of Brienne, another papal commander, expelled the imperial commander Rainald and his troops from the Patrimony of St. Peter. The dispatch by Gregory of a legate to Germany (Cardinal-Deacon Otto Candidus) in order to publicize the ban and visit the German church made, however, no impression on Frederick's position there.

Gregory excommunicated Frederick a fourth time on 30 August 1228. The emperor arrived in Acre on 7 September 1228. After he successfully negotiated a favorable peace treaty and a ten-and-a-half-year truce with the Egyptian sultan el-Kamil (18 February 1229) and also crowned himself king of Jerusalem (18 March 1229), a papal legate, Patriarch Gerold of Jerusalem, pronounced an interdict over the Holy Places. This penalty and the renewed excommunication furthermore prompted resistance to Frederick from the Templars, Hospitallers, and others. With no further progress in Outremer possible, the news of Gregory's other countermoves convinced the emperor to depart Outremer on 1 May and return on 10 June 1229 to Brindisi. When Frederick quickly raised troops and reconquered lost territories in the Regno, Gregory again excommunicated him and freed all of his subjects from fealty.

In the new military situation prompted by the emperor's return and rapid recovery of territory, Hermann von Salza, grand master of the Teutonic Knights, acted as honest broker for negotiations between pope and emperor. The peace accord between the two was reached in two stages at San Germano (23 July 1230) and Ceprano (28 August 1230), with conquered papal territories and confiscated property of papal partisans returned by Frederick in exchange for Gregory's lifting the sentence of excommunication and reinstatement of Frederick's subjects' fidelity. Frederick made further concessions regarding royal influence over the Sicilian church, not only recognizing the freedom of episcopal and abbatial elections, postulations, and confirmations, but also pledging to respect the inviolability of ecclesiastical immunities of persons and properties both as regards secular taxation and court jurisdiction. The role of the emperor in northern Italy and his ambition for a union of Italy and Germany remained unresolved and thus potential causes for future discord. The peace was confirmed by a personal meeting between pope and emperor a few days later, on 1 September 1230, in Anagni.

During the following spring (1231) Gregory complained, without effect, that the emperor had not returned confiscated Templar property as per the peace treaty. Frederick's promulgation of the Constitutions of Melfi in August/September 1231, with their expression of regal absolutism and restrictions of ecclesiastical liberties in his Sicilian kingdom, also earned the pope's displeasure but still did not upset the fragile peace. In December 1232 the pope also complained that the Saracens in Lucera, a town just within the kingdom's borders, had demolished a church. However, the Roman commune's offensive against Viterbo in 1232 and revolt against the pope in 1234 prompted the two rulers to close ranks to some degree. Frederick's armed intervention assured Gregory's safety; the participation of German troops proved an important factor in the complete submission of the Romans to the pontiff in 1235. For his part, in late 1234/early 1235 Gregory obligingly excommunicated Frederick's rebellious son, King Henry, and nullified oaths of allegiance to the latter. In another family matter, namely, the negotiations that led to the emperor's marriage in July 1235 to Isabella of England, the pope also acted as supporter and intermediary.

Another outstanding political situation did not, however, contribute to smooth imperial-papal relations. In 1232–33 Gregory served for a time with some success as an arbiter between Frederick and the rebellious Lombard League, but his renewed efforts to soothe this rivalry during 1235 were without effect, due both to the Lombards' unhelpful support for King Henry's rebellion and to the emperor's tough bargaining position. Frederick eventually concluded that Gregory actually wished to aid the truculent Lombard communes, whereas the pope continued to claim that he acted only as a peacemaker. But the activities of Gregory's legate, Cardinal James of Praeneste, in northern Italy during the summer of 1236 prompted renewed imperial accusations of partiality.

During the emperor's subsequent campaign in northern Italy he requested that the Lombard rebels be excommunicated by the pope; this elicited on 23 October 1236 Gregory's reply (*Si memoriam beneficiorum*) full of complaints, already voiced some months earlier, regarding both the oppression of the Sicilian church and the despoliation, arrest, and exile of some Sicilian clergy. During 1237 both emperor and pope conducted further negotiations for peace in Lombardy, but hopes for a solution were dashed by Venetian intransigence and the emperor's great military victory over the Lombard League at Cortenuova already mentioned. Frederick's demand for Milan's unconditional surrender merely hardened the Lombards' will to resist.

Tentative moves during 1238 and early 1239 toward improving relations between pope and emperor were thwarted by outstanding disagreements, as well as by actions of both men. It was becoming increasingly clear to Gregory that Frederick desired the creation of strong imperial centralized government in northern Italy as well as the integration of Rome itself into his imperial scheme. The exultant emperor sent the Romans the captured *carroccio* of the Milanese so that they might also celebrate his triumph. Gregory's legate in northern Italy, the notary Gregory of Montelongo, continued to be active in aid of the Lombards, while papal diplomacy in addition achieved a rapprochement of the usually rival Venetians and Genoese. The conflict erupted when Frederick dispatched his illegitimate son Enzio to Sardinia for marriage with Adelasia, a Sardinian noblewoman and heiress to Torre and Gallura. There Enzio entitled himself king of the island that Gregory, as had popes before him, considered subject to the papacy as a fief.

On 10 March 1239 the emperor sent the cardinals a letter (*Cum sit Christus*) stressing their power within the Roman church while condemning the pope's partisanship for the Lombards. The letter was intercepted before it reached its destination, and on 20 March 1239 Gregory excommunicated Frederick once again and likewise freed the latter's subjects from their fealty. The pope's sixteen charges included allegations of imperial assistance to rebellious Romans, imperial impediment of the crusade against the Albigensians, hindrance of protection of the Holy Places in Outremer and of the Latin Empire, and oppression of the Sicilian church through prevention of orderly filling of church vacancies, seizure of ecclesiastical property, imprisonment of clergy, and extortionary exactions of ecclesiastical income. Curiously enough, there was no explicit mention of the emperor's conflict with the Lombards.

In the ongoing propaganda war both emperor and pope resorted to encyclicals and manifestos. Probably during late March 1239 Frederick wrote again to the cardinals (*Conscientiam vestram*), suggesting that a general council would best judge the dispute between him and the pope. Gregory wrote on 7 April 1239 (*Sedes apostolica*), decrying the emperor's lack of gratitude for the church; the pope furthermore declared an interdict on any place where the emperor might reside. On 20 April 1239 Frederick published two letters. In the first (*Levate in circuitu*) to the imperial princes, he decried Gregory's support for Lombard rebels, his personal unworthiness for office and jurisdiction, and his support for heretical Milan. The pope was called the *author schismatis et amicus erroris*. The emperor again suggested that the cardinals convoke a general council to decide matters between him and Gregory, permitting the emperor an opportunity to defend himself. Finally, he reminded the princes that wrongs committed against him touched them as well. In the second letter (*Cum Roma sit*), this one to the Romans, the emperor called the pope *blasphemator noster* and requested assistance.

Gregory responded forcefully; his encyclical (variously dated 21 June/1 July 1239) *Ascendit de mare bestia* called Frederick the monster of blasphemy (*bestia blasphemie*, beast of the Apocalypse), a heretic, and a precursor of the Antichrist. The pope further charged that the emperor not only had rejected Christ's virgin birth, but even had maintained that the world had been deluded by three charlatans: Moses, Jesus, and Mohammed.

In July 1239 Frederick wrote *In exordio nascentis* to the cardinals; this letter contained both a confession of his Catholic faith and a vigorous defense against *Ascendit*. The emperor called the pope the false vicar of Christ and a pharisee seated on the chair of perverse dogma, anointed with the oil of wickedness. But the conflict was not solely fought on parchment.

Gregory was now in formal alliance with Genoa, Venice, Milan, and Piacenza. For his part, Frederick hermetically sealed the Regno off from the rest of Italy, expelled both Franciscans and Dominicans from the kingdom, and occupied the papal enclave of Benevento. The threat of interdict was nullified by the emperor's counterthreat to expropriate any who should heed it. Frederick's forces next invaded papal territories in the Marches and Spoleto (summer of 1239) and annexed them to the empire; he subsequently (winter of 1240) occupied Tuscany as well. The emperor's division of the peninsula north of the Regno into imperial vicariates and his movements against Rome itself underscored not only his determination to control all Italy, but also his oft-expressed opinion that the city was "head and origin" of the empire.

The pope did not lose heart in this perilous situation. Both his dramatic procession through the city on 22 February 1240 with relics of Peter and Paul and his appeal to the saints to protect Rome, if the inhabitants did not, energized support among the Romans to defend their homes. His legate Gregory of Montelongo continued to rally resistance against the emperor in Lombardy and in the Romagna.

But the picture north of the Alps provided little hope. Even before Frederick's second excommunication Gregory's legate Albert von Behaim had attempted in vain to construct an alliance hostile to the emperor between King Wenceslas I of Bohemia, Duke Otto II of Bavaria, and Duke Frederick II of Austria. After the 1239 papal excommunication the legate strove to capitalize on this penalty, but he instead aroused resistance from many secular and ecclesiastical princes. The legate finally tried to raise up an antiking in Germany, but no likely prospect could be induced to accept the offer. At the behest of the imperial princes some peace negotiations occurred during late 1239 and early 1240, but these eventually failed due to Gregory's insistence and Frederick's refusal to include the rebellious Lombards in any negotiated truce.

During January and February 1240 the emperor's forces invaded papal territories once again, but withdrew in March. On 16 March 1240 Frederick issued the encyclical *Triplex doloris aculeus*, which contained a litany of all of the injuries suffered by him at the hands of the pope, his associates, and his allies. In June 1240 imperial forces once again massed at the borders of the Patrimony of St. Peter. In his contemporary manifesto (*Collegerunt pontifices*) Frederick described the pontiff as a rapacious wolf, a deaf asp, and a lover of schism. Gregory replied with *Convenerunt in unum*, wherein he called Frederick the Antichrist, a basilisk, the Fallen Angel, a rapacious wolf, a beast-made-man, and a dragon. The emperor was further charged with the invasion of Petrine lands, contempt for the pope and clergy, the creation of an unsatisfactory situation within the Sicilian kingdom and the Holy Land, the loss of Jerusalem, and preferential treatment of heretics.

Thereupon Gregory summoned (9 August 1240) a general council to meet in Rome on the following Easter Sunday (1241) to deal with important matters affecting the church, that is, in other words, to judge the emperor. Frederick protested without effect against the calling of this council to the kings of England and France (Henry III and Louis IX), other princes, and loyal imperial subjects. Furthermore, he declared that he would offer no safe-conduct for potential participants in such a synod.

In December 1240 the pope concluded a treaty with the Genoese to transport transmontane participants by sea to the council. The synod's convocation was, however, sabotaged by the emperor's and Pisa's naval forces, which on 3 May 1241 southeast of Elba near the island of Montecristo decisively defeated the Genoese fleet transporting many of the French and Spanish prelates en route to the council, sinking three ships, capturing twenty-two others, and allowing only three to escape. Several of the prospective council participants perished, while about one hundred others were captured, two papal legates (James of Praeneste and Otto Candidus) among them. The prisoners were placed in confinement in Apulia, although the French subjects among them were eventually liberated at Louis IX's insistent request. The council was thus aborted, but Frederick's success soon boomeranged, for in the eyes of public opinion he no longer possessed the excuse that he fought merely against Gregory as an enemy, and not against the church as a whole.

During 1241 both pope and emperor were distracted by the appalling Mongol invasion of Eastern Europe and the consequent threat to Germany. Gregory proclaimed a crusade against the Asiatic invader and offered the same dispensation as for crusaders to the Holy Land. There were even some attempts at peacemaking during June 1241 sponsored by the English crusader Richard of Cornwall, but they came to naught due to the pope's demand for Frederick's unconditional submission. During July and August imperial forces once again closed in on Rome. Gregory responded with what would prove to be his final broadside (*Vox in Rama*). In apocalyptic tones he called Frederick the "vicar of the Ancient Dragon," who attacks the church, the Bride of Christ. To the standard list of the emperor's crimes some new ones were added, such as mistreatment of the people, bishop, and town of Benevento, bribery of the Romans to acts of disloyalty, and the capture and imprisonment of the hapless would-be conciliar prelates in the "dungeons of Pharaoh."

Gregory died in Rome on 21 or 22 August 1241 and was buried in St. Peter's Basilica. This signaled the end of Frederick's conflict with this particular pope, but not—as the pontificate of Gregory's eventual successor Innocent IV would show—with the papacy as such. At the great pontiff's death imperial forces were ordered by Frederick to withdraw to the Regno to await the imminent papal election and further events. Gregory IX personified the many faces of the medieval papacy. On the one hand, he was masterful, energetic, persistent, courageous, temperamental, tough, and at times unscrupulous. On the other hand, he was learned, devout, and mystical. Always mindful of past tradition, he was nevertheless sensitive to the cultural, political, and spiritual currents of his time. He had a taste for ceremony and hierarchy; he showed skill in arbitration, legislation, and administration. He earned both the admiration and animosity of his contemporaries. The devoted friend of Francis of Assisi as well as the unyielding opponent of Frederick II, he was a figure of epic and dramatic proportions.

SELECTED BIBLIOGRAPHY

Armstrong, Regis J. " 'Mira circa nos': Gregory IX's View of Saint Francis of Assisi." *Laurentianum* 25 (1984): 385–414.

Aubert, R. "Grégoire IX." In *Dictionnaire d'histoire et de géographie ecclésiastiques*. Paris: Letouzey & Ané, 1986, 21: 1437–38.

Auvray, Lucien, ed. *Les Registres de Grégoire IX: Recueil des bulles de ce Pape*. 4 vols. (final volume completed by Mme. Vitte-Clemencet and Louis Carolus-Barre). Bibliothèque des Écoles françaises d'Athènes et de Rome, 2e série. Paris: A. Fontemoing, 1896–1910, 1955.

Balan, Pietro. *Storia di Gregorio IX e dei suoi tempi*. 3 vols. Modena, 1872–73.

Bonmann, O. "Gregor IX." In *Lexikon für Theologie und Kirche*. Freiburg im Breisgau: Herder, 1960, 4:1186–87.

Brooke, Rosalind. *Early Franciscan Government: Elias to Bonaventure*. Cambridge: Cambridge University Press, 1959.

Esser, Kajetan. "Die Briefe Gregors IX. an die heilige Klara von Assisi." *Franziskanische Studien* 35 (1953): 274–95.

Fehling, Ferdinand. *Kaiser Friedrich II. und die römischen Kardinäle in den Jahren 1227 bis 1239*. Berlin, 1901.

Felten, Joseph. *Papst Gregor IX*. Freiburg im Breisgau, 1886.

Flood, David. "The Politics of 'Quo elongati.' " *Laurentianum* 29 (1988): 370–85.

Franzen, August, and Remigius Bäumer. *Papstgeschichte*. Freiburg in Breisgau, 1974, 206–11.

Grabmann, Martin. *I divieti ecclesiastici di Aristotele sotto Innocenzo III e Gregorio IX*. Miscellanea Historiae Pontificiae 5, coll. 7. Rome, 1941, 70–133.

Graefe, Friedrich. *Die Publizistik in der letzten Epoche Kaiser Friedrichs II*. Heidelberg, 1909.

"Gregorius IX papa." In *Repertorium fontium historiae Medii Aevi*, vol. 5. *Fontes*. Rome: Istituto storico italiano per il Medio Evo, 1984, 231–32.

Gross, Walter. *Die Revolutionen in der Stadt Rom, 1219–1254*. Berlin: Vaduz, 1934, 7–60.

Grundmann, Herbert. "Die Bulle 'Quo elongati' Papst Gregors IX." *Archivum franciscanum historicum* 54 (1961):3–25.

Holder-Egger, O., ed. *Philippi de Perusio Epistola de cardinalibus protectoribus Ordinis fratrum minorum*. Monumenta Germaniae Historica, Scriptorum (in folio) 32. Hannover and Leipzig: Hahn, 1913, 680–81.

Huillard-Bréholles, J.-L.-A. *Historia diplomatica Friderici Secundi*, vols. 3, 4, and 5, parts 1 and 2. Paris: Plon, 1852–59.

Jelicic, Vitomirus. "De mente Gregorii IX in adornanda collectione Decretalium." In *Acta congressus iuridici internationalis vii saeculo a decretalibus Gregorii IX et xiv a codice Iustiniano promulgatis*, vol. 3. Rome: Libraria Pontificio Instituti Utrisque Iuris, 1936, 3–20.

Joelson, Olga. *Die Papstwahlen des 13. Jahrhunderts bis zur Einführung der Conclaveordnung Gregors X.* Berlin: Ebering, 1928, 5–18.

Ladner, Gerhart B. *Die Papstbildnisse des Altertums und des Mittelalters*, vol. 2. Vatican City: Pontificio Instituto di Archeologia Christiana, 1970, 97–111.

Levi, Guido. "Documenti ad illustrazione del Registro del Card. Ugolino d'Ostia legato apostolico in Toscana e Lombardia." *Archivio della Società romana di storia patria* 12 (1889): 241–326.

Maleczek, Werner. *Papst und Kardinalskolleg von 1191 bis 1216: Die Kardinäle unter Coelestin III. und Innocenz III.* Vienna: Osterreichsche Akademie der Wissenschaften, 1984.

Mann, Horace K. *The Lives of the Popes in the Middle Ages*. Vol. 13. London and St. Louis: Kegan Paul, Trench, Trubner and Co., 1925, 165–441.

Manselli, Raoul. "Federico II e Gregorio IX: Appunti d'una ricerca." *Studi storici meridionali* 2 (1982): 3–14.

Marchetti Longhi, Giuseppe. "Ricerche su la famiglia di papa Gregorio IX." *Archivio della Deputazione romana di storia patria* 67 [n.s., 10] (1944): 275–307.

Michaud-Quantin, Pierre. "Remarques sur l'oeuvre législative de Grégoire IX." In *Études d'histoire du droit canonique dédiées à Gabriel Le Bras*, vol. 1. Paris: 1965, 273–81.

Moorman, John. *A History of the Franciscan Order from Its Origins to the Year 1517*. Oxford: Clarendon Press, 1968.

Potthast, A., ed. *Regesta pontificum romanorum* Vol. 1. Berlin, 1874. Reprint, Graz: De Decker, 1957, pp. 681–937, nn. 7862–11073.

Powell, James M. "Frederick II and the Church: A Revisionist View." *Catholic Historical Review* 48 (1963): 487–97.

Roberg, B. "Gregor IX." In *Lexikon des Mittelalters*. Munich and Zürich: Artemis Verlag, 1989, 4:1671–72.

Rodenberg, Carolus, ed. *Epistolae saeculi XIII e regestris pontificum romanorum selectae*. Vol. 1. Monumenta Germaniae Historica. Berlin: Veit et Socius, 1883, 261–728, 730–39.

Schaller, Hans Martin. "Das letzte Rundschreiben Gregors IX. gegen Friedrich II." In *Festschrift Percy Ernst Schramm*, ed. Peter Classen and Peter Scheibert. Wiesbaden: F. Steiner, 1964, 309–21.

Segl, Peter. "Gregor IX., die Regensburger Dominikaner, und die Anfänge der 'Inquisition' in Deutschland." In *Regensburg, Bayern, und Europa: Festschrift für Kurt Reindel zum 70. Geburtstag*, ed. Lothar Kolmer and Peter Segl. Regensburg: Universitatverlag, 1995, 307–19.

Selge, Kurt-Viktor. "Franz von Assisi und die römische Kurie." *Zeitschrift für Theologie und Kirche* 67 (1970): 129–61.

Spence, Richard. "Gregory IX's Attempted Expeditions to the Latin Empire of Constantinople." *Journal of Medieval History* 5 (1979): 163–76.

———. "Pope Gregory IX and the Crusade on the Baltic." *Catholic Historical Review* 69 (1983): 1–19.

Spirito, Silvana. "Étude sur deux protagonistes du mouvement franciscain au XIIIe siècle: Gregoire IX et Frère Élie." *Etudes franciscaines* 13 (1963): 181–99.

Thomson, Williel R. "The Earliest Cardinal-Protectors of the Franciscan Order: A Study in Administrative History." *Studies in Medieval and Renaissance History* 9 (1972): 39–52.

Van den Gheyn, J. "Lettre de Grégoire IX concernant l'empire latin de Constantinople." *Revue de l'orient latin* 9 (1902): 230–34.

Vita Gregorii papae IX. ex altero ms. Bibliothecae Ambrosianae. Ed. L.A. Muratori. In *Rerum italicarum scriptores*, vol. 3, 1. Milan: Typ. Societatis Palatinae, 1723, 574–75.

Vita Gregrorii papae IX. ex cardinali aragonio. Ed. L.A. Muratori. In *Rerum italicarum scriptores*, vol. 3, 1. Milan: Typ. Societatis Palatinae, 1723, 575–87. Reprinted in Paul Fabre and Louis Duchesne, *Le Liber censuum de l'eglise romaine*, vol. 2. Paris: 1910, 19–36.

Vita Gregrorii papae IX. ex ms. Bernardi Guidonis. Ed. L.A. Muratori. In *Rerum italicarum scriptores*, vol. 3, pt. 1. Milan: Typ. Societatis Palatinae, 1723, 570–74.

Wenck, Karl. "Die heilige Elisabeth und Papst Gregor IX." *Hochland: Monatsschrift für alle Gebiete des Wissens der Literatur, und Kunst* 1 (1903–4): 129–47.

Zarncke, Lilly. *Der Anteil des Kardinals Ugolino an der Ausbildung der Drei Orden des Heiligen Franz*. Leipzig and Berlin, 1930.

Zöllig, Benedikt. *Die Beziehungen des Kardinals Hugolino zum heil. Franziskus und zu seinem I. Orden*. Münster in Westfalen, 1934.

INNOCENT IV
(1243–54)

Thomas F. Madden

Sinibaldo Fieschi was born in Genoa, the fifth son of Count Ugo of Lavagna. He pursued his early studies at Parma, where his uncle was bishop, and soon became a canon of the cathedral there. Later, Fieschi went to the University of Bologna, where he studied Roman and canon law. Under the patronage of Cardinal Ugolino dei Conti di Segni (later Pope Gregory IX [1227–41]), Fieschi moved to Rome and was rapidly promoted in the papal curia. In 1226 he was appointed auditor. The following year Gregory IX made him a cardinal and vice-chancellor of the Holy See. In 1235 he was named rector of the March of Ancona. Besides his duties in the curia, Sinibaldo Fieschi remained a devoted student of law. He published many sophisticated legal tracts, including the *Apparatus*, a commentary on the *Decretals* of Gregory IX. His application of canon law throughout his pontificate was rigorous. He is perhaps best known for his attack on corporate excommunications, which punished the innocent for their proximity to the guilty.

The election of Sinibaldo Fieschi to the pontificate did not proceed immediately after the death of his predecessor. Pope Celestine IV had occupied the throne of St. Peter for less than a month when he died on 21 November 1241. His election had been a nightmare. Two of the cardinals were held captive by Frederick II, and the rest were imprisoned by the senator of Rome, Matteo Orsini, who demanded that they elect a candidate acceptable to him. The terrible living conditions that Orsini imposed on the captive cardinals in Rome proved fatal to one of them. It is no wonder, then, that when the death of Celestine IV was announced, five cardinals immediately fled Rome, taking up residence in the pope's summer palace at Anagni or in fortified positions elsewhere. Cardinal Giovanni Colonna, an open supporter of Frederick II, was arrested by Matteo Orsini before he could make his escape. Two other cardinals, one of whom was Sinibaldo Fieschi, remained in Rome. Two more, James of Palestrina and Otto of St. Nicholas, were still held captive by the emperor. Fieschi repeatedly called the cardinals back to Rome for an election, but to no avail. Frederick would not release his prisoners unless he was certain that a friendly pope would be elected. Orsini felt the same. The cardinals not languishing in jail cells refused to meet unless their colleagues were released and they could be assured of a free election. Eighteen months of stalemate began.

Frederick II was still under the ban of excommunication imposed by Gregory IX. He was determined that the next pope would be, from his point of view, more reasonable. If that meant that Christendom would have to survive without a pope for an extended period, so much the better. Yet as the months passed, pressure was building on Frederick to act. King Louis IX of France urged him to free his captives so that the rift between empire and papacy could be healed and Christendom could unite to fight its external enemies. Baldwin of Constantinople, who was desperate for aid to prop up his teetering empire, also begged Frederick to end the stalemate so that a new crusade could be called. Frederick acquiesced, at least partially. In August 1242 he released Cardinal Otto of St. Nicholas. Louis IX wrote to the other cardinals calling on them to do their duty and end the interregnum. According to Matthew Paris (who is by no means always reliable), the French clergy went so far as to threaten to elect a pope themselves if the cardinals would not get on with it. For his part, Frederick and his armies stepped up their attacks on papal territories near Rome. Still, the cardinals refused to meet until the emperor released Cardinal James of Palestrina.

In May 1243 Frederick was forced by public opinion to release his last captive cardinal and withdraw from the neighborhood of Rome. Once all the cardinals were assembled at Anagni, they wasted no time in electing Sinibaldo Fieschi on 25 June 1243. Despite his close association with Gregory IX, Fieschi had managed to remain on relatively friendly terms with Frederick II. He was a compromise: a new pope who could make peace with the emperor without compromising papal authority. By taking the name Innocent, Fieschi proclaimed his hope that he would proceed in that state, yet his choice was also surely meant to raise the specter of Innocent III to all those who would trample the rights of the church. Frederick received the news of the election with joy, expressing the desire to work out a peace with Innocent as soon as possible.

The emperor did not have long to wait. Within weeks of his election Innocent's envoys arrived in Frederick's court to negotiate peace. Frederick's greatest crime was the capture, imprisonment, and in some cases murder of a great many prelates, including bishops and cardinals, on their way to a council called by Gregory IX. In addition, Frederick had seized papal lands. The pope's envoys insisted that any peace must include reparation for these injuries to the church. If Frederick considered himself innocent of some or all of the crimes, they said, then the matter could be decided by a committee of clergy and princes. The envoys pointed out, however, that while the pope was willing to negotiate, he was not willing to abandon the Lombards who had rebelled against Frederick in support of the church. During the winter of 1243–44 Innocent received imperial envoys with counterproposals. With great effort, a peace plan was hammered out.

On Holy Thursday (31 March 1244) the papal curia, imperial representatives, and delegates from the Lombard towns assembled in Rome and announced the details of a peace settlement. It was agreed that the territorial map would return to its state before Frederick's excommunication in 1239. In addition, the emperor promised to make restitution for his capture of the prelates, undertake substantial works of charity, forgive those who had rebelled against him, and supply money and troops to princes whom the pope would later designate. The last condition was meant to provide support for Louis IX and his forming crusade, Baldwin of Constantinople, and German princes defending against the Tartars. In return for these concessions and acts of penance, Frederick would receive papal absolution.

Detail of fresco of Pope Innocent IV by Taddo Gaddi. (Courtesy of the Vatican Library)

The peace agreement was troubled from its very beginning. Shortly after it had been signed, Innocent demanded that Frederick return the papal lands that he had taken. Frederick replied that he was very willing to do so, but insisted that the pope first give him his absolution. That was impossible, Innocent replied, since without penance and tangible proof of repentance there could be no absolution. For the sake of peace the cardinals urged the pope to waive this objection and absolve Frederick. Baldwin of Constantinople, who was eager to return with imperial troops, also supported immediate absolution. But Innocent had too often seen Frederick receive papal favors in return for empty promises. He would not allow him to do so again.

With both sides unwilling to budge, Frederick suggested a face-to-face meeting. Innocent agreed. The two were to meet at Narni, just north of

Rome. In late May and early June both parties were converging on the city. On 7 June Innocent stopped at Civita Castellana. Word had reached the pope that Frederick had made plans to capture him. Innocent sent word to Genoa of his situation and asked his kinsmen there to send galleys to Civitavecchia so that he could make his escape. The galleys arrived almost three weeks later, on 27 June. On that day Innocent traveled to Sutri, where he ordered the cathedral to prepare for his celebration of the feast of SS. Peter and Paul on 29 June. In reality, the pope had no intention of attending. On the night of 28 June Innocent, disguised and accompanied by a few friends, rode out of Sutri. They arrived in Civitavecchia the following day. On 30 June Innocent boarded the waiting galleys and sailed for Genoa.

Innocent's reasons for failing to make the rendezvous at Narni have been variously argued. Some have suggested that at Narni Innocent foresaw another Canossa. In a face-to-face meeting Frederick could make a grand show of contrition, forcing Innocent into administering absolution in return for mere words. Those who view Innocent in the darkest terms believe that the pope wanted more from Frederick than the peace agreement promised. A meeting with the emperor would make that impossible. The scholarly defenders of Frederick, however, are forced to ignore or explain away the numerous sources that testify that Frederick was bringing armed men to capture the pope. If Innocent wished to avoid a meeting with the emperor, why then did he agree to it? If he planned to flee all along (as some argue), why did it take three weeks to arrange for boats to make his escape? Given Frederick's repeated use of kidnapping as a means of controlling the church, Innocent later explained, it is no wonder that he fled when he heard of the emperor's plans.

Innocent's escape was plagued by storms at sea, but he finally made it to Genoa on 6 July. He was very ill and would remain so for three months. In early October the pope left for Lyons, where he arrived on 2 December 1244. Lyons, "the first see of the Gauls," would host the pope and the curia for the next seven years.

On 27 December Innocent IV proclaimed a general council, the thirteenth ecumenical council, which would meet in Lyons on 24 June 1245. This was to be the council planned by Gregory IX but prohibited by Frederick II's capture of prelates traveling to Rome to attend. The call for the council captured the attention of the emperor, who now professed that he was willing to abide by the previous peace agreement. Yet when Innocent replied that Frederick should first return captured church lands, the emperor responded by increasing his arrests of papal adherents, including relatives of the pope. Given Frederick's refusal to honor his promises with anything other than words, in April 1245 Innocent renewed the excommunication of the emperor.

On 26 June 1245 the Council of Lyons was convened. Innocent opened the council by recounting the grievous threats to Christendom: the peril of the Latin Empire, the fall of Jerusalem, the invasion of the Mongols, and the persecution of Frederick II. In attendance were representatives from the Latin East, as well as Emperor Baldwin, and the patriarchs of Constantinople, Antioch, and Aquileia. Frederick had convened a diet in Verona, so he was not present at Lyons, but he did send the eloquent Taddeo da Suessa as his representative.

When the council turned its attention to Frederick, Innocent listed the emperor's numerous crimes, including waging war against the church, seizing its lands, capturing and murdering prelates, heresy, and tyranny over the Sicilian church. Taddeo da Suessa responded to the charges by extolling Frederick's character and ascribing the disputes to misunderstandings. The emperor was eager to abide by the peace treaty, he said, if a papal absolution was forthcoming. Once he had been absolved, Taddeo da Suessa assured the council, Frederick would prepare to lead three separate crusades: one each to Jerusalem, Constantinople, and Hungary. Innocent responded that such promises were made of straw; that Frederick had made similar oaths all of his life and had shown himself faithless in keeping them. Taddeo proposed, then, that the council delay its decision until Frederick could be there in person. The charge of heresy, he reminded the council, required examination. Frederick was not far, he said, and could be in Lyons in a matter of days. Innocent agreed, a fact that cripples theories that the pope wished to avoid a direct meeting with the emperor. Innocent gave Frederick twelve days to appear before the council. The emperor's bluff was called. Unable to bring troops into Lyons to make his case, he thought it best to avoid the whole thing entirely. When the emperor failed to appear, Taddeo da Suessa could do nothing but ask for additional delays. The council had waited long enough. On 17 July the pope deposed Frederick II. Shortly thereafter he proclaimed crusades against all of the enemies of Christ, including the German emperor. From the moment of Frederick's deposition, Innocent turned his attentions to the construction of a new order of Christendom, one without an emperor.

Frederick turned again to Louis IX of France. The war in Germany between Innocent's nominee for king of Germany, Henry Raspe, and those loyal to Frederick was draining recruits from Louis's forming crusade. If Louis could convince Innocent to absolve Frederick, the emperor promised to assist in Louis's holy enterprise. Louis and Innocent met at Cluny on 30 November 1245, but nothing substantial came of it. This was, however, the first time that the cardinals appeared in the new red hats that would signify their status for centuries. In May 1246 the archbishop of Palermo traveled to Lyons and proclaimed that he had examined Frederick for heresy and had found none. Innocent was not willing to accept this assessment, but he did again extend an offer to examine Frederick himself if he would come to Lyons and administer absolution if he showed contrition. Frederick was willing to come to Lyons, but not unarmed, and not to show contrition. Shortly after the death of Henry Raspe, in May 1247, Frederick assembled his troops and began marching toward Lyons. Quickly Innocent turned to Louis IX, who swore to protect the pope with French troops if necessary. It never came to that. Before Frederick could reach Lyons, he received news of the revolt of Parma.

Frederick's siege of Parma was difficult and long, and it took its toll on the aged man. While it dragged on, Frederick ordered the construction of an entirely new capital city within view of Parma. Victoria, as Frederick named it, was hurriedly built. As befitted an imperial capital, it became the new home of the imperial treasury, crown, and menagerie. Yet it lacked imperial fortifications. On 18 February 1248, while Frederick was hunting, the citizens of Parma attacked Victoria, seized its wealth, and burned it to the ground. Taddeo da Suessa was killed in the assault. Frederick abandoned the siege. When he heard the news, Innocent exclaimed, "Oh Victory, for the honor of Christ, you have been vanquished!"

Frederick, too, had been vanquished. His health was broken, although his pride remained intact. On 13 December 1250 he died. He apparently received absolution, albeit noncanonically, from the archbishop of Palermo. According to Matthew Paris, Frederick followed a Byzantine custom and became a monk just before his death. In his will he left a sizable sum for a future crusade and ordered that all he had taken from the church be returned. Had he done the same a few years earlier, he would have received the papal absolution he so desired.

Frederick had left his son Conrad as heir to Sicily and the empire. Since Conrad was engaged in Germany, Manfred, an illegitimate son, was designated regent in Italy until Conrad's return. Innocent was unwilling to accept this arrangement. Sicily was a papal fief, and Frederick was by no means a good vassal. Innocent had no intention of letting the Hohenstaufens retain these lands. Furthermore, the kingship of Germany was an elective position, and Innocent had his own nominee, William of Holland. During Holy Week 1251 William of Holland came to Lyons and led the papal horse. Innocent then left Lyons, heading ultimately back to Rome. In January 1252 Conrad arrived in Sicily and established firm control. Since he was unwilling to submit his claim to the pope, Innocent excommunicated Conrad and began searching for powerful lords to take over the region. He first offered it to Richard, earl of Cornwall, the brother of Henry III of England, who refused it. Then Innocent tried to entice Charles of Anjou, the brother of Louis IX of France. Charles was fascinated by the offer, and negotiations began, but in the end Louis's advisors forced Charles to decline. In October 1253 Naples, which had rebelled after Frederick's death, fell to Conrad. Innocent was desperate. He offered the crown of Sicily to the child Edmund, the second son of the king of England. Henry III accepted the title, but it was never more than that.

English nobles were lukewarm about the idea of involvement so far from home, so the whole project foundered and died. Despite numerous appeals for action from the pope, Henry never lifted a finger to defend his son's title.

On 21 May 1254 Conrad died at the age of twenty-four. The serious threat to the church evaporated. Conradin, who was only two, was designated by his father to be heir of Sicily and the empire and was committed to the care of the pope until he came of age. Innocent was willing to accept Conradin, but not his claims. Manfred and Conradin's regent, Berthold of Hohenburg, were at first reluctant to place Sicily in Innocent's hands, but at last relented. A few months later Innocent entered into the Kingdom of Sicily as its overlord. Manfred welcomed the pope and showed him every deference. Innocent traveled across the kingdom in a magnificent triumphal procession. This was his greatest victory, but it was short lived. Shortly after Innocent left the kingdom, Manfred rebelled against the pope, proclaiming himself as its heir. The armies of the pope marched south to crush the rebellion, but they were decisively defeated on 2 December 1254. A few days later, on 7 December, Innocent IV died in Naples.

SELECTED BIBLIOGRAPHY

Abulafia, David. *Frederick II: A Medieval Emperor*. London: Allen Lane, The Penguin Press, 1988.

Berger, É., ed. *Les Registres d'Innocent IV*. 4 vols. Paris, 1884–[1920].

———. *Saint Louis et Innocent IV: Étude sur les rapports de la France et du Saint-Siège*. Paris: 1893.

Burns, R.I. "A Lost Crusade: Unpublished Bulls of Innocent IV on Al-Azraq's Revolt in Thirteenth-Century Spain." *Catholic Historical Review* 74 (1988): 440–49.

Dehio, L. *Innozenz IV. und England: Ein Beitrag zur Kirchengeschichte des 13. Jahrhunderts*. Berlin: G.J. Goschensche Verlagshandlung, 1913.

Deslandres, P. *Innocent IV et la chute des Hohenstaufen*. Paris: 1907.

De Stefano, A. *L'idea imperiale di Federico II*. Florence, 1927.

Franchi, A. *La svolta politico-ecclesiastica tra Roma e Bisanzio (1249–1254)*. Rome, 1981.

Guerello, F. *Lettere di Innocenzo IV dai cartolari notarili genovesi*. Rome: Pontificia Univestia Gregoriana, 1961.

Haluscunskyi, Th., and M.M. Vojnar, eds. *Acta Innocentii PP. IV (1243–1254)*. Rome, 1962.

Hampe, K. "Aus verlorenen Registerbänden der Papste Innocenz III. und Innocenz IV." *Mitteilungen des Instituts für Osterreichische Geschichtsforschung* 23 (1902): 545–67; 24 (1903): 198–237.

Haskins, C. "Two Roman Formularies in Philadelphia." In *Miscellanea Francesco Ehrle*, vol. 4. Rome, 1924, 275–86.

Hauréau, M.B., ed. "Quelques lettres d'Innocent IV extraites des manuscrits de la Bibliothèque nationale." *Notices et extraits des manuscrits de la Bibliothèque nationale* 24 (1876): 157–246.

Huillard-Bréholles, J.-L.-A. *Historia diplomatica Friderici Secundi.* 6 vols. Paris, 1852–61.

Kantorowicz, Ernst. *Kaiser Friedrich der Zweite.* Berlin, 1931.

Mann, H.K. "Innocent IV, the Magnificent, 1243–1254." In *The Lives of the Popes in the Middle Ages*, vol. 14. London: Kegan Paul, Trench, Trubnes and Co., 1928.

Matthew Paris. *Chronica Majora.* Ed. H.R. Luard. 7 vols. Rolls Series. London: Longman & Company, 1872–84.

———. *Historia anglorum, sive, ut vulgo dictitur, Historia Minora.* Ed. F. Madden. 3 vols. Rolls Series. London: Longmans, Green, Reader, and Dyer, 1866–69.

Melloni, Alberto. *Innocenzo IV: La concezione e l'esperienza della cristianità come "regimen unius personae."* Genoa, 1990.

Pacaut, M. "L'Autorité pontificale selon Innocent IV." *Moyen âge* 66 (1960): 85–119.

Pagnotti, F., ed. "Niccolò da Calvi e la sua Vita d'Innocenzo IV con una breve introduzione sulla istoriografia pontificia dei secoli XIII e XIV." *Archivio della Società romana di storia patria* 21 (1898): 7–120.

Pansa, P. *Vita del gran pontefice Innocenzio Quarto scritta già da Paolo Pansa Genovese e da Tommaso Costa corretta e migliorata.* Naples: G. Carlino, 1601.

Podestà, F. *Papa Innocenzo IV.* Milan, 1928.

Powell, James M. "Frederick II and the Church: A Revisionist View." *Catholic Historical Review* 48 (1963): 487–97.

Puttkamer, G. von. *Papst Innocenzo IV.* Münster: Helios-Verlag, 1930.

Quintana Prieto, A. *La documentación pontificia de Inocencio IV (1243–1254)*, 2 vols. Rome: Instituto Espanol de Historia Eclesiastica, 1987.

Rodenberg, Carolus, ed. *Epistolae saeculi XIII e regestis pontificum romanorum selectae.* 3 vols. Berlin: 1883–1894, reprinted, Munich: Weidmann, 1982.

Salimbene. *Cronica.* Ed. G. Scalia. Scrittori d'Italia. Bari: G. Laterza, 1966.

Setton, Kenneth M. *The Papacy and the Levant (1204–157).* 4 vols. Philadelphia: American Philosophical Society, 1976, 1: 68–77.

Ullmann, Walter. "Frederick II's Opponent: Innocent IV as Melchisedek." In *Atti del Convegno internationale di studi federiciani.* Palermo: A. Renna, 1952, 53–81.

Van Cleve, T.C. *The Emperor Frederick II of Hohenstaufen, Immutator Mundi.* Oxford: Clarendon Press, 1972.

Watt, J.A. "The Theory of Papal Monarchy in the Thirteenth Century: The Contribution of the Canonists." *Traditio* 20 (1964): 179–317.

BONIFACE VIII (1294–1303): ABLE ADMINISTRATOR, IMPRUDENT POLITICIAN

RICHARD KAY

About 1235 the future pope was born Benedict Caetani (Gaetani), the younger son of a minor noble family in the small town of Anagni, thirty miles southeast of Rome, where he became a canon of the cathedral in his teens. But in 1252, when his uncle Peter Caetani became bishop of Todi, eighty miles to the north, Benedict went with him and began his legal studies, eventually acquiring a canonry there in 1260, not to mention the small nearby castle of Sismano. He never forgot his origins; in later life he repeatedly expressed his gratitude to Anagni, Todi, and especially the Caetani family. Probably he acquired most of his training in Roman and canon law in and around Todi, for he later described his study at Bologna as brief.

By 1264 he was a trusted member of the Roman curia, serving as secretary to Cardinal Simon of Brie on a mission to France. Similarly, he accompanied Cardinal Ottobono Fieschi to England (1265–68) and, after some years of inconspicuous employment, was sent to France to supervise the collection of a tithe in 1276 and was made a papal notary in the late 1270s. Meanwhile, he had accumulated some seventeen benefices, which he was permitted to keep when he was promoted, first to cardinal-deacon in 1281 and then to cardinal-priest in 1291. As cardinal, he often served as papal legate in diplomatic negotiations with France, Naples, Sicily, and Aragon.

In 1294, after a deadlock of twenty-seven months, the cardinals compromised on Peter of Morrone, a holy but illiterate hermit, as their new pope, Celestine V. Benedict became his most trusted advisor. When, after five months of capricious and incompetent government, Celestine wished to resign, it was Benedict who assured him that canon law permitted a pope to abdicate. The cardinals promptly elected Benedict Caetani himself as the next pope, Boniface VIII (24 December 1294).

With thirty years of experience in the curia, the new pope was at his best in introducing changes in its administration. The archives were re-organized and the library cataloged. The government of the Papal States was modified to improve relations between the communes and papal of-ficials. He founded the University of Rome (La Sapienza) and refounded the one at Avignon (1303). But most important, Boniface commissioned the first supplement to the *Decretals* of Gregory IX, which collected papal decrees issued since 1234 as the sixth book of *Decretals* and hence was known as the *Liber sextus* (published in 1298). Yet Boniface was not one of the great canonists. He lacked creative imagination; instead, his legal talent was for harmonizing existing laws and moderating them, and this he did extensively and effectively. For example, he defended the secular clergy from the mendicants (*Super cathedram*) and provided for their ed-ucation (*Cum ex eo*). Although he seems to have written his most important decretals himself, he took care to ensure their legal validity by discussing them with the cardinals.

If Boniface had done nothing else, he would be remembered as an en-ergetic, practical pope, but not as an outstanding one. He differs from most popes in his attempt to give practical effect to the exalted conception of the papal prerogatives that theologians and especially canon lawyers had developed over the last century. In this he was essentially a lawyer seeking to establish precedents by forcing the secular monarchs to acknowledge their subjection to the papacy "by reason of sin" (*ratione peccati*), so that the pope could judge a sinful ruler and eventually depose him if he did not repent. Boniface most notably insisted on his rights, however, not on principle but to get revenge for being humiliated by King Philip IV the Fair of France in their first conflict (1296–97).

War broke out in 1294 between England and France, and to support it, both Edward I and Philip IV taxed their clergy. Both the abbot of Cîteaux and the archbishop of Canterbury protested to Boniface, who responded with the bull *Clericis laicos* (24 February 1296), which forbade laymen from taxing the clergy without papal permission. In England the king quickly broke all resistance by outlawing the clergy, and the archbishop neatly avoided a confrontation by leaving compliance up to the conscience of individual clerics. But in France the crisis was more acute, for Philip the Fair brought financial pressure to bear on the curia by prohibiting the export of money from France, much of which would benefit Boniface, and by expelling all foreign merchants, including the pope's bankers. Boniface realized that he had overextended himself and in a succession of bulls gradually backed down. First, he allowed clergy to loan money to the

Crown for the defense of the realm; next, he authorized clerical financial aids to subsidize a just war; and finally, he declared that the secular ruler was to be the judge of whether his war was really a just one (*Etsi de statu*, August 1297). Despite these concessions, the next year he included *Clericis laicos* in the *Liber sextus*.

Boniface lost because he had overextended himself, not only by taking on England and France together, but also by simultaneously making war on the Colonna family. His passion to aggrandize his own family, the Caetani, was the cause. For more than twenty years he had been buying land for his relatives, and increasingly the Caetani came to compete with the Colonna for properties in the Roman Campagna. In May 1297 the Colonna forestalled one of Boniface's acquisitions by hijacking the convoy bearing money for the purchase. Boniface overreacted, first by deposing the two Colonna cardinals, James and Peter, and then by declaring a crusade against their family—the ultimate papal abuse of the crusading ideal. Finally, by an outright lie (*Inferno* 27.85–111) he took their stronghold, Palestrina, and razed it (1298). The Colonna cardinals retaliated in a series of manifestos that denounced Boniface as a usurper and a simonist (Dante agreed in *Paradiso* 27.22–24 and *Inferno* 19.52–57) and began the defamation of his character that was later to be continued by Philip the Fair, with whom they both took refuge in 1299.

Marble sculpture of Pope Boniface VIII by Arnolfo di Cambrio, 1296. (Courtesy of the Vatican Library)

Boniface celebrated the turn of the century by instituting the Jubilee of 1300—the first of its kind. This was a profitable variation on the now-impossible pilgrimage to the Holy Land; pilgrims to Rome that year were to receive a plenary indulgence for their sins. The event displayed Boniface's skill as an administrator and diplomat, for maximum participation was ensured by arranging safe-conduct to Rome and adequate food, housing, and public order while pilgrims were there.

Meanwhile, Boniface prepared an elaborate plan to revenge himself on

Philip the Fair by forcing him to admit that even the king of France was subject to the papacy *ratione peccati*. In July 1300 Philip was warned that his usurpations of ecclesiastical jurisdiction were sinful, even though they were incurred by taking bad counsel (*Recordare rex inclyte*). When Philip had ignored this warning for a full year, Boniface proceeded to the next step. He and the cardinals drew up a private letter to Philip (*Ausculta fili*, 5 December 1301) that listed in detail his sins against the church, for which he deserved to be excommunicated, and then informed the king that if he did not repent, he would be judged by the pope in an assembly he had convoked for 1 November 1302. For that purpose, Boniface summoned the bishops and principal abbots of France, together with representatives from every French cathedral chapter, to give him counsel in Rome; the summons also included the leading theologians and lawyers of the realm, although he did not insist that they attend. The pope's purpose was evidently to take counsel with everyone the king should have consulted before taking any action that affected the church. Presumably the king's proper counselors on church affairs would agree with Boniface that Philip had acted illegally, and hence the king would be personally responsible for seeking bad advice rather than good.

Philip by no means wished to be judged by a pope, with or without the counsel and consent of his clergy. He countered by forbidding the convokees to attend under pain of having their property confiscated by the Crown. This effectively vitiated Boniface's proposed consultation with the French clergy, for only a handful of the convokees subject to royal jurisdiction dared attend. But the prohibition greatly simplified Boniface's task, for he declared that anyone who impeded attendance was automatically excommunicated (31 May 1302), and when Philip persisted, the king was given a year to repent (September 1302). Although the convocation was duly held in November, it was an anticlimactic formality that served its purpose by being poorly attended.

Probably a draft of the bull *Unam sanctam* was discussed and approved as sound doctrine by the assembled prelates. The bull itself was promulgated on 18 November 1302, after the convocation was over, as popes usually did when acting with the advice of a church council. The bull is based on arguments that had long been familiar to theologians and canonists, as Jean Rivière shows, but the conclusion of *Unam sanctam* has the status of a dogma rather than a mere theory: "It is altogether necessary to salvation for every human creature to be subject to the Roman Pontiff." From the context it is clear that to Boniface this meant that "if the earthly power err, it shall be judged by the spiritual power," that is, *ratione peccati*. Boniface was therefore asserting the papal prerogative to interfere in secular affairs when sin is involved. The bull states in universal terms the same doctrine expounded privately to Philip in *Ausculta fili*. Philip understood very well that *Unam sanctam* subjected the governmental acts of the French Crown to review by the pope, and he did not rest until he had secured a permanent exemption from it for France, its king, and his subjects (*Meruit*, 1306). *Unam sanctam* was Boniface's attempt to convert the pope's position as moral arbiter of Christendom into a legal prerogative.

Boniface's French policy had repercussions in Italy. The pope was the feudal overlord of the Regno, the kingdom of southern Italy and Sicily, which he had granted as a fief in 1265 to the French count of Anjou, Philip the Fair's great-uncle. In 1282, however, the island of Sicily rebelled against its new French masters, and the nobles gave the crown instead to the king of Aragon, whose wife was the last of the Hohenstaufens, the dynasty that the Angevins had replaced. For the next twenty years popes attempted to recover the island. When the mainland Angevins proved inept, Boniface preached a new crusade against the Sicilians, and to lead it he hired Charles of Anjou, the brother of Philip the Fair (1298). While Boniface and Philip were maneuvering in 1302, Charles invaded the island in May and was still fighting when he was called home by his brother. With the loss of his champion, the Angevin king Robert of Naples was ready to make peace, and in August the Treaty of Caltabellotta recognized the independence of the island under its Aragonese king, Frederick. In May 1303 Boniface reluctantly confirmed the treaty, stipulating only that the new kingdom be known as Trinacria rather than Sicily. The loss of Sicily as a papal fief caused a major reconfiguration of Italian diplomacy that inclined later popes to withdraw from Italian politics and take up residence at Avignon.

At the same time, in May 1303, Boniface gained immense advantages for the papacy over the Holy Roman Empire. Albert I of Austria had killed the emperor-elect in battle and wished to succeed him. After five years of negotiation Albert bought Boniface's approval by conceding, as no emperor had done before, that the empire was subject to the papacy, that the pope could veto an imperial election, and that the emperor-elect must swear an oath of feudal loyalty and obedience to the pope. Again Boniface gave concrete, legal form to the theories cherished by the thirteenth-century canonists.

The climax of Boniface's plan to humiliate Philip the Fair was set for 8 September 1303, when the king was to be publicly excommunicated, precisely a year after he had been warned to repent. Boniface retired to Anagni, where he intended to publish the bull, *Super Petri solio*. But his plans were rudely upset by Philip's councilor, William of Nogaret. In line with the medieval concept of justice as tit for tat, the royal plan was the mirror image of Boniface's. Just as Boniface had called a council to judge Philip, so one would be called to judge the pope. In March, and again in June, Nogaret had presented the case against Boniface to royal assemblies at

Paris, which duly requested that the king summon a general council of the church to judge whether, as Nogaret alleged, Boniface was in fact not pope but rather an antipope and a heretic as well. Philip naturally obliged, and Nogaret was then sent to Italy to summon the pope, if not actually to bring him back. In order to serve the summons in person, he enlisted the help of Marquis Sciarra Colonna, who with the help of a small band of supporters enabled Nogaret to confront Boniface in his family palace at Anagni on 7 September. Accounts of the action differ widely, but it is unlikely that the pope himself was physically abused. It was enough that the summons was served and the excommunication forestalled. The triumph Boniface had anticipated was turned into a humiliating defeat. He never recovered: a week later he returned to Rome and died there on 12 October. Nogaret continued to press his charges, but they were eventually dropped in return for the cancellation of Boniface's hostile acts against Philip and France.

Boniface VIII is the most controversial of all popes. Certainly he is the most unpleasant pope on record, and unfortunately for his reputation, Philip the Fair saw to it that the record in this case is surprisingly detailed for the age. Boniface was a man consumed by pride, overconfident of his own considerable intellectual and administrative abilities, and consequently often arrogant to, and contemptuous of, almost everyone else. He ridiculed others publicly and frequently with abrasive, sarcastic remarks. No doubt his chronic kidney stones made him irascible, but far from seeking to bridle his passions, he indulged in outbursts of rage as well as prolonged temper tantrums.

Impatient of criticism and intolerant of opposition, he had few friends; instead, he reserved his affections for himself, his family, and his roots. He cultivated his own glory by commissioning statutes of himself, at least six of which survive; moreover, he invented the papal triple crown, or tiara, and on occasion even dressed himself in the imperial regalia. His unparalleled aggrandizement of his family and consequent persecution of the Colonna led eventually to the humiliation of Anagni.

Clearly Boniface was a capable administrator and diplomat, though he was more effective, it would seem, as a subordinate, since his own judgment was too often clouded by passion. Essentially, he was not an original thinker but a practical person, whose talent lay in advancing the ideas of others. Thus he undoubtedly contributed to the perfection of the system of canon law, and similarly his political goal was to make kings and emperors acknowledge in practice the theories of papal supremacy formulated by his predecessors. He was neither a holy man, like his predecessor, nor a heretic, as his enemies claimed; his piety was conventional and tinged with Aristotelian naturalism. In his own terms, his fatal flaw was a deficiency of regal prudence, which is the essential virtue of rulers.

SELECTED BIBLIOGRAPHY

Bautier, R.H. "Le Jubilé romain de 1300 et l'alliance franco-pontificale au temps de Philippe le Bel et de Boniface VIII." *Moyen âge* 86 (1980): 189–216.

Boase, Thomas S.R. *Boniface VIII.* Makers of the Middle Ages. London: Constable, 1933.

Boyle, Leonard E. "The Constitution *Cum ex eo* of Pope Boniface VIII." *Mediaeval Studies* 24 (1962): 263–302. Reprinted in his *Pastoral Care, Clerical Education, and Canon Law, 1200–1400.* Collected Studies Series 135. London: Variorum, 1981.

Chiomenti Vassalli, D. "Il nepotismo de Bonifacio VIII." In *Lunario Romano VIII: Fatti e figure del Lazio medievale,* ed. R. Lefevre. Rome: Palombi, 1979, 429–43.

Coste, Jean, ed. *Boniface VIII en procès: Articles d'accusation et dépositions des témoins (1303–1311).* Pubblicazioni della Fondazione Camillo Caetani, Studi e documenti d'archivo, 5. Rome: "L'Erma" di Bretschneider, 1995.

Curley, Mary Mildred. "The Conflict between Pope Boniface VIII and King Philip IV, the Fair." Ph.D. diss., Catholic University of America, 1927.

Denifle, Heinrich. "Die Denkschriften der Colonna gegen Bonifaz VIII. und der Cardinäle gegen die Colonna." *Archiv für Literatur- und Kirchengeschichte des Mittelalters* 5 (1889): 493–529.

Digard, Georges. *Philippe le Bel et le Saint-Siège de 1285 à 1304.* 2 vols. Paris: Librairie du Receil Sirey, 1936.

Dupré-Theseider, E. "Bonifacio VIII, papa." In *Dizionario biografico degli Italiani,* 12. Rome: Istituto della Enciclopedia Italiana, 1970, 146–70.

[Dupuy, Pierre.] *Histoire du differend d'entre le pape Boniface VIII. et Philippes le Bel, roy de France.* Paris, 1655. Reprint, Tucson, Ariz.: Audax Press, 1963.

Ehler, Sidney Z., and John B. Morrall, trans. and eds. *Church and State through the Centuries: A Collection of Historic Documents with Commentaries.* Westminster, Md.: Newman Press, 1954.

Fawtier, R. "L'Attentat d'Anagni." *Mélanges d'archéologie et d'histoire de l'Ecole française de Rome* 60 (1948): 153–79.

Finke, Heinrich. *Aus den Tagen Bonifaz VIII: Funde und Forschungen.* Vorreformationsgeschichtliche Forschungen 2. Münster i. W.: Aschendorff, 1902.

Franchi, A., and B. Rocco. "La pace di Caltabellotta, 1302, e la ratifica de Bonifacio VIII, 1303." *Theologos* 3 (Palermo, 1985): 331–424. Also published separately, Palermo: OFTES, 1987.

Gallina, F. "De potestate Ecclesiae in temporalibus iuxta doctrinam Bonifacii VIII." *Ephemerides iuris canonici* 45 (1989):9–37.

Gardner, J. "Boniface VIII as a Patron of Sculpture." In *Roma anno 1300: Atti della IV Settimana di studi di storia dell'arte medievale dell'Università di Roma "La Sapienza" (19–24 maggio 1980),* ed. A.M. Romanini. Mediaevalia 1. Rome: Bretschneider, 1983, 513–27.

Izbicki, Thomas M. "*Clericis laicos* and the Canonists." In *Popes, Teachers, and Canon Law in the Middle Ages,* ed. J.R. Sweeney and S. Chodorow. Ithaca, N.Y.: Cornell University Press, 1989, 179–90.

Kay, Richard. "*Ad nostram praesentiam evocamus*: Boniface VIII and the Roman

Convocation of 1302." In *Proceedings of the Third International Congress of Medieval Canon Law, Strasbourg, 3–6 September 1968.* Monumenta iuris canonici, ser. C, vol. 4. Vatican City: Biblioteca Apostolica Vaticana, 1971, 165–89.

Lévis-Mirepoix, duc de. *L'Attentat d'Anagni: Le conflit entre la papauté et le roi de France, 7 septembre 1303.* Trente journées . . . , no. 7. Paris: Gallimard, 1969.

Mann, Horace K. *The Lives of the Popes in the Middle Ages.* Vol. 18. St. Louis: Herder, 1932, 1–420.

Melville, Marion. "Guillaume de Nogaret et Philippe le Bel." *Revue d'histoire de l'église de France* 36 (1950): 56–66.

Muldoon, James. "Boniface VIII's Forty Years of Experience in the Law." *Jurist* 31 (1971): 449–77.

Powicke, F.M. "Pope Boniface VIII." *History* 18 (1934): 307–29. Reprinted in *The Christian Life in the Middle Ages and Other Essays.* Oxford: Clarendon Press, 1966, 48–73.

Les registres de Boniface VIII. Ed. G. Digard, M. Faucon, A. Thomas and R. Fawtier. 5 vols. Bibliothèque des Écoles françaises d'Athènes et de Rome, ser. 2 in 4, no. 4. Paris, 1884–1939.

Rivière, Jean. *Le problème de l'église et de l'état au temps de Philippe le Bel: Etude de théologie positive.* Spicilegium sacrum Lovaniense, Etudes et documents, 8. Louvain and Paris: E. Champion, 1926.

Ruiz, Teofilo F. "Reaction to Anagni." *Catholic Historical Review* 65 (1979): 385–401.

Runciman, Steven. *The Sicilian Vespers: A History of the Mediterranean World in the Later Thirteenth Century.* Cambridge: Cambridge University Press, 1958. Reprint, Baltimore, MD: Penguin Books, 1960.

Schmidt, Tilmann. *Der Bonifaz-Prozess: Verfahren der Papstanklage in-der Zeit Bonifaz' VIII. und Clemens' V.* Forschungen zur kirchlichen Rechtsgeschichte und zum Kirchenrecht, 19. Cologne and Vienna: Böhlau, 1989.

———, ed. *Libri rationum Camerae Bonifatii papae VIII (Archivum Secretum Vaticanum, Collect. 446 necnon Intr. et ex. 5)* Lettera Ant., 2. Vatican City: Scuola Vaticana di paleografia, 1984.

———. "Papst Bonifaz VIII. als Gesetzgeber." In *Proceedings of the Eighth International Congress of Medieval Canon Law San Diego, University of California at La Jolla, 21–27 August 1988,* ed. Stanley Chodorow. Monumenta iuris canonici, ser. C, vol. 9. Vatican City: Biblioteca Apostolica Vaticana, 1992, 227–45.

Scholz, Richard. *Die Publizistik zur Zeit Philipps des Schönen und Bonifaz' VIII: Ein Beitrag zur Geschichte der politischen Anschauungen des Mittelalters.* Kirchenrechtliche Abhandlungen 6–8. Stuttgart: Enke, 1903.

Seppelt, Franz X. *Geschichte der Päpste von den Anfängen bis zur Mitte des zwanzigsten Jahrhunderts.* Vol. 4. Ed. G. Schwaiger. Munich: Kosel-Verlag, 1954.

Strayer, Joseph R. *The Reign of Philip the Fair.* Princeton: Princeton University Press, 1980.

Ullmann, Walter. "Boniface VIII and His Contemporary Scholarship." *Journal of Theological Studies* 27 (1976): 58–87.

Waley, Daniel. *The Papal State in the Thirteenth Century*. London: Macmillan, 1961.

Watt, J.A. "Dante, Boniface VIII, and the Pharisees." *Studia Gratiana* 15 (1972); 201–15.

Wolter, Hans. "Celestine V and Boniface VIII." In *Handbook of Church History*, ed. Hubert Jedin and John Dolan, vol. 4, *From the High Middle Ages to the Eve of the Reformation*, by Hans-Georg Beck, Karl August Fink, Josef Glazik, Erwin Iserloh, and Hans Wotter. Trans. Anselm Biggs. New York: Herder & Herder, 1970, 267–81, 707–9.

Wood, Charles T., ed. *Philip the Fair and Boniface VIII: State vs. Papacy*. European Problem Studies. New York: Holt, Rinehart & Winston, 1967.

BIBLIOGRAPHIC NOTE

The bibliographies of the individual entries in this part for each of the notable medieval popes give some idea of the vast amount of Latin source material available for study of the medieval papacy. Some of the most important materials have been translated into English. On the early Middle Ages one should consult the following three volumes, which have helpful notes: *The Book of Pontiffs (Liber Pontificalis): The Ancient Biographies of the First Ninety Roman Bishops to AD 715*, translated with an introduction by Raymond Davis (Liverpool: Liverpool University Press, 1989); *The Lives of the Eighth-Century Popes (Liber Pontificalis): The Ancient Biographies of Nine Popes From AD 715 to AD 817*, translated with an introduction and commentary by Raymond Davis (Liverpool: Liverpool University Press, 1992); and *The Lives of the Ninth-Century Popes (Liber Pontificalis): The Ancient Biographies of Ten Popes from A.D. 817–891*, translated with an introduction and commentary by Raymond Davis (Liverpool: Liverpool University Press, 1995). Brian Tierney, *The Crisis of Church and State, 1050–1300* (Englewood Cliffs, N.J. Prentice-Hall, 1964); translates many papal documents from the later Middle Ages, with commentary embodying an American Catholic perspective.

Christopher Dawson, *Religion and the Rise of Western Culture* (Garden City, N.Y.: Image Books, 1958), gives an excellent overview of the entire period. Robert Bartlett, *The Making of Europe: Conquest, Colonization, and Cultural Change, 950–1350* (Princeton: Princeton University Press, 1993), though somewhat unevenly informed about the papacy itself, gives a more detailed and up-to-date presentation of the High Middle Ages. Glenn W.

Olsen, "The Changing Understanding of the Making of Europe from Christopher Dawson to Robert Bartlett," in *Actas del V Congreso "Cultura Europea"* (Pamplona: Aranzadi Editorial, 2000), 203–10, traces recent historiography. Isnard Frank, *A Concise History of the Mediaeval Church*, trans. John Bowden (New York: Continuum, 1995), centers on the papacy. Hubert Jedin and Jay Dolan, general eds., *Handbook of Church History*, vol. 3, *The Church in the Age of Feudalism*, ed. F. Kempf, Karl August Fink, Josef Glazik, Erwin Iserloh, and Hans Wolter (New York: Herder & Herder, 1968), and vol. 4, *From the High Middle Ages to the Eve of the Reformation*, ed. H.-G. Beck et al. (New York: Herder & Herder, 1970), are packed with information; see on the latter volume the review by Glenn W. Olsen, *Catholic Historical Review* 57 (1971): 478–80. Horst Fuhrmann, *Germany in the High Middle Ages, c. 1050–1200*, trans. Timothy Reuter (New York: Cambridge University Press, 1986), presents an excellent general study with much material on the papacy.

On Rome itself Peter Llewellyn, *Rome in the Dark Ages* (New York: Praeger, 1996), is useful; Jeffrey Richards, *The Popes and the Papacy in the Early Middle Ages, 476–752* (London: Routledge & Kegan Paul, 1979), is fundamental; and Paul Hetherington, *Medieval Rome: A Portrait of the City and Its Life* (New York: St. Martin's Press, 1994), has a particular interest in the history of art. On the latter see also Herbert L. Kessler, " 'Caput et speculum omnium ecclesiarum': Old St. Peter's and Church Decoration in Medieval Latium," in *Italian Church Decoration of the Middle Ages and Early Renaissance: Functions, Forms, and Regional Traditions*, ed. William Tronzo (Bologna: Nuova Alfa editoriale, 1989), 119–46.

Eamon Duffy, *Saints and Sinners: A History of the Popes* (New Haven: Yale University Press, 1997), is a general history of the papacy written to accompany a British television series of the same name by an accomplished Catholic historian who in some degree assesses the papacy according to a modern standard interested in the fostering or retarding of human freedom. This book ends with a lively bibliographical essay very useful for further reading. J.N.D. Kelly, *The Oxford Dictionary of Popes* (Oxford: Oxford University Press, 1986), is a reliable dictionary for orientation to specific pontificates. Richard P. McBrien, *Lives of the Popes: The Pontiffs from St. Peter to John Paul II* (San Francisco: Harper, 1997), on the other hand, is thoroughly unreliable if occasionally amusing. The survey of the medieval papacy by the hesitatingly Roman Catholic scholar Bernhard Schimmelpfennig, *Das Papsttum: Von der Antike bis zur Renaissance*, 4th ed. (Darmstadt: Wissenchaftliche Buchgesellschaft, 1996), is of excellent quality. This volume has been translated into English, but not well, from the third German edition: *The Papacy*, trans. James Sievert (New York: Columbia University Press, 1992). See the review by Mary Stroll in *Speculum* 69 (1994): 563–64. Schimmelpfennig included much material on Rome and the papacy in a volume he coedited with Ludwig Schmugge,

Rom im hohen Mittelalter: Studien zu den Romvorstellungen und zur Rompolitik vom 10. bis zum 12. Jahrhundert: Reinhard Elze zur Vollendung seines siebzigsten Lebensjahres gewidmet (Sigmaringen: J. Thorbecke, 1992). The older Catholic series by H.K. Mann, *The Lives of the Popes in the Early Middle Ages*, 18 vols. in 19 (London: B. Herder Book Co., 1902–32), remains useful on matters of fact.

For the beginnings of the Middle Ages, see R.A. Markus, *From Augustine to Gregory the Great: History and Christianity in Late Antiquity* (London: Variorum Reprints, 1983). Markus is a Catholic historian who disapproves of the development of papal monarchy after the time of Gregory the Great. Pierre Riché, *Petite vie de saint Grégoire le Grand (540–604)* (Paris: Desclee, 1995), is a brief, well-informed study. For England, see Henry Mayr-Harting, *The Coming of Christianity to Anglo-Saxon England*, 3rd ed. (University Park: Pennsylvania State University Press, 1991), a standard study; see also Glenn W. Olsen, "The Idea of the *Ecclesia Primitiva* in the Writings of the Twelfth-Century Canonists," *Traditio* 25 (1969): 61–86, on Gregory I, Bede, and the mission to England. Of Thomas F.X. Noble's many sharp and incisive contributions to the study of the early medieval papacy, the following might be highlighted: "Morbidity and Vitality in the History of the Early Medieval Papacy," *Catholic Historical Review* 81 (1995) 505–40; review of James C. Russell's *The Germanization of Early Medieval Christianity* in *American Historical Review* 100 (1995): 888–89; "Rome in the Seventh Century," in *Archbishop Theodore: Commemorative Studies on His Life and Influence*, ed. Michael Lapidge (Cambridge: Cambridge University Press, 1995); and *The Republic of St. Peter: The Birth of the Papal State, 680–825* (Philadelphia: University of Pennsylvania Press, 1984).

For the Carolingian period, see also Thomas F.X. Noble, "The Papacy in the Eighth and Ninth Centuries," in *The New Cambridge Medieval History*, vol. 2, *c. 700–c. 900*, ed. Rosamond McKitterick (Cambridge: Cambridge University Press, 1995), 563–86; and "Tradition and Learning in Search of Ideology: The *Libri Carolini*," in *"The Gentle Voices of Teachers": Aspects of Learning in the Carolingian Age*, ed. Richard E. Sullivan (Columbus: Ohio State University Press, 1995), 227–60. David F. Appleby, "Rudolf, Abbot Hrabanus, and the Ark of the Covenant Reliquary," *American Benedictine Review* 46 (1995): 419–43, discusses relations between the Carolingians and Rome. Though somewhat uneven, Willemien Otten, "The Texture of Tradition: The Role of the Church Fathers in Carolingian Theology," in *The Reception of the Church Fathers in the West: From the Carolingians to the Maurists*, 2 vols., ed. Irena Backus (Leiden: E.J. Brill, 1997), 1:3–50, is generally well informed. Jean Werckmeister, "The Reception of the Church Fathers in Canon Law," in the same volume, 51–81, considers topics such as the authority of the pope in medieval church law throughout our period.

Two careful studies of Karl Leyser examine European society before and during the investiture struggle: "Concepts of Europe in the Early and High Middle Ages," *Past and Present* 137 (1992): 25–47; and *Communications and Power in Medieval Europe: The Gregorian Revolution and Beyond*, ed. Timothy Reuter (London: Hambledon Press, 1994). Much discussion of this period centers on two books of the Lutheran scholar Gerd Tellenbach: *Church, State, and Christian Society at the Time of the Investiture Contest*, trans. by R.F. Bennett (Atlantic Highlands, N.J.: Humanities Press, 1959), an excellent characterization of the reform ideas of this period, and *The Church in Western Europe from the Tenth to the Early Twelfth Century*, trans. Timothy Reuter (New York: Cambridge University Press, 1993). See the reviews of this latter book by Uta-Renate Blumenthal, John van Engen, and Thomas F.X. Noble in, respectively, *Catholic Historical Review* 81 (1995): 255–56; *Speculum* 71 (1996): 496–99; and *American Historical Review* 100 (1995): 146–47. Hagen Keller, "Das Werk Gerd Tellenbachs in der Geschichtswissenschaft unseres Jahrhunderts," *Frühmittelalterliche Studien* 28 (1994): 374–97, gives an important evaluation of Tellenbach's views. Colin Morris, *The Papal Monarchy: The Western Church from 1050 to 1250*, Oxford History of the Christian Church (Oxford: Oxford University Press, 1989), is a wide-ranging book which treats many historiographical issues. On this book see the review by G.W. Olsen in *The Catholic Historical Review* 77 (1991): 503–5.

See also on the eleventh and twelfth centuries the detailed study of H.E.J. Cowdrey, *The Age of Abbot Desiderius: Montecassino, the Papacy, and the Normans in the 11th and Early 12th Centuries* (Oxford: Clarendon Press, 1983); Carl Erdmann, *The Origins of the Idea of Crusade*, trans. M.W. Baldwin and W. Goffart (Philadelphia: University of Pennsylvania Press, 1977), a classic work with much material on the papacy's role in the origins of the Crusades; and two works of I.S. Robinson: *Authority and Resistance in the Investiture Contest: The Polemical Literature of the Late Eleventh Century* (Manchester: Manchester University Press, 1978) and *The Papacy, 1073–1198: Continuity and Innovation* (Cambridge: Cambridge University Press, 1990). Robert L. Benson, *The Bishop-Elect: A Study of Medieval Ecclesiastical Office* (Princeton: Princeton University Press, 1968), is a very important study of, among other things, canon law and the papacy in the closing years of the Investiture Struggle and beyond. Glenn W. Olsen, "The Theologian and the *Magisterium*: The Ancient and Medieval Background of a Contemporary Controversy," *Communio* 7 (1980): 292–319, treats the authority of the pope in canon law in the twelfth and thirteenth centuries. Kenneth Pennington, *Pope and Bishops: The Papal Monarchy in the Twelfth and Thirteenth Centuries* (Philadelphia: University of Pennsylvania Press, 1984), is a fine book on this period. See also on the early-thirteenth-century papacy the review by Glenn W. Olsen of Wilhelm Imkamp, *Das Kirchenbild Innocenz' III (1198–1216)* (Stuttgart: A. Hiersemann, 1983), in *Church History* 54 (1985): 99–100, and Brenda Bolton, *Innocent III: Studies* on *Papal Authority and Pastoral Care* (Aldershot, Hampshire: Ashgate, 1995). Michael Borgolte, *Petrusnachfolge und Kaiserimitation: Die Grablegen der Päpste, ihre Genese und Traditionsbildung*, Veröffentlichungen des Max-Planck-Instituts für Geschichte 95 (Göttingen: Vanderhoeck and Ruprecht, 1989), an important book conveniently summarized in a review by Thomas F.X. Noble in *Catholic Historical Review* 81 (1995): 605–7, describes especially the ideological ties between Rome, Peter, the papacy, and the church in the latter part of this period. Christopher Ryan, ed., *The Religious Roles of the Papacy: Ideals and Realities, 1150–1300* (Toronto: Pontifical Institute of Mediaeval Studies, 1989), presents a wide range of scholarly studies, and Sylvia Schein, *Fideles Crucis: The Papacy, the West, and the Recovery of the Holy Land, 1274–1314* (Oxford: Clarendon Press, 1991), gives a thorough description of the role of the papacy in some of the later Crusades.

PART III

The Renaissance and Reformation Papacy

INTRODUCTION

Margery A. Ganz

The papacy during the Renaissance and Reformation was at a critical point in its history. Several of the themes that were developing during the Middle Ages continued during the period of the Avignon captivity of the church and its aftermath. Other themes that began once the popes returned to Italy continued for the rest of the period and into the early modern era.

The sources for this period are rich and varied. Beginning with a series of registers and other curial and cameral documents that survived from the Avignon captivity of the church, the collection of primary sources that have survived more than five hundred years is truly amazing. Some of the documents traveled with the popes from Avignon to Carpentras to Florence to Bologna to Ferrara and finally came home to Rome. Once Nicholas V founded the Vatican Library, many of these documents found a home in that library along with his and Eugenius IV collection of humanist manuscripts. It was Sixtus IV who began the division of administrative documents from literary and theological ones. Certain particularly precious documents were stored in Castel Sant'Angelo for safekeeping, and under Julius II there was an attempt to put the archives of the Camera Apostolica in order and to sequester all private documents. However, it took the Council of Trent to really establish a central archive of the church in the Vatican Palace, and it was not until Paul V in 1610 that the building of the present archive was begun. The Vatican archives eventually came to contain diplomatic documents, papal bulls, fiscal documents of the Camera Apostolica, private family archives of papal families, records of congregations, and other documents to make up the largest collection of documents pertaining to the Catholic church and its relationship, both religious and secular, to the rest of the world. Today these documents, studied by many of the historians listed in the bibliographies of popes from the Renaissance and Reformation, form an incredible source for historians of the papacy in particular and Christendom in general. Leonard Boyle's important work, *A Survey of the Vatican Archives and Its Medieval Holdings*, enables the researcher to know where to look in this vast collection that spans about one thousand years.

Generally the documents reveal that the trend toward a powerful papal monarchy competing for allegiance of the lay population with the strong secular rulers was stopped for a time by Philip IV (the Fair)'s kidnapping of Pope Boniface VIII in 1303. During the next seventy-plus years the popes lived as prisoners, albeit in a golden cage at Avignon, of the French kings. The years in Avignon further reduced the power and prestige of the papacy. Among the popes who reigned in Avignon but had a much greater influence were John XXII and Gregory XI. Among other things, John XXII (1316–34) will be remembered for his centralization of authority as well as creating a centralized financial system that increased papal revenues through control over ecclesiastical benefices, and the repression of religious dissent as heresy. When John XXII came to power after a two-year vacancy in the papacy, the papal bureaucracy was in a chaotic state and needed a firm hand to govern it. Pope John XXII possessed that firmness and was willing and able to exercise it. In addition, John XXII took the selling of church offices to new heights by increasing the number of people who were transferred every time a new bishop was appointed, and in that way the church continued to generate income for the papal treasury and various projects that were important to John and his successors.

John XXII was also committed to actually governing the church and publishing papal letters, bulls, and collections of canon law. In addition, John XXII believed that it was an essential part of a bishop's role to combat heresy; he could only do that if his diocese was of a reasonable size so that true control would be possible. During his pontificate the pope was also forced to decide issues between the Spiritual and Conventual Franciscans. Various issues surrounding the ideal of poverty were decided by John, who enforced his views on the Franciscan order. John's relations with secular rulers like Louis of Bavaria were also problematic, and over the last years of his reign the pope spent much of his energies fighting with Louis, who had become the holy Roman emperor and refused to acknowledge John XXII's vision of papal rule.

John XXII was criticized for his nepotism in awarding all kinds of appointments and gifts to members of his extended family. Criticism of John's extravagances can be found in the writings of both Dante and Petrarch. Spartan living was not something in which John XXII indulged, but he also left a substantial amount in the papal treasury while managing to give away large sums to the poor.

Several popes from the mid-fourteenth century onward tried to liberate the papacy from Avignon. Neither Innocent VI (1352–62) nor Urban V in 1367 proved able to do so. Clearly Rome was anxious to have the popes return to their traditional site because of the expected economic and political benefits. However, it was not to be in the mid-fourteenth century. Later, Gregory XI managed to bring an end to the Avignon captivity of the church. By the time Gregory XI began his reign in 1370, he had already had a major career in the papal bureaucracy due to his skills as a lawyer and the patronage of his uncle Clement VI, and he had served Urban V during his failed campaign to return the papacy to Rome. He was elected pope ten days after the death of Urban V. His quick election may have been due to his diplomatic abilities, the twenty-two years he had spent as a member of the sacred college of cardinals, and most probably the fact that six of the eighteen cardinals who met to elect the pope belonged to his family. Nepotism had once again led to the naming of a pope.

When he was elected pope, Gregory XI was only a simple deacon, so he had to be ordained a priest before he could actually be crowned pope on 5 January 1371. His pontificate was a continuation of the traditional themes already in place; a crusade against the Turks, the reform of the Dominican order and of the Hospitallers, the reestablishment of political stability in Italy, peace between England and France, which were engaged in the Hundred Years' War, and most especially, the return of the papal seat to Rome. Gregory took a firm stand against heretics and used the Inquisition to attempt to bring religious conformity throughout Western Europe by forcing secular rulers to enforce the laws on heresy.

Like many of his medieval predecessors, Gregory was committed to bringing the Holy Land under Christian control. The Turks had conquered the Latin kingdom of Jerusalem in 1291, and eighty years later there had been no truly organized attempt to retake that territory. Although Gregory XI certainly tried to change that, he was unsuccessful in achieving Christian hegemony over the Latin kingdom. Within six months of his election Gregory XI was busy trying to organize a crusade, which did not come to fruition until 1378 the year he died. However, he encountered obstacles because England and France were busy fighting each other while the holy Roman emperor, involved in the unstable political situation at home, proved unable to participate. Many of the Italian rulers who had previously committed to the enterprise, as well as the Byzantines, also withdrew their support of this papal project. The crusade, which finally began seven years after the papal call, came to a quick end when the

Christian army was successfully ambushed in April 1378. However, Gregory was spared the news of this disaster, dying a few weeks before the ambush.

Gregory's desire to return the papacy to Rome was paramount during his years as pope. Therefore, he was an extremely interested player in domestic Italian affairs. Papal policy had always been based on the independence of Rome and a papal state free from foreign intervention. During the early years of his pontificate Gregory's main opponent in this area was the Visconti family of Milan, which was engaged in expanding its hegemony over the Italian peninsula. Gregory supported the Tuscan city-states against the campaigns of the Visconti using them as a buffer between the Papal States and Milan. Gregory's problems vis-à-vis the Papal States stemmed from the fact that the pontiffs had been absentee landlords since the Avignon captivity began, and many Italian cities were not exactly anxious to have the pontiffs back in a position of dominance. As a neighbor of the Papal States, Florence was most suspicious about Gregory's expansionism and was suspicious of his moves in the peninsula. During the recurrence of plague and famine in the mid-1370s, the fact that the papal vicars refused to sell their surplus grain to many of the Tuscan city-states, including Florence, led to an escalating tension between the Holy Father and the rulers of Florence. Florence actually fomented rebellion within the Papal States in the 1370s, which led the pope to look for other allies from among northern Italian rulers as well as Naples. But all were wary of an increased papal presence. Certainly most secular Italian rulers were not anxious to have the popes back in Rome in a strong position. As with his crusade, Gregory died before the final victory and settlement of the war with Florence, which was negotiated by Pope Urban VI just months after Gregory's death.

Gregory XI's pontificate proved important. Throughout his career Gregory XI acted to hold on to the church's traditional role in maintaining peace and order within Christendom, destroying heresy, regaining the Holy Land, and returning the papacy to its traditional seat in Rome. He was interested in making the papacy strong and having papal authority recognized throughout the then-known world. While Gregory knew where he was headed, he often proved unable to get others to travel that route with him. Following his death, the papacy headed into the even more problematic period of the Great Schism (1378–1417).

During these tumultuous years, multiple popes existed in various places at the same time. Although Gregory had wanted to remove the papacy from Avignon, he was unable to ensure that only one pope existed in Rome. After his death there were popes in Rome, Avignon, and finally Pisa. This problem led directly to the Council of Constance, which began in 1414. It was the Council of Constance that brought an end to the schism and elected Oddo Colonna to reign as Pope Martin V (1417–31) in 1417, thus satisfying its first goal of restoring unity to the church. Its two other goals proved less successful: to purge the church of heresy and to reform it in both head and members. Martin V's pontificate began themes that were followed by his successors throughout the fifteenth century. The first trend was the weakening and then the defeat of the concept of conciliarism; second was the increasing control of national churches by secular rulers, with a corresponding emergence of the pope as a secular ruler in central Italy; and last of all was a rapprochement between the Eastern and Western churches. Neither Martin nor his successors were anxious to redistribute power within the church in favor of the conciliarists, nor were the secular monarchs willing to cede any power to the pope.

The schism had given secular monarchs increased control over national churches, while the cardinals had also strengthened their position vis-à-vis the papacy. Neither of these groups were willing to reduce the money they collected due to their respective positions. All needed a pope with whom they could work. Although Martin V was not the first choice of the cardinals, he was acceptable to both sides. Coming from a powerful Roman family, he had the network not only to bring the papacy back to Rome but also to restore its prestige there. Martin proved unwilling to allow the conciliarists to encroach on papal authority or privilege. The reform movement among those present at Constance also seemed to peter out after his selection. Pope Martin V made it absolutely clear that he was unwilling to entertain the idea of a pope under the council or even within it as the correct structuring of the church's hierarchy.

By the end of Constance, Martin clarified that his approach to governing Christendom would be to deal separately with secular monarchs. Although several reforms were promulgated by Constance, the council gave Martin the responsibility to negotiate the remaining issues with individual nation-states. The issues included, but were not limited to, the following: the composition of the college of cardinals, spiritual taxes to be imposed, which benefices would be appointed by the pope and which by secular rulers, and *annates* revenues for the year to be sent to Rome. By dividing the group of secular rulers, Martin was able to strengthen the papacy at their expense.

With the end of the Council of Constance, Martin turned his attention to his role as temporal ruler of an Italian state, a stance followed by the remaining popes of the fifteenth century. Martin and his successors were to spend much of their revenue and time trying to increase their control of the Italian peninsula while ensuring the aggrandizement of their own families. Although this was supposedly done in the name of the exaltation of the Holy See, many of Martin's policies were nothing short of increasing the power and monetary resources of the Colonna family.

Continuing the struggle against the conciliar movement was Gabriele Condulmer, who became Eugenius IV in 1431 and ruled until 1447.

Though he was raised to the cardinalate at age twenty-five in 1408 by his uncle Gregory XII, Gabriele, who was in the pro-Florentine camp during Martin's pontificate, served only in minor posts during that pontificate. It was, in fact, his minor role during Martin's term that made him acceptable to the college of cardinals in 1431. Eugenius quickly faced two problems: an insurrection in Rome due in part to his attempt to dismantle the power of the Colonna, which in turn led to his exile in Florence under the protection of his Medici bankers; and the convening of the Council of Basel, which he tried unsuccessfully to transfer to Bologna. The Council of Basel made a strong attempt to reform the papacy, reduce its financial independence, and make it subservient to ecumenical councils. Among its decrees was one that required each future pope to acknowledge conciliar supremacy. Yet Eugenius was to regain his position with regard to the conciliarists.

Because both the conciliarists and Eugenius agreed on the need to bring an end to the schism that had existed between the Eastern and Western churches since 1054, the conciliarists attempted to have the council moved to Avignon, but Eugenius's plan to reconvene the Council of Basel in Ferrara to try to effect the union of the Eastern and Western churches was the one the Greeks were willing to accept. By January 1439 Eugenius had moved the council to Florence, where it did achieve a fragile union of the two churches on 5 July 1439. Although the Council of Basel had deposed Eugenius on 25 June 1439, Eugenius's achievement in finally bringing together the Eastern and Western churches, with the Eastern church acknowledging Rome's primacy, marked the pinnacle of his pontificate. Many of his enemies began to acknowledge his position and to see the intransigence of Basel as detrimental to the unity of Christendom.

Eugenius gathered supporters for his program and returned to Rome in triumph in September 1443. For almost one hundred years no pope was constrained to leave Rome until Charles V sacked the city in 1527. In addition, papal claims to rule the Papal States were largely unchallenged as well. However, the union of Eastern and Western churches proved ephemeral at best, since most of the Greeks at home were unwilling to accept Eugenius's plan. Nonetheless, the prolonged presence in Florence of many Greeks helped lead to a revival of Greek studies in that city. Eugenius also employed several Greek scholars within his household. The rest of the Ferrara-Florence council was undistinguished. Although he spent years in Florence, the center of the Italian Renaissance, Eugenius seemed only slightly impacted by the art developing around him. Eugenius was willing to work on local reform, like reorganizing the University of Rome, improving the instruction of clergy, and getting the Observant rule accepted into Florentine monasteries, but he was unwilling to envision a broader, churchwide reform. Unlike his predecessors and many who would follow him at the head of the Holy See, he promoted only a few of his relatives and was able to turn over the church's patrimony intact to his successor, Nicholas V.

Tommaso Parentucelli, who was elected pope on 6 March 1447 and then took the name Nicholas V (1447–55), followed Eugenius's lead in returning the papacy to permanent residence in Rome. Although Eugenius IV had turned the papal treasury over to Nicholas without any major debts, it also had very few assets. It was Nicholas's responsibility to rebuild papal wealth and then to use that wealth to enhance the authority of the pope and the clerical hierarchy. Other themes of Nicholas's pontificate, which would continue throughout the remaining half of the century, included the patronage of humanists and artists and the construction of renewed urban life in Rome and the Papal States, as well as the founding of the Vatican Library. Unlike several of his predecessors, Nicholas V came from a relatively poor family who struggled to send him to the University of Bologna. Once there, however, he brought himself to the attention of the bishop of Bologna, Niccolò degli Albergati, who took the future Nicholas into his service.

The future pope worked for the bishop of Bologna and then Eugenius IV, distinguishing himself as a talented diplomat and negotiator. He later got credit for his work in Florence in helping unite the Eastern and Western churches as well as for leading the discussions that helped bring the Ethiopians and the Armenians into union with the Catholic church. Tommaso's successful negotiations on behalf of the church led Eugenius to make him bishop of Bologna 1444. Eugenius then sent him on several diplomatic missions that led to his appointment as a cardinal in 1446. The following year, to the surprise of many of the cardinals since he was relatively young and did not belong to a great family, he was elected pope after the death of Eugenius IV. Nicholas began his pontificate by reaching out to the Romans in order to ensure his peaceful coexistence with his fellow citizens of the Eternal City. By returning certain tax revenues to the Romans and granting them full exercise of their traditional statutes, he made friends of his neighbors and assisted them in rebuilding the walls of the city and bridges, castles within the Papal States, and ports within its greater dominion. Thus everyone benefited, and Rome came to appreciate its new pontiff. Because of his own experience as a papal legate, Nicholas appointed excellent men to represent the cause of the Holy See abroad. Recognizing the need for compromise to build bridges to former papal adversaries, he also saw the need to rebuild fortifications within the Romagna and to have a much smaller army of papal mercenaries to protect his dominion. Increasingly, the pontiffs were becoming secular princes in Italy during the pontificates of Eugenius and Nicholas and their successors. In terms of political activities, Nicholas's last years were marred by a planned Roman insurrection led by Stefano Porcari and the conquest of Constantinople by the Ottoman Turks. Although Nicholas called for a crusade to save the Eastern church lands, neither European monarchs nor the papal curia were interested in allocating scarce resources for that project.

Because of his early education and his time in Florence both before and during the Council of Ferrara-Florence, Nicholas was the first pope to be an active humanist. Many of his friends were found among the leading humanists of the day. He was an avid book buyer who was always hunting for special manuscripts, many of which found their way into the Vatican Library. Since Nicholas believed that the renewal of the church required an up-to-date knowledge of the writings of the Greek church fathers, he commissioned translations of the works of St. Basil, St. Gregory Nazianzen, St. Cyril, and St. John Chrysostom, among others. Nicholas invited the most eminent humanists to be part of his court in Rome for the purpose of reviving both the classics of the early church and those of pagan antiquity. One could also see his Roman building program as an attempt to restore the city to its ancient splendor and place the church in the center of this renewed city.

Pope Pius II, the former Aeneas Silvius Piccolomini, was elected pope in August 1458 and reigned until 1464. One of the most studied, documented, and controversial popes of the fifteenth century, Pius II is remembered for his autobiographical *Commentaries*, providing an insider's view of the pope's life and pontificate. Like many of his predecessors, Aeneas had a career within the papal bureaucracy before his accession to the See of St. Peter. During those years he served several cardinals and traveled as a papal diplomat for three pontiffs. In the 1430s Aeneas's abandonment of his earlier proconciliar views in favor of a more promonarchical position paved the way for his steady advancement in the papal bureaucracy. Subsequently he held two bishoprics, including that of his home town of Siena, and was raised to the cardinalate by Callistus III, before attaining the coveted triple tiara. Though he called for a crusade against the encroaching threat of the Turks, like his predecessors, he proved unable to get the commitments from secular leaders to make a success of the crusade. Other issues he faced included nurturing the unity of the church in the face of heresy, various doctrinal disputes, large-scale confrontations over papal sovereignty on ecclesiastical issues and, especially, appointments primarily in France and the Holy Roman Empire, and the continuing reconquest of the Papal States while keeping Italian rulers from aligning themselves against him and preventing foreign rulers from seizing these lands. All of these could be subsumed in his conversion to the idea of a strong papal monarchy at the expense of the conciliarist program. Like many other Renaissance popes, Pius II was committed to the political aggrandizement of his family in Siena, in this case, as well as within the papal administration. Other popes would carry this nepotism to even higher levels than Pius, although the urban redesign and creation of a new city named Pienza after the pope was certainly one of the high points of papal patronage. Although Pius II is perceived as a humanist, he never really promoted humanist scholarship or Renaissance art outside of the beautification of Pienza.

Francesco della Rovere became Pope Sixtus IV (1471–84) in 1471 and ruled until 1484. His was one of the most dramatic and tempestuous pontificates in the fifteenth century. Educated by the friars of San Francesco at Savona, the future Sixtus IV went on to become an active priest within the Conventual wing of the Franciscan order. During the 1450s and 1460s Francesco della Rovere made his name teaching philosophy and theology and writing important theological tracts. It was Pope Paul II who made him a cardinal presbyter with the title of San Pietro in Vincoli in 1467, although he did not endow the new cardinal with many benefices. Nonetheless, Francesco was elected to be the supreme head of the Apostolic See in September 1471. Some believed he owed his election to his nephew Pietro Riario, who promised many benefits to a group of cardinals. Thus began a problem that would dominate Sixtus's pontificate: reneging on his promise to reduce nepotism. Three months later Sixtus nominated two of his nephews, Pietro Riario and Giuliano della Rovere (later Pope Julius II), as cardinals when they were still too young to hold office. These appointments set the stage for the continuing simony and nepotism that would dominate Sixtus's pontificate. Ambition and nepotism seem to have been the guiding motives of his pontificate. While Giuliano was certainly committed to the papacy and to the building of the Papal States, Pietro Riario and his brother Girolamo simply seemed to seek profit. Their behavior epitomized the vision of a corrupt and secularized papal court. It was just a short step from Sixtus IV to Alexander VI, who elevated corruption and nepotism to new heights.

During the 1470s a series of incidents indicated the growing problems between the Medici, who functioned as the papal bankers, and the papacy of Sixtus IV. These came to a head with the Pazzi conspiracy in April 1478, when Sixtus and his nephews were deeply involved with the archbishop of Florence, Francesco Salviati, and the Pazzi family in plotting to murder Giuliano and Lorenzo de Medici in the Florentine cathedral at the elevation of the Host during Pentecost. The plot failed when only Giuliano was killed, and Sixtus was faced with a war against Medicean Florence and her allies. In addition to placing Florence under interdict and excommunicating Lorenzo de' Medici, Sixtus participated in a number of wars in the Italian peninsula that earned him the image of a bellicose Renaissance pope. Sixtus and his successors claimed the absolute sovereignty of the pope in ecclesiastical as well as temporal matters. Sixtus spent much of his pontificate trying to collect funds from ecclesiastical benefices in England, France, and Spain. Because his wars as well as his projected crusade against the threat of Turkish expansion were expensive, he was constantly trying to end the fiscal autonomy of many of the towns within the borders of the Papal States while also using plenary indulgences to raise needed funds.

Sixtus was known for renewing the urban fabric of Rome. He spent much of the Holy See's patrimony in widening and paving its streets, building bridges, including one named after himself, repairing the water systems, building new churches, dedicating a chapel to the Virgin at St. Peter's, reviving hospitals, and creating buildings of the University of Rome. Many would argue that he made Rome habitable. In addition to the building program, Sixtus officially founded the first public Vatican library and thereby brought to fruition the earlier project of Nicholas V. Because he also collected and then transferred many of the important documents of the medieval papacy to the Castel Sant'Angelo, he can be viewed as the founder of the Vatican Archives. He also built the Sistine Chapel, which he had decorated by Ghirlandaio, Perugino, Rosselli, Signorelli, and Botticelli. The frescoes in this chapel—depictions of the life cycles of Moses and Jesus—were used to express Sixtus's idea of papal sovereignty, representing the pope as the supreme and God-inspired lawgiver. The frescoes make manifest the unity of theology and politics that marked Sixtus's pontificate. In later years Sixtus's nephew, Julius II, would put Michelangelo to work on the ceiling of that same chapel.

Unfortunately for the papacy, the pontificates of Innocent VIII (1484–92) and Alexander VI (1492–1503) did nothing to cleanse the institution's reputation. Indeed, the reign of Rodrigo Borgia, who became Alexander VI, actually worsened the world's opinion of the pope. At the time of his ascension to the papal dignity, Alexander VI had four living children, including both Cesare Borgia and Lucrezia. All four were to receive great riches through their father, though some also suffered for their relationship to the pontiff. Whether Cesare was responsible for the death of one of his sister's husbands as well as of his brother, we shall never know, but the reputation of the family was certainly tainted. Rodrigo Borgia had bought his way into high position, and he then used that position to enrich his family and provide for the political survival of his family after his death. While he and his son Cesare planned for every possibility to continue the family reign, as Machiavelli revealed, he did not plan for fortune to have intervened in their family's affairs by striking Cesare with a grave illness while Alexander himself lay dying. The Borgia influence was canceled in the conclave that followed Alexander's death with the election of reform-minded Pius III, who died just a month later.

Giuliano della Rovere was elected Pope Julius II by the conclave on 1 November 1503 and then spent ten years as the head of the Holy See. Prior to his election the future Julius II (1503–13) had been made a bishop by his uncle Sixtus IV and almost immediately afterward a cardinal in his uncle's old church of San Pietro in Vincoli, but he eventually became the cardinal-priest of Ostia. In the next few years Giuliano held seven episcopal sees and served as cardinal-legate to the Marches, to Umbria, to Avignon, and to France, where he made a variety of allies who were to be essential to him later in his career. He played a large role in his uncle Sixtus's foreign policy, although his ideas often lost out to those of his Riario cousins. He and Rodrigo Borgia both worked under Pope Innocent VIII, and although they did not always agree, he voted to elect Rodrigo as Pope Alexander VI. Nonetheless, Giuliano soon was perceived by Alexander VI as the enemy and was forced to flee to safety in France, from which point he tried to ensure the safety and security of his brother Giovanni Maria, from whom would descend the della Rovere line and his nephew Francesco Maria. Although he was a strong contender in the conclave that elected Pius III, he was not chosen as pontiff. Yet when Pius III died a month later, Giuliano was elected as Julius II in great part because he had acquired a good reputation during his years as a cardinal. His earlier career had revealed him to be both a shrewd and effective administrator and a generous patron of both artists and humanists. Like many of his predecessors, he had children as well as mistresses whom he favored, but he was perceived to be a firm defender of the church and was elected unanimously on 1 November 1503. Julius limited what he bestowed on his family—he never had more than two of his nephews in the sacred college at one time.

Julius II was a reform-minded pope who tried to solve the differences among the various factions of the Franciscans and sought to stop the practice of simony in papal elections, in particular, but also in the assignment of episcopal sees. Like many of his predecessors, he recognized the need for a Holy League to launch a crusade to render Christendom safe from the Turks. His was a busy pontificate that witnessed Julius's determination to resist the encroachments of secular monarchs against his role as head of Christendom as well as to retrieve all the original territories of the Papal States. Julius was committed to securing the independence and integrity of his state. Julius II reneged on an earlier agreement to appoint Cesare Borgia as captain general of the church, wanting his own person in that vital position. He also won back both Perugia and Bologna, and in the later years of his pontificate, he reorganized the administration of the Papal States. Among his most important policies was to require an annual accounting from all of his secular lords and other administrators. He collected taxes and created a new coinage named after himself. He put the papacy back on a solid financial basis by amassing a large treasury to support his wars and his patronage.

Julius II was a great patron of the arts. During his reign he restored all the churches where he had spent his career prior to his election as pope. Perhaps his most famous commissions were the two to Michelangelo to decorate the Sistine Chapel ceiling as well as to create a funeral monument that would eventually entomb his remains. He commissioned Raphael to decorate his new papal apartments and to produce his portrait, and Bramante to construct the corridor that linked the Vatican Palace with the Belvedere Villa and, most important, to design a new St. Peter's. Julius's artistic and architectural commissions helped create an imperial style in early-sixteenth-century Rome. Julius spent most of his energy safeguarding the material aspects (including the actual territory, buildings, administration, and political independence) of the Apostolic See, but he failed to apply his great talents to the cause of spiritual reform on the eve of the Reformation and so left the church he had rebuilt vulnerable to the assault of Martin Luther.

Julius II was succeeded by Giovanni de' Medici, the son of Lorenzo the Magnificent, who had been selected for a career in the church at an early age. His father saw to it that he was educated by humanist tutors like Angelo Poliziano, Marsilio Ficino, and Giovanni Pico dell Mirandola, resulting in a lifelong commitment to learning and culture. Sixtus IV bestowed on the future Leo X the rank of apostolic protonotary at the age of eight as well as several canonries and a convent; several of his father's allies also bestowed gifts of benefices, including the important monastery of Monte Cassino. In 1489, when Giovanni was only thirteen, Lorenzo managed to convince Pope Innocent VIII to make his son a cardinal and so start Giovanni on his way to the papacy.

For Lorenzo, Giovanni's new status was a way to bind the Medici and the city of Florence more closely to the church. Maintenance of this link was certainly one of the goals of Leo X's pontificate as well as that of his cousin, Clement VII. It was Julius II's support of Giovanni and his family that helped reinstate the Medici in Florence in 1512 after eighteen years of exile. Just over a year later Giovanni de' Medici was elected pope and took the name of Leo X (1513–21). His early acts reveal his strong attachment to his family and the city of his birth: he supported the city's Monte di pietà through his papal bull approving the charging of interest, and he began the beatification of Florence's fifteenth-century archbishop Antonino, which would be completed by his cousin, the future Clement VII.

Trying to create a foreign policy that preserved both Florence and the integrity of the Papal States, Leo made a variety of alliances with King Francis I of France and also with the holy Roman emperor Maximilian and even Frederick of Saxony. There also were calls for a crusade. Leo's principal interest seems to have been directed to the arts and humanist learning. Among the men who enjoyed his patronage were Michelangelo, Raphael, Bramante, Cellini, Bandinelli, and Leonardo da Vinci. Indeed, Raphael painted the wonderful triple portrait of Leo surrounded by his cousin Giulio de' Medici, who would rule as Clement VII, and Cardinal Ludovico de' Rossi. Among the intellectuals who surrounded this Medici pope were Pietro Aretino, Zanobi Acciaiuoli, Pietro Bembo, Jacopo Sadoleto, Johannes Reuchlin, and even Erasmus.

Unfortunately, Leo's pontificate will always be marred by his failure to deal promptly and in a decisive manner with Martin Luther's demand for church reform. Although Leo could certainly grasp and then deal with the complicated issues that arose both in Florence and within a wider Italian context, he seems to have misunderstood Luther's threat to the universal church, busying himself with the continuation of normal papal business like the creation of cardinals, the selling of church positions, and the calling of church councils. Indeed, he presided over the Lateran Council of 1512–17. While this council issued proclamations against simony and multiple benefices, most of its members, including Leo, had benefited from the very abuses it railed against, and it was the license that Leo granted to Albrecht of Brandenburg to sell indulgences for eight years that proved to be the last straw for Martin Luther. In evaluating his pontificate, one could say that Leo was too preoccupied with rebuilding Rome, patronizing artists and writers, and especially dealing with affairs in Florence to attack the rampant corruption within the church and address the theological issues raised by Martin Luther. As was the case with the Borgia popes and to a lesser extent the della Rovere popes, Leo and later his cousin Giulio (Clement VII) were primarily concerned with issues relating to the power and dominion of their own families rather than questions of concern to Christendom.

Giulio de' Medici spent the early part of his career working in the shadow of his cousin Leo X. Just three years younger than his cousin Giovanni de' Medici, the future Clement VII became part of the retinue of Giovanni once the latter became a cardinal. Once Leo became pontiff, he appointed his cousin Giulio to be archbishop of Florence and later a cardinal. During these years Giulio worked to further the interests of both the institutional church and of the Medici family. Although Pope Hadrian VI ruled for two years between the Florentine cousins, what the church really experienced was approximately twenty years of Medicean rule.

Ruling under the name of Clement VII, Giulio de' Medici (1523–34) continued many of the policies begun during Leo's pontificate. However, he had more problems juggling the interests of family, papal alliances, and church administration than he had had when he was only a cardinal. The 1520s and 1530s were difficult times because of all that was going on in Italy, France, Germany, England, and Spain. Consequently, Clement VII was frequently forced to negotiate a variety of agreements with an ever-changing group of rulers who wanted to control the territory of Italy, including Charles V, who sacked Rome in 1527. In order to achieve a balance of power that would preserve the autonomy of the church and the Papal States, Clement continually tried to make alliances with Roman nobles like Cardinal Pompeo Colonna or other Italian powers. He spent the last years of his pontificate enmeshed in the affairs of his family, who once again were trying to get back into Florence after being thrown out in 1527. He was successful in this last endeavor and also in arranging the marriage of Catherine de' Medici to Henry of Orléans in 1533. Much of his energy was expended in his cultural patronage, which included Michelangelo's *Last Judgment* as well as many humanist tracts. He finished the process of canonizing his predecessor archbishop Antonino of Florence, and he created the Monte della Fede, the papal-funded public debt, copied from the Florentine model. Like his cousin Leo X, Clement VII tried to balance the competing concerns of his family dynasty by, among other acts, making his cousin Ippolito a cardinal while also unsuccessfully trying to negotiate settlements with foreign states to keep them out of Italy. Although his pontificate is generally seen as a failure, his years in power were a time of great turmoil and change in Europe. By the time he died, his family was firmly ensconced in Florence, but much of Italy was under Spanish domination.

The last pope to be included in the Renaissance and Reformation part of this volume is Paul III, who was born Alessandro Farnese in 1469 and came to rule as Paul III beginning in 1534. Like several of the previous popes mentioned, the future Paul III (1534–49) received a humanist education that became important as his career in the church progressed. He served in a variety of ecclesiastical offices due to the patronage of Innocent VIII and Alexander VI as well as Julius II, Leo X, and Clement VII. His pontificate embodied most of the themes already revealed by other popes of this period. He was a religious reformer, a politician and diplomat, a patron of the arts and learning, and also a man committed to the advancement of his family.

Paul III was certainly known for his patronage of art, of learning, and beautifying the city of Rome. He spent much of his energy in revitalizing Rome after the sack of the city in 1527. His many projects included the reconstruction of the Piazza del Campidoglio, the construction of the Cappella Paolina, the decoration of the Sala Regia and of Castel Sant'Angelo, and the completion of Michelangelo's *Last Judgment* for the Sistine Chapel. He renewed both the physical fabric of the University of Rome and its human fabric by recruiting distinguished professors in a variety of fields while he also expanded the holdings of the Vatican Library and gave it a new director. He was also active in urban planning and hired both Michelangelo and Antonio Sangallo, the younger, to function as engineers overseeing the building of fortifications to protect the Holy See and its surrounding city.

Like many of his predecessors, Paul III wanted to lead a crusade against the Ottoman Empire. However, that crusade never materialized because he was not successful in convincing enough of the ruling monarchs of

Europe to work together with him on this project. He had a certain type of pragmatic approach to diplomacy that was very modern, but though he was successful in other areas of diplomacy, he failed to get sufficient commitments to make the crusade a reality.

At least on the surface, Paul III appeared committed to a true reform of the Catholic church as it existed in the sixteenth century. Just after he was elected, Paul III announced his intention of calling a general council to reform the church in the areas of doctrine and practice. Among his policies were episcopal residence for bishops, approval of the Jesuit order as well as several other new religious congregations, and the revival of the Roman Inquisition as a method of preventing the spread of Protestantism. Nepotism and simony continued during his pontificate, as he appointed his son and grandsons as cardinals. Nonetheless, he promoted more reform-minded, well-educated men to the position of cardinal than any other sixteenth-century pope. He commissioned *Consilium de emendanda ecclesia* (1537) from this group of men and then used it as a part of the deliberations during the Council of Trent (1545–63), which he convened, keeping his earlier promise. Although he did not live to see the end of the Council of Trent, he did set its agenda and begin this council that had an important impact on the way the church would be administered until Vatican II.

As the reader will see in the following biographies with their attendant bibliographies, the papacy during the Renaissance and Reformation underwent a variety of changes. While it developed many modern programs and functions, it still bore a great similarity to the condition in which it existed in 1308. Certainly, many of the medieval elements of the papacy continued throughout the Renaissance and Reformation. Many themes listed at the beginning of this introduction—simony, nepotism, and the development of a powerful papal monarchy, to name only three—were practiced by the eleven popes listed in this part. Conciliarism, crusading, and reform of the church and its hierarchy were also on the agenda of many of these pontiffs. A significant percentage of the men who sat on St. Peter's throne during these 250 years were truly religious and devoted to the welfare of the Catholic church. Nonetheless, many others seemed more intent on enriching and empowering their own families and states than in contributing to the development of a strong, universal church and a united Christendom. The territory of the Papal States was constantly being used as a springboard for the activities of the families of the pontiffs. The development of a strong papal monarchy with a pragmatic view of politics and its possibilities as well as its limitations certainly had its start during the Renaissance and Reformation. These trends would continue during the early modern period.

JOHN XXII (1316–34)

CAROL LANSING

Jacques Duèse was born in 1244 and was elected pope in 1316 after a violent struggle of over two years' duration between Gascon, Italian, and Provençal factions within the college of cardinals. Ultimately, the cardinals were held locked in conclave by the troops of Philip, count of Poitiers and leader of the French embassy. This lasted from 28 June to 7 August 1316, when the Gascons compromised with their opponents to elect Jacques Duèse. They probably agreed to the choice, as the historian of the Avignon papacy Guillaume Mollat suggested, only because Duèse was already seventy-two years old and looked frail and ill. If so, he surprised them. John XXII was an energetic, competent, and pugnacious man who lived to be ninety and in crucial ways shaped the late medieval papacy and church. His legacy was the centralization of authority in the huge, sedentary papal bureaucracy at Avignon, the extension of control over ecclesiastical benefices, a centralized financial system that vastly increased papal revenues, and the increased repression of religious dissent as heresy, most important, works of Meister Eckhart, Marsilius of Padua, and Peter John Olivi, as well as the Spiritual Franciscans.

The oldest of five children of a prominent family in Cahors, in southern Aquitaine, Jacques Duèse was born in 1244. Significantly, his education and career were legal and administrative rather than theological. He studied with the Dominicans at Cahors, then pursued civil and canon law at Montpellier, where he received a degree in civil law, and then studied theology briefly, first at Paris and then in Orléans. After teaching civil law for a time at Cahors, he became a professor of canon law at the University of Toulouse.

His administrative career began in Toulouse when he was already over fifty years of age. In 1295 he became a counselor to Louis, younger son of Charles II of Anjou and the new bishop of Toulouse. In a letter of 1298 Charles II called Duèse "his counselor and familiar" and appointed him temporary chancellor at the University of Avignon. With Angevin patronage, Duèse became a canon of Puy and in 1300 bishop of Fréjus. In 1308 Charles II of Anjou made him a royal counselor and chancellor of the Kingdom of Sicily. In 1310 he moved into the papal orbit when Clement V appointed him bishop of Avignon. He was sent on a mission to Philip the Fair that perhaps concerned the king's campaigns against Boniface VIII and the suppression of the Templars. Duèse also served on a commission examining accusations of lay interference in church affairs at the Council of Vienne (1311–12). Shortly afterwards Clement made him cardinal-priest of St. Vitale and then cardinal-bishop of Porto. After Clement's death in 1314, Duèse's candidacy for the papal tiara was pressed by the count of Poitiers and King Robert of Naples. He was not universally popular. Shortly after his election there were rumors of a plot by four Gascon cardinals to murder him, and the arrest of two men sneaking a baptized wax image of the pope into Avignon revealed another plot, an elaborate scheme by Hugues Géraud, a bishop of Cahors who had recently been convicted of simony, to accomplish John's slow death by poison and sorcery.

John XXII was a harsh and autocratic old man who created a climate of inflexible authority at Avignon. He was without doubt a gifted administrator. At his election the papal bureaucracy was in disarray, a result of the two-year vacancy and the spectacular legacies of the previous pope, Clement V, which had exhausted the treasury. John XXII was crowned in Lyons, but despite hopes of a return to Rome, he quickly moved the papal court to Avignon and then kept it there. Avignon was familiar from his tenure there as bishop. Once there, he is said to have left his papal chambers only to visit the cathedral next door. This put an end to the pattern of the last two centuries, an itinerant papal court. Once the curia was freed from the constraints of mobility, it was reorganized, and papal control of church offices and sources of revenue was vastly expanded.

John enlarged the papal right of reservation: the right to set aside the ordinary collators, typically a local bishop or cathedral chapter, and confer a vacant benefice. Popes from Clement IV in 1265 had gradually expanded this right, and John's constitution *Ex debito* extended papal reservations to a large number of benefices. For example, the 1317 *Execrabilis* forbade clerics to accumulate benefices and claimed for the papacy the right to collate the benefices that were given up in consequence. Reportedly, John provided or disposed of some 5,000 benefices, most of them resulting general or special reservation. Some 800 of the vacancies were episcopal and 531 abbatial. Over time John XXII's measures came close to eliminating the election of bishops by cathedral chapters. In France during his papacy 13 bishops were chosen by cathedral chapters, and 230 episcopal vacancies were provided or disposed by the papal curia. Multiple transfers became common: the 1325 death of the bishop of Auxerre, for example, led to six transfers. It is not surprising that it was during John XXII's papacy that bishops began to style themselves "bishop by grace of God and the Holy See."

The election of Pope John XXII by the conclave (1311), after a long vacancy.
(Courtesy of the Vatican Library)

The expansion of papal fiscal administration was engineered by the talented Gasbert of Laval, papal chamberlain from 1319 to 1347. The major sources of papal funds were taxes on ecclesiastical benefices. One lucrative innovation begun by Clement V and firmly established by John XXII was the claim on *annates*: when a person received a benefice disposed of or conferred by the Holy See, the first year's revenues were reserved to the Apostolic Camera. John also reserved the right to collect the revenues of vacant benefices that were in the pope's conferment. This included any benefices held improperly, for a variety of reasons. The Apostolic Camera under John XXII claimed in addition the right of spoil, which meant the right to seize the house and goods of deceased incumbents of benefices reserved to papal collation. Most of these goods were sold, though the popes added jewels and valuable books to their own collections.

Expanded authority and sources of revenue necessitated expanded administrative machinery; again, it was John's establishment of a sedentary court at Avignon that made this possible. His staff probably numbered between 300 and 400 people; Mollat calculated that in the year 1329–30 he spent close to three millon gold francs on their maintenance and payment. R.W. Southern measured the expansion of papal business by the average number of papal letters generated per year: 280 for Innocent III, who died in 1216, and 3,646 letters per year for John XXII, just a century later. As a jurist, unlike his predecessor, John attended to the orderly publication of canon law.

John XXII considered himself a reforming pope who sought to end practices that he deemed abuses: again, the bull *Execrabilis* revoked dispensations by his predecessor Clement V that had allowed clergy to hold more than one benefice. John considered that episcopal failure to combat heresy was sometimes due to overlarge dioceses and broke up a number of French and Spanish dioceses, notably Toulouse. He sought to reform the Hospitallers, weakened by debt and divided by the deposition of an incompetent grand master. John reorganized their finances. He similarly reformed and reorganized the Order of Grandmont. John XXII also encouraged the expansion of the church, including efforts toward a mission to Persia, though he hesitated to respond to a request for baptism from the pagan king Gediminas of Lithuania for fear of alienating the Teutonic Knights. John used the rich spoils from the suppression of the Knights Templar to create two Iberian orders intended to combat the Moors, the Order of Montesa in Aragon in 1317 and the Order of Christ in Portugal in 1319.

John XXII was an astute and tenacious man, and the events of his papacy were shaped by his personality. A 1323 exchange in consistory recorded by an emissary from Aragon conveys John's autocratic temperament. When Pietro Colonna argued Louis's claim to rule by right of his election and coronation, John replied angrily, threatening a Decretal against the imperial view. When Giacomo Stefaneschi cautioned him to beware the fury of the German, he retorted that the German would have to suffer his fury.

In another famous anecdote he is said to have cackled with malicious laughter at the discomfiture of two ambassadors who had contradicted themselves in an audience.

John acted as a patron, attracting scholars and probably Italian painters to Avignon, notably Petrarch. He collected manuscripts for the papal library, including not only theological works but classical texts. When Nicholas Trevet offered to write a commentary on the Pentateuch, John suggested Livy instead. He acquired copies of writings of Thomas Aquinas, and many—not only theological works but the commentary on the *Politics* of Aristotle—have extensive annotations in his own hand. This suggests, as Malcolm Lambert has pointed out, the influence of Aquinas's views on John's position in the struggle over Franciscan poverty. His musical taste was conservative. John was horrified by the ars nova, a new style in music pioneered by Philippe de Vitry, and in *Docta sanctorum* in 1324–25 he stated that singers in the new style were inebriating rather than soothing the ear and discouraging religious devotion with lewd gestures.

John XXII had a reputation for personal austerity and frugality. However, Lambert points out that his testimony in the 1290s for the canonization of a Franciscan saint suggests that unlike many contemporaries, John had little sympathy for radical poverty. In fact, he indulged his supporters and was guilty of nepotism on a grand scale, lavishing appointments and perquisites on friends and family. They became cardinals, administrators, legates, scribes, clerks, or stewards in the papal household. His brother Pierre was given 60,000 gold florins to purchase lands and a title; his sisters, nephews and nieces, and more distant kin were enriched as well. This tendency to surround himself with old friends and family members and to reward their loyalty can be seen as a reasonable response to the sometimes-murderous schemes of his opponents.

Both Petrarch and Dante bitterly condemned the extravagance of the Avignon court. Papal account books reveal that criticism of luxurious consumption at the court was thoroughly deserved. Mollat details a dinner given by John XXII to celebrate the wedding of a great-niece in 1324. The guests consumed an astonishing 4,012 loaves of bread, 8¾ oxen, 55¼ sheep, 8 pigs, 4 boars, many fish, 200 capons, 690 chickens, 580 partridges, 270 rabbits, 40 plovers, 37 ducks, 50 pigeons, 4 cranes, 2 pheasants, 2 peacocks, 292 small birds, 3,000 eggs, 2,000 various fruits, and 11 barrels of wine. Nonetheless, he managed to hide away large sums for himself and his family.

It is a measure of John's miserly reputation that the Florentine chronicler Giovanni Villani believed that at his death he left 18 million gold florins and treasure worth 7 million more. In fact, he left a respectable 750,000 florins in the papal treasury. John XXII also did not neglect his obligation to the poor. It is characteristic that he organized his local charities, creating an office termed the Pignotte that kept meticulous accounts of its ministrations to the poor. The Pignotte distributed clothing, medicine, wine, and food, again on a grand scale: Mollat calculated that in an average week the office gave away 67,500 loaves of bread. John XXII gave lavishly: according to Mollat, 7.16 percent of his total revenues were expended on gifts. Among the recipients were secular and regular churches; he often gave them bells, facilitating the saying of the Angelus, associated with indulgences. Not all agreed with the way he dispensed favors, and many criticized his policies.

John XXII moved energetically against dissident groups, driven perhaps by a concern to impose administrative order and reinforce papal authority, as well as a preference for black and white over shades of gray. Clement V had had little interest in inquisitions against heresy. John revived them, and the large-scale inquisitions of the period took place under his aegis, including the work of Bernard Gui and Jacques Fournier, investigating Waldensians, Beguines, Cathars, and converted Jews. *Ad nostrum*, the 1312 decision of the Council of Vienne against what the council considered the heresy of the Free Spirit—which did not exist as an organized movement—was issued early in John's pontificate. *Ad nostrum* was directly used to question suspects, clause by clause, in interrogations that effectively created a heretical sect. John also, like some predecessors, charged his enemies with heresy, including Italian Ghibellines, the Visconti, and the Este.

In some instances John's policies could be unexpectedly mild. He defended Beguines who led stable lives and avoided theological disputation in the 1318 *Racio recta*. He made efforts to protect Jewish communities from the attacks of the Pastoureaux. However, John also renewed his predecessors' proscriptions of the Talmud, and when Jews were driven from papal territories, he aided in the foundation of chapels dedicated to the Virgin on the sites of synagogues. At the same time, he launched investigations into suspect theologians. Jean de Pouilly was a master at the University of Paris who maintained that the secular clergy received their jurisdiction directly from God, and denied the force of any contradictory privilege, even one that issued from the Holy See. John, recognizing in this a challenge to papal authority, summoned Jean de Pouilly to Avignon to debate his position and then condemned his errors in the 1321 bull *Vas electionis*. The writings of the great Dominican mystic Meister Eckhart were scrutinized, and in 1329 eight propositions were censured, eleven were determined to be suspected of heresy, and seven were declared heretical. Sometime between 1318 and 1320 a commission of eight theologians appointed by John to investigate the Franciscan theologian Peter John Olivi's *Lecture on the Apocalypse* reported that the commentary should be condemned. The work, influenced by the millenarian views of the twelfth-century Calabrian abbot Joachim of Fiore, prophesied that at the coming of the sixth age the carnal church (identified with the papacy) would be destroyed and the true church (comprised of those who observed the poverty of Christ and the apostles, the Spiritual Franciscans) would rule. Sixty propositions were censured in February 1326.

Immediately after his election John XXII was faced with petitions from both sides in the bitter division between Conventual and Spiritual Franciscans. In Provence unauthorized Spirituals held two convents, Narbonne and Béziers, by force. The new minister-general, Michael of Cesena, requested from the curia the suppression of the unauthorized groups from Tuscany as well as Provence. An investigation was held in Avignon in 1316–17 in which the Spiritual leaders Ubertino da Casale, Angelo da Clareno, the leader of the Provençal group, and two other friars were questioned, and Angelo was imprisoned. The pope then moved against both groups, summoning sixty-four friars from Provence to the curia. The immediate issues were their defiant insistence on wearing dramatic short, ragged habits and their refusal to store provisions. Their interview with the pope was disastrous; ultimately, as the friars called out, "Holy father, justice, justice," John ordered them detained to await his decision.

John XXII's bulls on the Franciscan question moved from questions of authority to an attack on the theology of poverty itself. On 7 October he issued *Quorumdam exigit*, requiring obedience to superiors over fidelity to poverty and the Rule. "Poverty is great, but unity is greater; obedience is the greatest good if it is preserved intact." The Spirituals believed that their Rule was "the form of the evangelical life," laid down by Christ himself and thus beyond the power of Franciscan superiors or even the pope. However, with *Quorumdam exigit*, the only alternative to obedience was heresy. The bull was directly used in questioning suspect friars: would they obey and admit papal authority to make these precepts? Most Spirituals within the order submitted and abjured the Spiritual interpretation of the Rule. Four who ultimately refused were burned for heresy. John then pursued Franciscan rebels in two bulls: *Sancta Romana* of 30 December 1317 excommunicated the *fraticelli*, Spirituals outside the order, and *Gloriosam ecclesiam* of 23 January 1318 condemned the Tuscan Spirituals and five errors in their beliefs.

The dispute over Franciscan poverty was bound up with the problem of the nature of papal authority. It began when John on 26 March 1322 issued the Bull *Quia nonnunquam* that claimed the right to revoke the edicts of preceding popes. This opened up the possibility of revocation of clauses of the August 1279 decretal of Nicholas III, *Exiit qui seminat*, which had accepted the evangelical basis of absolute poverty, the doctrine that Christ and the apostles had had no dominion over property. *Exiit* was, as Malcolm Lambert argues, the rock on which the Franciscan order's case rested. It allowed the Franciscans to renounce ownership by distinguishing between use and dominion, or possession: the papacy accepted dominion over goods that were used by the Franciscans. John's motives for attacking the bull have been debated; some argue that he perceived *Exiit* as an obstacle to the condemnation of Olivi's Apocalypse commentary, while others, notably Brian Tierney, report that he recognized that the Franciscan ideal was a fundamental indictment of the entire church that had long departed from the poverty of the apostles.

The Franciscans, meeting in late May 1322 in their general chapter, recognized the threat and responded with general encyclicals insisting that

Exiit was immutable. John, angered at this slight to papal authority, answered with *Ad conditorem* (8 December 1322, second version 14 January 1323), which did abrogate the clause in *Exiit* in which the papacy accepted dominion over the goods used by Franciscans. *Ad conditorem* in fact questioned the value of the renunciation of dominion that was at the heart of Franciscan poverty, stating that in things that could be consumed by use there could be no use without dominion. After a formal appeal from Bonagratia of Bergamo, the official Franciscan representative at the curia, the bull was revised, sharpened, and reissued. Subsequently, in *Cum inter nonnullos* of 12 November 1323, John directly condemned two doctrines of absolute poverty, the idea that Christ and the apostles owned nothing individually or collectively and the corollary that Christ and the apostles had "the simple use of fact" but no right of use, sale, or donation over the things they held. In November 1324 John published *Quia quorundam mentes*, which fully formulated his position. The bull is important not only to the history of Franciscan poverty but also for the debates over the history of the doctrine of papal infallibility: which decrees did John consider to be revocable, and which not? Brian Tierney has argued that John had understood the Franciscan idea that *Exiit* was irrecoverable as an attack on his sovereignty, but with *Quia quorundam mentes* shifted to a position that opened up the possibility of the claim of infallibility.

John XXII's attack ultimately drove a group of Franciscan leaders into schism. John summoned the minister-general Michael of Cesena to Avignon to defend his position and then detained him until the minister-general escaped on the night of 26–27 May 1328 and with Bonagratia of Bergamo and the brilliant English theologian William of Ockham took refuge with Holy Roman Emperor Louis of Bavaria. From the Franciscan convent in Munich Ockham fired off attacks on John's political and theological views, culminating in his *Opus nonaginata dierum*. John looked for support elsewhere.

Like the other Avignon popes, John XXII tended to support French policy and allowed considerable financial subsidy to the French Crown. Although the tenths of 1312 and 1333 were collected to fund crusades, the profits went to the French monarchs with little interest in a crusade. Other fiscal privileges were granted: Philip the Tall was actually allowed to collect *annates* in France, Navarre, and Burgundy for four years. Other monarchs allied with the papacy were at times granted financial aid, though not on this scale. The bulk of the expanded papal revenues were spent on military campaigns in Italy, where forces led by the papal legate, Cardinal Bertrand du Poujet, engaged in an endless military and diplomatic struggle against the Visconti of Milan and their allies. After Bologna yielded to the Roman church in 1327, John decided to transfer the curia there and make the town the center of the Papal States. Palaces were requisitioned, and the fortress La Galliera was adapted as a papal citadel. However, Bertrand du

Poujet was unable to subdue the region. In the rapidly shifting alliances of the period, the papal cause lost the support of the Florentines and that of Robert of Anjou. When the Bolognese successfully rebelled in August 1334 and razed La Galliera, the planned return to Italy proved premature.

John engaged in a prolonged struggle over the papal role in imperial elections. When Louis of Bavaria was named holy Roman emperor and his election was disputed by Frederick of Austria, John XXII claimed the right to administer the imperial throne during a vacancy and to decide between the claimants. Instead, Louis defeated Frederick in battle and then sent an army to establish a vice-regent in Italy. On 8 October 1323 John began a process of excommunication, calling for Louis to step down from the imperial throne. Louis answered in December by protesting obedience and defending his position in the Appeal of Nuremberg. In January 1324 he called in the Appeal of Frankfurt for arbitration from a general church council. On 23 March 1324 John excommunicated him. Louis in the Appeal of Sachsenhausen on 22 May labeled John a heretic for his condemnation of the Spiritual Franciscans and called for a general council to replace him. Louis's position was justified by the political theories of Marsilius of Padua. The *Defensor pacis*, published in 1324, restricted the church to spiritual matters, denying it, for example, the right to coerce. Marsilius argued that ultimate authority in the church resided in a general council of the people, convoked by civil authority. John condemned five statements in the *Defensor pacis* as heretical in October 1327 and excommunicated Marsilius.

The conflict escalated in 1328 as John issued bulls that deprived Louis of his fiefs and then freed his vassals of their oaths of loyalty; Louis deposed John as a heretic pope and had an antipope, the Franciscan Pietro of Corbara, crowned in Rome. John was ultimately able to bring the antipope to heel: the friar recanted in consistory in Avignon and ended his days imprisoned in the papal palace. But John was not able to compel obedience from Louis, perhaps because of the harshness of his position. The elderly pope had deprived Louis of the imperial title by decree and would not be reconciled until Louis resigned it. Despite formidable allies, John failed. Ultimately, Louis abdicated to Clement VI in 1343.

In a sermon of 1331 on All Saints' Day John XXII preached a new understanding of the Beatific Vision. The question raised by John broke with earlier debates, which concerned how a created intellect can have vision of the divine essence. John instead asked when. How can there be a collective Last Judgment if the souls of the just and those of the damned have already received their particular judgments? The Scholastics had argued that souls purified after death can enjoy the Beatific Vision, a vision that will be intensified after the Last Judgment. John preached instead that until the resurrection of the body, the souls of the just can enjoy no vision of the divine essence. They instead await the Last Judgment, contented with the vision of the glorified humanity of Christ. He elaborated this view in a series of sermons in which he preached that before the resurrection of the body the dead do not possess eternal life, true beatitude, or the beatific vision. Similarly, the damned will live in Hell only after the Last Judgment. Why did John take this position? William of Ockham commented that he was completely ignorant of theology. Andrea Tabarroni argues that John's position reinforced papal monarchy, in opposition to the separation of spiritual and temporal powers in the views of his opponents. John's position meant that the reign of Christ, as both God and man, of necessity extended until the Last Judgment. The current theory of papal monarchy, inherited from Innocent III, based the spiritual and temporal authority of the pope on the reign of Christ. Because Christ's rule was the foundation and model of that of the pope, the vicar of Christ, John's position assured the continuation of papal jurisdiction literally until the end of time.

The sermons opened up a major controversy. John's position was attacked as heretical by his opponents, including Michael of Cesena, Bonagratia of Bergamo, and William of Ockham; he was defended by others, including a group of Oxford masters. Ultimately, debate was joined even by European princes, notably Robert of Anjou. Cardinal Napoleone Orsini, plotting John's deposition with Louis of Bavaria, urged the convocation of a council to judge him for heresy. John fell ill and on 3 December 1334 recanted in the presence of the cardinals. He died the following day.

SELECTED BIBLIOGRAPHY

Albe, Edmond. *Autour de Jean XXII: Hugues Géraud, évêque de Cahors: L'affaire des poisons et des envoûtements en 1317*. Cahors: J. Girma, 1904.

Babylon on the Rhone: A Translation of Letters by Dante, Petrarch, and Catherine of Siena on the Avignon Papacy. Ed. Robert Coogan. Madrid: José Porrúa Turanzas; Potomac, Md.: Studia Humanitatis, 1983.

Baluze, Etienne. *Vitae paparum avenionensium*. Ed. G. Mollat. Vol. 1. 1916. Paris: Letouzey & Ané, 1914–27. 107–94. This contains seven accounts of John's life.

Bock, Friedrich. "Studien zum politischen Inquisitionsprozess Johanns XXII." *Quellen und Forschungen aus italienischen Archiven und Bibliotheken* 26 (1935–36): 21–142.

Brampton, C.K. "Personalities at the Process against Ockham at Avignon, 1324–26." *Franciscan Studies* 26 (1966): 4–25.

Burr, David. *Olivi and Franciscan Poverty: The Origins of the Usus Pauper Controversy*. Philadelphia: University of Pennsylvania Press, 1989.

Caillet, Louis. *La papauté d'Avignon et l'Église de France: La politique bénéficiale du pape Jean XXII en France, 1316–1334*. Paris: Presses universitaires de France, 1975.

Dykmans, Marc. "Nouveau Textes de Jean XXII sur la vision béatifique." *Revue d'histoire ecclésiastique* 66 (1971): 401–17.

————. *Pour et contre Jean XXII en 1333: Deux traités avignonnais sur la vision béatifique.* Studi e Testi 274. Vatican City: Biblioteca Apostolica Vaticana, 1975.

Göller, Emil. *Die Einnahmen der Apostolischen Kammer unter Johann XXII.* Paderborn: F. Schöningh, 1910.

Guillemain, Bernard. *La Cour pontificale d'Avignon, 1309–1376: Étude d'une société.* Bibliothèque des Écoles françaises d'Athènes et de Rome, fasc. 201. Paris: E. de Boccard, 1962.

Heft, James. *John XXII and Papal Teaching Authority.* Texts and Studies in Religion, vol. 27. Lewiston, N.Y. E. Mellen Press, 1986.

Housley, Norman. *The Avignon Papacy and the Crusades, 1305–1378.* Oxford: Clarendon Press; New York: Oxford University Press, 1986.

Lambert, Malcolm. "The Franciscan Crisis under John XXII." *Franciscan Studies* 32 (1972): 123–43.

————. *Franciscan Poverty: The Doctrine of the Absolute Poverty of Christ and the Apostles in the Franciscan Order, 1210–1323.* London: Church Historical Society, 1961.

Lettres communes, analysées d'après les registres dits d'Avignon et du Vatican, 1316–1334. Ed. G. Mollat. 16 vols. Bibliothèque des Écoles françaises d'Athènes et de Rome, 3rd ser. Paris: A. Fontemoing, 1904–46.

Lettres secrètes et curiales du Pope Jean XXII, 1316–1334, relatives à la France, extraits des registres du Vatican. Ed. A. Coulon and S. Clemencet. 3 vols. Paris: Bibliothèque des Écoles françaises d'Athènes et de Rome, 1906–72.

Maier, Anneliese. "Annotazioni autografe di Giovanni XXII in Codici vaticani." *Rivista di storia della chiesa in Italia* 6 (1952): 317–22. This details John XXII's revealing marginal comments on manuscripts now contained in the Vatican Library.

Mazeika, R.J., and S.C. Rowell. "Zelatores Maximi: Pope John XXII, Archbishop Frederick of Riga, and the Baltic Mission, 1305–1340." *Archivum historiae pontificiae* 31 (1993): 33–68.

Mollat, Guilaume. "L'Election du pape Jean XXII." *Revue d'histoire de l'Eglise de France* 1 (1910): 34–49, 147–66.

————. "Jean XXII fut-il un avare?" *Revue d'histoire ecclésiastique* 6 (1906): 34–45.

————. *The Popes at Avignon, 1305–1378.* Trans. Janet Love from the ninth French edition. New York: Thomas Nelson, 1963.

Renouard, Yves. *The Avignon Papacy, 1305–1403.* Trans. D. Bethell. London: Faber, 1970.

————. *Les relations des papes d'Avignon et des compagnies commerciales et bancaires de 1316 à 1378.* Bibliothèque des Écoles française d'Athènes et de Rome, 151. Paris: A. Fontemoing, 1941.

Les sermons de Jean XXII sur la vision béatifique. Miscellanea historiae pontificiae, vol. 34. Rome: Presses de l'Université grégorienne, 1973.

Southern, R.W. *Western Society and the Church in the Middle Ages.* Harmondsworth, England: Pelican Books, 1970.

Tabarroni, Andrea. *Paupertas Christi et Apostolorum: L'ideale francescano in discussione (1322–1324).* Rome: Istituto Palazzo Borromini, 1990.

Tarrant, Jacqueline. *A Study and Critical Edition of the Extravagantes Joannis XXII.*

2 vols. Ph. D. diss., Centre for Medieval Studies, University of Toronto, 1976. The *Extravagantes*, edited by Tarrant, are published in the Monumenta iuris canonici, ser. B, Corpus Collectionum. Vatican City: Biblioteca Apostolica Vaticana, 1983.

Tierney, Brian. *Origins of Papal Infallibility, 1150–1350: A Study of the Concepts of Infallibility, Sovereignty, and Tradition in the Middle Ages.* Leiden: Brill. 1972.

Trottmann, Christian. *La vision béatifique: Des disputes scolastiques à sa définition par Benoît XII.* Bibliothèque des Écoles françaises d'Athènes et de Rome, fasc. 289. Rome: École française de Rome, 1995.

Valois, N. "Jacques Duèse, pape sous le nom de Jean XXII." *Histoire littéraire de la France* 34 (1915): 391–630.

Villani, Giovanni. *Cronica: con le continuazioni di Matteo e Filippo*, ed. Giovanni Aquilecchia. Turin: Einaudi, 1979.

Weakland, John. "John XXII before His Pontificate, 1244–1316: Jacques Duèse and His Family." *Archivum historiae pontificiae* 10 (1972): 161–85.

Wood, Diana. *Clement VI: The Pontificate and Ideas of an Avignon Pope.* Cambridge: Cambridge University Press, 1989.

GREGORY XI (1370-78)

LAURA DE ANGELIS

Since Roman times history and tradition had bound the papal seat so closely to Rome that by the thirteenth century the idea that a pope could reside outside its city walls seemed impossible. Yet a sudden change occurred with Pope Clement V (1305–14), a native of Gascony, who was intimidated by the party struggles in Italy and had been convinced by the king of France, Philip the Fair, to remain in the safe land of France. From that point on the papal seat remained in Avignon for more than seventy years, the city having later been sold to the church by Joan I of Naples, countess of Provence. The removal of the papal seat to Avignon caused difficulties for the entire Italian peninsula and especially for Rome, which lost not only its position as the capital of Christendom, but also the economic benefits deriving from the presence of the papal court. Rome also lost its position among the other major cities in Italy and became prey to increasing political anarchy.

Innocent VI (1352–62) made the first attempt to restore the papal authority to Italy with the prospect of a quick return of the pope to Rome. This was possible under his successor Urban V in 1367, but the event, long awaited by the major part of devout Italians, lasted only the short period of three years. The second and definitive attempt was made by Urban's successor, Gregory XI, ten years later.

Pierre Roger II, the future Pope Gregory XI, belonged to a family of the petite noblesse of the Limousin that had transformed itself during the fourteenth century from small landlords into a very influential clan, enjoying relationships with the royal houses of both France and England.

The change in the family's status was ephemeral and rapid and can be explained by the positions of many of its members in the church hierarchy. The key for the family's achievements lay in Gregory XI's paternal uncle, Pope Clement VI, who granted several of its members substantial ecclesiastic benefices. Born around 1330 into such a family, the future Gregory XI began his ecclesiastical career before the age of ten with canonnies and prebends provided by his uncle, Pope Clement VI. Trained as a lawyer and an administrator of the church, he was destined for a rapid and brilliant career within its ranks. In August 1347 Pierre Roger was named a notary of the Holy See; in May 1348, barely eighteen years old and only a deacon, he became, to general perplexity, cardinal-deacon of Santa Maria Nova.

After his promotion Pierre Roger left Avignon and enrolled in civil law at the University of Perugia, where he also studied canon law, theology, and moral philosophy, all subjects that he then mastered brilliantly to general admiration, even that of his own teacher, the famous Pietro Baldo degli Ubaldi. For the five years he dedicated to his studies, very little evidence can be found of his actions in the papal registers. Also, for about ten years afterwards Pierre worked quietly in the sacred college and only rarely appears in the papal records. It took twenty years after his promotion to the cardinalate before he entered the higher ranks of the ecclesiastical hierarchy. He accompanied Pope Urban V in his first attempt to return the papacy to Rome. Fresh from the failure of the Roman project, Urban V died in Avignon on 19 December 1370. Ten days later, when the cardinals met in conclave, in less than a day they chose the new pontiff, Pierre Roger II. His rapid election was due to a series of factors, such as his diplomatic abilities, family connections (six cardinals of the seventeen or eighteen gathered in the conclave belonged to the Roger family), and the high consideration in which he was held by the cardinals, during his twenty-two years while he had been in the sacred college.

After his election, still being a simple deacon, he was ordained a priest and on 5 January 1371 was crowned pope under the name of Gregory XI. The main issues in his papal program were a crusade against the Turks, the return of the papal seat to Rome, and the reestablishment of political stability in Italy, as well as peace between France and England, which had been engaged in a long and destructive war. Before moving the papal court to Rome, Gregory wanted to restore order within the church, reform the Dominican order, and reduce the Hospitallers to the observance of their rule. His religious zeal was directed especially against the heretics. Europe was then shaken by religious movements that later would lead to the Reformation. Gregory used the Inquisition with a very firm hand and reinforced it, increasing the number of inquisitors and forcing noncooperative sovereigns to enforce the laws on heresy.

The continuation of the Crusades, one of the main tasks in his pontificate, also revealed Gregory XI's traditional view of society and would lead to his long and arduous attempt to weld together different military forces against the Turks and eventually, given the lack of cohesion among the Christian armies, to the failure of the project. The Kingdom of Jerusalem had been conquered by the Turks in 1291. In Christian hands remained only Lesser Armenia and the island of Cyprus, and of the three military orders, only the Hospitallers were willing to fulfill their mission in the East. Since then Christian countries had lacked any interest in new crusades, and this factor explains the pope's ceaseless efforts and disappointments in starting a new one. He first called for a crusade in the summer of 1371, with the declared intention of assembling Christian armies for the following March. The battle at the Maritza River on 26 September 1371, in which the Turkish army destroyed the Serbs and conquered Macedonia, raised awareness in the West that Hungary, Albania, and the Adriatic coast were also in the same danger, and for the first time allowed the papal plea for action to be heard. England and France, engaged in a war with each other, and Germany, where the emperor was in a very uneasy political situation, were unable to supply military assistance. One by one, the Italian powers, King Louis of Hungary, and the Byzantines, who had all promised to carry out the crusade, abandoned the project, and the pope was left alone with the Hospitallers.

Pope Gregory XI. (Hulton/Archive by Getty Images)

The crusade was delayed by the papal plan to return the papacy to Rome and by the necessity of selling some of the Hospitallers' land to sustain the expenditures for the campaign. Once the campaign started, in April 1378, it came to a very quick and sudden end: the Christian army was captured in an ambush, leading to a very miserable end to years of effort. Pope Gregory had died a few weeks earlier and was thus spared the sight of the inglorious end of his hopes.

Gregory knew, as did his predecessors, that the papal seat was in Rome and that they would eventually bring the papacy back to Italy. Therefore the Avignon popes were very interested in the political situation in the peninsula and continued the traditional policy of independence of Rome and the Papal States against any foreign intervention. The major enemy in this period was represented by the Visconti family in Milan, and Gregory assumed the task of stopping its expansionism with the same tenacity he had shown in organizing the crusade, although this time with much better results. He succeeded in stopping Bernabò and Galeazzo Visconti in their threat to control central Italy and its main city-states. The main reason for the papal wars against the Visconti was the effort to secure Tuscany as a sort of buffer state between the two major Italian powers. The papacy needed to protect the independence of the Tuscan city-states, and it also held the city of Bologna, which was a key to the Apennine passes into Tuscany and central Italy.

A few weeks before pope Gregory XI's election Bernabò Visconti sent help to three lords (of Sassuolo, Montegarullo, and Ferrara) in revolt against Niccolò d'Este, lord of Modena and Ferrara. The papal legate in Bologna saw this as a revolt against their rightful master, and the Visconti help was considered improper. The newly elected pope Gregory immediately sent military troops to his ally Niccolò d'Este and called for help for the papal legate in Bologna. The Malatesta of Rimini, Francesco da Carrara of Padua, and the Florentines also were urged to keep their troops ready. The campaign, whose preparation and diplomatic efforts on both sides to secure allies had lasted for years, ended with the Battle of Montichiari. The victory of the papal army, though, was not definitive, and the Visconti managed to maintain their power in Milan. Financing the campaign was a heavy burden on papal finances and eventually forced the pope to impose heavy taxes throughout Europe. Papal revenues suddenly increased, from an average of about 200,000 florins under Urban V and Clement VI to the incredible sum of 770,000 florins in 1373.

The difficulty of raising such enormous amounts of money played in favor of a short military campaign, and the growing hostility of Florence toward the papacy became an urgent concern. A truce was signed in June 1375 that allowed the Visconti to prepare themselves for a new and easier expansion project. The papacy, however, immediately engaged in a new and dangerous war to fight a rebellion within the Papal States under the leadership of Florence.

This represented a new and dangerous development in the Italian political scene because the usual relationship between the papacy and the cities of central Italy had always been one of alliance against outside opponents such as the German emperor or, more recently, the expansionist aims of the Visconti family. The transportation of the papal seat to Avignon had weakened the papal government, leaving the subject territory with more freedom and the independent city-states with an increasing influence in the area. The papal project to return to Rome, preceded by the reestablishment of the pontiff's dominance in his own state, was received with suspicion, skepticism, fear, and open opposition. Discontent spread in the Papal States as many towns complained of mismanagement and extortions by papal officials. The pontiff apparently did not know what was happening in the Papal States in his absence. Gregory had left control of his state to subordinates, who were known for their severity and who underestimated the extent of popular discontent. Moreover, the successful papal war to gain control of the city of Perugia, which ended in 1371, also marked the beginning of an uneasy relationship with Florence, which was worried by imperialist papal ambitions in central Italy.

Within Florence itself the political situation was difficult and confusing. The *gente nuova*, or rising new groups, were trying to obtain participation in Florentine politics and to win a permanent position in the city councils. In their struggle they found their toughest opponents to be the patricians gathered in the Parte Guelfa. One of the most acrimonious debates between the two parties concerned the city's traditionally propapal foreign policy, which the *gente nuova* considered more a burden than an advantage for Florence. Despite strong papal support, the Parte Guelfa was losing credibility especially because of the suspicion among Florentine citizens that the papacy would enlarge its borders at the expense of the Tuscan towns. On the other side, the pope was obliged to regain strength and consolidate power in his own state in order to be able to transfer his seat to Rome, as had already been announced in 1372. Small incidents occurred in the following years between the papacy and some Tuscan cities, especially Florence and Siena, until Florence was placed under an interdict. In 1374 Florence and other Tuscan cities formed a defensive alliance without including the papacy, to which they were bound in theory by a previous alliance.

During the recurrence of plague and famine in the years 1374 and 1375 the papal vicars Gerard du Puy and Guillaume Noellet, in spite of papal orders, refused to sell their surplus grain to cities like Savona, Lucca, Pisa, Genoa, Padua, and Florence. The Florentines, refusing to believe the pope's justifications, saw in this refusal a confirmation of their worst fear of Gregory's imperialist intentions. The imminent end of the Visconti war also further disturbed their precarious relations. Florence feared that the mercenary troops, once they were without pay, would ransack its territory. In a conference of the major Tuscan cities held in Florence in June 1375, nuncios from Avignon asked for a financial contribution that would help continue the war against the Visconti. However, perhaps because of confusion in transmission of the news, the papal negotiator in Milan signed the truce the day before the conference in Florence opened. When news of the truce arrived in Florence, the reactions were furious. While the mercenaries from the northern battlefields headed south, Florence decided to declare war on the papacy.

Florence managed, in its search for allies, to foment rebellion within the Papal States by preaching against Italian slavery under a French yoke. Rebellion actually arose in the Papal States between 1375 and January 1376, and Gregory had to react with strength. Therefore he turned to Giovanna, queen of Naples, for help, and also to some lords of northern Italy, even the Visconti of Milan. The answers he received were quite cautious, which is why the campaign was undertaken by two mercenary companies. Yet initially the military results were quite poor, and the situation improved only after the papal seat returned to Rome and the sentences of interdiction and excommunication against Florence attained their desired effects and allowed for negotiations. Because of the excommunication launched against Florence, Florentine merchants had been expelled from France, Britain, and the Iberian peninsula, causing a strong antiwar movement within Florence itself. Quickly the league against the pope dissolved. Florence sent several missions to the pope, but his excessive claims had the result of prolonging the war until 1378, when peace was attained through the mediation of Bernabò Visconti. Gregory died in March, before the final settlement of all discord with Florence. It was his successor, Urban VI, who saw the end of the war and the victory for the church.

The alliance with England and especially France was essential for the church in every enterprise the pope had envisaged. The Hundred Years' War removed the two powerful countries from any possibility of sending help to the pope when he needed it. Therefore Gregory did all he could to help settle the differences between the two countries, even if he was considered by the English as an interested mediator because of his nationality and his closeness to the French Crown. He tried, with no success, to organize peace talks and urged the two sovereigns to reach an agreement that could allow an alliance in the campaign against the Muslims. Understanding that his influence was very limited, the pope decided to sail for Rome without waiting for visible results of his own efforts to ensure a positive solution of the war.

In Rome the pope's energies were absorbed by the Italian affairs, the war against Florence and the rebellion in the Papal States, until his death on 27 March 1378. Throughout his life and pontificate Gregory was able to maintain intense and continuous work habits, engaging himself in enterprises aimed at reaffirming the central role of the church in maintaining peace and order in the world, destroying heresy, and regaining the Holy Land for the Christian faith. He was interested in culture, not just in theological and juridical matters; he also appreciated many humanistic authors for their use of classical culture. He had talent as a diplomat, and even if his natural inclination led him to slow decisions that many interpreted as lack of a strong character, he never lost a clear perception of his own goals.

The main problems Gregory encountered and that led to the failure of most of his enterprises were represented by the very purposes he set up for his pontificate, namely, those of the continuation of the traditional policies of the papacy and his lack of creative and innovative leadership.

With Gregory XI's death the papacy entered into a severe crisis that soon brought the church to the Great Schism.

SELECTED BIBLIOGRAPHY

Annales ecclesiastici. Vol. 26, 1356–80. Ed. Casare Baronio; newer ed. by A. Theiner. Bar-le-Duc, 1872.

Annali d'Italia dal principio dell'era volgare sino all'anno MDCCXLIX. Milan, 1819.

Antonelli, M. "La dominazione pontificia nel Patrimonio negli ultimi venti anni del periodo avignonese." *Archivio della Regia Società romana di storia patria* 30 (1907): 269–332; 31 (1908): 121–68.

Arnould, M. *Histoire générale des finances de la France.* Paris: 1806.

Atiya, A. *The Crusade in the Later Middle Ages.* London: Metheun, 1938.

Baluze, Etienne. *Vitae paparum avenionensium.* Ed. G. Mollat. 4 vols. 1693. Paris Letouzey & Ané, 1914–27.

Barber, M. *The Trial of the Templars.* Cambridge: Cambridge University Press, 1978.

Baudoin, I. *Les chevaliers de l'Ordre de S. Jean de Jerusalem.* Paris, 1629.

Berlière, U. *Les collectories pontificals dans les anciens diocèses de Cambrai, Thérouanne, et Tournai au XIV siècle.* Analecta vaticano-belgica, vol. 10. Rome: Institut historique belge de Rome, 1929.

Brucker, G.A. *Florentine Politics and Society, 1343–1378.* Princeton: Princeton University Press, 1962.

Bullarum, diplomatum, et privilegiorum sanctorum romanorum pontificum. Taurinensis editio locupletoir facta. Vol. 6, ed. A. Tomassetti, Turin: 1859.

Calendar of Entries in the Papal Registers Relating to Great Britain and Ireland: Papal Letters. Ed. W.H. Bliss and J.A. Twemlow, vol. 4. 1879. New York: Kraus Reprint, 1971.

Cerasoli, F. "Gregorio XI e Giovanna I di Napoli: Documenti inediti dell'archivio vaticano." *Archivio storico per le province napoletane* 23 (1898): 3–24; 24 (1899): 307–28, 403–27.

Chronicon Angliae. Ed. E.M. Thompson, London: Longman and Co., 1874.

Cochin, C. "Un manuscrit de Sainte-Croix de Jérusalem aux armes de Gregoire XI." *Mélanges d'archéologie et d'histoire* 27 (1908): 363–72.

Codex diplomaticus dominii temporalis Sanctae Sedis. Vol. 1, ed. A. Theiner. 1861. Reprint, Frankfurt: Minerva, 1964.

Cognasso, F. *I Visconti.* Varese: Dall'Oglio, 1966.

La correspondance de Pierre Ameilh, archevêque de Naples, puis d'Embrun (1363–1369). Ed. H. Bresc. Paris, 1972.

"Cronacha della città di Perugia dal 1309 al 1491, nota col nome di Diario del Graziani." Ed. A. Fabretti, *Archivio storico italiano* 16, pt. 1 (1850): 69–750.

Davies, R.G. "The Anglo-Papal Concordat of Bruges, 1375: A Reconsideration." *Archivum historiae pontificiae* 19 (1981): 97–146.

De Feo, I. *Giovanna D'Angiò, regina di Napoli.* Naples: F. Fiorentino, 1968.

Déprez, E. *Les préliminaires de la guerre de cent ans: La papauté, la France, et l'Angleterre (1328–1342)*. Bibliothèque des Écoles françaises d'Athènes et de Rome, fasc. 86. Paris: A. Fontemoning 1902.

Dupré Theseider, E. *I papi di Avignone e la questione romana*. Le Monnier, Florence: 1939.

———. "La rivolta di Perugia nel 1375 contro l'abate di Monmaggiore e i suoi precedenti politici." *Bollettino della Deputazione di storia patria per l'Umbria* 35 (1938): 69–166.

Dykmans, M. "La bulle de Gregoire à la veille du Grand Schisme." *Mélanges de l'École française de Rome: Moyen âge–temps modernes* 83 (1971): 389–438.

Ellis, J.T. *Anti-Papal Legislation in Medieval England (1066–1377)*. Diss., Washington, D.C.: 1930.

Epistolario di Coluccio Salutati. Vol. 1, ed. F. Novati. Rome: Istituto Storico Italiano per il Medioevo, Forzani, 1891.

Eubel, C. *Hierarchia catholica medii aevi*. Vol. 1. Regensberg, 1898. Reprint, Padua: II messaggero di S. Antonio, 1960.

Forot, V. *Les cardinaux limousins*. Paris: J. Schemit, 1907.

Froissart, Jean. *Chroniques*. 11 vols. Ed. Siméon Luce, G. Raynaud and L. Mirot. Paris: J. Renouard, 1869–99.

Gherardi, A. "Appendice: La guerra dei fiorentini con papa Gregorio XI detta la guerra degli Otto Santi." *Archivio storico italiano*, ser. 3, 6, pt. 2 (1867): 208–32.

———. "Di un trattato per far ribellare al comune di Firenze la terra di Prato, nell'anno 1375." *Archivio storico italiano*, ser. 3, 10, pt. 1 (1869): 3–26.

Glenisson, J. "Une administration médiévale aux prises avec la disette: La question des blés dans les provinces italiennes de l'État pontifical en 1374–1375." *Moyen âge* 57 (1951): 303–26.

———. "Les origines de la révolte de l'État pontifical en 1375." *Rivista di storia della Chiesa in Italia* 5 (1951): 145–68.

Les grandes chroniques de France. Vol. 9, ed. Jules Viard. Paris: Librairie ancienne H. Champion et C. Klincksieck, 1937.

Guillemain, B. *La cour pontificale d'Avignon, 1309–1376: Étude d'une société*. Paris: E. de Boccard, 1962.

Hale, J.R., J.R.L. Highfield, and B. Smalley, eds. *Europe in the Late Middle Ages*. London: Faber & Faber, 1965.

Hay, D. *Europe in the Fourteenth and Fifteenth Centuries*. London: Longmans, 1966.

Hodgson, F.C. *Venice in the Thirteenth and Fourteenth Centuries*. London: G. Allen & Sons, 1910.

Jordan, C. "Le Sacre College au moyen âge." *Révue des cours et conférences* 23 (1921–22): 128–41.

Lacaille, H. "Enguerran de Coucy au service de Grégoire XI, 1372–1374." *Annuaire. Bulletin de la Société de l'histoire de France* 32 (1895): 185–206.

Larner, J. *The Lords of Romagna: Romagnol Society and the Origins of the Signorie*. New York: St. Martin's Press, 1965.

Lea, H.C. *A History of the Inquisition of the Middle Ages*. 3 vols. New York: Harper & Bros., 1906.

Leonard, E.G. *Histoire de Jeanne Iere, reine de Naples, comtesse de Provence (1342–1382)*. 3 vols. Paris: 1932–37.

Lettere senili di Francesco Petrarca. Vol. 2, ed. G. Fracassetti. Florence: Le Monnier, 1869.

Lettres closes: Lettres "de par le roy" de Philippe de Valois. Ed. R. Cazelles. Paris: 1958.

Lettres communes analysées d'après les registres dits d'Avignon et du Vatican. Ed. Anne-Marie Hayez. Rome: Bibliothèque des Écoles françaises d'Athènes et de Rome, ser. 3, 6 bis.

Lettres secrètes et curiales du pape Grégoire XI (1370–1378) intéressant les pays autres que la France. Ed. G. Mollat. 3 vols. Paris: E. de Boccard, 1962–65.

Lettres secrètes et curiales du pape Grégoire XI (1370–1378) relatives à la France. Ed. L. Mirot, H. Jassemin, J. Vieillard, G. Mollat, and E.R. Labande. 5 vols. Paris: E. de Boccard, 1935–57.

Le Liber pontificalis. Vol. 2, ed. L. Duchesne. Paris: E. de Boccard, 1892.

Luttrell, A. "Gregory XI and the Turks, 1370–1378." *Orientalia christiana periodica* 46 (1980): 391–417.

Michel, L. "La défense d'Avignon sous Urbain V et Grégoire XI." *Mélanges d'archéologie et d'histoire* 30 (1910): 129–45.

Mirot, L. *La politique pontificale et le retour du Saint Siège à Rome en 1376*. Paris, 1899.

———. "La question des blés dans la rupture entre Florence et le Saint-Siège en 1375." *Mélanges d'archéologie et d'histoire* 16 (1896): 181–205.

Mollat, G. "Grégoire XI et sa legende." *Revue d'histoire ecclésiastique* 49 (1954): 873–77.

———. *Les papes d'Avignon*. 10th ed. Paris: Letouzey & Ane, 1965.

———. "Relations politiques de Grégoire XI avec les siennois et les florentins." *Mélanges d'archéologie et d'histoire* 67 (1956): 335–76.

Partner, P. *The Lands of St. Peter: The Papal State in the Middle Ages and the Early Renaissance*. Berkeley: University of California Press, 1972.

Pastor, L. *The History of the Popes from the Close of the Middle Ages*. 4th ed. Vol. 1. London: K. Paul, Trench, Truebner & Co., 1913.

Perrens, F.T. *Histoire de Florence*. Vol. 5. Paris: Maison Quantin, 1880.

Perroy, E. "The Anglo-French Negotiators at Bruges, 1374–1377." *Camden Miscellany* 19 (1952): i–xlvii.

Pinzi, C. *Storia della città di Viterbo*. Vol. 3. Viterbo: Tipografia Sociale Agnesotti, 1899.

Renouard, Y. *Les relations des papes d'Avignon et des compagnies commerciales et bancaires de 1316 à 1378*. Bibliothèque des Écoles françaises d'Athènes et de Rome, fasc. 151. Paris: E. de Boccard, 1941.

Rerum italicarum scriptores. Ed. L.A. Muratori; new ed. by G. Carducci and V. Fiorini. Vol. 18, tome one, ed., *Corpus chronicorum bononiensium*. Ed. A. Sorbelli. 1905.

Rodolico, N. *Il popolo minuto: Note di storia fiorentina (1343–1378)*. Florence: Olschki, 1968.

Ronzy, P. *Le voyage de Grégoire XI ramenant la papauté d'Avignon à Rome (1376–1377), suivi du texte latin et de la traduction française de l'Itinerarium Gregorii XI de Pierre Ameilh*. Florence: l'Institut français de Florence, 1952.

Runciman, S. *A History of the Crusades*. 3 vols. Cambridge: Cambridge University Press, 1951–54.

Thibault, P.R. *Pope Gregory XI: The Failure of Tradition*. Lanham, Md.: University Press of America, 1986.

Torelli, P. "La presa di Reggio e la cessione ai Visconti nei carteggi mantovani (1371)." In *Studi in onore di Naborre Campanini*, Reggio Emilia: 1921, 130–53.

Tozzi, M.R. *Gregorio XI, ultimo dei papi avignonesi che restitui a Roma l'apostolica sede*. Roma: Pia Società Figlie di S. Paolo, 1938.

Vetera monumenta historica Hungariam sacram illustrantia. Vol. 2, ed. by A. Theiner. Rome: Tipografia Vatcana, 1860.

MARTIN V (1417–31)

ALISON WILLIAMS LEWIN

The Council of Constance (1414–18) ended the Great Schism (1378–1417) by elevating Cardinal Oddo Colonna to the papal tiara. Taking the name of Martin V, Colonna gained recognition as the one true pope of a reunited Christendom—and found himself facing crises on every hand. The council had three goals: to restore unity in the church, to purge it of heresy, and to reform it in head and members. Though *Frequens*, the decree providing for the regular summoning of a general council, was formally passed on 9 October 1417, only the first of the Council of Constance's three goals was truly achieved. The resolution of the Great Schism and the pontificate of Martin V initiated a rather different program from the one envisioned by the notables at Constance.

Martin's rule, and that of his successors, featured three distinct trends: first, the weakening and ultimately the defeat of conciliarism and any efforts at internal reform; second, increasing control by secular monarchs over their regional or national churches, and a corresponding growth in the pope's position as the temporal ruler of central Italy; and, running a distant third, attempts to achieve a rapprochement between the Eastern and Western churches. Fifteenth-century popes, beginning with Martin, seemed far more willing to concede actual governance and profits of Western Christendom to secular rulers than to accept conciliar government or any real reform and redistribution of power within the church itself.

During the schism the control states exercised over their own local ecclesiastical institutions had grown steadily. Many secular rulers had no desire to reverse this trend. The cardinals too had grown stronger; their number was limited, their share of papal revenues substantial. It was they who pushed hardest for a papal election, moving it to the top of the conciliar agenda, ahead of Holy Roman Emperor Sigismund's plans for sweeping reform. The reform decrees of 30 October illustrate how successful the cardinals had been: the general reformation of the church had been dropped from consideration completely, and the council now would serve to assist the new pope to reform his office and curia in eighteen specified points. With the powers of reform and conciliarism already sharply reined in, Cardinal Oddo Colonna, who took the name Martin V, became pope on 11 November 1417.

Colonna, though not the first or unanimous choice of the cardinals, nonetheless was acceptable to all, as he was to the delegates from the five nations present at the council. Known as the poorest and simplest of the cardinals, of a genial and open nature, he had managed as much as was possible to remain neutral during the struggles that marked the first three years of the council. As a member of one of the two most powerful families of Rome, Martin would probably also restore the prestige of the papacy in Rome. Last, as a moderate and sensible man, he seemed likely to favor reform, which the church desperately needed.

The pope managed during the further sessions of the council to lay the foundations for two major trends of the fifteenth-century papacy. First, he made clear that conciliar reform would in no way encroach on papal prestige and authority. On the day after his election Martin edited and approved the rules of the Papal Chancery. By following tradition in affirming the procedures and privileges of this administrative branch of the papacy, Martin in effect protected papal prerogatives that were themselves the root of many abuses in the church. Martin thus revealed his priorities in his first official act: he would ignore reform in the church if it in any way threatened to diminish the powers of the Holy See.

Having elected a pope, the members of the council now seemed to lose their drive for reform as well. The reform commission, consisting of six cardinals and six representatives from each nation, produced little of substance over the next two months. When they presented their moderate recommendations to Martin in January 1418, he accepted the minor encroachments upon papal prerogatives contained therein, but dismissed the definition of the causes for which a pope could be admonished or deposed. He remarked, "It does not seem good to us, as it did not to several nations, that on this point anything new should be determined or decreed" (Creighton, *A History of the Papacy*, II, 107). As he had during the first years of the council, Martin stayed above most quarrels and let differences among the various nations undo most plans for reform.

The ability to check conciliarism as well as to forestall reform also appeared early in Martin's tenure. Most prelates and princes in attendance at Constance perceived the two main issues confronting the church: internal governance and heresy. Martin managed to pronounce on the former while addressing the latter. John of Falkenburg, urged on by the Teutonic Knights, had written a libel against the king of Poland, asserting that he and his people "ought to be exterminated like pagans." Not surprisingly, the Poles took offense at this, and the Commissioners in Matters of Faith had condemned the libel, as they had also the writings of the Burgundian apologist Jean Petit. Both condemnations, however, awaited official pronouncement by the new pope. Wishing to offend neither the duke of Burgundy nor the Teutonic Knights, Martin demurred. When a protest by Poles and French alike left Martin unmoved, the Poles began to murmur of appealing to a future council. To this Martin did respond, promulgating a constitution asserting, "No one may appeal from the supreme judge, that is, the apostolic seat or the Roman pontiff, Vicar on earth of Jesus Christ, or may decline his authority in matters of faith" (Creighton, II, 109). Martin here directly undercut the very idea of pope under council, or even of pope in council, as the right structuring of the church's hierarchy.

The tomb of Pope Martin V in the basilica of St. John Lateran, sculpted by Isiah of Pisa. (Courtesy of the Vatican Library)

The second major tendency of Martin's pontificate, namely, negotiating with separate secular entities rather than the church hierarchy as a whole, was manifest in the final resolutions on reform. The eighteen points for reform presented in the decree of 30 October 1417 still remained on the table with the stipulation that the pope agree to them. On a few points all participants agreed: on 21 March the council approved statutes in which the pope withdrew exemptions and incorporations granted since 1378; condemned simony; abandoned papal claims to ecclesiastical revenues during vacancies; promised not to exact tenths except in real emergencies, and then only after consulting a kingdom or province's bishops; withdrew dispensations from discharging the duties of ecclesiastical offices while receiving the revenues therefrom; and enjoined greater regularity in clerical dress and deportment.

Because of dissension among the nations, however, the council agreed that Martin would negotiate concordats with the individual nations at Constance about the remaining provisions. No overarching schema of reform or even of reorganization united the concordats. In fact, in several key points they contradicted one another. Common to all were statements about the size and composition of the college of cardinals and limitations on the spiritual taxes the papacy could impose on the various nations. The specifics of which rulers could nominate or appoint to which benefices, or what percentage of *annates* were to be remitted for what period of time, varied from agreement to agreement. England's agreement was unique in having no provision regarding benefices, an omission that tacitly recognized a statute of 1351 that had confirmed the king's effective control over appointments. Martin subsequently, and unsuccessfully, sought to have the statute revoked.

The acceptance of these flawed agreements by all parties at Constance indicates how futile negotiations had become and how eager all participants at Constance were simply to leave. By gaining the ability to come to separate agreements with the various nations, Martin was able to weaken any concerted attempts by the church united to address concerns about his own powers. Without himself contributing to division, Martin was nonetheless able to reap the benefits of it. He was, however, simultaneously forced to recognize the various degrees of control secular rulers exercised over church offices and revenues within their boundaries.

The only area in which Martin might be said to have acted in full harmony with the spirit of the council concerned the third and least important issue, reconciliation with the Greek church. Envoys from the Greek church had been in attendance at Constance with the noble mission of reconciling the Eastern and Western churches in order to address the far more pressing and practical matter of dealing with the growing presence of the Turks in the East. Though the Greeks were treated with courtesy, they were unable to interest the Western church, still wrestling with its own internal affairs, in any serious negotiations. Martin did, however, establish friendly relations with the Greek emperor, relations that eventually led to the Council of Ferrara-Florence under Martin's successor, Eugenius IV.

With the dissolution of the Council of Constance in 1418, Martin turned from matters of internal church governance and reform to the more concrete problems of his position as a temporal ruler in Italy. When Martin became pope, the Papal States were a shambles. The condottiere Muzio Attendolo Sforza was pressing his own interests in Naples; the city of Florence supported Braccio da Montone of Perugia against him. Martin also faced the threat of Spanish resurgence in Italy through Alfonso of Aragon's claim to the Neapolitan throne under the aegis of the now antipope Benedict XIII.

Martin entered Italy in the autumn of 1418 with little in the way of resources or holdings. He stayed at the monastery of Santa Maria Novella in Florence from February 1419 until September 1420, listening to street urchins chant, "Braccio the Great conquers every state; poor Pope Martin is not worth a farthing." Through the efforts of Niccolò da Uzzano and Giovanni di Bicci de' Medici, Martin could at least rest assured that Baldassare Cossa, the Pisan antipope John XXIII, would not accept Braccio da Montone's offers of alliance. Instead, the Florentines secured Cossa's release and persuaded him to submit in June 1419 to Martin, who reinstated him as a cardinal of the Roman church.

Though short of funds, Martin was not completely powerless. His brother had secured control over much of Rome by 1420, and other brothers had received substantial feudal holdings from the queen of Naples, whose kingdom was technically itself a papal fief. In the Papal States many lords who had illegitimately seized lands and positions during the schism were anxious to have Martin confirm their rule as papal vicars, even at the price of substantial annual payments. Martin concluded the most important of these agreements with Braccio, whose rule of much of Umbria and the March of Ancona he recognized in 1420. Still smarting from the mocking comparisons made between Braccio's status and his own, however, Martin decided that the time had come to establish himself as a ruler in fact as well as in name. After mobilizing various tyrants of the Romagna to crush a rebellion in Bologna, Martin entered Rome in September 1420. There he found only houses in decay, churches in ruins, and empty streets.

While attempting to put his principal city in order, Martin found the peace he had established in Italy short lived. Martin had followed traditional papal policy in announcing in November 1419 that he would invest Louis II of Anjou as the successor of Queen Joanna II of Naples, should she die without an heir. Such action proved unacceptable to the Neapolitan court; Joanna instead accepted Alfonso of Aragon as her adoptive son and heir in September 1420. Soon Sforza was fighting as the papacy's condottiere against Braccio, the Aragonese champion. This war consumed all annual papal revenues and ended with both candidates agreeing to leave the kingdom.

To counter Braccio's presence and his friendly ties with Florence, Martin was willing to condone Filippo Maria Visconti of Milan's presence in the Romagna. Giorgio Ordelaffi's death in 1422 left Forlì with a minor as heir; rebellion against the widow in May 1423 was a sufficient excuse for Milanese troops to occupy the city. War erupted between Florentine and Milanese mercenaries, in which Martin remained officially neutral.

The unexpected death of Sforza in January 1424 tipped the scales in favor of Florence, but the equally unexpected death of Braccio in June of the same year left Martin much stronger in his own states. Martin marshaled his troops and officials and quickly cleansed the Papal States of Braccio's supporters. Some *signori* fled; some were disciplined and reinstated. Most important, the city of Perugia accepted direct papal rule.

During Martin's pontificate reform of the church figured only minimally; his main goals were clearly recovery of the temporal state and exaltation of the Holy See. Given the drastic reduction in papal revenues from Europe during the Great Schism, Martin's focus on regaining control over what was now his most reliable source of papal income appears completely understandable. While he followed the Council of Constance's mandate to hold a council, as specified by the decree *Frequens*, Martin's 1423 council at Pavia, later moved to Siena, was strictly pro forma. In part because of its Italian location, in part because of internal crises in England, France, and the Holy Roman Empire, the council was poorly attended. Martin's physical absence from the council, together with his arrangements for the safe-conducts of those attending, further undermined any optimism the prelates at the council might have felt about strengthening either the conciliar or the reform movements of the church. The curial party managed successfully to exploit tensions among the nations and to derail any steps toward meaningful reform. The council produced only condemnations of heresy and exhortations to union within all Christendom, including the Greek church. As its members trickled away, only a few voices protested.

On other fronts, the death of the French king Charles VI led his successor to issue in 1425 a decree reestablishing papal power as it had been in the days of the schism; despite the Parlement's refusal to register the decree, no calls for reform from the University of Paris's theologians would threaten Martin's papacy. With somewhat more effort and less success, Martin campaigned to have the English Crown remove all restrictions on the exercise of papal rights. He succeeded only in publicly humbling the archbishop of Canterbury and strengthening the position of the papal legate in England. Given his own tenuous position in central Italy, it is not surprising that Martin chose to sacrifice real power and revenues in lands that he had no real hope of controlling in order to focus more completely on the temporal domain he could realistically establish.

Wishing to forestall independent efforts at reform, Martin judged it prudent to issue his own constitution for reform, which he published on 16 May 1425. Most of its provisions were recycled from earlier reform decrees and aimed at correcting members of the clergy. Martin addressed the attire and behavior of members of the curia, especially the cardinals. As usual, archbishops, bishops, and abbots were enjoined to keep strict residence and to hold provincial synods regularly. Nothing in any way restricted the pope's power or increased that of those whom he clearly saw as subordinates. Apparently Martin's efforts to intimidate the ecclesiastical aristocracy of the curia succeeded; an ambassador for the Teutonic Knights reported that the cardinals were so afraid of Martin "that they stammered like awkward children in his presence" (Creighton, II, 161).

The constant need for money and Martin's own desire to serve his family meant that his court was far from uncorrupt, however. Large "presents" ensured that the pope would hear ambassadors' presentations quickly and favorably; despite his rigor in examining candidates for ecclesiastical appointments, Martin was not able to resist conferring the rich archdeaconry of Canterbury on his fourteen-year-old nephew. Driven by a constant need for funds, Martin and his nephews invested in the Florentine public debt (*monte*), which cost him leverage in negotiating with that state. His elevation of the Colonna family, his residence in the familial rather than the papal palace, and the intensification of the long-standing rivalry with the Orsini family betray Martin's aristocratic, Roman orientation. Like Martin's concern for the Papal States and his own revenues, aggrandizement of the Colonna family easily overrode even his mildest impulses toward reform.

Even had Martin been sincerely dedicated to reforming the church, he would have had little time to devote to it. The deaths of Sforza and Braccio relieved much of the pressure around Naples, but the Milanese lord Filippo Maria Visconti's growing ambitions led in 1426 to a Venetian alliance with Florence and raised concerns about stability in northern Italy. Though Martin lukewarmly supported Milan, his approbation did not suffice to keep Visconti from considering external allies, such as Sigismund or Alfonso, either of whose presence in Italy could be detrimental to Martin in both ecclesiastical and political terms. Through constant vigilance and negotiation Martin managed to preserve the precious hard-won stability of the Papal States and to begin the ambitious rebuilding of the city of Rome.

Overall, Martin succeeded in balancing allies and enemies with his cautious, somewhat unscrupulous adherence to his fixed goal of recovering and stabilizing the temporal state of the papacy. Despite considerable success in reclaiming a large portion of the Papal States and revenues therefrom, the fundamental weakness of Martin's position was revealed in his inability to impose papal rule on Bologna, the crucial northern anchor of the Papal States. Rebellion broke out in the summer of 1428; a military campaign to crush it proved expensive and ineffectual. In September 1429 Martin had to sign a peace with the city that failed to punish instigators of the rebellion, failed to restore direct rule of the church, and even made Martin responsible for the other side's expenses and ransoms. In April 1430 new rioting drove Martin's legate from Bologna, and Martin was considering laying siege to the city. Thus even the temporal control that Martin had made the focus of his pontificate was far from secure at the time of his death in 1431.

Similar mixed success showed in efforts to check heresy and to use councils to reform the church by 1431. Before the next reform council was to meet in that year at Basel, the Hussites had won a major victory at Taus. Cardinal Cesarini, whom Martin had charged with organizing the council, convinced the pope that only major reform could check the spread of heresy. Emperor Sigismund fully supported this agenda. Martin agreed to it, but then died shortly after the Council of Basel opened. His successor Eugenius IV refused any negotiations with the Hussites; when the council invited their leaders to attend, Eugenius declared the council dissolved in December 1431, thus precipitating the last significant resurgence of conciliarism in the West.

Later popes would pronounce on the ordering of the cosmos, on the relationships between sun and earth, God and his heavens. Martin and his immediate successors focused instead, with varying degrees of success, on ordering their own temporal states and the relationships between pope and council, the Holy See and secular rulers. For his success in achieving long-absent stability in central Italy, Martin's tombstone called him "the happiness of his times." On the positive side, Martin's hardheaded and practical policies enabled his successors to live with security and even splendor as temporal rulers of Rome and of central Italy. After the unfortunate Eugenius IV, no more would popes flee Rome in the middle of the night or wander throughout Italy seeking refuge. On the negative side, Martin also set the precedent of trading real papal prestige and revenues north of the Alps for material and military power in Italy. In the final analysis, the stubborn refusal of Martin V and his successors to condone any reform that lessened their prerogatives or allowed for any collective governance of the church and their deafness to the very real complaints of both clergy and laity concerning the church's organization and its mission proved disastrous for Catholicism. The splendor of the Roman curia in the sixteenth century originated in the hardheaded and practical policies of Martin V; unfortunately for the church, so did the Protestant Reformation.

SELECTED BIBLIOGRAPHY

Barraclough, Geoffrey. *The Medieval Papacy*. London: Thames & Hudson, 1968.

Bizzocchi, Roberto. *Chiesa e potere nella Toscana del Quattrocento*. Bologna: Società editrice il Mulino, 1987.

Caravale, Mario, and Alberto Caracciolo. *Lo stato pontificio da Martino V a Pio IX*. Turin: Unione Tipografico-Editrice Torinese, 1978.

Creighton, Mandell. *A History of the Papacy from the Great Schism to the Sack of Rome*. London: Longmans, 1907–11. Vol. 2 of 6. 1909.

Crowder, C.M.D. *Unity, Heresy, and Reform, 1378–1460: The Conciliar Response to the Great Schism*. New York: St. Martin's Press, 1977.

Duffy, Eamon. *Saints and Sinners: A History of the Popes*. New Haven: Yale University Press, 1997.

Guiraud, Jean. *L'État pontifical après le grand schisme: Étude de géographie politique*. Paris: Librairie Thorin & fils, 1896.

Hay, Denys. *The Church in Italy in the Fifteenth Century*. Cambridge: Cambridge University Press, 1977.

Jedin, Hubert. *A History of the Council of Trent*. Trans. Ernest Graf. Vol. 1. London: Thomas Nelson & Sons, 1957.

Jones, P.J. *The Malatesta of Rimini and the Papal State: A Political History*. Cambridge: Cambridge University Press, 1974.

McBrien, Richard P. *Lives of the Popes: The Pontiffs from St. Peter to John Paul II*. San Francisco: HarperSanFrancisco, 1997.

Oakley, Francis. *The Western Church in the Later Middle Ages*. Ithaca, N.Y.: Cornell University Press, 1979.

Ozment, Steven. *The Age of Reform, 1250–1550*. New Haven: Yale University Press, 1980.

Partner, Peter. "Florence and the Papacy in the Earlier Fifteenth Century." In *Florentine Studies: Politics and Society in Renaissance Florence*, ed. Nicolai Rubinstein. London: Faber & Faber, 1968, 381–402.

———. *The Lands of St. Peter: The Papal State in the Middle Ages and the Early Renaissance*. Berkeley and Los Angeles: University of California Press, 1972.

———. *The Papal State under Martin V*. London: British School at Rome, 1958.

Pastor, Ludwig. *The History of the Popes*. Trans. Frederick Ignatius Antrobus. London: Routledge & Kegan Paul, Vol. 1. 1949.

Prodi, Paolo. *The Papal Prince: One Body and Two Souls: The Papal Monarchy in Early Modern Europe*. Trans. Susan Haskins. Cambridge: Cambridge University Press, 1986.

Raynaldus, Odericus. *Annales Ecclesiastici*. Vols. 27–28. Paris: Victor Palmé, 1874.

Southern, R.W. *Western Society and the Church in the Middle Ages*. Hammondsworth: Penguin Books, 1970.

Thomson, John A.F. *Popes and Princes, 1417–1517*. London: George Allen & Unwin, 1980.

Tierney Brian. *Foundations of the Conciliar Theory*. Cambridge: Cambridge University Press, 1955.

EUGENIUS IV (1431–47)

Jacqueline A. Gutwirth

In 1989, on the occasion of the 550th anniversary of the Council of Ferrara-Florence, the city of Florence hosted two separate conferences commemorating the union of the Greek and Latin faiths. Fragile though this accord between the Eastern and Western churches would prove to be, it marked the high point of Eugenius IV's reign. The celebration in the cathedral of Florence provided a moment of unalloyed triumph in a pontificate marked by bitter dissension and a single-minded struggle for primacy against a powerful and popular conciliar movement. Whatever the ultimate assessment of Eugenius IV's personality and policies may be, he indisputably restored papal preeminence at a time when such an eventuality hardly seemed likely.

Gabriele Condulmer, born in 1383 to a prosperous and noble Venetian merchant family, did not seem given by nature to temporal ambition. Indeed, together with his cousin Antonio Correr, he became a founding member of the newly reformed secular canonry at S. Giorgio in Alga and retained a lifelong attachment to promoting its fortunes. Contemporaries agree that he was not interested in material possessions, reporting that he gave away his own quite considerable fortune. His quiet life was interrupted by the election of his maternal uncle, Angelo Correr, to the papacy as Gregory XII (1406–15). Both Gabriele and Antonio were summoned to the Roman court, and within a year—although a papal dispensation was necessary, given his youth—Gabriele was appointed bishop of Siena. By 1408, only twenty-five years old, he, together with his cousin, was elevated to the position of cardinal.

Gabriele's promotion to the sacred college must be seen against the background of the Great Schism that, since 1378, had rent the church apart. By 1409 the majority of cardinals of both the Roman (Gregory XII) and Avignonese (Benedict XIII) popes had defected from their respective courts and, assembling in Pisa, deposed both popes, declaring their respective cardinalates null and void. Their selection of Alexander V initiated a third, the Pisan, line of popes. It was not until the Council of Constance (1414–18) that unity was restored. The two non-Roman claimants to the papal throne were deposed; Gregory XII abdicated with the understanding that his college of cardinals be recognized as legitimate. In the light of this chain of distressing events, Gabriele's decision to serve his uncle marked at once his loyalty to kin and his adherence to the Roman line of popes. Whatever the psychological cost of witnessing his uncle's resignation may have been, surely Eugenius's uncompromising commitment to the primacy of the Roman See and to its jurisdictional supremacy over conciliar decisions was forged in the early years spent in Gregory's service.

The pope elected at Constance, Martin V (ruled 1417–31), a scion of the Colonna family, had impeccable Roman credentials. Unabashedly given to nepotism and scornful of his cardinals, he had little use for Gabriele. While he did appoint him legate of the March of Ancona and, in August 1423, governor of Bologna, Gabriele was relieved of the latter post because of his obvious pro-Florentine (and anti-Milanese) sympathies. In future years Gabriel's partisan politics would serve him in good stead, but for the remainder of Martin V's pontificate he never again held an administrative post.

It was precisely because Gabriele played so small a role in the political affairs of Martin V that his candidacy was acceptable to the college of cardinals. Yet scarcely had Eugenius IV acceded to the papal throne when he faced a dual threat to his position. In the first instance, he had to deal with an uprising in Rome and rebellion in the Papal States, engendered in good measure by his harsh handling of the Colonna, whose fiscal and territorial privileges gained under Martin V he sought to curtail. Although for a time he was able to regain a tenuous hold on Rome, a popular insurrection that threatened his life forced him to flee in 1434. Disguised as a monk, he reached Ostia, where a galley, dispatched by the Florentine Signoria, which had not forgotten his earlier partiality, brought him to Leghorn. Several days later he was in Florence, where the Medici, already papal bankers, served as his protectors. He lived in the papal apartments originally established for Martin V in Santa Maria Novella and, except for relatively brief stays in Bologna and Ferrara, would remain there for the duration of his exile. Although Giovanni Vitelleschi, the bishop of Recanati, rapidly restored order in Rome, it was not until 1443 that Eugenius felt it safe to return. Thus, of the sixteen years he was in office, over nine were spent in exile.

The second challenge—so it was perceived by Eugenius—was the convening of the Council of Basel in July 1431, in accordance with the decree *Frequens* issued by the Council of Constance. Despite having sworn to honor conciliar decrees, in December Eugenius issued a bull that dissolved the council and called for the assembly to reconvene in Bologna in eighteen months' time. By so doing, he hoped to move the council from the jurisdiction of Sigismund of Luxemburg and other secular princes back into papal territory. At issue was the critical question of whether a pope

Painting of Pope Eugenius IV surrounded by cardinals. (Courtesy of the Vatican Library)

could dissolve or even transfer a council without its consent. In a letter written somewhat later to the doge of Venice, Eugenius made his position clear. For Eugenius it was inconceivable that the papal office be made subordinate to the council, and he was determined that he not be the first to set such a precedent.

The council's response to Eugenius's unilateral prorogation of its proceedings was not long in coming. In February 1432 Basel reaffirmed *Haec sancta* issued at Constance, by which it declared itself superior to the pope.

Eugenius's capitulation was precipitous. Within a year, forced by pressure from the cardinals (the vast majority of whom supported Basel) and the successful foray of Duke Filippo Maria Visconti of Milan into papal territory at, so he claimed, the council's behest, Eugenius conceded. In *Dudum sacrum* (15 December 1433) Eugenius rescinded his decree of dissolution and declared Basel ecumenical in origin and proceedings. By 1435 the council voted to remove papal rights to *annates* and benefices, with catastrophic results for the papal coffers. It has been estimated that between 1427 and 1436 papal revenues dropped by two-thirds. The following year Basel undertook to reform the curia and the college of cardinals. It further declared that upon election popes would have to adhere to the decree of *Sacrosancta*, expressing conciliar supremacy as an article of faith. With the ratification of Basel's measures by France, in the Pragmatic Sanction of Bourges (1438), and Germany, in the Acceptance of Mainz (1439), the council's preeminence seemed secured.

Yet Eugenius was to regain the advantage. There was one issue on which both Basel and Eugenius were in agreement: that of unifying the Eastern and Western churches. But the questions of under whose aegis the council was to be held and where the council was to be located were bitterly contested. Ludwig Pastor has argued that of the three parties involved in the negotiations—the Greek emperor, the Council of Basel, and Eugenius IV—only the last truly cared about the union for its own sake. That is, the Greeks were prepared to submit to the West only to gain military aid against the Turks, while the council was hoping to bolster its stature by winning the Eastern adherence. Surely, however, Eugenius understood the larger moral, as well as the political, advantage that would accrue to the papal position should the two rites be reconciled. The issue of imputed motivations aside, the fact remains that the Greeks, partly for reasons of its greater proximity to the East, preferred to meet in Ferrara rather than in Avignon, the council's suggested location. Coupled with this purely practical reason for accepting Eugenius's site was the widespread feeling among the Greek prelates that for an agreement to be truly ecumenical, it had to have the approbation of the Roman pontiff.

Taking the offensive, Eugenius dissolved Basel in September 1437 and ordered its transfer to Ferrara. He quickly dispatched four Venetian galleys to transport some seven hundred Greek dignitaries from Byzantium to Italy. Among those who attended the council—moved in January 1439 to Florence—were the emperor, John VIII Paleologus, and his brother, John II, the patriarch of Constantinople, Mark of Ephesus, Bessarion of Nicaea, and Gemistus Plethon. Undeterred by the pope's success in assembling the Greeks to his conclave, Basel countered by declaring itself the sole legitimate council. Within two months, on 25 June 1439, the Council of Basel deposed Eugenius, but just ten days later, on 5 July, the document ending the schism in effect since 1054 was signed. The following day, amid much acclamation and solemn ceremony, the union decree, *Laetentur coeli*, was read in both Latin and Greek in the cathedral of Santa Maria del Fiore. Eugenius stood triumphant. An ecumenical council had declared him the head of the universal church.

Without question, the union of the two churches marked the high point of Eugenius's career. Not only had the Greeks accepted the primacy of the Roman See, but churchmen who had formerly opposed him, among them Nicholas of Cusa and Cardinal Cesarini, supported the position that popes were superior to councils. Moreover, the intransigence of the Council of Basel—particularly its ill-advised election of Duke Amadeus VIII of Savoy (Felix V, 1439–49)—resulted in ever-diminishing support. When Eugenius prudently reached an accord with King Alfonso of Aragon (withdrawing his former support for René of Anjou) and recognized his claim to the throne of Naples, the council lost its most ardent supporter. Alfonso's defection, together with that of Filippo Maria Visconti in August 1443, stabilized Eugenius's position in Italy. With the conciliar problem solved, Eugenius could return to his domain. In September 1443 Eugenius entered Rome in triumph. Until the city was sacked in 1527, no pope was to leave Rome under duress, and papal claims to authority in the states of the church remained, on the whole, unchallenged.

It is perhaps from this vantage point of a restored papacy that Eugenius's life and career might best be assessed. It should be noted that the Council of Ferrara-Florence could not ensure the union of the churches. For one thing, it was totally unacceptable to the majority of Greeks at home. Beyond that, the crusade called by Eugenius to counter the Turkish advance won little response from the European monarchs. Even before the fall of Constantinople in 1453, the ignominious defeat of the Western army at Varna in 1444 had diminished all hope of a continuous and strong Latin presence in the East. Although several other churches were later to sign a decree of union—among them, the Armenians, Copts, Syrians, Chaldeans, and Maronites of Cyprus—they too would eventually fall away.

If these were events over which Eugenius had no control, the same cannot be said about the utter failure of the Council of Ferrara-Florence—in sharp contrast to Basel's efforts—to address the pressing matter of churchwide reform. Here Eugenius must, in large measure, be held accountable. Certainly it is true that he was active in reform on the local level. Vespasiano da Bisticci reports his particular efforts to get the Observant rule accepted in the monasteries of Florence. He was also devoted to improving the instruction of clergy and almost totally reorganized the University of Rome. Additionally, he tried to broaden the college of cardinals. Of the seventeen appointments he made in December 1439, only five of the new cardinals were Italian. Still, Eugenius's negligence in implementing broad and deep change—however much he felt beleaguered by Basel—would have resounding consequences. In bypassing serious reform the Church would later find itself beset by a challenge that it could not deflect. The Reformation would challenge papal primacy in ways never imagined even by the most ardent conciliarists.

A happier consequence of the Council of Ferrara-Florence was the opportunity it provided for sustained contact between members of the Greek delegation, their counterparts in the papal curia, and Florentines educated in the humanist tradition. In particular, the rediscovery of Platonic thought in the West has been linked to the lectures on Platonic and Neoplatonic philosophy given by Gemistus Plethon. While Eugenius himself had little interest in classical learning, his protracted residence in Florence allowed him to employ some of the foremost Italian humanists of the day, among them Leonardo Bruni, Poggio Bracciolini, Flavio Biondo, and Ambrogio Traversari. Moreover, extensive negotiations with the Eastern patriarchs led Eugenius to introduce Greek scholars into his court. He hired Nicolas Sagundinus of Siponto and George of Trebizond as papal secretaries, as well as the Italian Hellenists Cristoforo Garatone and Giovanni Aurispa. With new men in the curia, the culture of the papal bureaucracy inevitably changed, although Eugenius, unlike his successors, remained personally untouched by the humanist program.

Austere and devout, Eugenius seems to have been similarly unmoved by the extraordinary artistic achievements that everywhere surrounded him. It is telling that during his sojourn in Florence the single most important work of art he commissioned was a papal tiara, designed by Lorenzo Ghiberti and worn on the occasion of the union of the two churches. Even when he returned to Rome, he commissioned few new projects, the most notable of which were Filarete's bronze doors for St. Peter's and Fra Angelico's frescoes in the Chapel of the Blessed Sacrament at the Vatican. Still, he diligently worked to restore the city's existing churches, many of which were in virtual ruin.

The restraint demonstrated by Eugenius in aesthetic matters is entirely consonant with accounts of his ascetic nature. Disdaining personal wealth, he gave lavishly to the poor. Moreover, in an office, that most often saw rulers succumb to flamboyant nepotism, Eugenius's was restrained. He elevated only two family members to the rank of cardinal: his cousin Francesco Condulmer and, although he was only twenty-three, his nephew, Pietro Barbo, later Paul II (1464–71). While he deployed others of his relatives in important positions, he rigorously abstained from rewarding them with ecclesiastical territories, and the estates of the church were intact at his death on 23 February 1447.

It is perhaps the very virtues for which he was esteemed—his personal probity and sincere piety—that, when viewed from another angle, explain his often-impolitic actions and his willingness to risk enmity and division to see his view of papal prerogative triumphant. Indeed, Eugenius's compelling need to win the princes of Europe away from Basel and the doctrine of conciliarism led him to compromise some of the historic freedoms of the church. In the Concordat of Vienna, drawn up between Eugenius IV and Frederick III (and signed by Nicholas V in 1448), the emperor affirmed his adhesion to the papacy. In exchange, Frederick won the right to nominate specified bishoprics and received a payment of 221,000 ducats. John B. Toews's remark, is trenchant: "Eugenius chose to exhaust the pontifical treasury rather than impair the traditional claims of the papacy" (*Church History*, 187). The long-range effect of this practice—which was adopted by ensuing popes from Nicholas V to Leo X—was to strengthen the role of national monarchies in the affairs of their local churches. At the same time, his successors came to identify church interests with ever more narrow political ends, shaping their policies to meet the demands of administering and preserving a territorial state. The cost to the papacy of ensuring the Papal States a role as one of Italy's five principal powers, together with the decision to cede some of its customary liberties to the princes, was a loss of its spiritual influence. Eugenius had secured the papacy's claim to an absolute and indivisible authority; he could not, however, assure its moral suasion.

SELECTED BIBLIOGRAPHY

Alberigo, Giuseppe, ed. *Christian Unity: The Council of Ferrara-Florence, 1438/39–1989.* Leuven: Leuven University Press, 1991.

Beck, Hans Georg, et al. *From the High Middle Ages to the Eve of the Reformation.* Vol. 4 of *Handbook of Church History.* Ed. Hubert Jedin, trans. Anselm Biggs. New York: Crossroad, 1982.

Biondo, Flavio. *Le Decadi.* Trans. A. Crespi. Castrocaro Terme: a cura del comune di Forlì, 1963.

Bisticci, Vespasiano da, *The Vespasiano Memoirs.* Trans. William George and Emily Waters. New York: Harper and Row, 1963.

Black, A.J. *Monarchy and Community.* Cambridge: Cambridge University Press, 1970.

———. "The Political Ideas of Conciliarism and Papalism, 1430–1450." *Journal of Ecclesiastical History* 20 (1969): 45–65.

Blouin, Francis X, Jr., ed. *Vatican Archives: An Inventory and Guide to Historical Documents of the Holy See.* New York: Oxford University Press, 1998.

Boyle, Leonard. *A Survey of the Vatican Archives and of Its Medieval Holdings.* Toronto: Pontifical Institute of Mediaeval Studies, 1972.

Caccamo, D. "Eugenio IV e la Crociata di Varna." *Archivio della Società romana di storia patria* 3rd ser., 10 (1956): 35–87.

Caravale, Mario, and Alberto Caracciolo. *Lo stato pontificio da Martino V a Pio IX.* Vol. 14 of *Storia d'Italia*, ed. Giuseppe Galasso. Turin: UTET, 1978.

Concilium Florentinum documenta et scriptores. 11 vols. Rome: Pontificium Institutum Orientalium Studiorum, 1940–76.

Creighton, Mandell. *A History of the Papacy from the Great Schism to the Sack of Rome.* 6 vols. New York: Longmans, Green & Co., 1907–11.

Fedalto, Giorgio, ed. *Acta Eguenii Papae IV (1431–1447)*. Roma: Pontificia Commissio Codici Iuris Canonici Orientalis Recognoscendo, 1990.

Fink, K.A. *Das vatikanische Archiv*, 2nd ed. Rome: Bibliothek des Deutschen Historischen Insituts in Rom, 1951.

Geanakoplos, Deno J. "The Council of Florence 1438–9 and the Problem of Union between the Greek and Latin Churches." *Church History* 24 (1955): 324–46.

Gill, Joseph. *The Council of Florence*. Cambridge: Cambridge University Press, 1959.

———. *Eugenius IV: Pope of Christian Union*. Westminster, Md.: Newman Press, 1961.

———. *Personalities of the Council of Florence*. Oxford: Basil Blackwell, 1964.

Gottlob, Adolf. *Aus der Camera Apostolica des 15 Jahrhunderts*. Innsbruck: Wagner, 1889.

Gualdo, Germano, ed. *Sussidi per la consultazione dell'archivio Vaticano*. Vatican City: Archivio Vaticano, 1989.

Hay, Denys. *The Church in Italy in the Fifteenth Century*. Cambridge: Cambridge University Press, 1977.

Hazard, H.W., ed. *The Fourteenth and Fifteenth Centuries*. Vol. 3 of *A History of the Crusades*, ed. Kenneth Setton. Madison: University of Wisconsin Press, 1975.

Infessura, Stefano. *Diario della città di Roma*. Ed. by Oreste Tommasini. Vol. 5 of *Fonti per la storia d'Italia*. Roma: Forzani, 1890.

Jedin, Hubert. *A History of the Council of Trent*. Trans. Ernest Graf. Vol. 1. London: Thomas Nelson & Sons, 1957.

Kirshner, Julius. "Papa Eugenio IV e il Monte Comune: Documenti su investimento e speculazione nel debito pubblico di Firenze." *Archivio storico italiano* 127 (1969): 339–82.

Mercati, Angelo. *Raccolta di concordati su materie ecclesiastiche tra la Santa Sede e le autorità civili*. Rom: Tipografia Poliglotta Vaticana, 1919.

Müntz, Eugène. *Les arts à la cour des papes pendant le XVe et le XVIe siècle*. Vol. 1. Paris: E. Thorin, 1878.

Muratori, Lodovico. *Annali d'Italia dal principio dell'era volgare sino all'anno 1749*. Vol. 9. Napoli: Giuseppe Ponzelli, 1754.

———, ed. *Istorie di Firenze dall'anno 1406 fino all 1438*. In *Rerum italicarum scriptores*, vol. 19. Milan: ex typografia Societatis Palatinae in Regia Curia, 1734.

———, ed. *Vita Eugenii*. In *Rerum italicarum scriptores*, vol. 3, pt. 2. Milan: ex typografia Societatis Palatinae in Regia Curia, 1734.

Ottenthal, Emil von. *Die Bullenregister Martins V und Eugens IV*. Innsbruck: Mittheilungen des Instituts für Oesterreichische Geschichtsforschung 1 (1885): 401–589.

Ozment, Steven. *The Age of Reform, 1250–1550*. New Haven: Yale University Press, 1980.

Partner, Peter. "Florence and the Papacy in the Early Fifteenth Century." In *Florentine Studies*, ed. Nicolai Rubinstein. Evanston: Northwestern University Press, 1968, 357–80.

———. *The Pope's Men*. Oxford: Clarendon Press, 1990.

Pastor, Ludwig. *The History of the Popes*. Vol. 1. Trans. Frederick Ignatius Antrobus. 5th ed. St. Louis: Herder, 1949.

Peterson, David. "An Episcopal Election in Quattrocento Florence." In *Popes, Teachers, and Canon Law in the Middle Ages*, ed. James Ross Sweeney and Stanley Chodorow. Ithaca, N.Y.: Cornell University Press, 1989, 300–325.

Petriboni, Pagolo di Matteo, and Matteo di Borgo Rinaldi. *Priorista, 1407–1459*. Ed. and introd. Jacqueline A. Gutwirth. Studi e testi del Rinascimento Europeo, vol. 10. Roma: Edizioni di Storia e Letteratura, 2001.

Piccolomini, Aeneas Sylvius (Pius II). *De gestis Concilii Basiliensis commentariorum*. Ed. and trans. Denys Hay and W.K. Smith. Oxford: Clarendon Press, 1992.

Prodi, Paolo. *The Papal Prince*. Trans. Susan Haskins. Cambridge: Cambridge University Press, 1987.

Sacchis, Bartolomeo de (il Platina). *Liber de vita Christi ac omnium pontificum*. Ed. Lodovico Muratori. In *Rerum Italicarum Scriptores*, 2nd ser., vol. 3, pt. 1. Città di Castello: S. Lapi, 1933.

Setton, Kenneth. *The Papacy and the Levant (1204–1571)*. Vol. 2. Philadelphia: American Philosophical Society, 1978.

Ševčenko, Ihor. "Intellectual Repercussions of the Council of Florence." *Church History* 24 (1955): 291–323.

Stieber, Joachim. *Pope Eugenius IV, the Council of Basel, and the Secular and Ecclesiastical Authorities in the Empire: The Conflict over Supreme Authority and Power in the Church*. Leiden: E.J. Brill, 1978.

Tanner, Norman P., ed. *Decrees of the Ecumenical Councils*. Vol. 1. London: Sheed and Ward, 1990.

Thomson, John A.F. *Popes and Princes, 1417–1517*. London: George Allen and Unwin, 1980.

Toews, John B. "Pope Eugenius IV and the Concordat of Vienna, 1448—An Interpretation." *Church History* 34 (1965): 178–94.

Tuleja, Thaddus V. "Eugene IV and the Crusade of Varna." *The Catholic Historical Review* 35 (1949): 257–75.

Viti, Paolo. ed. *Firenze e il Concilio del 1439*. 2 vols. Florence: Leo S. Olschki, 1994.

NICHOLAS V (1447–55)

JAMES R. BANKER

Pope Nicholas V led the Christian church in Rome in the middle of the fifteenth century after 150 years of division and frequent papal absence from Rome. Nicholas restored the papacy to permanent residence in Rome and specifically in the Vatican and to its near-absolute monarchical power within the church, established several of the patterns of the Renaissance papacy, including its patronage of humanists and artists and construction of a renewed urban Rome, shared in the founding of the Vatican Library, and began the practice of accenting the wealth of the church as a means of enhancing the authority of the pope and the clerical hierarchy.

Born in Sarzana north of Pisa in 1397 into a modest family as Tommaso Parentucelli di Baliante, the future pope Nicholas established himself as an excellent student at the University of Bologna. Despite his impoverished origins, he completed his liberal arts degree before he was eighteen years of age. His future clerical career was constructed on his open and liberal character as well as his familiarity with the literature of the church fathers, medieval learning, and the new studies of classical antiquity. His learning enabled him to obtain positions as a tutor for the sons of two of the most eminent families of Florence, those of Rinaldo degli Albizzi and Palla di Nofri de' Strozzi, between 1415 and 1417. Particularly in the palace of Palla Strozzi, Tommaso Parentucelli would have encountered the most progressive humanists, who stirred in the future pope two passions, love of ancient learning and the desire to construct edifices in the new antique style.

After this two-year sojourn in Florence he returned to Bologna to complete a doctorate in theology at twenty-two years of age. Tommaso's achievements attracted the attention of the pious bishop of Bologna, Niccolò degli Albergati, who took the recently laureated Tommaso into his service, charging him with oversight of his house, and in 1423 ordained him as a priest. The bishop and Tommaso forged a close relationship, and when Bishop Niccolò was made a cardinal and went to Rome in 1426, he took Tommaso with him. Thus the early career of Tommaso was tied to the bishop of Bologna, who distinguished himself with Tommaso at his side as a papal legate to negotiate conflicts in France, Burgundy, and Germany and within Italy.

When conflicts in Rome compelled Eugenius IV to reside in Bologna, Ferrara, and Florence from 1434 to 1443, Cardinal Niccolò and Tommaso accompanied the pope as part of his entourage. In Florence Tommaso renewed his acquaintance with the humanists and shared with them his learning and passion for classical culture. According to Tommaso's contemporary and biographer, Vespasiano da Bisticci, every evening and morning the young cleric would join the humanists Leonardo Bruni, Giannozzo Manetti, Poggio Bracciolini, and Carlo Marsuppini outside the papal residence in Florence for discussions. Already by 1437 he had become an assiduous searcher for ancient texts and possessed a considerable library. At the Council of Florence, amid the efforts to reunite the Greek Orthodox and Roman Catholic churches, Pope Eugenius IV commissioned Tommaso to lead the discussions with the Ethiopians and Armenians, and it is said that he brought these two churches into union with the Catholic church.

During his residency in Florence Tommaso established himself as an able negotiator, skilled in argument, who had amicable relations with the many high clerics and communities resident in Florence. Tommaso inspired confidence in all his acquaintances with his liberality, honesty, and openness. As the chief assistant of Cardinal Niccolò Albergati, he obtained access to clerical commissions and introductions to many in the clerical hierarchy of the Eastern and Western churches. Despite the fact that he had been a tutor to two families that the Medici had exiled in 1434, Tommaso enjoyed entrance to the Florentine elite, particularly with its humanistic clients.

Tommaso's abilities and services to the papal curia at the Council of Florence led Eugenius to make him apostolic subdeacon. When Cardinal Albergati died in 1443, Eugenius became his new patron and made him bishop of Bologna in 1444. Unable to return to his diocese due to conflicts, Tommaso resided in Rome and served Pope Eugenius, most noticeably to repair strained relations between King Alfonso of Naples and Florence and as legate to France and Germany. On his return from Germany in 1446, Pope Eugenius made him cardinal. Within months the pope died, and to the surprise of all, Tommaso Parentucelli was selected as his successor.

Within a period of little more than two years he had been selected bishop, cardinal, and pope; it is no surprise, then, that some regarded his elevation to the chair of Peter as directed from God, especially since he was barely fifty years of age. His biographers wrote of Pope Eugenius foreseeing the elevation of Tommaso to the papal throne and Tommaso himself doing so in a dream. In addition to his relative youth, Tommaso

Coronation of Pope Nicholas V by Emperor Frederick III in 1452. (Courtesy of the Vatican Library)

had no great family and apparently did not belong to any specific faction within the college of cardinals.

On his ascension to papal authority in 1447, Nicholas V faced several problems that had occupied Pope Eugenius IV in the latter part of his rule: disrespect for papal authority, most critically expressed in the Council of Basel and usurpers of papal political authority in the papal lands, both resulting in an empty papal treasury; conflicts between the major states of

Italy; conflicts within the Greek Orthodox church over its union with the Roman church that were made more significant by the growing power of the Turks and the Islamic religion in the eastern Mediterranean; and the unquiet restoration of Rome as the capital of Christendom and papal residence, which required a pacification of the Roman communal spirit and the restoration of its urban fabric.

Nicholas addressed these problems with a conciliatory spirit and plans for the peaceful restoration of papal power. The pope immediately addressed his relationships to the Roman commune and the nobles of the city and countryside, who had caused his immediate predecessors many problems. On 1 May 1447 he granted to the communal government the full exercise of its traditional statutes and liberties as well as the income from the wine tax for the University (Stadium generale) with any surplus to be expended on the walls of Rome and the needs of the city. Moreover, the decisions on where this income was to be spent were left to the discretion of the conservators, the chief executives of the Roman commune. The conservators and all other offices of the city and district were henceforth to be limited to Roman citizens, and the most important offices were salaried. Finally, the income from the ports and bridges of the city were only to be assigned for their repair. Nicholas also initiated a peaceful relationship toward the Roman nobility, forgiving past disputes and permitting the powerful to rebuild unfortified palaces.

Pope Nicholas sought to restore respect for the papacy through an assertion of traditional papal rights coupled with a willingness to appoint excellent legates who would negotiate with a long-suffering and conciliatory spirit. Though the pope was not a warring prince, he saw the necessity within the papal lands of central Italy to couple this negotiating stance with the presence of some mercenaries and the construction of fortifications. Working outward into the Papal States, Nicholas also labored to implement his policies of compromise and restoration based on negotiation and respect for the former papal adversaries. Most of the feudatories were confirmed in their cities and territories as ruling with papal authority. The pope balanced the ambitions of Francesco Sforza with those of Alfonso, king of Naples, and eventually forced the first to return to Milan, where, after the futile attempts of the republicans of that city to oppose him, Sforza became its lord. Nicholas released the greater part of the mercenary soldiers that Eugenius IV had maintained at great expense in the Papal States.

The pope also sought the aid of the weak German king, Frederick III, against the antipope and the German princes who supported church reform. This strategy included the last coronation of a German king by a pope when in 1452 Nicholas crowned Frederick emperor amid extravagant display but little enhanced imperial authority. The support of Frederick III, however, had been instrumental in the defeat of the antipope Felix V and the schismatic Council of Basel. Upon taking office, Pope Nicholas addressed the problem of the split within the church and sent the learned German Nicholas of Cusa, whom he had recently made a cardinal, to negotiate with Frederick III and the German princes, some of whom had banded together into an anti-Roman league. Nicholas of Cusa succeeded in convincing Frederick to accept Nicholas as pope and to threaten Basel with an interdict. This resulted in the capitulation of Basel to imperial and papal authority and in the concordat of 1448, which ended many German-papal disputes. Papal and monarchical pressures on Felix V compelled him to resign after recognizing Nicholas V as the rightful vicar of Christ. As part of Nicholas's diplomatic style, Felix was given an honorable place within the church and his appointments to church offices recognized as valid.

Through his papal legates in Germany Nicholas had promised an attack on the recognized church and clerical abuses, even if necessary by calling a church council in some undefined form. Failure of its implementation is the most formidable criticism of Nicholas and his pontificate. Ample were the discussions and publications on the plenitude of papal power that came from the papal curia and the supporters of papal monarchy, particularly in the tract of 1450 entitled "Summa against the Enemies of the Church" from the pen of the Spanish canonist Juan de Torquemada.

Another early success was the jubilee of 1450. Despite a visitation of the plague in the summer, and a disastrous pushing incident on the bridge of S. Angelo over the Tiber that resulted in the substantial loss of life in December, the jubilee was a grand occasion for the men and women of Christendom, who demonstrated their devotion by their great numbers in Rome and by filling the treasuries of the city of Rome and the papacy. In fact, Manetti held that this income allowed Nicholas V to rebuild Rome, purchase manuscripts, and support humanists in Greek and Roman studies.

Contemporaries praised the knowledge of Nicholas. Aeneas Sylvius Piccolomini wrote to Frederick III shortly after Nicholas ascended the papal throne: "In the seven arts that are called the liberal, he has been versed since childhood, so that everything stands at his command. He knows all the philosophers as well as the historians, poets, cosomographs, and theologians, for he is also initiated in sacred knowledge. He is acquainted with civil and canon law and medicine is not foreign to him. What is unknown to him lies beyond human knowledge" (Vespasiano da Bisticci, 37). Vespasiano claimed that he had an encyclopedic knowledge that included all the patristic and medieval writers, especially all the works of St. Augustine and Latin and Greek writers, and that he had memorized the Bible. As well, he had an excellent hand as a scribe and set forth a system for organizing libraries when so requested by Cosimo de Medici.

Vespasiano stated that as a young man, the future pope had two passions: "Buy books and build houses. During his pontificate he did both" (Manetti, 925). Manetti asserted that Nicholas ascribed to the humanist's advocacy of glory as a valid human end. This commitment to elements of humanism led the pope to support a large number of humanists in Rome and to plan, but not realize, "a library at St. Peter's for the general use of the Roman court." But it is clear that he possessed a large library because Vespasiano noted that the Aretine Giovanni Tortelli served as Nicholas's librarian and Manetti stated that Nicholas possessed five thousand books.

The election of Tommaso Parentucelli had raised the hopes of humanists in Florence, Rome, and elsewhere that their friend and cosearcher for manuscripts would make the Roman curia a center of humanistic studies, and Nicholas did not disappoint the humanists. He brought Giannozzo Manetti to Rome and appointed him a papal secretary, and later the Florentine humanist became his intimate client and personal secretary. Many other humanists were encouraged by Nicholas to search for and transcribe manuscripts, but perhaps the greatest achievement of his pontificate was the large number of Greek works translated into Latin. Vespasiano mentioned the translation of the *Iliad* of Homer, the *De situ orbis* of Strabo, for which Nicholas gave the translator Guarino da Verona 1,500 florins, the histories of Herodotus and Thucydides translated by Lorenzo Valla, the histories of Xenophon and Diodorus translated by Poggio Bracciolini, the *Republic* of Plato and numerous other translations by George of Trebizond, and many others as well. Nicholas was also animated by his belief that the rebirth of the church required a renewed knowledge of the writings of the Greek church fathers. He therefore commissioned translations of St. Basil, St. Gregory Nazianzen, St. John Chrysostom, and St. Cyril, among many others.

Nicholas wanted the most eminent of the humanists in his court for the purpose of reviving classics of the early church and pagan antiquity. He believed that there was nothing contradictory in that program or any threat in knowledge of the writings of non-Christians. Though some have accused Nicholas of attempting to tame possible pagan or Epicurean tendencies in humanism by channeling the movement through the papacy, it is clear that Nicholas saw humanism as part of the church's renewal and a means of enlarging the prestige of the papacy.

All the quattrocento biographers of Nicholas emphasized his project of rebuilding Rome as a means of restoring the city to its ancient splendor. This urban renewal was viewed as part of the humanistic revival, and many have seen the mind of Leon Battista Alberti behind the project. But Nicholas's contemporaries credited the pope with the animating spirit for Rome's new urban form. Nicholas V concentrated on rebuilding upon the Capitoline Hill, where he sponsored the construction of the Palazzi del Senatore and dei Conservatori for the communal government of Rome while reconstituting the Castel Sant'Angelo as the site of papal government, repaired the forty station traditional churches of indulgences and seven grand churches, and planned a complicated reorganization of the Borgo from Castel Sant'Angelo to St. Peter's and the Vatican Palace and its garden. Castel Sant'Angelo separated the communal government of the Roman people on the Capitoline from papal government in Trastevere. He also made plans to reform the Vatican Palace as the center of rule of the church and worked to create a new garden there.

In his "Testament," recorded on his deathbed by Manetti with the cardinals present, Nicholas V explained his building projects as based on two "principles." First, the buildings were to convey Christian doctrine to the illiterate so that the new holy city, "as if built by God," served a didactic function that images were said by Pope Gregory I to have served. The unlettered were to visualize God's government for humanity in the physical forms and their organization in Rome. The second principle of his building new and repaired walls for Rome and castles in the papal lands was undertaken to regain the authority of the church and to relieve the persecution of the Lands of Peter. Hence Nicholas directed the strengthening of Castel Sant'Angelo and the walls of Rome and the Borgo as well as walls and *castelli* throughout the papal territory.

Had the pontificate of Nicholas V ended in 1452, the pope could have died content in his accomplishments and the general state of the admittedly unreformed but now subordinated church. However, the years 1452 and 1454 and the first months of 1455 until the death of the pontiff in March witnessed disaster after disaster, all made worse for Nicholas by his physical weakness deriving from his ever more painful gout.

The first of these disasters occurred in Rome in January 1453 and destroyed much of Nicholas's trust in others and his earlier conciliatory style of papal rule. From the moment of his elections there had been Romans who attempted to raise popular support for some form of republican government in the city of Rome. The leader of this republican faction, Stefano Porcari, was himself a humanist and frequent leader in several central Italian cities, including a period as captain of the people in Florence in 1427. In that city he gained the friendship and admiration of the same group of civic humanists that supported the pontiff. Eugenius IV and Nicholas V had attempted to pacify Porcari through appointing him to rule in papal lands, but the republican continued to agitate in Rome, so Nicholas was compelled to exile him to Bologna with a yearly pension of three hundred ducats. Escaping the watchful eye of Cardinal Bessarion, the papal legate in Bologna, Porcari returned to Rome with the intention of capturing the pope and cardinals and establishing a Roman republic. The conspiracy rapidly came unraveled, and Porcari was captured and executed in January 1453.

Pope Nicholas's reaction was to fear the Romans and to turn to mercenaries and soldiers for his protection. He became less accessible and more suspicious. This conspiracy of Porcari and his admirers had been fomented despite what the pope believed to be his generous policy toward the citizens of the city.

But this easily forestalled republican insurrection had hardly been calmed when it became apparent that the long-developing thrust of the Ottoman Turks into Byzantium threatened the immediate loss of Constantinople and the possibility that much of Western Christendom would also fall to the forces of Islam. Papal enthusiasm for a grand crusade to protect Constantinople was dampened by what a large number in the papal curia viewed as the hostility of many in Byzantium to the union of the Eastern and Western churches of 1439. On his deathbed Nicholas felt compelled to respond to the criticism that he had done too little to defend the Eastern church. He reminded the cardinals of his involvement in Italian state conflicts and the paucity of general European support for a crusade to defend Constantinople. In truth, Nicholas had tied full papal support to an unequivocal acceptance of papal supremacy by the Eastern church; moreover, in purely political terms the Papal States had little to gain from supporting Constantinople against the Turks.

These difficulties of the last two years of the pontificate of Nicholas were made more difficult by his weakening health. Our present knowledge and conception of Nicholas V is essentially the same as that formed by his contemporaries and friends, Michele Canensi, Manetti, and Vespasiano. A man of culture, a supporter of the humanistic endeavor to reestablish patristic and classical studies, the rebuilder of Rome, and a supporter of peaceful diplomacy, Tommaso Parentucelli in their eyes sought to reestablish Rome and the papacy as the centers of a revived Christian civilization. That his later years were a disappointment to him, to his supporters, to the Western and Eastern churches, and to hopes of a reformed church do not detract from Nicholas's pacific character, his place in the history of humanism, and the revival of the city of Rome.

SELECTED BIBLIOGRAPHY

Bisticci, Vespasiano da. *Vite di uomini illustri del secolo XV*. Trans. into English as *Renaissance Princes, Popes, and Prelates: The Vespasiano Memoirs: Lives of Illustrious Men of the XVth Century*. Trans. William George and Emily Waters. Paperback ed. New York: Harper Torchbooks, Harper & Row, 1963, 31–58.

Canensi, Michele. *Ad Beatissimum D.N. Nicolaum V Pontificum . . . de ipsius laudibus et divina electione*. In Massino Miglio, "Una vocazione in progresso: Michele Canensi, biografo papale." *Studi Medievali*, ser. 3, no. 12 (1971): 463–524.

Cipolla, Costantino. *L'azione letteraria di Niccolò V nel Rinascimento*. Frosinone: Tipografia "Claudio Stracca," 1900.

D'Amico, John F. *Renaissance Humanism in Papal Rome: Humanism and Churchmen on the Eve of the Reformation*. Baltimore: Johns Hopkins University Press, 1983.

Gregorovius, Ferdinand. *History of the City of Rome in the Middle Ages*. Trans. A. Hamilton. London: G. Bell & Sons, 1894–1902. See vol. 7 book 13, chap. 2, pp. 101–49.

Infessura, Stefano. *Diario della Città di Roma*. Ed. Oreste Tommasini. Rome: Forzani, 1890.

Magnuson, Torgil. *Studies in Roman Quattrocento Architecture*. Stockholm: Almquist & Wiksell, 1958.

Mancini, G. "Giovanni Tortelli: Cooperatore di Niccolò V nel fondare la Biblioteca Vaticana." *Archivio storico italiano* 88, no. 2 (1930): 161–282.

Manetti, Giannozzo. *Vita Nicolai V, summi pontificis*. Ed. L.A. Muratori. In *Rerum italicarum scriptores*, vol. 3 pt. 2. Milan, 1734, cols. 908–60.

Onofri, L. "Sacralità, immaginazione, e proposte politiche: La *Vita* di Niccolò V di Giannozzo Manetti." *Humanistica Lovaniensia* 28 (1979): 27–77.

Pagnotti, J. "La *Vita* di Niccolo V scritta da Giannozzo Manetti." *Archivio della Società romana di storia patria* 14 (1891): 411–36.

Paschini, Pio. *Roma nel rinascimento*. Storia di Roma, 12. Bologna: Cappelli, 1940, 169–87.

Pastor, Ludwig *The History of the Popes from the Close of the Middle Ages*. 7th ed. Vol. 2. London and St. Louis: Routledge & Kegan Paul and B. Herder Book Co., 1949, 3–314.

Ramsey, P.A., ed. *Rome in the Renaissance: The City and the Myth: Papers of the Thirteenth Annual Conference of the Center for Medieval and Early Renaissance Studies*. Medieval and Renaissance Texts and Studies. Binghamton, N.Y.: Center for Medieval and Early Renaissance Studies, 1982.

Sforza, G. *Ricerche su Niccolò V: La patria, la famiglia, e la giovinezza di Niccolò V*. Lucca, 1884.

Toews, J.B. "Formative Forces in the Pontificate of Nicholas V." *Catholic Historical Review* 54 (1968/1969): 261–84.

Vasoli, Cesare. "Profilo di un papa umanista: Tommaso Parentucelli." In *Studi sulla cultura del Rinascimento*. Manduria: Lacaita, 1968, 69–121.

Westfall, Carroll W. *In This Most Perfect Paradise: Alberti, Nicholas V and the Invention of Conscious Urban Planning in Rome, 1447–55*. University Park: Pennsylvania State University Press, 1974.

PIUS II (1458–64)

EDWARD D. ENGLISH

Pope Pius II is one of the most documented, studied, and controversial pontiffs of the fifteenth century. Among the reasons for his notoriety is the survival of his well-written and autobiographical *Commentaries*, in which he discusses the political and diplomatic policies of his reign and draws marvelous descriptions of the movements of his court through interesting countrysides. These are, moreover, all interwoven with a certain amount of self-reflection. An able and experienced diplomat and prolific humanist writer, Pius was faced with several exceedingly intractable problems during his active pontificate. His character, both before and after his election, and his intentions, successes, and failures have been subjected to close, and not always favorable, scrutiny. This versatile Renaissance figure has been portrayed as an amoral egotist, a cultured and urbane dilettante, who was vain, grasping, inconsistent, hypocritical, careerist, and sybaritic. Although ultimately and apparently sincerely religious, Pius fits well into the Burckhardtian view of the versatile, self-made, and active intellectual. Within this personal and interpretive context, this complex, ambitious, and restless pontiff reigned at the heart of an important era in papal and European history.

Aeneas Silvius Piccolomini was born in Corsignano overlooking the Val d'Orcia near Siena in southern Tuscany on 18 October 1405. Both his mother's (Vittoria Forteguerri) family and the Piccolomini were old Sienese noble families that had suffered political and economic decline over the course of the fourteenth century. Aeneas grew up in rustic Corsignano but had enough resources and connections to escape to Siena for a university education in 1423. While initially studying the law there and in Florence, he heard the sermons of San Bernardino and met Andrea Biglia, Francesco Filelfo, and Mariano Sozzini, among other humanist teachers. In 1432 he initiated a series of relationships with several patrons, both ecclesiastical and lay, by gaining an appointment as secretary to Domenico Cardinal Capranica, with whom he attended the early meetings of the Council of Basel (1431–49). By 1435 he had started his career as a diplomat, traveling with or acting for several other prelates, such as Niccolò Cardinal Albergati. These assignments included missions to Scotland and to Germany, where he began to make his name as a skillful negotiator and representative of revived papal interests north of the Alps.

In the spring of 1436 he was named as *scriptor* and *abbreviator* for the Council of Basel, thus enabling him to speak and take part in its strongly conciliarist proceedings. An opponent of Eugenius IV, he eventually became a secretary to the antipope Felix V. This connection led him to the Diet of Frankfurt in 1442, where Emperor Frederick III (1440–93) took him into his service, even crowning him poet laureate on 27 July 1442. At the same time, the once-ardent conciliarist began to doubt conciliarist ideals and values. After an illness and as part of a conscious conversion to a more upright life, Aeneas switched parties by a reconciliation with Eugenius in 1445. After taking orders in 1446 and in conjunction with Nicholas of Cusa, he brought the neutral Frederick III and Germany into the papal camp in February 1447. Shortly thereafter he was ordained on 4 March 1447.

Such accomplishments soon brought rewards to the refashioned Aeneas in the form of an appointment as bishop of Trieste by Pope Nicholas V in 1447. Even while maintaining his political relationship with Frederick III by serving in various capacities, Aeneas became bishop of Siena in 1449, an event marked by joy in that city, but also with some suspicion and consternation regarding his local political agenda. The Sienese recognized him as a scion of a once-powerful family now excluded from the spheres of influence but with ambitions to be brought back into the ruling regime, a regime that the Piccolomini could conceivably come to dominate. According to his *Commentaries*, Bishop Aeneas was innocent of any such ambitions, proclaiming his respect for the regime, his desire for peace, and his loathing of factionalism. Beside dramatically noting that there may have been a plot against his life, Aeneas praised the party in power and recalled that the withdrawal from government might have been "voluntary." Despite such a gesture on the part of the nobles, the "people" or regimes forced them further out of power and into "an almost servile existence" by allowing them only a few offices and excluding them from service on the ruling council. This deprived them of any liberty or ability to serve as members of an organic state. After his old friend and patron, the emperor Frederick III, had passed pompously but uneventfully through the city,

Aeneas wrote in the *Commentaries* that the regime had come to accept him more readily. In the *Commentaries*, however, Aeneas later complained of several instances of his service to the commune not being appreciated. He asserted that the commune sometimes acted without honor and was unworthy of pity in its self-inflicted factional problems. Other than these minor bouts of wariness on the part of the bishop and the city, his reign as bishop was reasonably tranquil.

After negotiating with Alfonso the Magnanimous of Naples, undertaking a trip to heretical Bohemia, and laboring tirelessly for the interests of the Holy See, Aeneas was promoted by Pope Callistus III. Recognizing his abilities, these accomplishments, and a mutual commitment to the crusading enterprise, the Catalan Callistus raised him to the rank of cardinal-priest of Santa Sabina on 16 December 1456.

While continuing to further papal ambitions and diplomacy in Italy and across the Alps during the decade between 1446 and 1456, Aeneas wrote a number of impressive works on various topics and in several genres. Not all of these worked to his advantage. He had already written conciliarist tracts before his personal conversion and political change of heart that were to be held against him for the rest of his life, especially by his enemies in Germany during his pontificate. On top of leading a life unmarked by any devotion to chastity, including the fathering of several children, he had already written two famous books before his conversion around 1445. *Chrysis* was an erotic comedy, and *The Two Lovers (Lucretia and Euryalus)* was about the amorous deeds in Siena and at the imperial court of Frederick III's chancellor and patron of Aeneas, Caspar Schlick. Both works were popular and notorious.

In the 1430s he had written tracts in favor of conciliarist ideas that were later to be explicitly rejected by him as pope in various retractions and bulls, es-

Drawing of Pope Pius II by O. Pauvinius. (Courtesy of the Vatican Library)

pecially *In minoribus agentes* of 26 April 1463. These included a sympathetic description of the controversial and then barely discredited Council of Basel (*De gestis Basiliensis concilii*). It might be suggested that for Aeneas, soon to become Pius, the vision of conciliar cleansing of the church was to be replaced by one in which a crusade, conducted by a united Christendom under papal tutelage, would accomplish the same end.

He had produced other works before his election in 1458 that were less scandalous and had given credence to his literary and humanist talents.

These included *De curialium miseriis*, on the problems of courtiers, the *Pentalogus*, a visionary manual for governing compiled for the emperor, and *De liberorum educatione*, a collection of suggestions, almost a humanist program, for educating the children of princes. To quote Eugenio Garin, Aeneas intended "the 'scientific' preparation of leadership cadres for the achievement of the common good of humanity through the conscious elaboration of the moral sciences in their historical dimension" (40). His histories of Bohemia and of the reign of Frederick III contributed to his reputation as a fine Latin stylist and acute and skillful observer of nature and politics, deriving history from what seemed to be nature. Garin again defines Aeneas as a practical and active intellectual linking his historical reflection to the real world. Eugenio Garin thinks that for Aeneas the study of history and geography should lead to gaining a true wisdom that should then govern one's life. Nonetheless and despite this rhetorical commitment to ethical conduct, his numerous opportunistic changes of patrons and views on the governance of the church lend themselves only too well to skepticism about his motives, character, and constancy. Many of his contemporaries doubtless interpreted his motivation as based on personal advantage, political expedience, and pursuit of power.

Aeneas Silvius's life took a dramatic turn in the late summer of 1458 with the death of Callistus III on 6 August and that of his old patron, Cardinal Capranica, who died a few days later. Capranica had been the most likely successor, so the election was thrown open, with William Cardinal d'Estouteville, the favorite of France, now seemingly next in line. The sacred college assembled on 16 August, equally divided between nine Italians and nine non-Italians. As had become the custom, the assembled cardinals cynically agreed to a set of capitulations that were supposed to weaken the power of any new pope with respect to the college of cardinals. Although his description was censored from the sixteenth-century edition of the *Commentaries*, we possess a classic and detailed account by Aeneas of the various maneuvers, skillfully carried out by himself, leading to his election. Aeneas picturesquely portrayed himself as bucking the deals made among the cardinals in the latrines of the conclave. Employing all his diplomatic skill and self-aggrandizement, the prematurely aged and chronically ill Aeneas was elected on 19 August after the second scrutiny when Rodrigo Cardinal Borgia, the future Alexander VI, began the *accessus* process of swaying the tide to the cardinal of Siena. Playing on Vergil, Aeneas took the name Pius II and hoped that everyone might forget the amatory and conciliarist Aeneas and think only of the ascetic Pius.

The new pope faced problems common to his predecessors and successors in the fifteenth century. It is upon Pius's successes or failures and his methods and approaches that any evaluation of his reign must stand. The issues of his complex papacy can be defined as the promotion and leadership of a crusade; the fostering of the unity of the church in the face of heresy, especially in Bohemia, and doctrinal disputes; the confrontation over sovereignty on ecclesiastical issues and appointments in France and Germany; and the continuation of the reconquest of the Papal States while maintaining a balance of power among the states of Italy and keeping foreign rulers out. Last and most fundamental, he sought to ensure the triumph of papal primacy over conciliarist ambitions. The minor issues of his reign concerned minimal attempts at curial reform and the promotion of his family interests in Siena and in the papal administration. In a wider sense, his cultural activity involved little support for the new humanist culture, an inconsistent commitment to protect the surviving monuments of the classical civilization to which he was allegedly so dedicated, and the promotion of a few artistic projects, in particular, the rebuilding of his hometown Corsignano into Pienza and the staging of elaborate ceremonies and artistic projects for the reception of the head of St. Andrew into Rome from Greece. The common thread through all of these problems and policies was the desire to confront the threat of a revival of conciliarism and thus a weakening of the monarchical papacy to which Pius had become dedicated. Conciliarism had only been barely allayed in the 1440s, but continued to exercise a possible threat to papal sovereignty over the institutional church. In reality only a truce reigned, or so it seemed to contemporaries. Pius might have been inconsistent and vacillating in his policies, but they were all aimed at ensuring the primacy of the successor of St. Peter. These are the topics that he emphasizes himself in the *Commentaries*, and they will be now covered topically in the rest of this biography.

The decade of the 1450s was one of relentless progress by the Turks throughout the Balkan peninsula after their conquest of Constantinople in 1453. The Turks, under Mehmed II, were now on the doorstep of Western Europe and continuing their conquest of the Balkans. Pius's pontificate marked their absorption of the Morea in Greece, Lesbos in the Aegean, Trebizond and Sinope on the Black Sea, and Serbia and Bosnia in the peninsula. Hungary, central Europe, and even Italy were not far away. The papacy had long been considered one of the catalysts and sponsors of the crusade, if not the most important of all. To the new and ambitious pontiff, a crusade seemingly offered a way to unite the Christian powers and bring internal peace and a moral regeneration of both the laity and the clergy, all fostered by and under the leadership of the Holy See. It also could with great justification be called a true defense of Western Europe from an imperial and ambitious Islamic state.

On 12 and 13 October 1458 Pius began his efforts to launch a crusade by calling for a congress to meet on 1 June of the following year at Mantua or Udine. It was to be attended by all of the princes of Christendom. Venice refused to let the congress meet at Udine, so Mantua in the summertime became the place of meeting. After a series of generally triumphant entries through central Italy, Pius arrived at Mantua on 27 May, where he failed to find any princes to welcome him and anxious to go on crusade. They trickled into the congress over the next several months. Even the first sitting of the congress had to be put off until 26 September. Until then, numerous speeches about the value of a military enterprise were made. No power wanted to refuse to cooperate with the project of the pope, but none can be said to have actually furthered it either.

The merchant republics of Florence and especially Venice were reluctant to destroy their lucrative markets with the Turks. No prince seemed to see the leadership of such an enterprise as being in his best interest. Bogged down by squabbling about papal primacy in the north and conflict over the Neapolitan succession in Italy, the congress collapsed in January 1460. Within this context of abject papal failure, Pius issued the bull *Execrabilis* on 18 January. Although it was not much cited until the end of the century, this bull condemned an appeal to a council over the head of the pope. Pius then left Mantua and attempted to deal with the other problems facing the Holy See. He never gave up the concept of a crusade under the leadership of the pope, but he did little about it for the next few years except write a strange, but never-sent, letter to Mehmed II urging conversion and systematically attempting to refute the Koran. The sultan who had captured Constantinople was to play the role of Constantine uniting a utopian world under the true Christian faith.

The French monarchy, German princes, and some prince-bishops north of the Alps were often threatening to call another council outside of papal control in order to threaten Pius. However, any efforts along these lines would encounter an almost universal reaction of local, rather nationalist, negative response. These responses were to be exemplified by strong and consistent desires for sovereignty by lay governments over ecclesiastical institutions, benefices, and taxes.

In France Pius had to negotiate with the notoriously wily Louis XI, who succeeded his father Charles VII in 1461 and ruled until 1483. Louis consistently sought papal support for René of Anjou's claims on the Kingdom of Naples by offering to revoke the Pragmatic Sanction of Bourges (7 July 1438), which had effectively eliminated papal influence over ecclesiastical appointments in France. Despite this attractive offer and papal hopes for a crusade led by Louis, Pius steadfastly backed the Aragonese claim. Louis actually revoked the edict, but on Pius's failure to change sides, he restored Gallican control of the church by royal decree. Pius kept the French out of Italy but failed to regain papal pretensions within the Crown's domain.

When he was elected, Pius half-seriously referred to himself as the cardinal of Germany and the North. Despite his great experience there, or perhaps because of it, he was not to have an easy relationship with secular rulers and prelates from north of the Alps. National and regional issues and the personal ambitions on the part of both secular and lay rulers made Pius's desire for reconciliation with the Holy See a rare event in German affairs during his reign. The incompetence of Emperor Frederick III, Pius's old patron, compounded the difficulties of settling complaints by cities, princes, and feudal churchmen about fiscal rapacity resulting from the financing of the crusade. The specter of conciliarism was constantly evoked in disputes in Brixen, Mainz, Cologne, Brandenburg, and the Tyrol. Learned tracts on the issue of papal sovereignty were produced by apologists for both sides, such as the antipapal Gregor Heimburg and Teodoro Laelio and the propapal Gabriel Biel. Pius attempted to defend Roman primacy on every occasion, especially in the decretal *In minoribus agentes* issued on 26 April 1463. This uncompromising document built on the *Defensorium obedientiae apostolicae* written by Biel the year before. While gaining victories in conflicts over minor issues and the occupancies of particular offices, Pius did not succeed in any significant way either in settling the complex issue of Roman primacy or in raising support for the crusade.

As supreme pontiff and pastor, he also had to confront heresy and promote uniformity of belief and practice. This issue and duty were most acute in still partially Hussite Bohemia. Pius had some experience in Bohemia, having served as nuncio in 1451 and having been involved at the Council of Basel when the Compacts of 1433 were worked out. The Compacts had not really quelled the issues of purgatory, prayers for the dead, the use of images of the saints, and Communion under both species or utraquism. There was also the thorny issue of the old confiscations of church property carried out decades earlier. Even conservative Hussites had taken the Compacts as acceptance of their ideas, or at least that was how Pius had come to read events. The pontiff did work for union throughout his reign. This consisted of trying to get George of Podebrady, the king of Bohemia (1458–71), to accept papal authority and then embark on a crusade. George vacillated for years, never feeling secure enough in his throne to accept Roman primacy and impose conformity with its practices or rituals. Considering George duplicitous in the extreme and seemingly confusing Hussitism with Taboritism, Pius resorted, after lengthy but vain negotiations, to sanctions. The pontiff rashly and formally abrogated the Compacts on 31 March 1462. In the consistory on 16 June 1464 he went further and declared George a perjured and relapsed heretic, summoning him for judgment. The bull was not issued before Pius died the following August.

Pius, moreover, knew that he must face the completion of the reconstruction of the Papal States begun under Martin V several decades earlier. This became even more crucial with the discovery of alum at Tolfa near Civitavecchia during Pius's reign, thus breaking the lucrative Turkish monopoly and providing the Holy See with thousands of ducats in new income. This restoration of control had also to be accomplished to ensure that the Holy See was not under the control of any lay power in Italy or of any monarchy from outside Italy. In addition, by the mid-fifteenth century the financial value of the Papal States had once again become significant factors in the pope's and curia's income. The unreliable princes dominating cities in the Papal States, such as Borso d'Este and Sigismondo Malatesta, were always ready to challenge any papal pretensions to actual lordship or sovereignty in north central Italy. The new pope had to balance his ambitions in Italy among merchant republics obsessed with their commercial interests, of which the most prominent were Florence and Venice, the latter city and its fleet being absolutely necessary for any crusading plans. Pius was also caught between the wary diplomacy of the closely allied Duchy of Milan of Francesco Sforza and the Kingdom of Naples then being fought over for most of his reign by Angevin and Aragonese claimants to the throne, in reality a battle between French and Aragonese ambitions for Italy.

Although wavering at various moments, Pius provided crucial support for the victorious Aragonese claimant Ferrante of Naples (1458–94), the natural son of Alfonso V the Magnanimous. Always in close alliance with Francesco Sforza, the duke of Milan, and ardently opposed to the extension of French or Angevin power in Italy, Pius reestablished much of papal authority in the states of the church. He maintained control of Rome and Lazio and won his well-publicized war to the death with Sigismondo Malatesta, which included the famous inverted canonization in hell of Sigismondo. In the end, he restored a great deal of papal control over the Papal States, although this was limited by the lukewarm support, if not opposition, of many of the states on the peninsula. Despite these successes, they did not translate into any kind of Italian unequivocal support for the crusading enterprise of 1464.

Underlying all these matters of state, the reform of ecclesiastical institutions, practices, and clerical mores was a well-acknowledged need, but one constantly blocked by entrenched clerical and lay interests. Even a powerful and skillful occupant of the chair of St. Peter could only contemplate undertaking such a mission with great trepidation. Pius seemed to assume that the mustering of a crusade would have the added effect of reinvigorating the clergy and the Roman curia itself. The financing and recruitment of an army for the Balkans and its success would go far to eliminate clerical misconduct and spiritual malaise. Thus little was done except to threaten the lifestyles of the members of the college of cardinals, and all came to hang on the success of the armed mission to the East.

Within this grandiose plan there was a draft program for a bull, never issued, for the moral reform of the clergy in 1460, aimed specifically at cleaning up the households of the curia and the sacred college. These establishments were to be cleansed of actors, gamblers, and male and female concubines. Taverns and blaspheming were to be avoided by all members. As for the pontiff himself, he led an ascetic life, in fact spending the least on his itinerant household and court of any fifteenth-century pope. Beside caustically disciplining Rodrigo Borgia for his personal excesses and those of his entourage, he produced charming accounts of the joys of meeting his own court in the open air under the trees on Mont Amiato south of Siena near his hometown. Curial offices were put up for sale during his administration, with membership in the newly created college of abbreviators in 1463 bringing in 30,000 ducats.

Pius did rely on his relatives in important administrative posts, especially the children of his sister Laudomia, who had married Nanni Todeschini of Siena. His nephew Antonio Piccolomini Todeschini married the natural daughter of Ferrante of Naples, the Aragonese claimant to the throne. This was only one of a series of advantageous marriages that revived the fortunes of the Piccolomini family. Antonio occupied a number of strategic offices in Rome and the Papal States. Antonio's brother, Francesco, became bishop of Siena at twenty years of age and, soon thereafter, a legate in the Marches. After an exemplary personal life and numerous missions for three popes, he was elected Pope Pius III in September 1503, only to die a month later. Based on research in three Vatican registers, Richard Hilary has calculated that about 15 percent of Pius II's appointments could be classified as nepotistic, mostly to positions demanding reliability and trust. Like many popes and secular politicians, Pius II had to rely on family relationships, regional origins, and recommendations from trusted friends to carry out his political agenda.

The capitulary of the 1458 conclave did begin discussions about pluralities, simony, residence, and monastic discipline, but it seemingly was more for electoral show than for any genuine intent on the part of its adherents. At times hostile to the friars except for the Observants, Pius was unable to do much about their reform, since they played such key roles in his preaching for his crusading programs. Even the efforts of Nicholas of Cusa and Domenico de Domenichi, carried out periodically throughout Pius's reign, led nowhere beyond the discussion of systematic visitations to enforce conformity. The mundane problems of the mid-fifteenth-century church were recognized: the regulation of hospitals and convents of nuns, fraudulent indulgences and relics, bogus miracles, bleeding Hosts, the enforcement of the laws on usury and adultery, clerical misconduct, and magical practices. He also tried to protect newly converted Africans from the slave trade, then only a few decades old. But in the end all hope of reform was left to the accomplishment of a military mission to be assembled and conducted against all odds.

Pius II was primarily concerned in his relationship with Siena with the reintegration into the governing regime of certain noble families and also of members of one of the main parties of the city, the Dodici or Twelve. He constantly maintained that solutions to communal problems and the maintenance of good order would naturally result from the full and active participation in the government of some of Siena's most able citizens.

They were now unfortunately handicapped with political disabilities. As supreme pontiff and a Sienese, he tried to encourage harmony within a broadly based ruling class in a renewed polity. Sound government and policies based on concern for the common good could only arise when a regime had the benefit of the assistance and cooperation of its social, if not economic, elite. Of course, such a restoration could also benefit the new participants and their families, especially his family, the revived Piccolomini.

A few months after Pius's election in August 1458, he, as the commune had long feared, demanded the readmission of the nobles and the Twelve. In a letter of 4 November 1458, noting the long service of Sienese nobles and the Piccolomini to the state, their voluntary resignation of power (citing old tactical maneuvers on their part in the major changes of government in 1355 and 1369), and their subsequent unfair treatment by succeeding regimes, Pius expected the complete readmission of the nobles into the ruling coalition. He further wanted them eligible for all of the offices of the state. His family had already been partially rehabilitated as soon as word reached Siena of his election, but the pope now wanted all of the Monte of the Gentlemen to be brought back to full political rights. According to the *Commentaries*, the regime was "violently excited by this demand," backed as it was by a threat of the potentially lucrative papal entourage avoiding Siena and staying elsewhere, even in Florence.

Negotiations and threats such as these dominated Pius's relationship with his hometown through most of his papacy when he was both in the city and very nearby. By organizing expensive ceremonies for Pius when he was in Siena and appointing several committees to look into the matter, the Sienese of the ruling regime resisted and delayed implementation of Pius's proposals as long as they could. This was done in the face of papal threats of abandonment of the city to its enemies and despite the incentives promised to the city. These included the concessions of strategic strongholds in the countryside, the lucrative presence of the papal court, the canonization of St. Catherine, the implementation of beneficial architectural projects, and the official recognition of the University of Siena. Minor deals were worked out. However, as soon as Pius died in 1464, most of the concessions made by the commune were recalled, except for those granting the Piccolomini limited participation in the government and bureaucracy of the city.

Pius II was accused during his life, and especially after his death, of neglecting to support his fellow humanists. Francesco Filelfo was particularly outspoken regarding the failure of his former student, now with the disposal of much patronage, to repay his mentor's earlier letters of recommendation. The truth of these charges on a wider scale is not easy to evaluate. The authoritarian Pius, forgetting Aeneas, did little for those scholars of a republican bent and the defenders of selective liberty, except initially for the chameleon Giannozzo Manetti and the elderly Poggio Bracciolini, both of whom died in 1459. Playing the odd role of the leader of the republic of letters now in charge of the church, Pius was not much interested in sponsoring humanists seemingly not equal to his own accomplishment. The Sienese pope did befriend Flavio Biondo, Lodrisio Crivelli, and Giannantonio Campano, but mostly employed his fellow Sienese intellectuals in curial positions, such as Agostino Patrizi, Jacopo Ammanati, and Goro Lolli. While his reign cannot be described as much of a golden age for humanist patronage, Pius in his own person brought together a sometimes-uneasy reconciliation of religious belief with some of the new humanist thought. This was not an accommodation made by all of his successors.

As for his artistic patronage, Pius devoted his efforts primarily to turning Pienza, the new name for his hometown, Corsignano, into a much more impressive place including a new cathedral and palaces for cardinals, the newly created bishopric, and the Piccolomini family. Bernardo Gambarelli, nicknamed Rosellino, was the principal architect. This monument to himself and his family remains intact to this day. After his death his relatives, now much better established economically, built over the course of the rest of the century impressive palaces in Siena, a loggia, and a library, attached to the cathedral, decorated by Bernardino Pinturrichio. Beside being feted in elaborate entrances in Viterbo and several other cities, Pius sponsored complex ceremonies in Rome for the entry of St. Andrew's head during Easter week in 1462.

The main architectural projects for that event were the construction and decoration of a new chapel for that saint, inside the church, and the building of new steps and a loggia of benediction or pulpit and the sculptures by Paolo Romano of the fraternal saints Peter and Andrew, all in front of old St. Peter's. St. Andrew's head had been rescued from Patras in front of the approaching Turks in 1460. The expensive ceremonies in Rome were to welcome him to the Holy See, provide propaganda for the crusade, and drum up support for the deposed despot of Morea, Thomas Paleologus. It was only after the completion of these projects that Pius issued a bull to protect the ruins of Rome from pillaging for marble. Pius had been fairly silent about crusading after the failure of the congress at Mantua two years earlier. With these events and ceremonies completed, he now began to reflect again on the second, and almost equally ill-fated, supreme effort to attack the Turks in the Balkans under papal leadership. Moreover, they certainly must have been linked with Pius's own ambitions for his subsequent reputation, since he closely associated the whole festival with himself and intended to be buried, and was, in the new chapel inside St. Peter's.

In September 1463 Hungary and Venice entered into an offensive alliance against the Turks in the Balkans. Pius quickly took notice and returned to his old concept, even going so far as proposing in a consistory on 23 September to take the cross himself. He spent the rest of his reign raising money and manpower for this project while cajoling princes and republics to embark with him. With the succession to Naples settled and with early evidence of adherence by a few princes such as Philip, the duke of Burgundy, Pius was initially able to be more optimistic about its possibility. Although the duke ultimately reneged and Venice was to dither until the last moment, Pius, though sick and worn out, went to Ancona to cross the Adriatic in the summer of 1464. The pontiff arrived there on 19 July, having formally taken the cross on 18 June. A Venetian fleet eventually entered port on 12 August, most likely intent on merely reclaiming lost commercial colonies in the Peloponnesus. By then, however, many of the assembled crusaders had despaired of transport and had left the plague-ridden and hot city. This climax of disillusionment for Pius only shortly preceded his death on 14 August 1464. He was never able to overcome the enmities and conflicting interests of the princes or to convince the Venetians that their interests were best served by a crusade.

It is not easy to sum up the accomplishments and failures of Pius II, nor can one pass easy judgments about his character. Perhaps more research, using all of the available sources, would make that more possible and credible. Most of his reign was spent trying unsuccessfully to launch a crusade against the Turks, who had become a genuine threat to the heartland of Europe. Although this project was intended to further other reforms in the church, they too were ultimately neglected. Pius sought to play a major political role in Italy and the rest of Christendom and to restore the papal monarchy to a position of eminence and respect. Most of his political goals were not reached, despite his lengthy and worldly diplomatic experience before his election. He did consolidate papal influence, if not control, over most of the Papal States in Italy. He did restore the fortunes of his family. There can be little doubt that he consistently articulated a strong defense of the primacy of Rome and the Holy See. Whether he convinced many of his contemporaries is another matter. He did, nonetheless, manage to avoid the meeting of another council outside papal control during his reign. His most lasting monument must, however, be the literary and historical record that he left in the *Commentaries*.

SELECTED BIBLIOGRAPHY

Ady, C.M. *Pius II (Aeneas Silvius Piccolomini): The Humanist Pope*. London: Methuen & Co., 1913.

Andrews, A.D. "From the Piccolomini Papers." *Library Chronicle* 26, no. 1 (Winter 1960): 17–29.

Battaglia, F. *Enea Silvio Piccolomini e Francesco Patrizi: Due politici senesi del quattrocento*. Siena: Istituto comunale d'arte e di storia, 1936.

Bernetti, G. *Saggi e studi sugli scritti di Enea Silvio Piccolomini Papa Pio II (1405–1464)*. Florence: S.T.I.A.V., 1971.

Bianchi, R. *Intorno a Pio II: Un mercante e tre poeti*. Messina: Sicania, 1988.

Brosius, D. "Breven und Briefe Papst Pius II." *Römische Quartalschrift* 70 (1975): 212–23.

Bürck, G. *Selbstdarstellung und personenbildnis bei Enea Silvio Piccolomini (Pius II)*. Basler Beiträge zur Geschichtswissenschaft, 56. Basel and Stuttgart: Helbing & Lichtenhahn, 1956.

Burckhardt, Jacob. *The Civilization of the Renaissance in Italy*. Trans. S.G.C. Middlemore. Oxford: Phaidon Press, 1944.

Cardini, F. "La Repubblica di Firenze e la crociata di Pio II." *Rivista di storia della chiesa in Italia* 33, no. 2 (1979): 455–82.

Carli, Enzo. *Pienza: La città di Pio II*, Rome: Editalia, 1966.

Casanova, E. "Un anno della vita privata di Pio II." *Bullettino senese di storia patria* 38, no. 1 (1931): 19–34 (based on two volumes of account books of Pius II in the state archives in Rome).

Casella, N. "Recenti studi su Enea Silvio Piccolomini." *Rivista di storia della chiesa in Italia* 26 (1972): 473–88.

"Convegno storico piccolominiano (Ancona, 9 maggio 1965)." *Atti e memorie della Deputazione di storia patria per le Marche*, ser. 8, 4, no. 2 (1964–65): 5–233.

Crivelli, L. "De expeditione Pii papae II adversos Turcos." In *Rerum italicarum scriptores*, vol. 23, pt. 5, ed. Giulio C. Zimolo. Bologna: Nicola Zanichelli, 1950.

D'Amico, J.F. "Pope Pius II." In *Contemporaries of Erasmus: A Biographical Register of the Renaissance and Reformation*, vol. 3, ed. Peter G. Bietenholz and Thomas B. Deutscher. Toronto: University of Toronto Press, 1987, 97–98.

English, E.D. "An Elite at Work: The Gaining and Preserving of Wealth, Power, and Salvation in Late Medieval and Renaissance Siena." In *Work and Workers in the Late Middle Ages*, ed. Claire Dolan. Toronto: Pontifical Institute of Mediaeval Studies, 1991, 303–31.

Fosi, I.P. " 'La comune, dolcissma patria': Siena e Pio II." In *I ceti dirigenti nella Toscana del Quattrocento*, ed. Riccardo Fubini. Florence: Francesco Papafava, 1987, 509–21.

Galand-Hallyn, P. "La poétique de jeunesse de Pie II: La 'Cinthia.' " *Latomus* 52, no. 4 (October–December 1993): 875–96.

Garin, E. "Aeneas Sylvius Piccolomini." In *Portraits from the Quattrocento*. New York: Harper & Row, 1972, 30–54.

Haubst, R. "Der Reformentwurf Pius der Zweiter." *Römische Quartalschrift* 49 (1954): 188–242.

Head, C. "Pope Pius II and the Wars of the Roses." *Archivum historiae pontificiae* 8 (1970): 139–78.

Hilary, Richard B. "The Nepotism of Pope Pius II, 1458–1464." *The Catholic Historical Review* 64 (1978): 33–35.

Hoffmann, G. "Papst Pius II. und die Kirchenheit des Ostens," *Orientalia christiana periodica* 12 (1946): 217–37.

Housley, N. *The Later Crusades, 1274–1580: From Lyons to Alcazar*. Oxford: Oxford University Press, 1992.

Kaminsky, H. "Pius Aeneas among the Taborities," *Church History* 28, no. 3 (September 1959): 281–309.

Kisch, G. *Enea Silvio Piccolomini und die Jurisprudenz*. Basel: Helbing & Lichtenhahn, 1967.

Klauser, T. *Die abendlandishche Liturgie von Aeneas Silvius Piccolomini bis heute: Erbe und Aufgabe*. Vortrage der Aeneas-Silvius-Stiftung an der Universität Basel, 1. Basel: Helbing & Lichtenhahn, 1962.

Lesage, G.-L. "La titulature des envoyés pontificaux sous Pie II (1458–1464)," *Mélanges d'archéologie et d'histoire* 53 (1941–46): 206–47.

Maffei, D., ed. *Enea Silvio Piccolomini (Atti del convegno per il quinto centenario della morte)*. Siena: Accademia senese degli Intronati, 1968; see the especially valuable articles by Cecil H. Clough, Nicholi Rubinstein, and Alfred A. Strnad.

Mitchell, R.J. *The Laurels and the Tiara: Pope Pius II, 1458–1464*. Garden City, N.Y.: Doubleday, 1962.

Morrall, J.B. "Pius II: Humanist and Crusader." *History Today* 8 (January 1958): 27–37.

Naville, C.E. *Enea Silvio Piccolomini: L'uomo, l'umanista, il pontifice (1405–1464)*. Locarno: Analisi, 1984.

Nederman, C.J. "Humanism and Empire: Aeneas Sylvius Piccolomini, Cicero, and the Imperial Ideal." *Historical Journal* 36, no. 3 (September 1993): 499–515.

Paparelli, G. *Enea Silvio Piccolomini: L'umanesimo sul soglio di Pietro*. 2nd ed. Ravenna: Longo, 1978.

Piccolomini, A.S. (Pius II). *Aeneae Silvii "De curialium miseriis epistola."* Ed. Wilfred P. Mustard. Baltimore: Johns Hopkins Press, 1928.

———. *Aeneae Silvii "De liberorum educatione": A Translation, with an Introduction*. Ed. Joel Stanislaus Nelson. Studies in Medieval and Renaissance Latin Language and Literature, 12. Washington, D.C.: Catholic University of America Press, 1940. Also translated in 1897 and published as "The Treatise of Aeneas Sylvius Piccolomini, Afterwards Pius II, 'De liberorum educatione,'" in *Vittorino da Feltre and Other Humanist Educators*, ed. William Harrison Woodward. Cambridge: Cambridge University Press, 1897. Reprint, New York: Teachers College, Columbia University, 1963.

———. *Epistola ad Mahomatem II (Epistle to Mohammed II)*. Ed. and transl. Albert R. Baca. New York: Peter Lang, 1990.

———. *Pii II Commentarii rerum memorabilium que temporibus suis contigerunt*. Ed. Adrian Van Heck. 2 vols. Studi e testi, 312–13. Vatican City: Biblioteca Apostolica Vaticana, 1984. For a complete English translation, see *The Commentaries of Pius II*. Trans. Florence Alden Gragg with notes by Leona C. Gabel., 5 vols. Smith College Studies in History, 22, 25, 30, 35, 43. Northampton, Mass.: Smith College, 1937–57.

Platina, B. "Liber de vita Christi ac omnium pontificum (AA. 1–1474)." In *Rerum italicarum scriptores*, vol. 3, pt. 1, ed. Giacinto Gaida. Città di Castello: S. Lapi, 1932, "Pius II," 346–63.

Poggi Bracciolini, Giovanni Francesco. "De Pio II pontifice maximo." In *Le Liber pontificalis*, 3 vols. Ed. Louis Duchesne. Paris: Ernest Thorin, 1886–92. Reprint, Paris: E. de Boccard, 1981, 2:559–60.

Reinhard, W. "Papa Pius: Prolegomena zu einer Sozialgeschichte des Papsttums." In *Von Konstanz nach Trient: Beiträge zur Geschichte der Kirche von den Reformkonzilien bis zum Tridentinum: Festgabe für August Franzen*. Munich: Ferdinand Schöningh, 1972, 261–99.

Robin, D. *Filelfo in Milan: Writings, 1451–1477*. Princeton: Princeton University Press, 1991.

Rospigliosi, W. "Part II: Aeneas Silvius Piccolomini (Pius II)." In *Writers in the Italian Renaissance*. London: Gordon & Cremonesi, 1978, 103–46.

Rowe, J.G. "The Tragedy of Aeneas Sylvius Piccolomini (Pope Pius II): An Interpretation." *Church History* 30 (1961): 288–313.

Rubinstein, R.O. "Pius II as a Patron of Art, with Special Reference to the History of the Vatican." Ph.D. diss., University of London, 1957.

Rutger, F. "Ein Sammelband über Papst Pius II." *Quellen und Forschungen aus italienischen Archiven und Bibliotheken* 50 (1970): 462–74.

Santayana, S.G. *Two Renaissance Educators: Alberti and Piccolomini*. Boston: Meador Publishing Company, 1930.

Schimmelpfennig, B. "Der Amterhandel an der römischen Kurie von Pius II. bis zum Sacco di Roma (1458–1527)." In *Amterhandel im Spätmittelalter und im 16. Jahrhundert: Referate eines internationalen Colloquium in Berlin vom 1. bis 3. Mai 1980*. Berlin: Colloquium Verlag, 1984, 3–41.

Schmidinger, H. *Romana regia potestas: Staats- und Reichsdenken bei Engelbert von Admont und Enea Silvio Piccolomini*. Vorträge der Aeneas-Silvius-Stiftung an der Universität Basel, 13. Basel: Helbing & Lichtenhahn, 1978.

Schürmeyer, W. *Das Kardinalskollegium unter Pius II*. Historische Studien, 122. Berlin: Emil Ebering, 1914. Reprint, Vaduz: Kraus Reprint, 1965.

Schwoebel, R. "Pius II and the Renaissance Papacy." In *Renaissance Men and Ideas*. New York: St. Martin's Press, 1971, 67–79.

Silvestri, A. "Gli ultimi anni di Pio II." *Atti e memorie della Reale Deputazione romana di storia patria* 20–21 (1940–41): 1–58.

Smith, L.F. "Lodrisio Crivelli of Milan and Aeneas Sylvius, 1457–64." *Studies in the Renaissance* 9 (1962): 31–63.

Soranzo, G. *Pio II e la politica italiana nella lotta contra i Malatesti (1457–1463)*. Padua: Drucker, 1911.

Strnad, A.A. "Pio II e suo nipote: Francesco Todeschini Piccolomini." *Atti e memorie della Deputazione di storia patria per le Marche*, ser. 8, 4, no. 2 (1964–65): 35–84.

Tarugi, L.R.S., ed. *Pio II e la cultura del suo tempo: Atti del I convegno internazionale, 1989*. Milan: Edizioni Angelo Guerini, 1991.

Toews, J.B. "Dream and Reality in the Imperial Ideology of Pope Pius II." *Medievalia et humanistica* 16 (1964): 77–93.

———. "The View of Empire in Aeneas Sylvius Piccolomini (Pope Pius II)." *Traditio* 24 (1968): 471–87.

Totaro, L. *Pio II nei suoi "Commentarii": Un contributo alla lettura della autobiografia di Enea Silvio de Piccolomini*. Bologna: Pàtron, 1978.

Ugurgieri della Berardenga, C. *Pio II Piccolomini con notizie su Pio III e altri membri della famiglia*. Biblioteca dell'Archivio storico italiano, 18. Florence: Leo S. Olschki, 1973.

Valentini, G. "Le crociata di Pio II dalla documentazione veneta d'archivio." *Archivum historiae pontificiae* 13 (1975): 249–82.

Veit, L.M. *Pensiero e vita religiosa di Enea Silvio Piccolomini, prima della sua consacrazione episcopale.* Analecta gregoriana, 139. Rome: Università gregoriana, 1964.

Vivanti, C. "I *Commentarii* di Pio II." *Studi storici* 26, no. 2 (April–June 1985): 443–62.

Voigt, G. *Enea Silvio de' Piccolomini, als Papst Pius der Zweite, und sein Zeitalter.* 3 vols. Berlin: Georg Reimer, 1856–63. Reprint, Berlin: Walter de Gruyter, 1967.

Widmer, B. *Enea Silvio Piccolomini in der sittlichen und politischen Entscheidung.* Basler Beiträge zur Geschichtswissenschaft, 88. Basel and Stuttgart: Helbing & Lichtenhahn, 1963.

Zimpolo, G.C. "La 'Vita Pii II P.M.' del Platina nel cod. Vat. Ottoboniano latino 2056." In *Studi in onore di Carlo Castiglioni.* Fontes ambrosiani, 32. Milan: A. Giuffrè, 1957, 875–904.

SIXTUS IV (1471–84): THE FIRST MODERN POPE-MONARCH

Lorenz Böninger

The pontificate of Francesco della Rovere, who was elected pope on 9 August 1471 and adopted the name of Sixtus IV, marks one of the most tempestuous and dramatic periods in Italian history in the fifteenth century. Ever since, he has been one of the most controversial popes of all time. Francesco was born the son of the merchant Leonardo della Rovere and Luchina di Monleone on 21 July 1414 in Celle Ligure not far from Savona on the Ligurian coast. At the age of nine he was sent to the Franciscan convent of Savona. Although his parents were of rather modest origin and wealth, later reports of a childhood spent in misery are not borne out by the facts. For approximately five years Francesco was taught by the friars of San Francesco at Savona until his novitiate and his formal vows to enter the order (c. September 1429). From then on his career was closely linked to the history of the Conventual wing of the Franciscan order, which in the following decades was confronted with the rising internal opposition of the Observant movement. For approximately three years Francesco studied dialectics (1429/30), natural philosophy (1430/31), and metaphysics (1431/32) at different convents in Savona, Chieri, and Pavia before gaining the degree of bachelor of dialectics at Pavia in 1432.

For the next three years Francesco possibly taught dialectics at an unknown convent. From 1435 to 1439 he studied and read theology with the Franciscans in Bologna. In these years he also entered the priesthood. His academic itinerary then took him back to Pavia and Venice. For three years after 1441 Francesco mastered a theological course at Padua at the Convent of Sant'Antonio, and there in 1444 he gained his theological licentiate and doctorate. The presence of the head of the faculty of arts, the Greek humanist Ioannes Argyropulos, at the academic ceremony of the doctorate attests to the scholarly status Francesco had already gained. After his doctorate he frequently served as a headmaster (*regens*) of the Minorite convent at Padua until 1449; it has also been argued that he was already present at the important general chapter of the Franciscan order at Montpellier (1446), where the separation of the Conventualist and Observant wings became manifest. His function in the order (still dominated by the Conventualists) after 1446 was that of an assistant (*socius*) of the general, Antonio Rusconi da Como, who also took him to the next general chapter at Santa Croce in Florence in 1449.

Francesco's rapid rise in the institutional hierarchy of the order was interrupted by the death of Rusconi, and Francesco resumed his academic career in Bologna (1449/50), where he first met Cardinal Bessarion, and then at the Franciscan convent of Santa Croce in Florence (1450/51). After this brief period he taught philosophy and theology for several years at the convents of Perugia and Siena, where he was said to have attracted large crowds of listeners also from the general public (1451–60). At the general chapter of the Minorities in Rome in 1458 Francesco, with the strong support of Bessarion, who later in that year was appointed general protector of the order, was already one of the contenders for the office of the general. For the next two years, however, Francesco still served as *socius* of the newly elected General Sarzuela before becoming the general procurator of the order in Rome (1460/61) and subsequently head of its Genoese and Roman provinces (1461–64). With the advent of Pope Paul II, Francesco was finally elected the minister-general of the Franciscan order, once in 1464–67 and again in 1467–69.

From the 1460s emerge the three most important theological writings by Francesco, which were first printed in 1471 and 1473: a treatise on the nature of the blood of Christ (1463; second version, 1467; third version and dedication copy to Pope Paul, 1470), a second one on the power of God (c. 1467–70), and finally a treatise on the problem of the future contingents and the foreknowledge and immutability of God (c. 1470). In these writings he proved to be a valid and mature theologian and logician in the tradition of the fourteenth-century Franciscan master Duns Scotus. The first treatise had its immediate cause in a long and bitter theological controversy between the Dominican and Franciscan orders, which culminated in a formal academic debate in the Vatican before Pope Pius II. Not only did famous theologians like Domenico Dominichi or Giacomo della Marca contribute to the controversy, but also professors of medicine from the University of Padua. Although Francesco defended the Franciscan point of view in his text on the nature of the blood of Christ, his treatment and conclusion of the problem proved to be conciliatory.

With regard to the highly sensitive question of the nature of certain Christian relics, which lay at the heart of the argument and which was also touched upon by Francesco, the discussion was terminated by Pope Pius II in 1464 when he forbade further statements on this topic. The other two theological writings composed by Francesco treated more traditional arguments of the Scholastic culture of the Middle Ages. At least one of the two, *De futuris contingentibus*, was written at the direct request of Cardinal Bessarion as an official contribution to a contemporary theological disputes that had previously erupted at the university at Louvain. Again in this treatise, which examined several propositions claimed to be heretical,

Detail of a painting by Melozzo da Forli of Pope Sixtus IV (right) and his nephew Riario. (Courtesy of the Vatican Library)

Francesco manifested a moderate approach and opened the road to a peaceful settlement of the dispute in 1473.

When on 18 September 1467 Pope Paul II nominated Francesco cardinal-presbyter with the title of San Pietro in Vincoli, this was probably due to the influence of Bessarion, who was looking for a successor to take over his own role in the college of cardinals. Several sources also indicate the support of the commune of Florence, where earlier in that year Francesco had held the general chapter of the Franciscan order. His fame as a cardinal rested upon both his experience as an able theologian and as an aspiring and successful planner. In the four years of his cardinalate he held only a few church benefices. He deliberately refused "worldly" interventions (like that of the lords of Milan) in the procedure for the nomination of ecclesiastical dignitaries, and as a consequence he was lacking the economic means of his fellow cardinals. Despite this handicap, in the September 1471 conclave he was elected pope as the successor of Paul II, and he assumed the name Sixtus IV.

Sixtus's tenure as the supreme head of the Apostolic See has chiefly been judged in the light of certain negative developments under his pontificate, mainly the sale of offices (simony) and nepotism. In fact, contemporary sources maintained that his surprising election, after two fruitless previous attempts that had seen other cardinals as favorites, was due to the intervention of his nephew Pietro Riario, who had made generous promises to some of the eighteen cardinals. The capitulations of the conclave, signed by Sixtus before the election, would have greatly enlarged the authority of the cardinals in respect to their revenues and their power to co-opt new members; further regulations were intended to secure a reform of the church "in its head and members" and the institution of a general council to be convoked by the pope every three years. Like most of his predecessors, Sixtus felt bound only by the first of the capitulations, which obliged him to organize a military campaign against the Turks, which was to be financed by the income of the pontifical alum mines. The ruinous economic situation of the curia at his advent forced him to pay many debts with the sale of some of the treasures the luxury-loving Paul II had amassed during his reïgn. Sixtus's plans to organize a large-scale military response to the Turkish threat in the Mediterranean soon had to be revised in light of the lack of international support. In 1472 a Venetian-Neapolitan fleet under the command of Cardinal Oliviero Carafa reconquered Smyrna, and this victory was duly celebrated by the pope in Rome.

The nomination of two of his nephews as cardinals on 16 December 1471, the young Pietro Riario—said to have secured Sixtus's election—and Giuliano della Rovere (the later Pope Julius II), ignored the capitulations, since both were not yet thirty years of age and had not been approved by the college. Probably this important step was already a consequence of the mounting opposition in the college itself, but the assignment of central roles in the papal government to both cardinals was in the tradition of previous popes. Large incomes were assigned to them, and Riario was also appointed archbishop of Florence. According to the pope's plans, Riario's role as papal legate was to be that of a "secretary of foreign relations," whereas della Rovere was initially only in charge of the "interior and defense." To the energetic pope, the internal problems of the states of the church appeared nearly as pressing as the Turkish threat. While the formation of national states in Europe and the centralization and rationalization of governments and administrations all over Italy led to the irreversible process of "state building," the checkered territories of the church were still partly governed by papal vicars or "tyrants," who often collaborated with other local powers in not paying taxes and levies to the Roman government. A second problem for Sixtus was the situation of many still largely autonomous communes in Umbria, torn by strife and the clash of political factions, where the influence of Tuscan neighbors like Siena and Florence and of feudal lords like the Montefeltro was traditionally very strong.

If Sixtus's choice of the zealous and unyielding Giuliano della Rovere proved to be a fortunate one, the other two most influential papal nephews, Pietro and Girolamo Riario, did everything to distort the image of an austere and strict church government. In fact, the immense private expenses, lavish manners, and simonistic handling of ecclesiastical matters by Cardinal Pietro Riario created discontent and fueled the picture of a secularized and corrupt Roman court. The first serious political crisis originated with Lorenzo de' Medici in 1473, when the duke of Milan was preparing to sell the town of Imola in the Romagna. The cardinal intended to acquire it as a state for his brother Girolamo, who in that year was betrothed to Caterina Sforza, the duke's illegitimate daughter. Lorenzo, who was against this design due to Florence's own long-term strategic interests in the region, finally had to bow to the growing pressure. Nonetheless, despite the fact that his bank served as the pope's depository, the Medici refused to lend Sixtus the necessary sum for the acquisition.

An even more dangerous conflict broke out one year later at the Umbrian town of Città di Castello. The control of this town in the states of the church was of vital strategic importance for Florence. According to the papal point of view, it was governed by the "tyrant" Niccolò Vitelli and could only be liberated with military force led by the legate Giuliano della Rovere. Lorenzo de' Medici, however, was sustaining Vitelli, and when a compromise was finally reached in 1476, the political relations between the church and Florence were at a historical low. It was in this situation, following the earlier death of Cardinal Pietro Riario (1474), that his brother Girolamo, the count of Imola, succeeded in convincing the pope that a change of regime in Florence would considerably alter the expansive tendencies of the commune. Sixtus was fully informed of the conspiracy against Lorenzo de' Medici that in 1478 united Riario, the archbishop of Pisa, Francesco Salviati, and several members of the Pazzi family. Although the pope reportedly urged Riario to avoid any bloodshed, the conspirators ordered the murder of the two brothers Lorenzo and Giuliano during the celebration of Pentecost in the Florentine cathedral. Their assault, however, only killed Giuliano, the younger brother. The subsequent upheaval and revenge of Lorenzo's partisans led to the assassination of the archbishop of Pisa and others involved in the plot.

Sixtus's reaction to these events could not have been more intransigent and damaging: on 1 June 1478, just over five weeks after the attempted assassination, Lorenzo, the Signoria, and the colleges as well as the whole commune of Florence were excommunicated or placed under interdict. Church troops led by Federico da Montefeltro and the son of the king of Naples invaded Florentine territory. After a series of military defeats Lorenzo in the winter of 1479/80 succeeded in concluding a Florentine-Neapolitan peace with King Ferrante in March 1480 and achieved the cancellation of the papal interdict in December. Soon after, new military expenditures of the Italian states became necessary when the Turks conquered the town of Otranto in southern Italy and were only expelled in 1481. The Venetian threat against Ferrara led to another Italian war (1482–84), in which Sixtus confronted the prospect of military defeat by the troops of King Ferrante of Naples at the Battle of Campomorto on 21 August 1482. Although the Peace of Bagnolo was signed on 7 August 1484, ending the war, Sixtus failed to reach any of the strategic and political goals he and Riario had fought for in the Romagna.

The image of the belligerent Renaissance popes was formed during Sixtus's pontificate. His political strategies have often been justified by citing the disastrous influence Riario exerted on his uncle, or the sudden change of the pope's personality from a peaceful friar to a cynical and violent warlord. These explanations undervalue not only the guiding spirit behind Riario's activities, but also the coherence and consistency with which Sixtus pursued his goals. One example of his method of governing was the constant rivalry between Girolamo Riario and Giuliano della Rovere. Another example was the cruel persecution of the Roman baronial family of the Colonna in 1484 at the hands of Riario, who was clearly executing the papal will. Accusations that the possession of Imola mainly served to install a new dynasty and create a "private" state for Riario were correct. It must be stressed, however, that papal nepotism in itself was one of the traditional (and in the later age of the Counter-Reformation even "institutionalized") strategies to secure the efficient government of the church. The great number of relatives of Sixtus who during his pontificate could be found in the highest functions of the church hierarchy has also to be considered under this "functional" aspect.

Sixtus has been declared the first modern pope-monarch in the sense that he and the theologians in his service, such as Domenico Dominichi, claimed the absolute sovereignty of the pope not only in ecclesiastical and temporal matters, but also in an "absolutist," "secular" sense. As the bewildered ambassador of Emperor Frederick III had to learn in Rome in 1473, there was only one real emperor and monarch, Sixtus himself. From the beginning, the pope's pontificate was marked by bitter conflicts on the problem of the collation of ecclesiastical benefices with important European powers like France, Spain, and the Holy Roman Empire. Although the French king, Louis XI, in 1472 had agreed to a flexible application of the Pragmatic Sanction of 1438, later the relations between the two powers were extremely strained. In 1478 Sixtus attempted to avert the threat of conciliarism by renewing a bull of Pius II (*Execrabilis*, 1460) in which any appeal to a general council without the consent of the pope had been automatically declared heretical. When Lorenzo de' Medici, at the climax of the war following the Pazzi conspiracy in 1479, appealed to a general council of the church, Louis XI lent him his support. Criticism of the conduct of church affairs and the call for a general council, including the attempt by the bishop of the Kraijna, Andreas Zamometic, to reestablish the Council of Basel (1482), resounded so loudly throughout Europe that there was fear of a new schism of the church.

The enormous costs of several years of wars not only deeply affected the economy of richer Italian states like Florence or Venice, but above all that of the Papal States. Although Sixtus attempted and even partly succeeded in centralizing and putting an end to the financial autonomy of many of the subject towns, his halfhearted attempts to reform the Roman curia and the church government and administration in ecclesiastical and fiscal matters must be judged a failure. A spreading practice to fill the gaps in the papal balances was the sale of all sorts of dignities and offices in the church hierarchy, from the cardinalate to the newly created colleges of 72 abbreviators (1479), 100 solicitors (1482), and 72 notaries of the curia (1483). On eight different dates Sixtus created not less than 34 cardinals (his predecessor Paul II had appointed only 10 cardinals), of whom 6 were his own relatives. His attempts to reform the college of cardinals itself only led to a hypothetical ban on the cardinals' absence from Rome without papal permission (1478); another reform bull on this topic was never published. The rapacious demands for offices became one of the most important sources of income of the Roman court.

A characteristic new feature of Sixtus's pontificate was the sale of indulgences on a large scale, which in the following decades became a major scandal and later one of the chief causes of the German Reformation. In 1475 the inflation of the formerly limited indulgences to the so-called plenary indulgence was already notorious when Sixtus declared the year of the jubilee and pilgrims from all over Europe flocked to the Holy City. Preaching for the crusades by the mendicant orders in Europe under Sixtus was directly linked to the sale of indulgences: the earnings were to serve the financing of the campaigns. The discomfort caused by these sales was aggravated by a papal bull in 1476 that stated that indulgences under certain circumstances could also be effective for the deceased. This surprising (if not totally new) theological doctrine provoked a heated controversy and required a second declaration by the pope (27 November 1477).

Sixtus's determined preference of the conventualist wings of some religious orders led to indignation among observants. The granting of a long series of privileges to Dominicans, Franciscans, and Carmelites and the canonization of a Minorite friar, Bonaventura da Bagnoregio (1482), have to be seen in the light of the pope's Mendicant origins. He also supported the fervent preaching of the mendicant orders against moneylending and the creation of public banking institutes (*monti di pieta*), but in a few cases this preaching was also followed by anti-Semitic excesses (Trent, 1475). Sixtus was not only the first pope to take measures against the printing of "heretical" or dangerous books, but he also acknowledged the creation of the Spanish Inquisition (1478). His personal devotion to the Virgin and the Immaculate Conception was deep and reflected the position of his order. In 1477 he issued an apostolic constitution in which the dates of her celebrations were fixed. Already as a young friar in 1448, Sixtus had written a sermon on the subject of the Immaculate Conception, and as pope, he dedicated a chapel to the Virgin at St. Peter's and renewed her liturgical cult (in the *Psalterium Beatae Mariae Virginis*).

Sixtus won much praise with his attempts to "modernize" the urban structure of the Holy City, which he repeatedly extolled as the only center and capital of the world. Although a malicious report by the Roman diarist Stefano Infessura claimed that the broadening of streets was mainly due to a recommendation by the king of Naples in order to dominate the town more easily, the pope's merits in this respect were clear. In fact, his predecessors Nicholas V and Paul II had already taken important steps in this direction. In the jubilee year 1475 Sixtus regulated the conditions of real-estate ownership in the Holy City, where illegal private building was common. In the same year he completed the Ponte Sisto, the bridge named after himself, which connected the quarter of Trastevere and the economic center of Parione. At the same time he opened the street called Via Sacra from the Ponte Sant'Angelo to St. Peter's Square, while the new Via Sistina ran from Ponte Sant'Angelo in a northwesterly direction. Many new edifices were furnished with classical-like inscriptions that recorded and praised the pope's commission. Sixtus declared the widening and paving of the Roman streets to be one of the chief goals of his building program. An equally important aspect of his urban policy was the repairing of the water-supply system of the city, a program that carried on the initiative of pope Nicholas V, who had already installed several fountains. When in 1471 the pope donated a collection of antique Roman bronze statues like the *She Wolf* (*Lupa Capitolina*) or the famous *Thorn Drawer* to the Roman commune, this was regarded as the foundation of the Capitoline Museum.

The most ambitious new church built by Sixtus was the important Renaissance Church of Santa Maria del Popolo, erected between 1471 and 1477, which also became the burial site for three members of his family. A second project, possibly executed by the same architect, Baccio Pontelli, was the Church of Santa Maria della Pace, built on the former site of Santa Maria della Virtù and renamed to commemorate the peace with Naples of 1482. Sixtus had Santo Spirito in Saxia, one of the oldest hospitals of Rome, rebuilt; it served partly as a hospital for the pilgrims and the poor and partly as an asylum for orphans and children abandoned by their parents. This hospital was run by the Confraternity of the Holy Spirit, which was favored by Sixtus with a series of privileges, donations, and honors. A cycle of frescoes in the hospital, painted by unknown masters from around 1477/80 to after the canonization of Bonaventura (1482), records its history and in thirty-nine depictions praises the devoted and generous life of its restorer, the pope, from earliest infancy through various moments in his life and his final assumption into Heaven. The University of Rome seems to have flourished during Sixtus's pontificate, especially in the fields of canon law, civil law, and medicine. Renowned humanists like Francesco Filelfo, Pomponio Leto, Bartolomeo Fonzio, Domenico Calderini, and Porcellio Pandone read there. However, because necessary funding was withheld, the financial crisis of the institution was never resolved.

Sixtus diligently collected books and commissioned translations of rare ancient texts, but his indifference in matters of secular scholarship has been noted as well. Whereas papal libraries before his pontificate had mostly been private, on 15 June 1475 he officially founded the first public Vatican library, thus realizing an older project of Nicholas V. Initially it included only three rooms in the Vatican Palace, which were partly frescoed by the painters Domenico and Davide Ghirlandaio, Antoniazzo Romano, and Melozzo da Forlì. The humanist Bartolomeo Platina served as its first appointed librarian. By transferring some of the most important medieval documents of the Apostolic See from the papal library to Castel Sant'Angelo in 1475, Sixtus has also been regarded as one of the founders of the Vatican archives. The private chapel of the pope's singers, who seem to have performed mostly music in the tradition of the Gregorian chant and not yet polyphonic music, was the forerunner of the more famous later choirs. Sixtus's funeral monument by Antonio del Pollaiolo (1493), a marvelous bronze work now in the museum of St. Peter, depicts a pope surrounded by representations of the Disciplines and Virtues.

The most telling manifestation of the governing ideology of Sixtus's pontificate may be seen in the famed fresco cycle on the walls of the Sistine Chapel in the Vatican. The architect Giovannino de' Dolci erected the chapel on the site of the former medieval palace chapel between 1475/77 and 1481, after a design by Baccio Pontelli. Sixtus dedicated it to the Assumption and in August 1483 celebrated the first mass in it. Possibly by the early summer of 1482, however, most of the paintings of the cycle were already finished. Their painters were the most renowned Florentine and Umbrian masters of their period: Sandro Botticelli, Domenico Ghirlandaio, Pietro Perugino, Cosimo Rosselli, and Luca Signorelli. The original cycle of seventeen narrative paintings on the walls depicts the lives of Moses and Jesus, so that each scene corresponds to a parallel event from the life of the other (*The Assumption*; *Moses Saved from the River* to *The Nativity of Christ*; *The Circumcision of Moses' Son* to *The Baptism of Christ*;

The Trials of Moses to *The Temptation of Christ*; *The Crossing of the Red Sea* to *The Calling of the First Apostles*; *The Delivery of the Tablets of the Law* to *The Sermon on the Mount*; *The Punishment of Korah* to *The Delivery of the Keys to St. Peter*; *The Testament of Moses* to *The Last Supper*; *The Archangel Michael Defending the Body of Moses* to *The Resurrection of Christ*). The common typology of the two lives lies in their role as predecessors of the pope himself, especially in the unity of the regal, sacerdotal, and legislative powers that Moses and Jesus, and consequently his vicar on earth, possessed.

Although the Pauline typology of Moses as the predecessor of Christ was already popular in the Middle Ages, it was only in the fifteenth century that the popes had discovered this tradition as an eloquent expression of their own universal claims. Scholars have variably read the doctrinal background of this important cycle and its explicit or implicit allusions to contemporary events. Whereas older explanations sometimes stressed the direct military background of certain depictions like Moses' crossing of the Red Sea, more recent readings have attempted to reconstruct the theological program in its whole. The Franciscan typology of Moses, Jesus, and St. Francis has been emphasized, as much as possible, in references to the Roman liturgy of Lent. The direct references to the pope as supreme and God-inspired lawgiver, who by virtue of this power condemned the contemporary tendencies of conciliarism (seen in Botticelli's fresco depicting the punishment of Korah), are, however, very evident. The fresco cycle of the Sistine Chapel manifests a unity of theology and politics that was characteristic of Sixtus's pontificate. One could posit that this union was one of the strongest and most astonishing motives in the life of a man who by formation really was a professional academic theologian.

SELECTED BIBLIOGRAPHY

Bauer, C. "Studi per la storia delle finanze delle papali durante il pontificato di Sisto IV." *Archivio della Società romana di storia patria* 50 (1927): 319–400.

Benzi, F. *Sisto IV renovator urbis Sixtus: Architettura a Roma, 1471–1484.* Rome: Officina Edizioni, 1990.

Buddensieg, T. "Die Statuenstiftung Sixtus IV. im Jahre 1471." *Römisches Jahrbuch für Kunstgeschichte* 20 (1983): 34–73.

Bullarium Franciscanum continens constitutiones, epistolas, diplomata, romani pontificis Sixti IV ad tres ordines S.P.N. Francisci spectantia. Ed. Francesco Ioseph M. Pou y Marti. New ser., vol. 3 (1471–84). Rome: Quaracchi, 1949.

Cenci, C. "Ad bullarium Sixti IV supplementum." *Archivum Franciscanum historicum* 83 (1990): 491–535; 84 (1991): 51ff.

Clark, N. *Melozzo da Forlì, pictor papalis.* London: Sotheby's Publications, 1990.

Cortese, D., ed. *Francesco Della Rovere: L'orazione della Immacolata.* Padova: Centro Studi Antoniani, 1985.

Cortese, D., and L. Cortese. "Un papa al tavolo anatomico." *Il Santo* 26 (1986): 479–491.

Dessi, R.M. "La controversia sull' 'Immacolata Concezione' e la propaganda per il suo culto in Italia nel XV secolo." *Cristianesimo nella storia* 12 (1991): 265–95.

Di Fonzo, L. vol. 1, *L'età dei Della Rovere*. Vol. 2, *Sixtus* (Savona: Atti e memorie della Società Savonese di Storia Patria, new ser., 24–25, 1988; *V Convegno Savonese [Savona, 7–10 novembre 1985]*).

———. *I pontefici Sisto IV (1471–84) e Sisto V (1585–90)*. Roma: Edizioni Miscellanea Francescana, 1987.

———. *Sisto IV: Carriera scolastica e integrazioni biografiche (1414–1484)*. Roma: Edizioni Miscellanea Francescana, 1987.

Ettlinger, L.D. *The Sistine Chapel before Michelangelo: Religious Imagery and Papal Primacy*. Oxford: Oxford University Press, 1965.

Fubini, R. *Italia quattrocentesca: Politica e diplomazia nell'età di Lorenzo il Magnifico*. Milan: FrancoAngeli, 1994.

Gherardi, Iacopo. *Il Diario Romano di Iacopo Gherardi da Volterra dal VII settembre MCCCCLXXIX al XII agosto MCCCCLXXXIV*. Ed. Enrico Carusi. In *Rerum italicarum scriptores*, 2nd ser., vol. 23, pt. 3. Città di Castello: 1904.

Giudici, B. de'. *Apologia iudaeorum. Invectiva contra Platinam. Propaganda antiebraica e polemiche di curia durante il pontificato di Sisto (1471–1484)*. Ed. Diego Quaglioni. Roma: Roma nel Rinascimento, 1987.

Goffen, R. "Friar Sixtus IV and the Sistine Chapel." *Renaissance Quarterly* 39 (1986): 218–62.

Howe, E.D. *The Hospital of Santo Spirito and Pope Sixtus IV*. New York: Garland Pub., 1978.

Iacobus de Marchia, S. (1394–1476). *De sanguine Christi*. Ed. Dionisio Lasic. Ancona: Biblioteca Francescana, 1976.

Infessura, Stefano. *Diario della città di Roma di Stefano Infessura scribasenato*. Ed. Oreste Tommasini. Fonti per la Storia d'Italia 5, Rome: Instituto Nazionale di Studi sud Rinascimento, 1890.

Lee, E. *Sixtus IV and Men of Letters*. Roma: Edizioni di storia e letteratura, 1978.

Lewine, C. *The Sistine Chapel Walls and the Roman Liturgy*. University Park: Pennsylvania State University Press, 1993 (see the review by Charles L. Stinger, *Catholic Historical Review* 80 [1994]: 585–86).

Lightbown, R.W. *Sandro Botticelli: Life and Works*, vol. 1, *Life and Work*; vol. 2, *Complete Catalogue*. 2 vols. London: Elek, 1978.

Mannucci, U. "Le capitolazioni del Conclave di Sisto IV (1471): Con notizia di un codice fin qui ignorato sui Conclavi dei sec. XV e XVI." *Römische Quartalschrift* 29 (1957): 73–90.

Mayberry, N. "The Controversy over the Immaculate Conception in Medieval and Renaissance Art, Literature, and Society." *Journal of Medieval and Renaissance Studies* 21 (1991): 207–24.

Medici, Lorenzo de'. *Lettere*. Vols. 1–7 (1460–1484). Ed. Riccardo Fubini, Nicolai Rubinstein, and Michael Mallett. Florence Giunti, 1977–90.

Miglio, M., Francesca Niutta, Diego Quaglioni, and Concetta Ranieri, eds. *Un *pontificato ed una città: Sisto IV (1471–1484): Atti del Convegno, Roma, 3–7 dicembre 1984*. Littera Antiqua, 5. Vatican City: Scuola Vaticana di Paleografia, Diplomatica e Archivistica, 1986.

Monfasani, J. "A Description of the Sistine Chapel under Pope Sixtus IV." *Artibus et historiae* 7 (1983): 9–18.

Pastor, L. *Storia dei papi dalla fine del medio evo*. Nuova versione italiana sulla IV edizione originale. Vol. 2. Roma: Desclée, 1911.

Petersohn, J. *Ein Diplomat des Quattrocento: Angelo Geraldini (1422–1486)*. Bibliothek des Deutschen Historischen Instituts in Rom, 62. Tübingen: Max Niemeyer, 1985.

Pfeiffer, H.W. "Gemalte Theologie in der Sixtinischen Kapelle." *Archivum historiae pontificiae* 28 (1990): 99–159 (but see the review in *Roma nel Rinascimento*, 1992, 288–90).

Platina, Bartolomeo. *Platynae historici liber de vita Christi ac omnium pontificum (aa. 1–1474)*. Ed. Giacinto Gaida. *In Rerum italicarum scriptores*, 2nd ser., vol. 3, pt. 1. Città di Castello: 1932.

Pontani, Gaspare. *Il Diario Romano di Gaspare Pontani già referito al 'Notaio del Nantiporto' (30 gennaio 1481–25 luglio 1492)*. Ed. by Diomede Toni. *In Rerum italicarum scriptores*, 2nd ser., vol. 3, pt. 2. Città di Castello: 1907–8.

Properzi, V. "Sisto IV: Le arti a Roma nel primo Rinascimento: Palazzo della Cancelleria Apostolica—Ex Convento di S. Salvatore in Lauro, Roma, 23–25 Ottobre 1997." *Roma nel Rinascimento*, 1997, 283–86.

La querelle des futurs contingents (Louvain: 1465–1475). Ed. Léon Baudry. Études de Philosophie médievale 38. Paris: Librairie Philosophique J. Vrin, 1950.

Redig de Campos, D. "I 'tituli' degli affreschi del Quattrocento nella Cappella Sistina." *Atti della Pontificia accademia romana di archeologica. Rendiconti*, ser. 3, 41 (1968): 299–314.

Ruysschaert, J. "La bibliothèque vaticane dans les dix premières années du pontificat de Sixte IV." *Archivum historiae pontificiae* 24 (1986): 71–90.

Schwarz, U. "Die Papstfamiliaren der ersten Stunde: Zwei Expektativenrotuli für Sixtus IV (1. Januar 1472)." *Quellen und Forschungen aus italienischen Archiven und Bibliotheken* 73 (1993): 303–86.

Sevesi, P.M "Lettere autografe di Francesco della Rovere da Savona, ministro generale (1464–1469) e cardinale (1467–1471) (poi Sisto IV, 1471–1484)." *Archivum Franciscanum historicum* 28 (1935): 198–234; 477–99.

Shearman, J. *La costruzione della cappella e la prima decorazione al tempo di Sisto IV la Cappella Sistina: I primi restauri: La scoperta del colore*. Novara: De Agostini, 1986.

Sisto IV e Giulio II, mecenati e promotori di cultura: Atti del Convegno Internazionale di Studi, Savona, 1985. Ed. Silvia Bottaro, Anna Dagnino, and Giovanna Rotondi Terminiello. Savona: Coop Tipograf., 1989.

Stinger, C.L. *The Renaissance in Rome*. Bloomington: Indiana University Press, 1985. *Umanesimo a Roma nel Quattrocento. Atti del Convegno*. Ed. Paolo

Brezzi and Maristella de Panizza Lorch. Roma: Istituto di studi romani; New York: Barnard College, 1984.

Vasoli, C. "Sisto IV professore di teologia e teologo." In idem *Tra "maestri" umanisti e teologi: Studi quattrocenteschi*. Firenze: Le Lettere, 1991, 173–211.

JULIUS II (1503–13)

Nelson H. Minnich

Giuliano della Rovere was born on 15 December 1444 in the town of Albizzola Superiore just north of the port town of Albizzola Marina that lies two miles northeast of Savona on the Gulf of Genoa. His paternal grandfather, Leonardo della Rovere, was a cloth shearer, engaged in commerce, held many responsible posts in the city government of Savona, and saw to the marriage of his children into the better families of that city. His son Raffaele, about whom little is known, married Theodora Manerola, of Greek origins. They had four sons (Leonardo, Giuliano, Giovanni Maria, and Bartolomeo) and a daughter (Luchina, who eventually married Gianfrancesco Franchiotti and then Gabrielle Gara). In later life Giuliano, who always enjoyed nautical affairs, told the story of how as a boy he had taken some onions to market in Genoa in a small boat. In his satirical *Julius Exclusus* Erasmus claimed that as a youth Giuliano was a lowly paid oarsman.

His education was entrusted to his paternal uncle, Francesco, who was a noted Franciscan theologian and held many offices in the order, culminating in his election as minister-general in 1464. Destined for an ecclesiastical career, Giuliano apparently studied canon and civil law at the Franciscan friary in Perugia. Whether he ever entered the Franciscan order is unclear; however, in a polyptych of the Nativity commissioned by his uncle in 1483 Giuliano is depicted in the habit of a Franciscan. While he was in Perugia, he was ordained to the priesthood. Soon after Francesco's election as Pope Sixtus IV, Giuliano was appointed bishop of Carpentras, and two months later, in the first promotion of 16 December 1471, he was named cardinal-priest of San Pietro in Vincoli, succeeding to the titular church of his uncle, a title he retained until his own election as pope some thirty-two years later.

Giuliano held a number of other church offices. As a cardinal-priest he resigned from, but retained the title of, the church of San Pietro in Vincoli to become cardinal-bishop of Sabina in 1479, and he was transferred to the cardinalitial sees of Ostia and Velletri in 1483. In 1474 he was appointed grand penitentiary. In succession he held seven episcopal sees: Carpentras (1471–72), Lausanne (1472–76), Coutances (1476–77), Viviers (1477–78), Mende (1478–83), Bologna (1483–1502), and Vercelli (1502–3). He simultaneously held the see of Avignon (1474–1503), which was raised to metropolitan status in 1475. He held in administration his native see of Savona (1499–1502). Through the process of *in commendam*, the grant of an annual pension upon resignation, he received revenues from numerous Benedictine, Camaldolese, and Vallombrosan monasteries. The most important of his monastic holdings was probably Grottaferrata (1472 onwards), which he rebuilt. He also served as cardinal-legate to the Marches (1473); to Umbria (1474), where he ended factional fighting; to Avignon and France (1476), where he resolved the conflict over the loss of legatine powers by Charles de Bourbon, an ally of the French king Louis XI, who feared papal support of his rival, the duke of Burgundy, for control over Provence; again to France (1480–82), where he secured the release from prison of a bishop and a cardinal and worked for peace between France and the Holy Roman Empire regarding the Burgundian inheritance; to Bologna (1483), where he exercised good governance; and to the Marches (1487), where he worked to put down the rebellion at Osimo. His competence in carrying out his legations increased his reputation in Rome.

Giuliano gradually became a powerful cardinal. Under his uncle Sixtus IV (1471–84) he often vied unsuccessfully for influence over foreign policy with his Riario cousins, the cardinals Pietro and Raffaele and the layman Girolamo. Giuliano initially allied himself with the Ghiblline Colonnas, favored Genoese independence from Milanese control, backed Ferrante of Naples in his conflict with Ludovico Sforza of Milan, and opposed the Ferrarese war. Once the duplicity of subordinate agents in his legations of 1476 and 1480–81 was exposed, he established good personal relations with the French king Louis XI (1461–83). He skillfully advanced the career of his younger brother Giovanni Maria, helping him marry Giovanna de Montefeltre (1474), acquire title to the town of Senigallia in the Marches of the Papal States (1474), inherit the duchies of Arce and Sora in Naples (1475) that had been given to his elder brother Leonardo (d. 1475) when he married Giovanna d'Aragona, and secure the office of prefect of Rome (1475, also left vacant by Leonardo's death). From Giovanni Maria would descend the della Rovere dynasty.

Giuliano's rivalry with Cardinal Rodrigo Borja (Borgia) came to the fore toward the end of the pontificate of Innocent VIII (1484–92). They had both worked for his election. Giuliano was most influential on papal foreign policies during the years 1481 to 1486 and from 1491 to 1492. He turned against the Colonnas when they affronted papal authority. He backed the Neapolitan barons in their conflict with King Ferrante in part because his brother Giovanni Maria's wife was the sister-in-law of one of the leading rebel barons. While Giuliano was raising troops in Genoa, peace between Innocent VIII and Ferrante was restored (1486), in part on the urging of Borja. Eventually Giuliano made his own peace with the Neapolitan king. His conflict with the Spanish cardinal was evident to all in the final hours of Innocent's pontificate. While Giuliano favored, Borja strongly opposed honoring the deathbed wishes of Innocent VIII favoring his Cibò relatives.

Pope Julius II. (Courtesy of the Library of Congress)

In the conclave of 1492 Giuliano successfully blocked the candidacy of the worldly Milanese Ascanio Sforza and eventually joined in the unanimous election of Rodrigo Borja as Alexander VI (1492–1503). Under this pope and his chief advisor Sforza, Giuliano became a leader of the opposition in the college of cardinals. Upon the death of his protector, the Neapolitan king Ferrante (1494), Giuliano fled from his fortress at Ostia to exile in France, where he urged King Charles VIII (1484–98) to invade Italy to claim the crown of Naples and also depose Alexander VI by means of a council. He raised his own troops and money in Genoa and accompanied the French king in Italy. Charles VIII instead negotiated with Alexander VI his own safe passage through the Papal States and Giuliano's restoration to ecclesiastical titles and lands. Following the ultimate failure of the Neapolitan campaign, Giuliano retired to his see of Avignon. Concern for the security of his brother Giovanni Maria (d. 1501) led him to continue backing the French. Although he was reconciled once again with the pope by the new French king Louis

XII (1498–1515), Giuliano waited until the death of Alexander VI in 1503 to return to Rome, in the meantime protecting himself and his nephew Francesco Maria (1490–1538) from the intrigues of the Borjas. Although he was a strong contender in the conclave of September 1503, he lost out this time to another reformer, Pius III, who reigned but a month.

Prior to his own election Giuliano had established a good reputation among his colleagues. His heavy involvement in shaping and executing earlier papal policies had shown him to be a shrewd and effective administrator. He was in touch with the culture of his times, supporting the work of artists and humanists, even if he himself showed little personal interest in learning. His munificence and generosity were well known. He seems to have followed the social mores of his day. Not considered promiscuous, he nonetheless came down with syphilis in April 1498. He admitted to having fathered a daughter, Felice. Her mother was Lucrezia, who later married and bore a son, the future Cardinal Giandomenico de Cupis. Whether Giuliano also had children by his mistress Masina is unclear. Although he was recognized as someone who readily promoted the interests of his relatives, he was viewed more as a trustworthy and ardent defender of the church's liberty and dignity who openly opposed the degradation suffered by the papacy under Alexander VI. Whether out of a desire to put the era of the Borjas firmly behind them or persuaded by his many offers of offices and favors, the cardinals, with only Giuliano voting differently, unanimously elected him pope on 1 November 1503 in the briefest conclave on record. He was crowned pope on the steps of St. Peter's Basilica on 26 November and took possession of his episcopal throne at St. John Lateran on 6 December. As a condition of his election he had sworn to a series of capitularies, promising to convoke a council, implement church reform, and launch a crusade.

Julius took various measures to promote church reform. He generally favored the election of reform-minded friars to leadership positions in their orders for example, appointing as vicar-general Egidio Antonini of Viterbo for the Augustinian Hermits and Tommaso de Vio of Gaëta for the Dominicans. Having been the cardinal-protector of the Franciscans (1474–1503), he was keenly aware of their internal divisions. In 1506 he assembled in Rome a meeting of various factions. When no agreement emerged except to update the statutes, he ordered the smaller groups to join either the Observants or Conventuals and forbade the Observants from taking over any more Conventual houses. Due to their inadequacies, he later refused to approve the revised statues that tried to impose on all factions a common observance of stricter rules. He seems to have foreseen the need to divide the Franciscans permanently into two separate orders. Having secured his own election as pope by practices considered simoniacal, he drew up a bull against simony in papal elections, *Cum tam divino*, that was dated from St. Peter's in Rome on 14 January 1506, but was not promulgated as a papal decree until 11 October 1510 in Bologna and 25 October 1510 in Rome and later confirmed as a conciliar constitution at the fifth session (16 February 1513) of the Fifth Lateran Council, four days before his own death. This bull invalidated any such election, allowed clergy and laity to refuse obedience to a pope so elected, deprived from office any cardinal accepting such bribes, and authorized the uncorrupted cardinals to elect a new pope or convoke a general council.

He skirted the question of simony in the papal appointment of bishops by requiring the appointee to resign first into the hands of the pope any curial office he might have and, if he had none, to obtain one in order to resign it. By the creation and sale of curial offices he increased papal revenues. In an effort to head off demands for more radical reforms of the curia, he issued on the eve of the Fifth Lateran Council the decree *Et si Romanus Pontifex* of 30 March 1512, which reduced fees and eliminated some of the more scandalous practices. These reforms he had confirmed by the Lateran council at its fourth session on 10 December 1512. With the help of the Fifth Lateran Council, which he convoked on 18 July 1511 and opened on 3 May 1512, Julius II seems to have intended a more sweeping reform of the curia and church, but the conciliar commissions had not yet completed their work when he died.

During its first year the council was preoccupied with defeating the rival Pisan council and made little progress on its other goals. Despite his election promise to call a crusade and his occasional reaffirmation of this intent, as in the aims assigned to the Holy League and the Lateran council, Julius did little to realize that goal beyond establishing the necessary preconditions for a successful crusade by restoring peace to Italy and amassing funds to finance it. An ardent defender of the prerogatives of the papacy, he resisted the encroachments of secular governments, most notably those of Venice, imposing sanctions on it in 1509 for having appealed to a council against a papal decision and securing its agreement in 1510 to papal appointments to its bishoprics. He promoted missionary activities in the newly discovered lands, establishing dioceses in the Caribbean islands (1504, 1511) and reluctantly granting to the Spanish monarchs in 1508 the right of royal patronage in America. On questions of religious belief and practice he was personally traditional, he supported the work of moderate inquisitors, and he actively promoted various devotions to Christ and the saints.

As head of the Papal States, Julius II tried to reassert papal control over local lords and towns and secure the independence and territorial integrity of his state. Until he had built up the papal treasury so that he could hire troops, he temporized and used diplomacy to restore peace to his lands and to pressure Venice to respect papal sovereignty and navigational rights. Instead of appointing Cesare Borja as captain general of the church, as promised, Julius II pressured him into surrendering his fortresses. When

Borja fled to Naples, the pope got Spanish authorities to arrest him and then ship him off to Spain. Once backed by an army, Julius II secured in 1506 the submission of Gianpaolo Baglioni of Perugia and the exile of Giovanni Bentivoglio from Bologna, whose government he reorganized. Despite the pope's insistence that Venice restore all the territories it had seized in the Romagna and along the Adriatic coast, the Republic refused to return the principal cities. Not until march 1509 did Julius II join the League of Cambrai, formed by France, the Holy Roman Empire, Aragon, and others to force Venice to restore to their original overlords the numerous lands and cities it had conquered. When the league's stunning victory at Agnadello in May 1509 caused Julius II to fear the power of his allies, especially France, the Venetian government quickly came to terms with him, restoring all the cities, acknowledging papal navigational rights, and accepting papal appointments to its bishoprics.

By making a separate peace with Venice in February 1510, Julius II violated the terms of the league. As a justification for his actions, he claimed that France had already violated the agreement by confiscating income from ecclesiastical benefices. Louis XII, whose French troops had helped restore papal authority in the Romagna, was even more incensed by Julius II's repeated attempts (July–October 1510) to drive the French from Genoa. The king retaliated by restoring the Bentivogli to Bologna and convoking the Synod of Tours (September 1510), which urged peace and called for a church council. Having won the support of Spain and Venice and a month later of England, Julius II formed on 4 October 1511 an anti-French league, called the Holy League because of its announced intention of protecting the Papal States and preparing for a crusade. The papal vassal, Ferrara, however, refused to join this new alliance and continued to support Louis XII.

With the support of this king, of Emperor Maximilian I, of three French and two Spanish cardinals, and of a couple dozen French bishops, the anti-Julian Pisan council opened in early November, but due to a lack of wider support, local opposition, and the inability of French forces to provide adequate protection, it transferred to Milan and then to Asti and came to a dismal end in Lyons one year later. Militarily, the French won the Battle of Ravenna on 11 April 1512 and overran the Romagna, only to be forced to retreat from Italy due to the extensive losses suffered, the withdrawal of imperial forces, and the entry of the Swiss into the services of the Holy League. With the departure of the French, Duke Alfonso d'Este of Ferrara made peace with the pope, the propapal Medici were restored to Florence and the Sforza to Milan, and the papacy was given Parma and Piacenza. Julius II was hailed as "Liberator of Italy." In order to win over Emperor Maximilian I to support the Lateran council, however, Julius II agreed in November 1512 to an alliance with him that supported imperial claims to Venetian territory. Instead of making the pope "the lord and master of the world," the treaty led the Venetians to negotiate an alliance with France that would prolong the war for years after he died.

Julius II is considered the restorer, even the second founder, of the Papal States. Not only did he win back lost territories and assert effective control over local lords, but he also made all of his officials render an annual accounting of their administration. He strengthened the authority of secular courts, put tight controls on revenues, and introduced a new coin (the silver *giulio*) whose worth he carefully regulated and in whose denomination he required taxes to be paid. By careful tax collection (without extortions), the sale of offices and indulgences, and the traditional confiscation upon death of the cardinals' and curialists' wealth derived from church offices, he amassed a large treasury to support his wars, administration, patronage, and crusade fund.

Julius II was a great connoisseur and patron of art. As a cardinal, he restored his titular church of San Pietro in Vincoli and built a new palace next to it. He also renovated his other residence at the Church of the Twelve Apostles and rebuilt the fortress at Ostia. He embellished his cathedral churches at Avignon and Savona with paintings and rich furnishings. As pope, he hired Donato Bramante to construct the corridor that connected the Vatican Palace with the Belvedere Villa and partially enclosed the ascending gardens, in the uppermost portion of which he placed his collection of ancient statuary. This architect also designed a new St. Peter's Basilica whose cornerstone Julius laid on 18 April 1506. For its new choir chapel the pope endowed a group of cantors, known as the Cappella Giulia, and commissioned the sculptor Michelangelo Buonarroti to carve his elaborate tomb (1505-45) that was to be placed there. The pope also pressured Michelangelo to fresco the ceiling of the Sistine Chapel (1508-12). Unwilling to reside in the Borja apartments, he had a new series of rooms (*stanze*) constructed above them and commissioned Raphael to decorate them with frescoes (1508-17). This artist also painted his formal portrait (1512). For the city of Rome, Julius II planned a straight street (the Via Giulia) to connect the Ponte Sisto to a new bridge (never built, the Ponte Giulio) near the Vatican at the site of the ruined Pons Triumphalis. Paralleling this street on the other side of the Tiber he laid out the Via della Lungara that connected the Borgo Leonino with Trastevere. Along the Via Giulia he hoped to build a Palazzo dei Tribunali, but was able only to lay its huge foundation stones. By his various building projects Julius II tried to give to Rome an imperial style of architecture.

Julius II was a remarkable man. He set for himself grand goals and was relentless in their pursuit. His contemporaries stood in awe of him, calling him *il terribile*. Tall in stature, he was full of boundless energy, impetuous, and given to swings of emotion, from warmhearted kindness to outbursts of anger. When the siege of Mirandola dragged on, he went in person to the snow-laden camp to urge on his troops. He was frank in his speech and seems to have had few close advisors. He even kept his relatives at a distance. There were never more than two nephews at a time appointed by him to the sacred college, and he did not allow relatives to act as intermediaries or political councilors. Nonetheless, they were beneficiaries of his nepotism. Several were appointed as bishops. He lavished on his ungrateful youthful nephew Francesco Maria the Duchy of Urbino, the lordship of Pesaro, and the office of captain general of the church. He formed alliances with the baronial families of Rome by three marriages: of his illegitimate daughter Felice to Giovanni Giordano Orsini, of his nephew Niccolò Franchiotti to Laura Orsini (daughter of Orso Orsini and Giulia Farnese), and of his niece Lucrezia Gara to Marcantonio Colonna. By contemporary standards, he was moderate in his nepotism and usually limited it to worthy relatives. What seems to have guided most of his actions as pope was a determination to safeguard the independence, authority, and majesty of the Apostolic See. By concentrating his efforts on a material restoration of the papacy (its territorial integrity, political independence, and administrative and cultic buildings in Rome), he failed to devote sufficient attention to a spiritual renewal of the church, desperately needed on the eve of the Reformation.

SELECTED BIBLIOGRAPHY

Brosch, Moritz. *Papst Julius II. und die Gründung des Kirchenstaates*. Gotha: Friedrich Andreas Perthes, 1878.

Bullarum diplomatum et privilegiorum sanctorum romanorum pontificium Taurinensis editio. Ed. Francesco Gaude et al. 25 vols. Turin: Sebastiano Franco, Enrico Dalmazzo, et aliis editoribus, 1857–72, 5 (1860), 399–537.

Burchard, Johannes. *Liber notarum ab anno MCCCCLXXXIII usque ad annum MDVI*. Ed. Enrico Celani. In *Rerum italicarum scriptores: Raccolta degli storici italiani del cinquecento al millecinquecento*, vol. 32. Città di Castello: Tipi della casa editrice S. Lapi, 1906–42.

D'Amico, John F. *Renaissance Humanism in Papal Rome: Humanists and Churchmen on the Eve of the Reformation*. Baltimore, MD: John Hopkins University Press, 1983.

de la Brosse, Olivier. "Latran V." In *Latran V et Trente I*, by Olivier de la Brosse, Joseph Lecler, Henri Holstein, and Charles Lefebvre. Histoire des conciles oecuméniques, 10. Paris: Éditions de l'Orante, 1975, 13–114.

Dykmans, Marc. "Le conclave sans simonie ou la bulle de Jules II sur l'élection papale." In *Miscellanea Bibliothecae Apostolicae Vaticanae*, vol. 3. Studi e testi, 333. Vatican City: Biblioteca Apostolica Vaticana, 1989, 203–55.

Erasmus, Desiderius. *Julius Excluded from Heaven: A Dialogue. "Dialogus Julius exclusus e coelis."* Trans. and annotated Michael J. Heath. In *Collected Works of Erasmus*, vols. 27–28, ed. A.H.T. Levi. Toronto: University of Toronto Press, 1986, 155–97, 489–508.

Gilbert, Felix. *The Pope, His Banker, and Venice*. Cambridge, Mass.: Harvard University Press, 1980.

Grassi, Paride de. "Le cinquième Concile du Latran d'après le Diaire de Paris de Grassi." *Annuarium historiae conciliorum* 14 (1982): 271–369.

———. *Le due spedizioni militari di Giulio II tratte dal diario di Paride Grassi Bolognese*. Ed. Luigi Frati. Documenti e studi pubblicati per cura della reale deputazione di storia patria per le provincie di Romagna, I. Bologna: Regia tipografia, 1886.

Guicciardini, Francesco. *Storia d'Italia*. Ed. Costantino Panigada. 5 vols. Scrittori d'Italia, 120–24. Bari: Giuseppe Laterza & Figli, 1929, reprinted 1967.

Julius II. "Speech of Julius II." Ed. Nelson H. Minnich in his "Concepts of Reform Proposed at the Fifth Lateran Council." *Archivum historiae pontificiae* 7 (1969), 163–251, here Appendix 1, 237–38.

Klaczko, Julian. *Rome and the Renaissance: The Pontificate of Julius II*. Trans. John Dennie from the French 1898 edition. New York: G.P. Putnam's Sons, 1903.

Luzio, Alessandro. *Isabella d'Este di fronte a Giulio II negli ultimi tre, anni del suo pontificato*. Milan: Casa editrice L.F. Cogliati, 1912.

Partridge, Loren, and Randolph Starn. *A Renaissance Likeness: Art and Culture in Raphael's "Julius II."* Berkeley: University of California Press, 1980.

Pastor, Ludwig. *The History of the Popes from the Close of the Middle Ages*. Trans. and ed. Frederick Ignatius Antrobus et al. 40 vols. St. Louis: B. Herder Book Co., 1923–53. See especially vol. 6 (based on the 1895 German edition), 208–659.

Rodocanachi, Emmanuel Pierre. *Histoire de Rome: Le pontificat de Jules II (1503–1513)*. Paris: Librairie Hachette & Cie., 1928.

———. *Le Première Renaissance: Rome au temps de Jules et de Léon X, la cour pontificale, les artistes et les gens de lettres, la ville et le peuple, le sac de Rome en 1527*. Paris: Librairie Hachette & Cie., 1912.

Seneca, Federico. *Venezia e Papa Giulio II*. Padua: Liviana Editrice, 1962.

Shaw, Christine. *Julius II: The Warrior Pope*. Cambridge, Mass.: Blackwell, 1993.

Stinger, Charles L. *The Renaissance in Rome*. Bloomington: Indiana University Press, 1985.

Ullmann, Walter. "Julius II and the Schismatic Cardinals." In *Schism, Heresy, and Religious Protest*, ed. Derek Baker. Studies in Church History, 9. Cambridge, Eng.: University Press, 1972, 177–93.

LEO X (1513–21)

CAROL BRESNAHAN MENNING

The house of Medici, Lorenzo de' Medici wrote his young son Giovanni, went hand-in-hand with the city. Lorenzo deemed Giovanni clever and wise. Later events would prove the father's estimation well founded, for it would be to Giovanni that the Medici largely owed their return to Florence in 1512 after nearly two decades of exile. Throughout his career in the church he would prove a tireless advocate of the house of Medici. He was much less successful, however, in solving the serious problems facing the Catholic church during his pontificate, which coincided with the first years of the Reformation.

Born in 1475, Giovanni di Lorenzo di Piero de' Medici was but three years old at the time of the Pazzi conspiracy in 1478, from which his father barely escaped alive. During the ensuing war Lorenzo sent his family to the Medici villa in Cafaggiolo for safety. Giovanni's older brother, Piero, reported that the elder children practiced writing and that Giovanni, not even five years of age, already knew how to spell. As Giovanni's education progressed, humanist tutors like Angelo Poliziano, Marsilio Ficino, and Giovanni Pico della Mirandola instilled in him a lifelong interest in learning and culture.

A second son, Giovanni was groomed for a career in the church. Lorenzo recorded the boy's tonsure in 1483 and Pope Sixtus IV's bestowal on him the rank of apostolic protonotary and its accompanying honorific, "Messer." The youth also accepted canonries and the convent of Passignano. Louis XI of France offered an abbey and promised an archbishopric. Not to be outdone, the king of Naples presented Giovanni with Monte

Cassino, the most venerable center of Benedictine spirituality, while the duke of Milan endowed him with the abbey of Morimondo. This Renaissance potlatch helped to forge relationships and extend networks of patronage and *amicizia* (friendship) between the house of Medici and these rulers, but it was also symptomatic of problems in the church: while still a boy, Giovanni de' Medici held twenty-two benefices.

In 1489, at a cost of tens of thousands of ducats allegedly siphoned from public funds, Lorenzo persuaded his brother-in-law, Pope Innocent VIII, to nominate Giovanni as a cardinal. Lorenzo considered Giovanni's cardinalship to be the greatest achievement of the House of Medici. Between 1489 and 1491 Giovanni, thirteen at the time of his nomination and thus underage, bided his time in Pisa, studying canon law and theology. In 1492 he took his place in the college of cardinals and moved to Rome, where, he told his father, Innocent received him warmly. Lorenzo replied with what turned out to be one of the last letters of his life. He warned his son that Rome was a sink of all iniquity. He urged on Giovanni regular exercise, a plain diet, and an early start to a long workday. Finally, Lorenzo shrewdly suggested, "You ought to . . . show that you prefer the honor and and state of the church . . . to every other consideration. Nor, while you keep this view, will it be difficult for you to favor your family and your native place. On the contrary, you should be the link to bind this city closer to the church, and our family with the city" (Sourcebook of the Italian Renaissance, trans. Marrick Whitcomb, Philadelphia: University of Pennsylvania Press, 1903, 82–86). Despite his father's advice, by the time he became pope, Giovanni would be notoriously lazy and visibly corpulent; one historian compared him to a Persian cat. Like the feline, he also became an avid hunter. But Giovanni would never fail to heed the last part of his father's advice, for he was an indefatigable advocate of his family's fortunes.

Shortly after Lorenzo's death in 1492 Innocent VIII appointed Giovanni papal legate to Tuscany. Two years later sixty thousand French troops marched into Italy in the first of a wave of invasions by those whom Niccolò Machiavelli called "barbarians." Florentines rebelled against what Francesco Guicciardini termed the "rash" leadership of Piero de' Medici, who along with Giovanni and other family members was declared a rebel and was forced to flee. Medici dwellings were sacked, and the property itself was confiscated by the state.

Giovanni spent much of his exile traveling. In Rome, Venice, Bavaria, the Rhineland, Flanders, and France he made important contacts with powerful men, including the holy Roman emperor, Maximilian and, according to his first biographer, Paolo Giovio, with Cardinal Giuliano della Rovere. With Piero de' Medici's death in 1503, leadership of the family fell to Cardinal Giovanni. The same year saw the election of Rovere to the papacy as Julius II, who proceeded to confer appointments on his Medici friend. On the pretext that the Florentines had supported the council of Pisa, regarded by the papacy as schismatic, the new pope gave Giovanni the welcome orders to make war on the Florentine republic with the aid of papal and Spanish forces. The Florentine oligarchy was overthrown in 1512 in a virtually bloodless coup, and the triumphant Medici reentered Florence after eighteen years of exile. The Florentine patrician and Medici adherent Paolo Vettori urged Cardinal Giovanni to show a firm hand in reestablishing the Medici in the city. Giovanni was reminded that, unlike his Medici forebearers, he would have to use force to control his state.

Giovanni stationed Spanish troops at the entries to the Piazza della Signoria in a show of the *forza* that Vettori had urged. Shortly thereafter there was put in place a constitution that, while retaining the facade of the republic, allowed the Medici to rule behind the scenes.

On 11 March 1513 a rump college of cardinals—the others, mostly French, remained loyal to the Pisan council—elected Giovanni de' Medici pope, apparently believing that his delicate health would make for a brief reign. After hastily receiving holy orders on 15 March, he became bishop of Rome on 17 March and was crowned two days later in a spectacular pageant that left the entire city in awe. Giovio recorded that the new pope took the name Leo after a dream that his mother had had the night before giving birth. Clarice, so the story went, saw an image of herself delivering not a child but a gentle lion; hence Leone. Whether the story is literally true or not, it illustrates Leo's keen sense of his family heritage.

Pope Leo X. (Courtesy of the Library of Congress)

Contemporaries suggested that Giovanni's elevation to the papacy in 1513 brought about a change in Medici behavior in Florence. According to the contemporary historian Bernardo Segni's *Istorie fiorentine*, before the promotion of Giovanni to the papacy, [The Medici] went about dressed in citizen's clothing and without bodyguards but once Giovanni became pope, they assumed a grandeur in both appearance and deed.

An excellent example of Leo's degree of control over Florence appeared in his treatment of that city's Monte di pietà. The bylaws of the *monte*, a civic pawnshop that extended secured small loans at 5 percent interest, called for it to return any profits to its borrowers. In 1519 Leo ordered its overseers instead to donate profits to the Company of the Good Men of San Martino, a pet Medici charity. At the Fifth Lateran Council Leo's bull *Inter multiplices* ensured the continued fiscal health of *monti di pietà* by extending general approbation to their practice of charging interest, a decision that lay behind Pope Pius X's canon 1543, the Catholic church's modern statement on usury. Similarly, Leo's ability to use his office to influence affairs in Florence was reflected in his effort to secure the canonization of the city's late archbishop, Antonino. In 1516 Leo paid a visit to the Dominican monastery of San Marco, hostile to the Medici since the time of Savonarola. The pope sprang a surprise on the brothers: he vowed to see to the canonization of Antonino and placed his cousin, the archbishop of Florence, in charge of it. A letter from the canon of the Duomo shrewdly noted that Antonino's sainthood would bring honor to the whole city, the Medici, and the pope. The friendly relations between the late archbishop and Leo's great-grandfather, Cosimo Pater Patriae, would now be mirrored in friendship between Florentines and the pope. The letter also hinted that Leo would bestow other favors on the city. The bull of canonization was published during the reign of Leo's cousin, Clement VII. Leo thus showed himself capable of using not only the stick—*forza*—but the carrot.

Given the political vicissitudes of early-sixteenth-century Europe, Leo needed to make foreign policy a high priority. Threats to the papacy included Turkish expansion, the presence of foreign troops in the peninsula, and claims by northern monarchs, especially the French king, to parts of Italy. To oppose the first, Leo called for crusades. To counterbalance the last two, Rome joined Spain, the Holy Roman Empire, and England in the League of Mechlin in 1513, defeating forces of the French king Louis XII at the Battle of Novara in June of that year. In the ensuing peace treaty Louis agreed to withdraw his support for the Council of Pisa; its consequent collapse was a decisive victory for the pope and a blow against the conciliarists.

Louis's successor, Francis I, determined nonetheless to press his claims to Naples and Milan shortly after taking the throne in 1515. Aware of the disastrous consequences of the French invasion of 1494 for both the papacy and the Medici, Leo undertook secret negotiations with the French king. The result was the Concordat of Bologna, issued in the form of the papal bull *Primitiva* on 18 August 1516. Leo surrendered to the French monarchy the power to nominate many high church officials in France while retaining, at least in theory, veto power. Not until the French Revolution would this agreement between church and state be abandoned.

Having reached a modus vivendi with the French king, Leo now needed to check the ambitions of the holy Roman emperor, a problem that became acute in 1519 with the death of Maximilian. His likely successor, his grandson Charles I, already held the Spanish crowns and the Hapsburg Netherlands. Alarmed at the prospect of this young man's addition of the imperial crown to his titles, Leo threw his support behind the candidacy of Francis I and then, ironically, behind Frederick of Saxony, Luther's prince and protector. Leo X proved unable to prevent Charles's election and was therefore forced to reach accommodation with the new emperor, who took the title Charles V.

Leo X was devoted to the arts and learning and spent, by one estimate, some 400,000 ducats on patronage; as Machiavelli's friend Francesco Vettori remarked, the pope was completely incapable of saving money. Having studied with the Dutch composer Henricus Isaac, Leo loved both secular and sacred music, and during his papacy the choir for the Sistine Chapel increased to thirty-six singers. His architect, Donato Bramante, designed a plan to rebuild St. Peter's that remained the basis for Michelangelo's later reconstruction. Leonardo da Vinci, Baccio Bandinelli, Raphael, Benvenuto Cellini, and Michelangelo himself were among the artists who worked for Leo. Raphael, who according to Giorgio Vasari received "countless favors" from Leo, left a remarkable triple portrait showing Leo X flanked by Cardinals Giulio de' Medici (Giovanni's cousin and the future Clement VII) and Ludovico de' Rossi. Dressed in richly textured robes, Leo holds a magnifying glass, the better to read the book before him. His corpulence testifies to his inability to defeat the sin of gluttony. The painting nonetheless pleased Leo, if Vasari is to be believed, for he rewarded Raphael with both generous payment and future commissions.

Although the historian John D'Amico has dismissed mistaken characterizations of Leo as the quintessential humanist, arguing that humanism in Rome began its decline under his reign, he also acknowledged that the Medici pope made significant efforts to support learning. Leo employed Pietro Aretino for a time until the latter's scurrilous writings made his continued presence in Rome untenable. Leo established a Greek college and appointed humanists to important posts: Zanobi Acciaiuoli became prefect of the Vatican Library, and Pietro Bembo and Jacopo Sadoleto took positions in the reorganized papal secretariat. The German humanist Johannes Reuchlin dedicated his treatise on the kabbala to Leo, though Leo later silenced Reuchlin for his support of Jewish literature. Erasmus, who said that the pope welcomed him fraternally, dedicated his translation of the New Testament to his patron Leo, who in 1517 authorized the discontented monk to accept benefices and go about without wearing the monastic habit. By 1520 Erasmus was squirming to avoid Leo's pressure to oppose Luther publicly, ruefully noting to a friend, "A bishopric is waiting for me if I choose to write against Luther" (J. Huizinga, *Erasmus of Rotterdam*, London: Phaidon Press, 1952, 146).

It was not, however, by patronage of artists and friendship with humanists that Leo's pontificate would be judged. His reign coincided with the first years of the Protestant Reformation. Astute in managing Florentine affairs, he seemed bewildered by the issues that drove Luther and the reformers. Rather, Leo resorted to the most obvious kind of politicking, such as his creation on a single day in 1517 of thirty-one new cardinals in an attempt to stack the college in response to an unsuccessful conspiracy by several cardinals to poison him. Another of his political aims was to confirm by the bull *Inter graves* Pope Julius II's goal to reconquer the Papal States. He was aware of the need to confront corruption in the church and oversaw the Fifth Lateran Council, which met from 1512 to 1517.

The council, called by Julius II but presided over for most of its duration by Leo, was attended mainly by Italian cardinals. In many ways it foreshadowed the Council of Trent (1545–63). Doctrinal issues concerned it but little. Rather, it issued proclamations against abuses like simony and multiple benefices, approved a mechanism for press censorship, and urged stricter moral rules on clerics. Yet it failed to implement its high-minded principles. Those who attended were, after all, the same men who benefited from many of the practices it denounced. Foremost among these was Leo himself, whose desire to rebuild St. Peter's created a tremendous demand for money.

To raise it, Leo put up for virtual auction the vacant archbishopric of Mainz. The high bid of ten thousand ducats, the cost of a papal dispensation for the holding of multiple sees, along with fourteen thousand for the *annate* (a year's income from the see paid by the benefice holder to the pope), came from Albrecht of Brandenburg, a younger son of the house of Hohenzollern. To help Albrecht to finance his new post, the pope authorized the sale of indulgences in his territory for an eight-year term. Popes had declared indulgences efficacious in reducing time in purgatory for the souls of those who confessed their sins, showed contrition, and made a donation. Indulgences had evolved into highly marketable certificates because many of the faithful believed—erroneously, according to doctrine—that they actually forgave sins. It was this sale that led Martin Luther, a priest in nearby Saxony, to post his ninety-five theses on the night of 31 October 1517.

This episode marked the beginning of the Protestant Reformation. It also provided fodder for generations of Protestant pamphleteers. Typical was a Puritan writer in late-seventeenth-century England who accused Leo of dissolution and greed. Leo, the writer claimed, promised forgiveness of sins and entry into heaven to those who purchased indulgences, which, the allegation continued, the pope was "selling" for his rebuilding projects in Rome. Even Francesco Guicciardini, who abhorred Luther's doctrine, denounced the sale of indulgences, which, he believed, "were being granted only to extort money" (Francesco Guicciardini, *The History of Italy*, trans. Sidney Alexander, New York: Macmillan, 1969, 319).

Luther at first avoided conflict with Leo, calling him a lamb amid wolves. Preoccupied with the imperial election, the pope reacted slowly. Not until 1520 did he issue the bull *Exsurge Domine*, threatening the Augustinian with excommunication and ordering him to burn his heretical works. Luther burned the papal bull instead and soon was calling Leo the Antichrist. Henry VIII of England rallied to the pope's side with his *Assertio septem sacramentorum*, which won for the future founder of the Church of England the title "Defender of the Faith" from the grateful Leo.

Whether any pope could have steered a safe course among the storms of early-sixteenth-century Europe is debatable. Even after the Council of Trent the total income from church benefices to cardinals alone came to over a million scudi. The persons with the power to effect reform were often those who most benefited from the status quo. Even observers who pointed out the abuses of the church and of papal policy were often caught up in them. Machiavelli, for instance, could attack the popes for preventing any one prince from unifying Italy while being unable to do so themselves, and at the same time dedicate works to Leo, whose pontificate continued the state of affairs that caused Machiavelli such despair. Leo himself presided over the Fifth Lateran Council, which condemned simony, multiple benefices, and nepotism, while showing himself a master of all three. Although he succeeded in reforming the Franciscans by giving control over the order to the Observant branch, he was not successful in implementing wide-ranging reform of the church.

Leo's inability to resolve the important issues facing him was apparent to many observers. Francesco Guicciardini concluded that he had failed to fulfill the expectations aroused at his assumption. Guicciardini's history documented Leo's preoccupation with carving out a state in central Italy for the Medici as well as his failure to stem the Lutheran heresy. The writer also understood keenly the role that the pope played; to hold their state, the Medici line required Popes. The greatest Italian poet of the age, Ludovico Ariosto, frustrated at his inability to win appointments and favors from his erstwhile friend Leo, immortalized the pope's foolishness in two satires. The satirist complained that although he was an old friend of the pope, nonetheless Leo promoted—according to a parable in the satire—the least little magpie in his retinue rather than men of talent like Ariosto himself. The poet resigned himself to staying in solitude.

Critical judgments of the Medici popes continued into the nineteenth and twentieth centuries. Jacob Burckhardt's *Civilization of the Renaissance in Italy* referred to the "gay corruption" of Leo's court at Rome. The great ottocento historian of the papacy, Leopold von Ranke, suggested that while Leo might have been kindly, learned, and liberal (echoing Lorenzo de' Medici's "savio"), these very traits distracted him from the serious problems confronting the church. Leo was thus preoccupied with rebuilding Rome, patronizing artists and writers, and directing affairs in Florence rather than attacking the corruption of the church and addressing the serious theological issues raised by Martin Luther. Even the Catholic historian Ludwig Pastor related an anecdote that sums up opinion about Leo: upon his election in 1513 he was supposed to have remarked that since he had been given the papacy, he was now going to enjoy it. Thus the received view of Leo is of an able politician and a discerning patron, but a venal man.

It is impossible to understand his goals and accomplishments if one fails to keep in mind that even after becoming pope, Leo X remained in many ways Giovanni de' Medici. He sought the establishment of the Medici in a secure position in Florence and in Tuscany. This concern became preeminent, and critics have rightly pointed out that he pursued *la politica della casa*—dynastic politics—at the expense of other matters. His successful effort to take the Duchy of Urbino from Francesco Maria della Rovere and give it to his own nephew Lorenzo nearly bankrupted the papal treasury and illustrated the short lifespan of papal gratitude: the dispossessed Francesco Maria was the nephew of Julius II. Yet when he was elected in 1513, the Medici had been back in Florence for only a year. When he died suddenly in 1521, they rested more securely in Florence because of his efforts. As the historian Peter Partner wrote that Leo, and later his cousin Giulio, placed the dynastic needs of the house of Medici above those of the papacy or church. How could Leo have served so successfully as an advocate of his family's interests and have been so unsuccessful by almost every measure as pope? The answers come both from his personality and from the larger circumstances in which he found himself.

First, his career illuminated several serious problems in the church. Even as he condemned simony, absenteeism, and multiple benefices, Leo sold some two thousand offices, with the proceeds amounting to about one-sixth of ordinary papal income. He appointed his cousin Giulio de' Medici archbishop of Florence, cardinal, and vice-chancellor, having first been obliged to grant a dispensation for his illegitimate birth followed with the absurd declaration that Giulio's parents had in fact been secretly married. Both Medici represented the stranglehold that younger or bastard sons of the elite maintained over high church offices. For transalpine Europeans, Leo X was the perfect example of the Italian domination over the church, a fact that had long alienated northerners from Rome. With the exception of two Borgia popes and Hadrian VI, every pontiff from the Renaissance until John Paul II was Italian. By the 1450s Martin Mair, chancellor of the archbishop of Mainz, had complained that the papacy "despised the German nation" and drained it of its wealth. The reply by Cardinal Aneas

Silvius Piccolomini, later Pope Pius II, revealed the gravity of the estrangement. "The grievances . . . catalogued by Mair either do not exist," he pronounced, "or are trivial" (Strauss, 39). His dismissive approach was repeated by Leo, who could not comprehend the strength, determination, and commitment of reformers like Martin Luther.

Leo thus failed to comprehend the magnitude of the problems, some inherited, others of his own making, that faced his pontificate. At the same time, he operated during a tumultuous period of history that demanded action on behalf of *casa* and *città*. In this arena he achieved remarkable success. The historian Giorgio Spini concluded that the Medici regime was nothing other than the fruit of the tenacious and often intelligent will of popes and princes of the line to construct a state. In the task of state building Leo attempted, with notable success, to place his family at the head of a territorial state whose structures remained largely intact until the Napoleonic era.

SELECTED BIBLIOGRAPHY

Ackerman, James S. "The Planning of Renaissance Rome, 1450–1580." In *Rome in the Renaissance: The City and the Myth*, ed. P.A. Ramsey. Binghamton, NY: Center for Medieval and Early Renaissance Studies, 1982.

Ady, Cecilia M. *Lorenzo dei Medici and Renaissance Italy*. New York: Collier Books, 1962.

Aretino, Pietro. *The Works*. 2 vols. New York: Covici-Friede, 1933.

Bainton, Roland. *Here I Stand: A Life of Martin Luther*. New York: Mentor, 1978.

Bullarium Romanum. Vol. 5. Turin: Franco et Enrico Dalmazzo, 1855.

Burckhardt, Jacob. *The Civilization of the Renaissance in Italy*. Trans. S. Middlemore. 2 vols. New York: Harper Torchbooks, 1958.

Caravale, Mario, and Alberto Caracciolo. *Lo stato pontificio da Martino V a Pio IX*. Turin: Unione Tipografico-Editrice Torinese, 1978.

Cellini, Benvenuto. *The Autobiography*. London: Penguin, 1956.

D'Amico, John. "Humanism in Rome." In *Renaissance Humanism: Foundations, Forms, and Legacy*, ed. Albert Rabil, vol. 1. Philadelphia: University of Pennsylvania Press, 1988.

———. *Renaissance Humanism in Papal Rome: Humanists and Churchmen on the Eve of the Reformation*. Baltimore: Johns Hopkins University Press, 1983.

Fanelli, Vittore. "Il Ginnasio greco di Leone X a Roma." *Studi romani* 9 (1961).

Guicciardini, Francesco. *The History of Italy*. Trans. Sidney Alexander. New York: Macmillan, 1969.

———. *Ricordi*. Ed. Raffaele Spongano. Florence: G.C. Sansoni, 1951.

Huizinga, J. *Erasmus of Rotterdam*. London: Phaidon Press, 1952.

"Instructione al Magnifico Lorenzo." Ed. Tommaso Gar. *Archivio storico italiano, appendice*, no. 1 (1842–44).

Lettera di Raffaello d'Urbino a Papa Leone X. Rome: Tipografia delle Scienze, 1840.

Machiavelli, Niccolò. *Il principl Scritti politici*. Milan: U. Mursia ed., 1977.

Menning, Carol Bresnahan. *Charity and State in Late Renaissance Italy: The Monte di Pietà of Florence*. Ithaca, N.Y.: Cornell University Press, 1993.

Minnich, Nelson. "Participants at the Fifth Lateran Council." *Archivum historiae pontificiae* 12 (1974).

Mitchell, Bonner. *Rome in the High Renaissance: The Age of Leo X*. Norman: University of Oklahoma Press, 1973.

O'Reilly, Claire. " 'Without Councils We Cannot Be Saved': Giles of Viterbo Addresses the Fifth Lateran Council." *Augustiniana* 27 (1977).

Partner, Peter. *Renaissance Rome, 1500–1559*. Berkeley: University of California Press, 1976.

Picotti, G.B. *La giovinezza di Leone X*. 1928. Milan: Hoepli, 1981.

Polizzotto, Lorenzo. "The Making of a Saint: The Canonization of St. Antonino, 1516–1523." *Journal of Medieval and Renaissance Studies* 22 (1992).

Roscoe, William. *The Life and Pontificate of Leo the Tenth*. 7th ed. 2 vols. London, 1872.

Segni, Bernardo. *Istorie fiorentine*. Florence: Barbera, Bianchi, 1857.

Setton, Kenneth. "Leo X and the Turkish Peril." *Proceedings of the American Philosophical Society* 113 (1969).

Spini, Giorgio. "Questioni e problemi di metodo per la storia del principato mediceo e degli stati toscani del Cinquecento." *Rivista storica italiana* 58 (1941).

Stinger, Charles L. *The Renaissance in Rome*. Bloomington: Indiana University Press, 1985.

Storia d'Italia. Ed. Costantino Panigada. 5 vols. Bari: Giuseppe Laterza & figli, 1929.

Strauss, Gerald, ed. *Manifestations of Discontent in Germany on the Eve of the Reformation*. Bloomington: Indiana University Press, 1971.

Vasari, Giorgio. *The Lives of the Artists*. Harmondsworth, Eng.: Penguin, 1965.

Vaughan, Herbert M. *The Medici Popes*. 1908. Reprint, Port Washington, N.Y.: Kennikat Press, 1971.

———. *Studies in the Italian Renaissance*. 1921. Reprint, Port Washington, N.Y.: Kennikat Press.

Winspeare, Fabrizio. *La congiura dei cardinali contro Leone X*. Florence: Leo Olschki, 1957.

CLEMENT VII (1523–34)

Kenneth Gouwens

Clement VII is among the least studied of the "Renaissance" popes. No doubt this neglect has resulted in part from the spectacular political and ecclesiastical failures of his administration, such as the sack of Rome (1527) and the loss of Henry VIII's England from the Catholic fold. His pontificate has also been seen to lack cultural distinction, constituting a lull between the "high Renaissance" and the Counter-Reformation culture of Paul III's Rome. Recent research has shown, however, that Clement was in fact a discerning cultural patron who intervened actively in the projects he commissioned. Considerable evidence suggests, too, that his political strategies were less bankrupt than has sometimes been supposed, reflecting not so much his diplomatic naïveté as the depressing range of options that confronted him. Seeking to further both familial and papal interests and to promote Renaissance cultural values in the dawning age of the Reformation, Clement VII could only meet with disappointment and disaster.

Giulio de' Medici was born on 26 May 1478, one month after the brutal murder of his father Giuliano (brother of Lorenzo the Magnificent) in the cathedral of Florence by political enemies of the Medici family. Scholars have been unable to identify the illegitimate Giulio's mother with any certainty, nor do we know anything of his first seven years other than that he may have spent them in the care of the architect Antonio da Sangallo. Thereafter he lived in the Palazzo Medici in Florence with his uncle, Lorenzo, and with his cousins Giuliano and Giovanni, alongside whom he probably enjoyed the tutelage of humanist scholars such as Gentile Becchi. When Giovanni assumed his cardinal's duties in early 1492, Giulio joined his sixteen-year-old cousin's retinue and thereafter spent nearly three decades in Giovanni's ample shadow.

Just weeks after Giovanni's elevation to the cardinalate, however, Medici fortunes were severely disrupted by the death of Lorenzo. The eldest son, Piero, lacked Lorenzo's political acumen, and in 1494, when the French king Charles VIII's army directly threatened Florence, the Medici were exiled from the city. Initially under the guidance of the Dominican preacher Savonarola, Florence entered upon two decades of political experimentation that ended only with the return of the Medici in 1512. In the intervening years Giulio fell into the role of furthering family interests as his cousins defined and directed them. In 1509, for example, he was instrumental in arranging the marriage of Piero's daughter, Clarice, to the prominent Florentine banker Filippo Strozzi—one of many moves designed to reestablish the Medici in Florence. It was only with the assistance of Spanish troops in September 1512, however, that the Medici at last returned to power in the city, which they would control until shortly after the sack of Rome in 1527.

Soon after Giovanni de' Medici was elevated to the papacy as Leo X (11 March 1513), he appointed Giulio archbishop of Florence and created him cardinal, in which capacity Giulio gained numerous benefices, both from his cousin and from people seeking influence with the pope through his agency. Throughout Leo's pontificate Giulio worked to further the interests both of the institutional church and of the Medici—goals that were frequently conjoined, as in the suppression of Savonarolans in Florence in 1515. In 1517 he became vice-chancellor of the church, and he gained an estimable reputation as administrator and diplomat. By the time of Leo's death in December 1521, in part through Giulio's efforts, the papacy had become firmly aligned with the Spanish king and holy Roman emperor-designate, Charles V, a policy that reflected both the perceived seriousness of the French threat in Italy and a desire to encourage Charles's efforts to combat the Lutheran heresy.

Although Giulio emerged as the favorite in the conclave that followed, his candidacy was blocked by two factors: (1) French threats of a schism should he be elected and (2) the opposition of two influential cardinals, Pompeo Colonna and Francesco Soderini. Sensing electoral gridlock and concerned for the stability of Medicean control of Florence, Giulio himself nominated the Imperialist loyalist Adrian of Utrecht, a clear supporter of the imperial cause, but one whose candidacy was less threatening to Giulio's Italian antagonists. This compromise candidate was quickly elected (Hadrian VI, 1522–23), but died after a brief reign distinguished by moral conservatism and fiscal prudence.

Subsequently Giulio again emerged as the leading candidate for the See of Peter. This time, through a combination of promises and threats, he managed to obtain the support of the proimperial Cardinal Colonna and was elevated as Pope Clement VII on 18 November 1523. Adherents heaved a sigh of relief at the election of another apparent ally of Charles V. Meanwhile, humanists in Rome and Florence, delighting in the prospect of a return to the lavish patronage they had enjoyed under Leo X, hailed the news as marking the beginning of a new golden age. They could hardly have been more wrong.

From the outset of his pontificate Clement had difficulty juggling the interests of family, papal alliances, and church administration as success fully as he had done under Leo X. After initially maintaining the alliance with Charles V, the new pontiff soon showed himself loyal above all to protecting family interests and to preserving the papacy's political autonomy. In pursuit of the latter goal, Clement therefore aimed to prevent either France or Spain from becoming dominant in Italy. This was, in effect, the policy that he had earlier executed for his cousin Leo X, and that had led the papacy to forge the alliance with the emperor. But as the growing northern territorial states increasingly dwarfed the Italian powers, the prospects for the policy's success moved ever farther from Clement's diplomatic reach. In 1524 he tried to strike a pose of neutrality, but that autumn, Francis I led an army into Italy, taking Milan on 28 October, and the subsequent descent of Spanish troops into Lombardy compelled Clement to take sides. In part because of the immediacy of the French threat to the Papal States in central Italy, Clement opted for an alliance with France. But the sound defeat of the French at the Battle of Pavia (24 February 1525), in which Francis I was himself taken prisoner, at once

Sixteenth-century painting of Pope Clement VII by Sebastiano del Piombo. (Courtesy of the Vatican Library)

transformed the political landscape. Soon Clement entered into negotiations with Lannoy, the imperial viceroy of Naples, and they reached an agreement (1 April) that included guarantees of imperial protection for the Papal States and for Medicean control of Florence.

The failure of the imperialists to adhere to the manifold terms of this treaty prompted Clement to incline again toward the French, a tendency that became a commitment after Francis I regained his freedom in March

1526 and promptly reneged on the concessions he had made to Charles in the Treaty of Madrid (January 1526), which had included the renunciation of French claims to Milan. Swayed by the arguments of his pro-French counselor, the papal datary Gian Matteo Giberti, Clement feared that Spanish hegemony in the Italian peninsula would end any possibility of papal political autonomy, and so he joined with Francis I, Florence, Venice, and Milan in the League of Cognac (22 May) against Charles V. The efforts of the imperial envoy Ugo da Moncada in mid-June to sway Clement to abandon the league met with no success. Thereafter the sides became polarized. On 23 June Clement sent a forceful letter to Charles, itemizing the emperor's offenses against him. That autumn Charles responded in kind, adding on a call for a council, which Clement rightly took as a threat to his autonomy. Meanwhile, as tensions increased, the papacy suffered a series of political disappointments and military reverses, including the Turkish victory at Mohacs, and its allies continued to provide insufficient support. Worse still, Charles V was preparing to lead a fleet to Italy. By mid-September the disillusioned pope was considering the possibility of betaking himself to Barcelona to negotiate directly with the emperor. But just then, on 20 September, Cardinal Pompeo Colonna and his brothers led a military assault on the Vatican in a brazen attempt to seize power from Clement and possibly even to kill him. The beleaguered pope took refuge in the papal fortress, Castel Sant'Angelo, and the following day he accepted an armistice brokered by Moncada, guaranteeing amnesty to Colonna.

Once the immediate threat had abated, Clement sought to avenge his humiliation, excommunicating Pompeo Colonna, stripping him of his ecclesiastical rank, and ordering the destruction of some of the family's properties. But this move had the inadvertent effect of driving the Colonnesi even farther into the imperial camp. In the months that ensued Clement's political position became ever more tenuous as an imperial army led by Charles of Bourbon moved inexorably southward toward Rome. For months Clement alternately sought terms of peace and forestalled their conclusion, in accordance with the papacy's shifting military fortunes and expectations. By late March the situation was desperate enough that Clement at last concluded an armistice with Lannoy, the imperial viceroy of Naples. But the truce proved ineffective, since Bourbon and his men refused to accept its provisions, and on the morning of 6 May they attacked the city of Rome. Clement again fled to Castel Sant'Angelo, but this time the situation was far more grave: by sunset nearly the entire city was under imperial control. Bourbon had been killed in the initial assault, leaving the Spanish and German troops without a unifying leader. While Clement remained effectively a prisoner for six months, the imperial troops lorded it over their captives, looting and destroying buildings, desecrating relics, and torturing and murdering priests and citizens. When Clement at last escaped to Orvieto on 6 December, he did so only with the assistance of the now-dominant Cardinal Colonna, whose consistent loyalty to the emperor—possibly to the point of colluding with Bourbon in plotting the assault on Rome—was now being rewarded.

Once freed, Clement resumed his efforts to create political space for papal autonomy, exploring the possibilities of renewing alliances with one side or the other. Hoping to regain territories that the papacy had lost, he also aimed to restore the Medici to power in Florence, from which they had been driven shortly after the sack of Rome. By the autumn of 1528, however, the failure of the French to conquer Naples, combined with his own inability to conclude a favorable accord with northern Italian powers such as Venice, inclined Clement once again to seek an alliance with the understandably skeptical Charles V. The progress of negotiations was halted in January 1529 when Clement became gravely ill. Sensing an urgent need to provide for the future of the Medici in the church, he made his young nephew Ippolito a cardinal, a move that the latter actually resented, since he aspired to control Florence. Once Clement recovered, however, negotiations resumed, and on 29 May Clement and Charles reached terms of peace, including imperial support for the return of the Medici to Florence. That autumn pope and emperor met in Bologna, where, the following February, Clement officially crowned Charles as holy Roman emperor. That summer Spanish troops restored Medicean control of Florence, and in 1532 the illegitimate Alessandro de' Medici—who, historians speculate, may well have been Clement's son—became duke of Florence. Thus the Medici once again ruled Florence, but only under the aegis of the emperor.

The issue of the *libertà d'Italia* at last having been resolved, Clement turned his attentions ever more to family concerns, including arranging the marriage of Catherine de' Medici to Henry of Orléans, which took place in October 1533. The issue of church reform, necessarily subordinated to the wars of the 1520s, also came to the fore. Here, as in politics, Clement had continued the Fabian tactics of his cousin, Leo X, but it was again during Clement's reign that the situation became untenable. On 24 March 1534, after delaying resolution of the issue for years, Clement officially recognized the validity of Henry VIII's first marriage. By that time, however, the English schism was already well under way. Meanwhile, Clement's occasional talk of convening a church council came to nothing. When he died on 25 September 1534, Giulio de' Medici left behind a papacy severely impoverished, a church weakened by multiple schisms, and an Italy largely under Spanish domination.

It would not be fitting, however, to conclude on so negative a note. Clement did in fact make important contributions during his pontificate, continuing to support literature and the arts much as he had while a cardinal, and commissioning lasting monuments such as Michelangelo's painting of the *Last Judgment* in the Sistine Chapel. Moreover, despite his shortcomings as an administrator, in 1526 he created the Monte della Fede, the papal-funded debt, which constituted a major innovation over more traditional hand-to-mouth expedients for raising revenue. At the outset of his papacy he evidenced interest in reform by discouraging the holding of multiple benefices and refusing, until the desperate political straits of early 1527, to create cardinals as a means of raising revenue. The political circumstances rendered even more dangerous than usual the convening of a council, which he feared would provide an occasion for enemies to depose him on the grounds of illegitimate birth.

It is more appropriate, then, to end somewhat more charitably with the observation that Giulio de' Medici had inherited an untenable position. Contemporaries marveled at how his fortunes changed once he was elevated to the papacy. There was talk among Florentines that Giulio had worked hard to gain a good reputation as a cardinal but squandered it after he became pope. If this outcome resulted in part from Giulio's temperament, which inclined him to consider all options, to resist commitment to a given policy, and to vacillate endlessly when left to his own devices, it also resulted from his advocacy of values that would become increasingly problematic in the age of the Reformation: the oft-conflicting desires to promote family interests, to maintain the political "liberty" or autonomy of the papacy and of Italy despite the growth of northern states, and the desire to embellish the papal image with the grandeur of humanist rhetoric and the lasting beauty of exceptional artistic works.

SELECTED BIBLIOGRAPHY

Bullard, Melissa Meriam. *Filippo Strozzi and the Medici: Favor and Finance in Sixteenth-Century Florence and Rome*. Cambridge and New York: Cambridge University Press, 1980.

Chastel, André. *The Sack of Rome, 1527*. Trans. Beth Archer. Princeton: Princeton University Press, 1983.

De Caprio, Vincenzo. *La Tradizione e il trauma: Idee del Rinascimento romano*. Manziana: Vecchiarelli, 1991.

Gaisser, Julia Haig. *Pierio Valeriano on the Ill Fortune of Learned Men: A Renaissance Humanist and His World*. Ann Arbor: University of Michigan Press, 1999.

Gouwens, Kenneth. *Remembering the Renaissance: Humanist Narratives of the Sack of Rome*. Leiden: Brill, 1998.

Guicciardini, Francesco. *The History of Italy*. Trans. and ed. Sidney Alexander. New York: Macmillan, 1969.

———. *The Sack of Rome*. Trans. and ed. James H. McGregor. New York: Italica Press, 1993.

———. *Storia d'Italia*. 3 vols. Ed. Silvana Seidel Menchi. Turin: Einaudi, 1971.

Hook, Judith. *The Sack of Rome, 1527*. London: Macmillan, 1972.

Pastor, Ludwig. *The History of the Popes from the Close of the Middle Ages: Drawn from the Secret Archives of the Vatican and Other Original Sources.* Trans. Frederick Ignatius Antrobus. London: Kegan Paul, 1901–33.

Prosperi, Adriano. "Clemente VII, papa." In *Dizionario biografico degli italiani*, vol. 26. Rome: Instituto della Enciclopedia Italiana, 1982, 237–59.

———. *Tra evangelismo e Controriforma: G.M. Giberti (1495–1543).* Rome Edizioni di storia e letteratura, 1969.

Reiss, Sheryl E. "Cardinal Giulio de' Medici as a Patron of Art, 1513–1523." 3 vols. Ph.D. diss., Princeton University, 1992.

Reynolds, Anne. *Renaissance Humanism at the Court of Clement VII: Francesco Berni's "Dialogue against Poets" in Context.* Studies, with an edition and translation. New York: Garland, 1997.

Stinger, Charles L. *The Renaissance in Rome.* Bloomington: Indiana University Press, 1985; rev. ed., 1998.

Zimmermann, T.C. Price. *Paolo Giovio: The Historian and the Crisis of Sixteenth-Century Italy.* Princeton: Princeton University Press, 1995.

PAUL III (1534–49)

William V. Hudon

Alessandro Farnese, the man who would become Pope Paul III, was born in Canino on 29 February 1469. His family held lands around Lago di Bolsena, near modern Lazio's border with Tuscany. As the son of Pier Luigi Farnese and Giovannella Gaetani, he possessed impeccable noble credentials in what became one of Rome's most prominent families. He received an education that reflected the Renaissance cultural ideals of such families. That education began under the tutelage of the humanists Pomponio Leto and Giovanni Battista Pio and was later crowned by studies at the University of Pisa and at the famous court of Lorenzo de' Medici (*il magnifico*, 1449–92) in Florence.

He served in a variety of ecclesiastical offices, initially due to the patronage of Pope Innocent VIII and Rodrigo Borgia, the future Pope Alexander VI (1492–1503). His association with the latter might not have been wholly dependent on Borgia's intimate relationship with Farnese's sister, Giulia, although after becoming cardinal in 1493 he was known by the nickname "cardinal Petticoat." As cardinal, but prior to his priestly ordination in 1519, Farnese kept a mistress and fathered four children, three of whom (Pier Luigi, Paolo, and Ranuccio) were legitimized during the reigns of Julius II (1503–13) and Leo X (1513–21).

Sometimes the "great" and most "notable" of popes are quite difficult to characterize succinctly, and Paul was one such pope. After a three-day conclave (11–13 October 1534) and an election greeted by popular acclaim, he commenced a series of actions that reflect a curious, even inexplicable, blend of personal characteristics that some might consider almost mutually exclusive. Paul exhibited extraordinary, deep contradictions in the way that he acted—and apparently thought—during the course of his pontificate. These contradictions can be identified in Paul's work as a religious reformer, as a politician and diplomat, and as a patron of art and learning.

Many consider Paul the first pope committed to efficacious reform of the Catholic church in the sixteenth century. The reasons for this begin, of course, with the inaction of his predecessors, but include Paul's election announcement of an intention to hold a general council to discuss and sketch out reform of church doctrine and practices. The reasons also include his nearly consistent promotion of more qualified candidates to the rank of cardinal. Among those competent, well-educated, and reform-minded cardinals were Gian Pietro Carafa, Gregorio Cortese, Gasparo Contarini, Reginald Pole, and Jacopo Sadoleto. Paul commissioned from them and others the reform document *Consilium de emendanda ecclesia* (1537), which expressed ideas that had a considerable effect upon the deliberations at and the decrees of the council he later convened, the Council of Trent (1545–63).

He shared the view of episcopal power and how it ought to be exercised held by these cardinals, for he had personally conducted a visitation of his north central Italian diocese of Parma in 1516, long before such responsible behavior became fashionable. That view of the office of bishop became the centerpiece of the Tridentine reform plan that served as the administrative aim of the church until Vatican Council II. Paul presided over the approbation of the Society of Jesus (or Jesuit order) and encouraged other new religious congregations like the Theatines, the Barnabites, the Somaschi, and the Ursulines, in addition to supporting confraternal organizations throughout Rome. These were all actions that promoted the process of reform and reflected a commitment to ideals concerning religious practice that motivated continuing, post-Tridentine action. In 1542 he designed a revival of the Roman Inquisition for similar ends. He placed Carafa at its head and intended that it operate moderately in coordinating efforts to limit the spread of Protestant doctrines in Italy.

While taking all these actions, however, Paul also demonstrated the sizable limitations of his commitment to reform. He unabashedly promoted the interests of his family through the papal office in the Renaissance tradition he must have learned, in part, from Alexander VI. Paul's nepotism undercut the otherwise consistently high quality of his cardinalatial appointments. His two teenaged grandsons, Alessandro Farnese and Guido Ascanio Sforza, ultimately proved themselves talented enough to do good work as cardinals, but their promotions came against considerable opposition. Paul decided to bestow the papal properties of Parma and Piacenza as a duchy upon his son Pier Luigi against similar opposition to the gross nepotism it reflected, and ironically, the 1545 bull granting these territories was separated by less than five months from the bull opening the Council of Trent.

Although Paul was personally attracted to the model of episcopal residence that was prescribed for all bishops at Trent, he did not require it of his grandson Alessandro, but instead showered him with benefice upon lucrative benefice in perfectly unreformed fashion. Although Paul restricted unjust inquisitorial prosecution of Jews in Spain and Portugal and had no intention of utilizing his new Roman tribunal against them, he installed perhaps the most infamous anti-Judaic cleric of the age, Gian Pietro Carafa, as head of that revived inquisition. Paul convened the Council of Trent in a difficult political context with great diplomatic skill, but it was clear that he feared the prospect of conciliarism there and appeared to be an indecisive procrastinator to his closest advisors—like Marcello Cervini (1501–55, Pope Marcellus II, 1555)—when matters at the meeting required swift action. These facts reduce Paul's stature to that of one who began, but lacked consistency in applying, the reform many desired.

Paul has often been viewed as the consummately political Renaissance pope. Signs of his skill in diplomacy appeared from the very beginning of his curial career. Paul was, after all, able to remain in the good graces of both Julius II and Leo X, who were implacable enemies. As a result, Paul gained the experience that lay behind his own sometimes-successful papal foreign policy. He served as legate to the Marches for Julius II between 1504 and 1507, there attempting to implement the pope's military and diplomatic poli-

Pope Paul III. (Courtesy of the Library of Congress)

cies. Paul was assigned, among other things, to rid the territory—by military force, if necessary—of troublemakers from the local nobility who challenged papal control. Leo X entrusted to him and others a task that he considered of great importance: negotiation of a diplomatic solution to the problems raised by the schismatic Council of Pisa (1511–12), especially over the dispensations it had granted. Through that undertaking Paul gained experience in working with French diplomats. He enjoyed the highest confidence of Pope Clement VII (1523–34), who named him legate in

Rome in 1529 and hence in charge of negotiations with the representatives of Emperor Charles V. Clement considered Paul so capable, some historians have said, that he would have bequeathed the papacy to Paul, had it been in his power.

All of that experience made Paul comfortable in foreign affairs, but his policies as pope were not always successful. This was due, at least in part, to his own errors and inconsistencies. At times his diplomatic skill at compromise became a detriment instead of an asset. That was clear when Paul attempted to formulate policies that would simultaneously satisfy the arch-rivals Charles V (holy Roman emperor, 1519–56) and Francis I (king of France, 1515–47) while maintaining his own neutrality in the seemingly continual conflict between the two rulers. Both imperial and French loyalists, as well as observers committed fully to neither one side nor the other, noted the dissimulation and duplicity required to even attempt such a contradictory position. Paul went so far as to conduct personal embassies in the interest of securing a truce in the Hapsburg—Valois conflict to facilitate convocation of the Council of Trent. When agreement on the truce was attained, it was gained more through the exhaustion of French and imperial combatants than through the efforts of Paul and his diplomats between 1537 and 1544. In addition, although historians frequently uphold Paul and some of his early modern colleagues as examples of modern, pragmatic state building, this pope had plans thwarted by his own ideal-istic, and sometimes highly impractical, views. He attempted to systemat-ically reinforce fortifications and defense systems along the coast of Italy to protect trade from piracy, for example. In the long run, however, his pragmatist's plan became a crusader's hope: to lead a multinational force against Ottoman corsairs in the Mediterranean. Paul exhibited unreason-able confidence that self-aggrandizing heads of state would cooperate, in-stead of squabbling among themselves, in order to repulse infidels under his leadership. With this attitude he resembled his deceased medieval fore-bears far more than he resembled any early modern secular absolutists. In the final analysis, he was anything but single minded in political policy making.

Although Paul has been considered magnanimous, well intentioned, and even populist for some policies—like his defense of the rights of New World natives in the 1537 bulls *Veritas ipsa* and *Sublimis Deus* and his promotion of popular carnival festivities at papal expense—at times he also sacrificed public to private goods. In 1540, for example, Paul squashed rebels in Perugia opposing a salt tax with techniques he probably learned from Julius II, and the rebellion itself has been considered the last gasp of the Umbrian capital's communal, democratic government expiring under papal and imperial control. Deciding to carve a duchy out of papal territory for his son was thus not one of Paul's choices that can be considered wholly unprecedented or out of character.

No careful analysis of this pontificate can omit Paul's extensive patronage of art, of learning, and of the city of Rome itself. A large number of the major monuments and artworks of the late Renaissance were produced through his support, including the Capella Paolina, reconstruction of the Piazza del Campidoglio, the decoration schemes in the Vatican Sala Regia and in Castel Sant'Angelo, and of course, the *Last Judgment* in the Sistine Chapel. His relationships with Raphael and Michelangelo are perhaps best known, and for the latter he arranged not only an enormous income, but also control over all artistic projects for the Vatican Palace. Paul physically and intellectually restored the university of Rome La Sapienza, reconstructing its buildings destroyed in the 1527 sack of Rome and supporting the recruitment of distinguished professors in medicine, rhetoric, theology, and philosophy.

In 1548 he placed the Vatican Library under the directorship of the humanist Marcello Cervini, enhanced its holdings at considerable cost, and insisted on both the expansion of its cataloging and the preservation of its treasures. He reconvened the painting school of Raphael, whose members had scattered after the sack. He utilized Michelangelo, Antonio da Sangallo the Younger, and a host of others in extensive building and fortification projects in towns throughout the Papal States. Paul also undertook urban-planning efforts in Rome, which anticipated the later work of Sixtus V (1585–90). He left no doubt that the years of austerity following the sack were over.

Even in this patronage of humanist learning and art Paul stood as a man of contradictions. While he supported the creation of art and architecture that is unsurpassed in the Western world, he also spent considerable sums patronizing less-than-high-level cultural production. His court may have been a haven for the most learned humanist poets, philosophers, and historians of the day, but it also harbored astrologers who were consulted before every decision of importance and sycophantic pseudoscholars who produced, among other things, a Farnese genealogy tracing back to Noah's Ark. Although the money he spent served to endow the artistic heritage of both the church and the nation of Italy in the long run, Paul funded many undertakings that possessed a strong element of self-interest, not to say self-aggrandizement. Sangallo's completion of the Palazzo Farnese near Campo del Fiori that now serves as the French Embassy in Rome, for example, became increasingly splendid as it neared completion.

Only a 250 percent increase in his salary under Leo X permitted then Cardinal Farnese to even consider construction of the palace he desired. Once he attained the papal throne, however, money was no object. Some churches and monasteries in Rome and—for all practical purposes—whole towns like Frascati were reconstructed at least in part due to Paul's desire for multiple summer residences. Even in the absence of Giorgio Vasari's portraits of Paul as Alexander the Great, it is easy to see why some have concluded that this pope's patronage was a form of self-identification with great emperors of the past.

Perhaps one of the best sources available to comprehend Paul's view of the papal office is the *ricordi* or memoir that he composed on the "practice" of the papacy. He wrote it shortly before his death and addressed it to his grandson Alessandro. Although early in the document Paul cautioned that no one should actively seek the papacy, and that service to the church ought to be the principal motive of a pope, his idealistic and high-minded rhetoric ended there. With arrogance he referred to the time when God would call Alessandro to the throne, and he told him to maintain a position of deference with those who had become cardinal before him. Paul indicated that the creation of a new pope from among those cardinals he had appointed would be a great honor, but not necessarily useful to Alessandro. Then, in the centerpiece of his statement, Paul provided specific information on certain cardinals and the behavior Alessandro should expect from them in future conclaves, as well as cautions about the potential dangers lurking among rival Roman noble families.

Thus Paul III acted as politician and nepotist to the very end and indeed bequeathed this character, in a manner of speaking. He entered his final illness and died in 1549 in the context of renewed conflict over the disposition of Parma and Piacenza. This time the conflict involved his grandson, Ottavio Farnese. Despite his anger over Ottavio's rebellion in demanding possession of Parma, Paul dictated the political concession virtually at the hour of his death. It was the last act of a truly inveterate nepotist.

Historians are mistaken to depict Paul III's pontificate as the end or beginning of any era. Arguments could easily be constructed, and many have been, to assert that he was the last representative of the "Renaissance" papacy or the first "Counter-Reformation" pope. All such arguments really miss the point, since Paul can be considered either a "Renaissance" or "Counter-Reformation" pope only by first defining the nature of these complex periods in broad, unspecific terminology and then oversimplifying the personality of a complicated man. Neither one of these operations serves the need we have to understand historical personages in their full humanity. Paul was nepotist and reformer, self-aggrandizing monarch and humanistic patron, a haughty aristocrat who could not resist guffawing at the carnival, a man who was simultaneously committed to conciliar reform and scared to death of it. Perhaps, as Ludwig von Pastor said, he was a transitional figure between the age of Renaissance and the age of reform, but these very terms lose their meaning as more and more such transitional figures are identified. The same could be said—albeit for different reasons—of the three popes who succeeded Paul: Julius III (1550–55), Marcellus II (1555), and Paul IV (1555–59). Men with humanist scholarly credentials continued to be elected pope. They continued to teeter on the tightrope trying to retain papal power while promoting reform. They continued to patronize artists and architects. They never fully rid themselves of the desire to make nepotistic use of ecclesiastical property. Very few occupants of the papal throne in the "Renaissance" or the "Reformation"— no matter how one defines either of these periods—can be simply or easily characterized. To do so with Paul III would rob him of his rich humanity and fascinating personality.

SELECTED BIBLIOGRAPHY

Adorni, Bruno. *L'architettura farnesiana a Piacenza, 1545–1600*. Parma: Luigi Battei, 1982.

Batiffol, Pierre. *La Vaticane de Paul III à Paul V*. Paris: E. Leroux, 1890.

Brizzi, Gian Paolo, et al. *Università, principe, Gesuiti: La politica farnesiana dell'istruzione a Parma e Piacenza, 1545–1622*. Rome: Bulzoni, 1980.

Buschbell, Gottfried von. *Reformation und Inquisition in Italien um die Mitte des XVI. Jahrhunderts*. Paderborn: Schöningh, 1910.

Capasso, Carlo. *Paolo III, 1534–1549*. 2 vols. Messina: G. Principato, 1923–24.

Capece, Scipione. *De principiis rerum ad Paulum III, pontifex maximus*. Patavii: J. Cominus, 1777.

Cardanus, Ludwig, ed. *Nuntiaturberichte aus Deutschland, I Abteiling, 1533–1539, Legation Farnesus und Cervinus*. Berlin: A. Bath, 1909.

Concilium Tridentinum. 13 vols. Freiburg: Herder, 1901–38.

Da Campagnola, Stanislao. "Un crocifisso di legno contro Paolo III Farnese durante la Guerra del Sale del 1540." *Laurentianum* 34 (1993): 49–66.

DeMolen, Richard L., ed. *Religious Orders of the Catholic Reformation*. New York: Fordham University Press, 1994.

Edwards, W.H. *Paul der Dritte; oder, Die geistliche Gegenreformation*. Leipzig: J. Hegner, 1933.

Fragnito, Gigliola. "Evangelismo e intransigenti nei difficili equilibri del pontificato farnesiano." *Rivista di storia e letteratura religiosa* 25 (1989): 20–47.

Gaeta, Franco, ed. *Nunziature di Venezia*. Rome: Istituto storico italiano per l'età moderna e contemporanea, 1967.

Gaudioso, Filippa M.A., and Eraldo Gaudioso, eds. *Gli affreschi di Paolo III a Castel Sant'Angelo: Progetto ed esecuzione, 1543–1548*. 2 vols. Rome: De Luca, 1981.

Gleason, Elisabeth G. "Who Was the First Counter-Reformation Pope?" *Catholic Historical Review* 81 (1995): 173–84.

Hallman, Barbara McClung. *Italian Cardinals, Reform, and the Church as Property, 1492–1563*. Berkeley: University of California Press, 1985.

Hudon, William V. "Countering 'the Turk': Papal and Genoese Naval Policy, 1535–1536." *Archivum historiae pontificiae* 30 (1992): 351–62.

———. *Marcello Cervini and Ecclesiastical Government in Tridentine Italy*. De Kalb: Northern Illinois University Press, 1992.

Jedin, Hubert. *Geschichte des Konzils von Trient*. 5 vols. Freiburg: Herder, 1950–75.

Lesseps, Monique de. *Paul III, pape de transition*. Paris: Tolra, 1965.

Metzler, Josef, ed. *America Pontificia: Primi saeculi evangelizationis, 1493–1592*. 2 vols. Vatican City: Libreria Editrice Vaticana, 1991.

Navenne, Ferdinand de. *Rome, le Palais Farnese, et les Farnese*. Paris: Librairie Albin Michel, 1914.

Pastor, Ludwig Freiherr von. *The History of the Popes from the Close of the Middle Ages*. Vols. 11 and 12. Trans. Frederick Ignatius Antrobus. Ed. Ralph Francis Kerr. St. Louis: Herder, 1950.

Prodi, Paolo. *The Papal Prince: One Body and Two Souls: The Papal Monarchy in Early Modern Europe*. Trans. Susan Haskins. Cambridge: Cambridge University Press, 1987.

Querini, Angelo Maria. *Imago optimis principis in gestis Pauli III Farnesii expressa*. Brixiae: J.M. Rizzardi, 1745.

Robertson, Clare. *Il gran cardinale: Alessandro Farnese, Patron of the Arts*. New Haven: Yale University Press, 1992.

Romani, Marzio A., and Amedeo Quondam, eds. *Le corti farnesiane di Parma e Piacenza, 1545–1622*. 2 vols. Rome: Bulzoni, 1978.

Stinger, Charles. *The Renaissance in Rome*. Bloomington: Indiana University Press, 1985.

BIBLIOGRAPHIC NOTE

The most important repository for papers of the Renaissance and Reformation popes is the Archivio Segreto Vaticano (ASV), which houses those from Boniface VIII to Paul III. The Biblioteca Apostolica Vaticana (BAV) is also important. Original documents can be found in the *Registra Lateranensia* and the *Registra Supplicationum*, while the papal account books are found in the *fondo* labeled *Introitus et Exitus*. Leonard Boyle's *A Survey of the Vatican Archives and Its Medieval Holdings* (Toronto: Pontifical Institute of Medieval Studies, 1972) enables the researcher to know where to look in this vast collection that spans more than one thousand years. Also useful in finding one's way through the Vatican Archives is Francis X. Blouin, Jr.,'s *Vatican Archives: An Inventory and Guide to Historical Documents of the Holy See* (New York: Oxford University Press, 1998). Ludwig Pastor's *The History of the Popes from the Close of the Middle Ages*, trans. and ed. Frederick Ignatius Antrobus et al., 40 vols. (St. Louis: B. Herder Book Co., 1923–53), provides an overview of all the popes of this period. Peter Partner's *The Lands of St. Peter: The Papal State in the Middle Ages and the Early Renaissance* (Berkeley: University of California Press, 1972) remains an excellent survey of the Papal States, while his companion volume *The Pope's Men: The Papal Civil Service in the Renaissance* (Oxford: Clarendon Press, 1990) examines the administration of the See of St. Peter. For additional references and manuscripts written by and for popes, see Paul Oskar Kristeller's *Iter Italicum accedunt alia itinera: A Finding List of Uncatalogued or Incompletely Catalogued Humanistic Manuscripts of the Renaissance in Italian and Other Libraries*, 6 vols. (Leiden: E.J. Brill, 1963–92).

On John XXII's career, see Guillaume Mollat's "Jean XXII fut-il un avare?" *Revue d'histoire ecclésiastique* 6 (1906): 34–45, and also his "L'Election du pape Jean XXII," *Revue d'histoire de l'Église de France* 1 (1910): 34–49, 147–66, as well as N. Valois's "Jacques Duèse, pape sous le nom de Jean XXII," *Histoire Littéraire de la France* 34 (1915): 391–630, and, finally, John Weakland's "John XXII before His Pontificate, 1244–1316: Jacques Duèse and His Family," *Archivum historiae pontificiae* 10 (1972): 161–85. Etienne Baluze's *Vitae paparum Avenionensium*, ed. G. Mollat, vol. 1 (Paris: Letouzey & Ané, 1914), 107–94, contains seven accounts of John's life, while Emil Göller's *Die Einnahmen der Apostolischen Kammer unter Johann XXII* (Paderborn: F. Schöningh, 1910) is an edition of the papal account books. Canon law sources for John XXII include Jacqueline Tarrant's *A Study and Critical Edition of the Extravagantes Joannis XXII*, 2 vols. (Ph.D. diss. University of Toronto, 1976). The *Extravagantes*, also edited by Tarrant, are published in the Monumenta iuris canonici, ser. B, Corpus Collectionum (Vatican City: Biblioteca Apostolica Vaticana, 1983). For further reading on John's policies, see Louis Caillet's *La papauté d'Avignon et l'Église de France: La politique bénéficiale du pape Jean XXII en France 1316–1334* (Paris: Presses universitaires de France, 1975). Also useful are James Heft's *John XXII and Papal Teaching Authority*, Texts and Studies in Religion, vol. 27 (Lewiston, N.Y.: E. Mellen Press, 1986), and Malcolm Lambert's "The Franciscan Crisis under John XXII," *Franciscan Studies* 32 (1972): 123–43, which both add details to the picture.

On Gregory XI, especially his political undertakings, including his fight with Florence and his work for a crusade, see A. Luttrell, "Gregory XI and the Turks: 1370–1378," *Orientalia christiana periodica* 46 (1980): 391–417, and L. Mirot, *La politique pontificale et le retour du Saint-Siège à Rome en 1376* (Paris: 1899), as well as G. Mollat's "Grégoire XI et sa legende," *Revue d'histoire ecclésiastique* 49 (1954): 873–77, the same author's "Relations politiques de Grégoire XI avec les siennois et les florentins," *Mélanges d'archéologie et d'historie* 67 (1956): 335–76, and his "Préliminaires de la guerre des Otto Santi (1371–1375)," *Comptes rendus de l'Académie des inscriptions et belles-lettres*, 1955, 113–16. For an overview of the Avignon papacy, see G. Mollat, *Les papes d'Avignon*, 10th ed. (Paris: 1965), and Y. Renouard's *Les relations des papes d'Avignon et des compagnies commerciales et bancaires de 1316 à 1378*, Bibliothèque des Écoles françaises d'Athènes et de Rome, fasc. 151 (Paris: 1941).

Two recent publications, *Saints and sinners: A History of the Popes* by Eamon Duffy (New Haven: Yale University Press, 1997) and *Lives of the Popes: The Pontiffs from St. Peter to John Paul II*, by Richard P. McBrien (San Francisco: HarperSanFrancisco, 1977) provide solid overviews of Martin V's reign. Chapter 1 of Hubert Jedin's *A History of the Council of Trent*, trans. Ernest Graf (London: Thomas Nelson & Sons, 1957), provides an excellent guide to understanding some of the structural and constitutional problems articulated at the Council of Constance. A more extensive analysis is C.M.D. Crowder's *Unity, Heresy, and Reform, 1378–1460: The Conciliar Response to the Great Schism* (New York: St. Martin's Press, 1977). For an extensive, well-documented examination of Martin's Papacy in ecclesiastical context, Mandell Creighton's *History of the Papacy*, (London: Longmans, 1909), presents a thorough account of the events at Constance, Martin's election, the issues confronting Martin at the outset of his pontificate, and all major events of his reign. Those interested in the pope's role as temporal ruler can profit by two books of Peter Partner: *The Lands of St. Peter* already cited and *The Papal State under Martin V* (London: British School at Rome, 1958), as well as his short article "Florence and the Papacy in the Earlier Fifteenth Century," in *Florentine Studies: Politics and Society in Renaissance Florence*, ed. Nicolai Rubinstein (London: Faber & Faber, 1968). The chapter entitled "The Pontificate of Martin V" in P.J. Jones, *The Malatesta of Rimini and the Papal State: A Political History* (Cambridge: Cambridge University Press, 1974), outlines negotiations with other Italian powers, as does Denys Hay's *The Church in Italy in the Fifteenth Century* (Cambridge: Cambridge University Press, 1977).

Readers who wish to know more about Eugenius IV should turn to Joseph Gill's *Eugenius IV: Pope of Christian Union* (Westminster, Md.: Newman Press, 1961), the single modern account of his life. For original sources, see *Acta Eugenii Papae IV* (1431–1447) ed. Georgio Fedalto (Rome: Pontificia Commissio Codici Iuris Canonici Orientalia Recognoscendo, 1990). Joachim Stieber's *Pope Eugenius IV, the Council of Basel, and the Secular and Ecclesiastical Authorities in the Empire: The Conflict over Supreme Authority and Power in the Church* (Leiden: E.J. Brill, 1978), although focused on Germany, is indispensable for anyone interested in the issues raised by the rival councils and the long-term political consequences of their irreconcilable differences. See Appendix A for an exemplary bibliographic essay on sources relevant to Eugenius's papacy. For primary sources related to the Council of Florence, see *Concilium Florentinum documenta et scriptores*, 11 vols. (Roma: Pontificium Institutum Orientalium Studiorum, 1940–76). The proceedings of the two conferences held in Florence to commemorate the 550th anniversary of the signing of the decree of union between the Greek and Latin faiths are published in *Christian Unity: The Council of Ferrara-Florence 1438/39*, ed. Giuseppe Alberigo (Leuven: Lauren University Press, 1991), and *Firenze e il Concilio del 1436*, ed. Paolo Viti, 2 vols. (Florence: Leo S. Olschki, 1994). Readers interested in the Varna crusade should consult Kenneth M. Setton, *The Papacy and the Levant (1204–1571)*, vol. 2 (Philadelphia: American Philosophical Society, 1978). Finally, the richest contemporary account of the ceremonial and ritual events attendant on Eugenius's residence in Florence is found in *Priorista (1407–1459)* by Pagolo di Matteo Petriboni and Matteo di

Borgo Rinaldi, edited by Jacqueline Gutwirth in *Studi e testi del Rinascimento Europeo*, vol. 8 (Rome: Edizioni di Storia e Letteratura, 2000).

As secretary of Nicholas V, Giannozzo Manetti wrote his panegyric (Manetti, *Vita Nicolai V, summi pontificis*, ed. L.A. Muratori, in *Rerum italicarum scriptores*, vol. 3, pt. 2. [Milan, 1734], cols. 908–60) in the year of the pope's death. Ignoring the failures of the last two years of Nicholas's pontificate, Manetti presented the pope as possessing humanistic knowledge and designs for a golden age. His work is especially strong on Nicholas as a patron of the arts. This *Vita* remains the best source for the pope's biography and his pontificate. In "Formative Forces in the Pontificate of Nicholas V," *Catholic Historical Review* 54 (1968/1969): 261–84, J.B. Toews attacked the traditional view that Nicholas was pacific and that his pontificate is best characterized by his support of humanism. Nicholas's intellectual preparation was legal, theological, and diplomatic, while his support of humanism and cultural resources generally was an effort to use them in the rebuilding of papal power. Toews stressed the military spending of Nicholas in the papal lands and papal repression of any independence there as an effort to organize a territorial state.

In "Profilo di un papa umanista: Tommaso Parentucelli," in *Studi sulla cultura del Rinascimento* (Manduria: Lacaita, 1968), 69–121, Cesare Vasoli provides a modern study of Parentucelli. He finds the early humanistic and Florentine experience formative in Nicholas's papal policies, including his conciliatory policies and his construction of a court with a large number of laymen. In *Vite di uomini illustri del secolo XV*, translated into English as *Renaissance Princes, Popes, and Prelates: The Vespasiano Memoirs: Lives of Illustrious Men of the XVth Century*, trans. William George and Emily Waters (New York: Harper and Row, 1963), 31–58, the Florentine bookseller Vespasiano da Bisticci wrote an appreciative biography of Nicholas filled with important evidence of the pope's youth and education, his humanistic friends and interests, especially the library in the Vatican, and his death. Several elements were drawn directly from Manetti's *Vita*, but Vespasiano has his own anecdotes and a perceptive account of Nicholas's character. Finally, in his monograph *In This Most Perfect Paradise: Alberti, Nicholas V and the Invention of Conscious Urban Planning in Rome, 1447–55* (University Park: Pennsylvania State University Press, 1974), Carroll W. Westfall viewed Parentucelli's life as consistent from his humanistic training in Florence through the employment of humanism for the benefits of enhancing the authority of the church and the power of the pope. Though Alberti may have drawn the design of the new Rome, it was Nicholas's program that was constructed, based on humanistic ideals and his conception of the papacy. This makes him the first Renaissance pope. Westfall emphasized Nicholas's statement in his "Testament" that his buildings were to be read by the illiterate as doctrine and that they were to be placed within a relationship to all parts of the city.

There is no adequate modern biography of Pius II, but the old books by George Voigt, *Enea Silvio de' Piccolomini, als Papst Pius der Zweite, und sein Zeitalter*, 3 vols. (Berlin: Georg Reimer, 1856–63; reprint, Berlin: Walter de Gruyter, 1967), Cecilia Mary Ady, *Pius II: (Aeneas Silvius Piccolomihi) The Humanist Pope* (London: Methuen & Co., 1913), and Ludwig von Pastor, *The History of the Popes, from the Close of the Middle Ages*, vol. 3 (London: Kegan Paul, Trench, Trübner, & Co., 1894) remain valuable. The biography written by Berthe Widmer, *Enea Silvio Piccolomini Papst Pius II: Ausgewählte Texte aus seinen Schriften* (Basel and Stuttgart: Benno Schwabe & Co., 1960), is the best recent attempt. Much of the scholarship on Pius from the last century can be tracked in the *Bullettino senese di storia patria*; for references to studies in that journal and to reviews of studies published elsewhere, see the bibliographical index published as volume 76–81 (1969–74), especially pages 204, 208–209. Pius produced numerous works that have survived in various manuscript and printed editions from the fifteenth century to the present. Some of them, such as the *Commentaries*, now have excellent modern editions. Others can only be found in the fairly reliable *Opera quae extant omnia* collection printed at Basel in 1571. A somewhat out-of-date but good place to start is the Library of Congress's *Pre-1956 Imprints of the National Union Catalog* in volume 460 on pages 300–313. See also *Biographical and Bibliographical Dictionary of the Italian Humanists and of the World of Classical Scholarship in Italy, 1300–1800*, 6 vols. (Boston: G.K. Hall, 1962–67, especially 4:2809–24), which refers to numerous editions and secondary studies. The correspondence and records of his papacy survive in the Vatican Archives in *Registra Vaticana* 468–523, *Registra Lateranensia* 535–99, *Armaria* XXIX 7–10, XXXI, 31, 52, *Registra Supplicationum* 507–66, *Introitus et Exitus* 440–58, and many other collections. Immense numbers of documents and correspondence dealing with his papacy survive in archives throughout Europe and in Italy, especially in Milan and Venice. For other examples, see the state archives of Siena: *Concistoro (Deliberazini)* 548–79, (*Memoriali e duplicati*) 1417–23, and (*Lettere*) 1991–2009. Beside communal and papal correspondence, these Sienese records include discussions of policies toward the pope and account books for entries and entertainment for Pius, who spent months lingering near his hometown. There are hundreds of references to manuscripts related to Pius in Paul Oskar Kristeller's *Iter Italicum accedunt alia itinera: A Finding List of Uncatalogued or Incompletely Catalogued Humanistic Manuscripts of the Renaissance in Italian and Other Libraries*, 6 vols. (Leiden: E.J. Brill, 1963–92).

A useful approach to the politics and early writings of Francesco della Rovere (later Sixtus IV) when he was a friar and cardinal is Paolo M. Sevesi's "Lettere autografe di Francesco della Rovere da Savona, ministro generale (1464–1469) e cardinale (1467–1471) (poi Sisto IV, 1471–1484)," *Archivum Franciscanum historicum* 28 (1935): 198–234, 477–99. The most prominent contemporary narrative of Sixtus IV was written by the papal librarian, Bartolomeo Platina, *Platynae historici liber de vita Christi ac omnium pontificum (aa. 1–1474)*, ed. Giacinto Gaida, in *Rerum italicarum scriptores*, 2nd ser., vol. 3, pt. 1 (Città di Castello, 1932), 398–420. The severest contemporary critic of the pope was the Roman chronicler Stefano Infessura, who wrote *Diario della città di Roma di Stefano Infessura scribasenato* ed. Oreste Tommasini (Roma: Fonti per la Storia d'Italia 5, 1890). For the diplomatic history of Italy in the years 1471 to 1484, see the fundamental edition of the first seven volumes of the *Lettere* of Lorenzo de' Medici, ed. Riccardo Fubini and others (Florence: Giunti, 1977–90). Various studies have contributed to a change of the critical fortune of Sixtus IV over the last decades. Critical editions of his writings and the interest in his theological doctrines have revealed his intellectual stature, but the themes that predominate in many modern monographs are the "renovatio urbis" and the artistic commissions in the period of his pontificate. Several international congresses on Sixtus IV have confirmed the actuality of these approaches (see Virginia Properzi, "Sisto IV: Le arti a Roma nel primo Rinascimento: Palazzo della Cancelleria Apostolica—Ex Convento di S. Salvatore in Lauro, Roma, 23–25 ottobre 1997" *Roma nel Rinascimento*, 1997, 283–86).

In "Latran V," in *Latran et Trente I* (Paris: Éditions de l'Orante, 1975) Oliver de la Brosse and his coauthors have produced a study of the general council called by Julius II to end the Pisan schism, reform the church, especially the curia, condemn doctrinal errors, make peace among Christian princes, and call a crusade. In *Julius Excluded from Heaven: A Dialogue. "Dialogus Julius exclusus e coeli,"* trans. and annotated Michael J. Heath, in *Collected Works of Erasmus*, vols. 27–28, ed. A.H.T. Levi (Toronto: University of Toronto Press, 1986), 155–97, 489–508, Desiderius Erasmus produced a satirical attack on Julius II. Another primary source for the study of Julius II is Francesco Guicciardini's *Storia d'Italia*, ed. Costantino Panigada, 5 vols., Scrittori d'Italia, 120–124 (Bari: Giuseppe Laterza e Figli, 1929, reprinted 1967), a classic, almost contemporaneous study of the foreign policy of Julius II based in part on archival materials. Felix Gilbert's *The Pope, His Banker, and Venice* (Cambridge, Mass.: Harvard University Press, 1980) is a study of Julius II's efforts to defend his temporal and spiritual prerogatives in his relations with Venice.

Loren Partridge and Randolph Starn's *A Renaissance Likeness: Art and Culture in Raphael's "Julius II"* (Berkeley: University of California Press, 1980) is a careful analysis of the context, commissioning, purposes, and iconographic details of Raphael's portrait of Julius II that reveals the personality, programs, and patronage of the pope. While Christine Shaw's *Julius II: The Warrior Pope* (Cambridge, Mass.: Blackwell, 1993) emphasizes the political aspects of his career, Charles Stinger's *The Renaissance in Rome* (Bloomington: Indiana University Press, 1985) places Julius II in the intellectual culture of his time, claiming that the pope saw himself as a new Julius Caesar. A well-written and balanced traditional presentation of the life and character of Julius II based primarily on older printed sources and literature is Ivan Cloulas, *Jules II* (Paris: Librairie Arthème Fayard, 1990). Finally, Ludwig Pastor's *The History of the Popes from the Close of the Middle Ages*, trans. and ed. Frederick Ignatius Antrobus et al., 40 vols. (St. Louis, MO: B. Herder Book co., 1923–53), especially 6:208–659, goes beyond politics to consider Julius II's role as head of the church and patron of culture.

For a readable account of the Medici family with special strength in Leo X's childhood and relations with his kin, see Cecilia M. Ady's *Lorenzo dei Medici and Renaissance Italy* (New York: Collier Books, 1962). Bonner Mitchell's *Rome in the High Renaissance: The Age of Leo X* (Norman: University of Oklahoma Press, 1973) presents a sketch of "the temper of life" in Leo's Rome. William Roscoe's *The Life and Pontificate of Leo The Tenth* (7th ed., 2 vols. London, 1872), in an older work, but still useful, and one of the few full English-language studies of Leo. For Leo's political views, examine Tommaso Gar, ed., "Instructione al Magnifico Lorenzo," *Archivio storico italiano, appendice* 1, no. 1 (1842–44), which reveals Cardinal Giovanni's political views. Kenneth Setton discusses Leo's call for a crusade in "Leo X and the Turkish Peril," *Proceedings of the American Philosophical Society* 113 (1969).

The most accessible primary source in English translation on Clement VII's reign is Francesco Guicciardini, *The History of Italy*, trans. and ed. by Sidney Alexander (New York: Macmillan 1969). The best survey of his career is that of Adriano Prosperi, "Clemente VII, papa," *Dizionario biografica degli italiani*, vol. 26 (Rome: Instituto della Enicplopedia Italiana, 1982), 237–59. See also Sheryl E. Reiss, "Cardinal Giulio de' Medici as a Patron of Art, 1513–1523," 3 vols. (Ph.D diss., Princeton University, 1992). Among older accounts, see the influential narrative of Ludwig Pastor, *The History of the Popes from the Close of the Middle Ages: Drawn from the Secret Archives of the Vatican and Other Original Sources*, ed. F.I. Antrobus et al. (London: Kegan Paul, 1901–1933), vols. 9 and 10. T.C. Price Zimmermann provides an elegant and concise narrative of Clement's policies in *Paolo Giovio: The Historian and the Crisis of Sixteenth-Century Italy* (Princeton: Princeton University Press, 1995), chaps. 6–8.

On intellectual and cultural themes of Clementine Rome, see André Chastel, *The Sack of Rome, 1527*, trans. Beth Archer (Princeton: Princeton University Press, 1983); Vincenzo De Caprio, *La tradizione e il trauma: Idee del Rinascimento romano* (Manziana: Vecchiarelli, 1991); Julia Haig Gaisser, *Pierio Valeriano on the Ill Fortune of Learned Men: A Renaissance Humanist and His World* (Ann Arbor: University of Michigan Press, 1999); Kenneth Gouwens, *Remembering the Renaissance: Humanist Narratives of the Sack of Rome* (Leiden, Brill, 1998); and Anne Reynolds, *Renaissance Humanism at the Court of Clement VII: Francesco Berni's "Dialogue against Poets" in Context* (New York: Garland, 1997).

There are very few sources available on Paul III in English. One of the oldest remains one of the finest: Ludwig Freiherr von Pastor's *The History of the Popes from the Close of the Middle Ages*, 40 vols. 3rd ed. (St. Louis: Herder, 1938–53). Volumes 11 and 12 still constitute the best extended study of Paul III and the only one in English. The work was originally published as *Geschichte der Päpste seit dem Ausgang des Mittelalters*, 21 vols. (Freiburg im Breisgau: Herder, 1854–1928). Additional information in English must be gathered piecemeal from studies focused on one of the myriad personalities, events, or movements with which Paul had contact. Literally hundreds of such studies are available, but some recent examples are Barbara McClung Hallman, *Italian Cardinals, Reform, and the Church as Property, 1492–1563* (Berkeley: University of California Press, 1985); Charles Stinger, *The Renaissance in Rome* (Bloomington: Indiana University Press, 1985); Paolo Prodi, *The Papal Prince: One Body and Two Souls; The Papal Monarchy in Early Modern Europe*, trans. Susan Haskins (Cambridge: Cambridge University Press, 1987); Clare Robertson, *Il gran cardinale: Alessandro Farnese, Patron of the Arts* (New Haven: Yale University Press, 1992); Richard L. DeMolen, ed., *Religious Orders of the Catholic Reformation* (New York: Fordham University Press, 1994); and Elisabeth G. Gleason, "Who Was the First Counter-Reformation Pope?" *Catholic Historical Review* 81 (1995): 173–84.

For the ambitious scholar who would like to produce that modern biography this character cries out for, a plethora of primary sources is available. The major archival collections related to his career as pope are in the Archivio Segreto Vaticano in the *Carte farnesiane*, *Fondo Concilium Tridentinum*, and *Registra lateranensia*, 1621–1664. Additional sources are scattered throughout other states archives and libraries in Italy, including the Biblioteca Apostolica Vaticana, the Biblioteca Palatina in Parma, the Archivio di Stato in Florence, and the Archivio di Stato in Naples. The latter possesses a large collection of documents from the Farnese family, also named *Carte farnesiane*. Portions of Paul's diplomatic papers and related correspondence appear in published collections like *Concilium Tridentinum*, 13 vols. (Freiburg: Herder, 1901–38); Gottfried Buschbell, *Reformation und Inquisition in Italien um die Mitte des XVI. Jahrhunderts* (Paderborn: Schöningh, 1910); J. Lestocquoy, ed., *Correspondance des nonces en France: Acta nuntiaturae gallicae*, vols. 1–6 (Rome: Gregorian University Press, 1961–66); Ludwig Cardanus, ed., *Nuntiaturberichte aus Deutschland. I Abteilung, 1533–1539, Legation Farnesus und Cervinus* (Berlin: A. Bath, 1909); Franco Gaeta, ed., *Nunziature di Venezia* (Rome: Instituto storico italiano per l'età moderna e contemporanea, 1967); and Josef Metzler, ed., *America Pontificia: Primi saeculi evangelizationis, 1493–1592*, 2 vols. (Vatican City: Libreria Editrice Vaticana, 1991).